COMPARATIVE
DEMOCRATIC
POLITICS

Comparative Democratic Politics

A Guide to Contemporary Theory and Research

Edited by
Hans Keman

SAGE Publications
London • Thousand Oaks • New Delhi

First published 2002

 SAGE Publications Ltd
6 Bonhill Street
London EC2A 4PU

SAGE Publications Inc.
2455 Teller Road
Thousand Oaks, California 91320

SAGE Publications India Pvt Ltd
32, M-Block Market
Greater Kailash -I
New Delhi 110 048

British Library Cataloguing in Publication data

A catalogue record for this book is available from the British Library

ISBN 0 7619 5476 7
ISBN 0 7619 5477 5 (pbk)

Library of Congress Control Number available

Typeset by SIVA Math Setters, Chennai, India
Printed in Great Britain by The Cromwell Press Ltd,
Trowbridge, Wiltshire

SUMMARY OF CONTENTS

CONTENTS

LIST OF FIGURES

LIST OF TABLES

NOTES ON THE EDITOR AND CONTRIBUTORS

Hans Keman is Professor and Chair of Political Science at the Vrije Universiteit in Amsterdam. He has previously taught at the University of Amsterdam, the European University Institute (Florence, Italy), the University of Leiden and was a Research Fellow at the Australian National University (Canberra) and the Netherlands Institute of Advanced Studies (NIAS). Currently he is co-editor-in-chief of the *European Journal of Political Research*. He has published on comparative politics and its methodology, public policy formation, the welfare state, economic policy-making and on party systems and the functioning of governments. Among his latest publications are *The Politics of Problem-Solving in Postwar Democracies* (1997) and with Paul Pennings and Jan Kleinnijenhuis: *Doing Research in Political Science. An Introduction to Comparative Methods and Statistics* (1999).

Klaus Armingeon is Professor of Political Science at the University of Berne (Switzerland). Before this he taught at the universities of Konstanz, Tübingen, Mannheim and Heidelberg in Germany. His work focuses on trade unions, corporatism, consociational democracy, social and economic policies, political participation, party systems and voting behaviour in comparative perspective. Recent publications in English include articles on the Swiss welfare state and economic policy. In addition he has published on Swiss federalism and on the effects of negotiation democracy. Among his publications are *Der Nationalstaat am Ende des 20 Jahrhunderts* (The Nation-State at the end of the 20th Century, 1996) and 'The Effects of Negotiation Democracy' (*European Journal of Political Science*, 2002).

Uwe Becker is Senior Lecturer in Political Science at the University of Amsterdam. He has been a visiting fellow in Australia, Sweden, the USA and at the European University Institute (Italy). He has published and edited books on class theory, political science, Dutch politics in comparative perspectives and lately (1999) on European democracies. Most of his recent articles deal with welfare state and labour market developments in the Netherlands.

Ian Budge has been Professor of Government at the University of Essex since 1976. He was the founding director of the Essex Summer School in Quantitative Social Science Methods and is former executive director of the ECPR. He has published on democratic theory, party behaviour, elections and party systems, and government formation from a comparative perspective. He is also director of the 'Manifesto Research Project' on party programmes, government declarations and public policy formation in Western democracies. Ian Budge has held visiting professorships and fellowships in Spain, Italy, Germany, The Netherlands, the United States and recently in Australia. He has also published several books, amongst which are: *The New Challenge of Direct Democracy* (1996), *Parties and Democracies. Coalition Formation and Government Functioning in 20 States* (1993, with Hans Keman), and *Mapping Policy Preferences: Estimates for Parties, Governments and Electors 1945–98* (with H-D. Klingemann, A. Volkens, and J. Bara, 2001).

Francis G. Castles is currently Professor of Social and Public Policy at the University of Edinburgh, having formerly held Chairs in Political Science at the Australian National University and the Open University in England. He has been convenor of a series of path-breaking comparative studies of the determinants of policy outcomes in Western democratic states. His most recent books are *Comparative Public Policy: Patterns of Post-war Transformation* published in 1998 and *The Welfare State Reader*, co-edited with Chris Pierson (2000).

Hans Daalder is emeritus Professor of Political Science at the University of Leiden. One of the founders of the ECPR he was first Head of Department of Political and Social Sciences at the European University Institute (Florence, Italy). He has published widely on comparative politics – in particular European politics in the area of political development and political parties in democracies – and on Dutch politics as well as on topics of political history. His latest contribution to the field of comparative analysis is: *Comparative European Politics. The Story of a Profession* (1997). He is now working on a political biography of the first social democrat to become Dutch Prime Minister: Willem Drees (1886–1988).

Svante Ersson is currently working at the University of Umeå. His main research concerns empirical comparative politics, and the development of comparable data on political behaviour and institutions. He has co-authored together with Jan-Erik Lane many books on European politics, institutions and governance and comparative politics.

Richard I. Hofferbert is Distinguished Professor Emeritus at the State University of New York at Binghamton, as well as Recurring Visiting Professor at the Wissenschaftszentrum-Berlin. He has published widely on policy analysis, political parties, and democratic performance. Among his books are *Parties, Policies, and Democracy* (1994, with Hans-Dieter Klingemann, Ian Budge and others) and *Parties and Democracy* (ed., 1998).

Kees van Kersbergen is currently Professor of National Political Systems and Dutch Politics at the University of Nijmegen (The Netherlands). Before that he was Senior Lecturer at the Vrije Universiteit Amsterdam and was attached to the European University Institute (Italy). He publishes widely on Dutch politics and policy-making as well as on the political development of welfare states from a cross-national perspective. In 1996 van Kersbergen was awarded the Stein Rokkan Prize for Comparative Social Research for his book *Social Capitalism. A Study of Christian Democracy and the Welfare State* (1995).

Jan-Erik Lane is Professor of Political Science at the University of Geneva and has previously taught in Umeå, Lund and Oslo. He has published widely on topics of political theory, comparative political economy and sociology as well as on public policy formation and public sector management. His latest books are *Politics and Society in Western Europe* (with Svante Ersson, 1998) and *The New Institutional Politics. Performance and Outcomes* (also with Svante Ersson, 2000).

Peter Mair is Professor of Comparative Politics at Leiden University in The Netherlands and previously taught at the University of Limerick, the University of Strathclyde, the University of Manchester, and the European University Institute. He has been co-editor of the journal *West European Politics*. He has published numerous articles on party system development, aggregate electoral development, parties and their organization and on comparative politics in general. Together with Stefano Bartolini he was awarded the Stein Rokkan Prize for Comparative Social Research in 1991 for their study of electoral volatility in Europe. He has co-authored *Representative Government in Modern Europe: Institutions, Parties and Governments* (3rd edition, 2000).

Malika Aït Mallouk is a graduate student in Comparative Politics and Assistant in the Department of Political Science at the Vrije Universiteit Amsterdam. She is working on employment policies in EU Member States in relation to EU decision-making during the 1990s.

Michael D. McDonald is Associate Professor and Chair of the Department of Political Science at Binghamton University (State University of New York). His research and publications focus on issues of democratic representation under various forms of electoral, party, and governmental systems.

Paul Pennings is Associate Professor at the Department of Political Science at the Vrije Universiteit Amsterdam. His research focuses on political parties and their institutional environment from a comparative perspective. Among his recent publications are *Comparing Party Systems* (co-editor with Lane, 1998) and *Democratizing Candidate Selection* (special issue of *Party Politics*, 2001). Together with Kleinnijenhuis and Keman he published *Doing Research in Political Science. An Introduction to Comparative Methods and Statistics* (1999).

Manfred G. Schmidt is the recently appointed Professor and Chair in Political Science at the University of Heidelberg. He was Director of the Centre of Social Policy Studies in Bremen (Germany). His major research interests are: political institutions and public policy in the Federal Republic of Germany; comparative public policy; and democratic theory. Manfred Schmidt was the winner of the Stein Rokkan Prize in Comparative Social Research in 1981. In 1995 he was awarded the Leibniz Prize of the German Research Foundation. His book publications include *Wörterbuch zur Politik* (Dictionary in Politics and Political Science, 1995), *Sozialpolitik in Deutschland. Historische Entwicklung und internationaler Vergleich* (Social Policy in Germany. Historical Development and International Comparison, 1998, 2nd edition) and *Demokratietheorien* (Theories of Democracy, 2000, 3rd edition).

PREFACE AND ACKNOWLEDGEMENTS

This edited volume is the result of the collaboration among a number of European political scientists, who all met each other regularly at Joint Sessions of Workshops organized by the European Consortium of Political Research (ECPR). Over the years we have worked together in various (nationally and internationally organized) research projects. All these research projects had, in one way or another, in common that they focused on democratic politics as a process, on the one hand, and on the political performances of democracy as a system, on the other hand.

Not too long ago we felt the urge to throw our experience and knowledge together in view of the recent developments in democracies across the world. The so-called 'established' democracies, stable as they (still) appear, show signs of fatigue as legitimate systems of public governance (considered by many as a result of the politicization of the European Union); whereas the recent 'waves' of democratization have not only increased the number of (constitutional) representative democracies, but also urge us to ponder the quality of existing insights in representative democracy, both as a political process and as a system of governance. Basically this is the underlying idea of this edited volume: to examine the present 'state of the art' and to update our collective knowledge and empirical applications of *comparative democratic politics*. In this sense this volume can be indeed considered as a 'guide to present theory and research'. We hope that this effort will be helpful to other colleagues, in particular those active in the field of 'comparative politics', as well as those who are concerned with or interested in understanding contemporary democracy.

Last, but not least, many others were involved in getting this book into a publishable format and helped us to gather the necessary information and data. First of all I am grateful for the support of my Faculty of Social-Cultural Sciences at the *Vrije Universiteit* (Amsterdam). I am particularly grateful to Sabine *Luursema*, who helped me to produce the manuscript. Without her it would not only have taken much longer, but it would not have looked like it does now. Also the assistance of Malika *Aït Mallouk* should not go unnoticed. She assisted me in collecting and analysing data as well as compiling the bibliography. In addition Lucy *Robinson* of Sage Publishers must be thanked for her support from the very beginning of this endeavour, and her patience with me, until the very end of producing this book. This quality was even more so demonstrated by my loving and caring friend Mieke *Rijkers*, whose patience has been beyond any measure.

Finally, I wish to thank the contributors, who bore with me and my requests, for their spirited and congenial co-operation. It goes almost without saying, of course, that I alone am responsible for any errors and mistakes that may have escaped my attention.

Hans Keman (Editor)
Riis – Fryslân, The Netherlands

PART ONE

THE COMPARATIVE APPROACH TO DEMOCRACY

The three chapters in this first part of the book are meant as a general introduction for what follows later. The main goal is to introduce the reader to the *comparative approach* in political science. Such an introduction is necessary because to many it is not self-evident that the comparative approach is a distinctive field within political science (Keman, 1993a). Yet, 'Comparative Politics' is distinctive and, at the same time, part and parcel of the discipline. In this book we advance the point of view that theory formation on the level of political systems requires a rigorous and systematic empirical foundation. And precisely, democracy, the central object of study throughout this book, arguably must be studied and discussed by means of comparative analysis.

The *first chapter* introduces the reader to the relationship between field of inquiry, the theoretical domain to which this field belongs, and how it can be systematically researched by means of comparative analysis. In *Chapter 2* the origins and development of 'Comparative Politics' is elaborated. Daalder shows that the comparative approach was not only developed as an analytical and methodological tool, but that it developed in response to the 'ups and downs' of democratic development during the 'interbellum'. In addition this essay makes clear that there is considerable variation among 'comparativists' in doing research. Amongst other things, these differences within the field of comparative political science concern: 'Few Cases and Many Variables *versus* Many Cases and Few Variables' (see also: Landman, 2000). This difference in comparative approach is often also denoted as the difference between quantitative or *variable-oriented* research and the qualitative or *case-oriented* approach of comparative politics (Ragin, 1987; Przeworski, 1987).

This debate is the starting point for *Chapter 3*. Here Keman attempts to demonstrate how far a more quantitative approach can travel in discussing the central topic of this book: representative democracy. In fact, this chapter shows in what way and to what extent it is possible to investigate cross-nationally the concept of 'Polyarchy' (cf. Dahl, 1971) *worldwide*. It is an example of how to relate (existing) theory to fresh empirical evidence. This chapter is then also intended to make the reader familiar with the *universe of discourse* of this book: the contemporary world of representative democracy.

1 THE COMPARATIVE APPROACH TO DEMOCRACY

Hans Keman

1.1 INTRODUCTION

This book aims at empirical and theoretical analyses with respect to the interactions between political and societal actors within the institutional arrangements that characterize representative democracy. In particular, we have set out to investigate the interactions of these actors in parliamentary and presidential democratic polities and their impact on public policy formation and related democratic performance. More specifically, this book aims to explain the format and consequences of *democratic politics* under socially diverse situations and varying economic circumstances. In fact, one may wonder how it has been possible to construct and consolidate democracy in such a fashion that most democratic countries appear to have developed into relatively stable and effective polities under political and economic circumstances where one would not always have expected it. In other words: how does one account for viable and enduring forms of 'democraticness' often in situations where the seeds of conflict are expected to prevail over consensus and may well have led to political dissatisfaction and threats to democracy?

Answering this question is not only of interest to professional political scientists, but is also highly relevant for a wider audience interested in the relation between politics and society in contemporary democracies. Particularly today it appears that turbulence and turmoil characterizes the relation between politics and society in many countries. As a result, party systems and governments appear to be in a situation of flux, both in terms of their partisan composition and in terms of public governance. This, in turn, affects the degree of acquiescence of societal actors and the extent of coalescence among political actors. Many commentators on current political affairs see this situation as conducive to a decrease in co-operative behaviour, affecting in the process of forming governments, and in a reduction in policy concertation affecting eventually policy performances. At the end of the day these developments appear to impair the domestic policy-making capacity of representative democracies.

Yet, this situation is historically not unique. On the contrary, political stability appears rather to be the exception to the rule.[1] Characteristic of democratic politics across the world and in (the 'new') Europe has been the swing back and forth between change and continuity (Bingham Powell, 1982; Mair, 1997; Budge et al., 1997). For politics is essentially the manifestation of conflicts arising from social heterogeneity, which sooner or later reach the political arena in terms of salient issues that have to be decided upon (Putnam, 1993; Keman, 1997b). This book is about the study of these developments and, more precisely, the extent to which democratic political systems are indeed capable of coping with societal change in the contemporary world.

The focus of the separate contributions to this volume is on the institutionalization of societal conflict and the extent to which this generates viable consensus formation among political actors that makes the attainment of public welfare by means of public policy formation feasible within representative democracies. Hence, the approach adopted here to account for change and continuity departs from the point of view that political institutions basically frame the process of political decision-making in these societies as well as shape the room to manoeuvre for political and societal actors to influence and direct public policy formation. We focus therefore on the democratic state and its political performance in order to understand the problem-solving capacity in contemporary democracies (Lane and Ersson, 2000).

The point of departure of this book is that *institutional arrangements* of representative democracies are to be considered as conceptual variables that vary across the various polities as well as over time. In addition, we hold the view that these variations in institutional arrangements influence the behaviour of politically relevant actors – representing societal interests – and thus their *room to manoeuvre* in reaching viable and feasible modes of policy formation. Democracy, from this point of view, facilitates and constrains conflicting interests that are an inherent feature of political life. This approach to the democratic process as a means of channelling or structuring, not eradicating, conflict runs through this book, recognizing, in the words of Lipset (1959: 1), that 'stable democracy requires the manifestation of conflict'. Yet, at the same time we think it equally crucial to study the extent to which these mechanisms of containing conflict and preserving the political order are a means of institutionalizing societal conflict and establishing a proper balance between conflict and consensus (Diamond and Marks, 1992: 12).

In the remainder of this introductory chapter the general framework of analysis, which structures the arguments of the separate chapters as well as their sequential logic, will be elaborated. First, in Section 1.2 a crucial dimension to study the relations between political action and related policy outcomes in representative democracies will be discussed, namely the paradox of 'conflict and consensus' (Keman, 1997a; Scharpf, 1998). It is argued that political actors can and must be conceived of as behaving rationally in order to understand the feasibility of a more or less stable political order. In Section 1.3 this perspective is elaborated by outlining the political context in which actors and institutions are relevant for the study of democratic politics. In Section 1.4, I shall move on to a short discussion of the 'new institutionalism' that will enable us to relate processes of collective decision-making to the process of public policy formation with respect to political performance within democracies (Guy Peters, 1996; Czada et al., 1998). The argument will be that institutions do not only offer crucial insights in these processes, but can also be meaningfully applied to explain the nexus between conflict and consensus in democratic politics. Finally, in Section 1.5 of this introduction, the framework of empirical analysis – the *political chain of democratic command and control* – which structures this book, will be presented.

1.2 THE PURSUIT OF POLITICAL ORDER: DEMOCRACY AND PERFORMANCE

In comparative politics many explanations have been offered, attempting to account for the paradoxical situation of simultaneous change and stability in representative democracies (see for an overview: Lipset and Rokkan, 1967; Daalder and Mair, 1983; Lane and Ersson, 1994). Yet, most of these explanations are flawed by the fact that they neither systematically link institutions to actors, nor relate the type and occurrence of political action systematically to the patterned variation of institutions affecting decision-making and the related democratic performance (Keman, 1997c; Scharpf, 1998; Schmidt, 2000).

It appears a necessary and a rewarding endeavour therefore to analyse these concepts more systematically, in terms of their conceptualization *and* from a cross-national perspective. In this way it will be possible to assess the strengths and weaknesses of institutional arrangements as theoretical concepts *and* as empirical concepts that can 'travel' cross-nationally without unduly 'stretching' them (Sartori, 1970; Collier and Mahon, 1993; Pennings et al., 1999; Landman, 2000). One of the aims is to discover the extent to which the institutional design – or arrangement – of contemporary democracy works under changing circumstances and differing conditions and is capable of furthering political consensus by means of public policy formation where deep-seated conflicts appear inevitable and destabilize society. In other words: to what extent is representative democracy capable of coping with change whilst maintaining an efficient and effective political order?

A crucial and central question in political science thus concerns the way societal conflicts can be handled in a genuinely problem-solving fashion. Conflicts appear to the participants more often than not as a zero-sum game. If and when societal conflicts are indeed 'solved' in a unilateral fashion (for instance by ignoring substantial minorities due to simple majority-voting), according to the logic of game theory, in the long run this will more often than not be conducive to a situation of sub-optimal outcomes for all participants, even for the winners (albeit, of course, in a different degree for winners and losers in a society). In formal political theory this situation has been described as a result of the (well-known) Prisoner's Dilemma, on the one hand, and will often lead to 'free ridership' as a consequence of collective action, on the other hand (Olson, 1982; Mueller, 1989; Scharpf, 1998).

Both explanations point to the so-called 'social choice' paradox of politics and society: *rational actors* pursuing their interests by means of societal inter-action whilst being dependent on others, must act strategically to achieve their individual utility. However, the eventual outcomes of this process tend to yield optimal results (instead of maximum pay-offs) for all actors involved (Scharpf, 1997: Shepsle and Bonchek, 1997). To some students of politics this paradox must (inevitably) lead to the creation of the state, which enforces solutions to (individual) actors within a society in order to enhance public welfare (which is then a macro-level solution to problems that may, at best, induce optimal results on the micro-level; e.g. Rawls, 1972; Nozick, 1974). To others political authority is not necessarily a consequence of social choice (e.g. Axelrod, 1984; Czada et al., 1998). In this alternative view, ration-ally behaving actors – in need of collective action to achieve optimal gains – can and will in due time co-operate voluntarily on the basis of 'tit-for-tat'. Hence, solving the 'social choice' paradox is a matter of *exchange*, either mutually or taking it in turns. If true, there would be a need for a separate authority and hierarchy to solve societal conflict by means of political con-sensus in order to enhance public welfare (Scharpf, 1998; Keman, 1999). From this it can be argued that the political process, embedded in the state – regulating societal conflict – becomes a separate segment of any society with its own institutions: in our case, the democratic state. It is important to note therefore that in this view the relationship between politics and society emphasizes the role of institutions and the way they work in overcoming societal conflict by means of consensus formation. Democratic institutions, however, may be necessary but in reality may not always be sufficient to produce a political consensus as well as an adequate policy performance at all times and under varying (social and economic) conditions. Vital for understanding these processes is the analysis of the role and functioning of political actors – parties and governments. This role is examined in *Part Two* of this book.

A good example is the way in which the majority rule in parliament regard-ing decision-making can create both theoretical and empirical stalemates, i.e. 'voting cycles' in democracies (Mueller, 1989: 63–89). In practice, these situations have been avoided in two ways: one, by means of compromises among decision-making actors (hence, exchange in order to co-operate); two, by adapting the formal procedures, introducing additional rules concerning agenda-setting and the rank-ordering of issues to decide on (Shepsle, 1997). It is precisely these practices, which laid the foundation of Lijphart's model of consensus democracy (as opposed to the 'majoritarean' types of democracy). In our view this signifies not only the importance of analysing the 'rules of the democratic game', but even more so that this type of interaction between actors and institutions can and should be discussed more fully in *comparative* terms (i.e. by means of cross-national studies). In this way the historicist and sociological biases of such models can be precipitated. This idea will be elaborated by means of cross-national analysis in *Part Three* of this book.

This conclusion signifies the need to develop empirically-based models of exchange relations between societal and political actors based on *a priori* statements, rather than taking country-specific findings or thick description of events as explanations of the relationship between politics and society in contemporary democracies. In this book, therefore, we will investigate the exchange relations typical for democratic politics in plural societies as paradoxical and that are manifested in a pendulum movement between the political process of decision-making and societal performance. In fact, one of the major aims of *Part Four* of this book is the attempt to explain the 'political' performance of representative democracies by applying the comparative empirical analysis of public policy-making (e.g. Keman, 1997; Castles, 1998; Lane and Ersson, 2000). It is important then to state clearly what is meant by the interactions between institutions and actors in terms of the core subject, i.e. the 'political'.

1.3 POLITICS, POLITY AND POLICY: TOWARDS AN INTERACTIVE MODEL OF ACTORS AND INSTITUTIONS

A point of departure is the idea that in representative democracies, time and again, societal conflicts are to be resolved by means of those institutions that facilitate the formation of acceptable and feasible agreements between opponents, inducing a viable consensus that is considered as an optimum (or best solutions on) for any of the participants[2] within the various modes of decision-making. This implies that societal conflict and political consensus are *complementary* notions that are *reciprocally* interrelated. The extent to which there is an institutionalized political order of society that is capable of producing a problem-solving balance between conflict and consensus, that is enduring and incurs a minimal loss to any individual or group within a society, is not only a measure of the relation between political order and the distribution of public welfare, but in particular of the viability of the political-institutional system. Such a condition is what we call a *structure-induced equilibrium* explaining the relative stability of the political order. From this it follows that the study of the development and working of *political institutions* is crucial to a better understanding of the paradox of societal conflict and political consensus (Colomer, 1996; Shepsle, 1997; Scharpf, 1998; Keman, 1999). This is particularly the case in representative democracies where the relations between state and society are by and large autonomously, albeit interdependently, organized (i.e. pluralism). These relations materialize in democratic polities through a variety of collective actors, such as political parties, interest groups and social movements.

The pursuit of political order must be analysed therefore by focusing upon those patterns of behaviour (i.e. modes and codes of conduct among actors) that are dependent upon certain formal and informal arrangements enhancing the *democratic governance* of societal conflicts. Institutional arrangements thus regulate the behaviour of *political* and *societal* actors who are both autonomous and interdependent in a democratic polity. These arrangements are at the same time only viable if the problem-solving decision-making (i.e. a political compromise by means of exchange) can be effectively implemented (i.e. by a legitimate authority) within society and induces an efficient redistribution and reallocation according to the political settlement, resulting in an adequate policy performance. If not, the political order will tend to be unstable and will probably be less enduring; the balance between conflict and consensus is then lacking and the *democratic governance* of society will be less or, indeed, will not be enhancing public welfare by means of policy formation (i.e. regulating societal conflict by means of public goods). In other words: the way democratic politics works is vital for achieving a *structure-induced equilibrium* in society. This brings us to the question of how to define the *political* as a concept that not only can travel (worldwide), but also allows for a meaningful differentiation of it from what is 'society' *per se*.

This concept can be conceived by means of three dimensions of democracy: *politics, polity and policy* (Keman, 1993a: 43–7). Politics is then what I would like to call the *political process*. On this level actors (mostly aggregates of individuals organized in parties, associations, or interest groups) interact with each other when they have conflicting interests or views regarding societal issues that cannot be solved by them (i.e. deficiency of self-regulation). This problematic will be discussed and examined in *Part Two* of this book. The process of solving those problems, which make actors clash, is more often than not visible through the *institutions* that have emerged in order to facilitate conflict resolution. Institutions help to develop coalescence and to achieve a consensus among conflicting actors through compromising alternative preferences. These institutions manifest themselves in the rules of the game in a society. This is what the term polity means and is elaborated in *Part Three* of this book. To put it more formally, rules are humanly devised constraints that shape political interaction. Institutions are here considered to be regulated both by formal rules, such as for instance those enshrined in a constitution, and which can be enforced by means of authority, and by informal rules, i.e. those that evolve over time and are respected and followed as a code of conduct by most actors involved.[3] The institutions available in a democratic society for political action allow the citizens to participate in the decision-making, albeit indirectly, and thus to influence, mainly through representation by parties, the process of public policy formation. This process is equivalent to what also could be called state intervention or the 'authoritative allocation of values in a society' by means of democratic governance. Actions of the state, or a related allocating agency, are in this conceptualization of the political viewed as relatively independent from societal interests (Skocpol, 1985: 45). That is to say, political action, i.e. the relation between politics and policy-making, requires a degree of autonomy in order to be feasible and effective. If this is not the case then the political process is merely ritual and indeed simply a reflection of societal features and developments. In short, a theory of the democratic process must assume that there exists a mutual and interdependent relation between politics and society, and that its organization is to a large extent independent from society. The issue at hand is then to investigate *empirically* to what extent and in what way this process can be observed and affects social and economic developments within a society.

Comparative research of political actors in relation to democratic institutions is essential to the study of the relationship between politics and policy formation in the attempt to resolve the paradox of societal conflict and political consensus. By such research we hope to shed more light on the development of democratic politics *per se*, and on processes of institutionalization as an explanation of the occurrence of structure-induced (dis)equilibria in representative democracies. An important, not to say crucial, factor in this respect is the extent to which political actors have indeed sufficient room to manoeuvre. In other words, what is the impact of institutions on the behaviour of political actors and hence on the processes of policy formation as well as the eventual political performance of democracies?

1.4 NEW INSTITUTIONALISM AND POLITICAL ROOM TO MANOEUVRE IN DEMOCRACIES

In recent times institutionalism has been revived by comparative analyses of the relation between politics and policy formation (Thelen and Steinmo, 1992; Weaver and Rockman, 1993; Schmidt, 1999; Keman, 1998; Guy Peters, 1996; Czada et al., 1998). Institutions are regarded in these studies as *intervening variables* to explain democratic policy formation and related policy performance. This type of research often provided empirical evidence demonstrating that political institutions added significantly to the understanding of the cross-national and inter-temporal variation in the problem-solving capacity of capitalist democracies (Keman, 1996; Scharpf, 1991; Steinmo et al., 1992). This development has been the result of a growing feeling of discomfort with the mainstream research into the political process focusing on actors that accompanied the so-called behavioural revolution that would have led to a political explanations and to 'reductionism' (Olsen, 1998). The main criticisms can be summarized as follows: Politics is predominantly considered as a result of exogenous factors, in particular sociological and cultural attributes of actors, which implies a type of determinism of political choices in which the 'political' is not considered as an autonomous variable but is rather explained by the *contextual* features of political actors participating.

An example of this contextual bias can be found in the original research on the 'consociational theme'. In fact these analyses were based on socio-cultural features of pluralistic societies and the way these developments shaped the behaviour of political agencies as well as the particular working of democratic institutions (e.g. Daalder, 1966; Steiner, 1974; Lijphart, 1975). In fact, case-description was conducive to theoretical explanations of political behaviour. Yet, it should be noticed that these analyses were important in complementing Anglo-Saxon theories with regard to stable government. In addition, these studies made understandable those democratic institutions which appeared as equifunctional from a comparative perspective but were in fact plurifunctional. In other words: the political actors within certain polities used identical rules of political decision-making differently, and, paradoxically enough, produced a structure-induced equilibrium. Hence, so it appears, it is *not* the context that explains the political process, but rather the way the *interactive* pattern of institutions and actors is shaped that seems to matter (Lijphart, 1999; see Chapter 7 in this book).

Another example is the view that 'politics' predominantly is considered as a result of individual behaviour or as aggregates thereof and thus the role of institutions cannot be considered as independent influences on political processes. Such a view often leads to *atomistic* biases in research designs dealing with actors operating on various levels. A good example of this can be found in the 'social choice' approach of political behaviour (Downs, 1957). Here voting behaviour is considered to be equivalent to market behaviour and is therefore conceivable as a supra-individual manifestation of social choice. Hence, aggregates of individual preferences determine political decision-making. In fact the Downsian approach of the political process is an – albeit sophisticated – elaboration of this idea. Yet, as is well known by now (see Barry, 1978), economic rationality is not necessarily identical to political rationality, and the manifestation of individual preferences in political decision-making is largely dependent on the institutions that *mediate and aggregate* individual choice (e.g. the type of electoral system and concurrently the way parties compete for office; Budge, 1993). In our view the institutionalization of political life – like the working of party systems or the relations between the executive and the legislative – is crucial for understanding the material and procedural performance of a political system (Heywood, 1997; see further Chapters 4 and 6 of this book).

Contextualism and atomism have more often than not displaced the role of politics as an autonomous explanation of political processes, and the emerging 'new institutionalism' can be seen as an attempt to restore the (traditional) approach of analysing the political process, but without denouncing all elements contained in the behavioural approach and the economic explanations of politics. What we do contend, however, and will stress throughout this book is the idea that the interactions between actors and institutions are crucial for explaining the working and quality of representative democracies, rather than the behaviour of political actors *per se* or their rational (self-interested) motives as such.

In our approach, institutional variables, conceptualized at the macro-level of analysis, are conceived as *intervening* variables, i.e. as mechanisms that link political inputs (electoral results, issue-formation, etc.) to policy outputs (e.g. measures and expenditures) across polities and over time (Putnam, 1993: 8–9). In accordance with the new institutionalist approach we see political decisions and policy-formation in whole or in part as being derived from political institutions and thus as 'irretrievable sources of political action' (Héritier, 1998: 33). For instance, March and Olsen (1989) define institutions in a somewhat loose manner as a number of interconnected rules and routines that indicate the relation between a (organizational) role and a (decision-making) situation within democracies. In other words, politics is only partially 'rational' and 'consequential', and the process of decision-making is neither dominated by actors *per se*, nor influenced by socio-cultural features or economic conditions of a society *alone*. On the contrary, as Olsen notes: 'Political institutions are the building blocks of political life. They influence available options for policy-making and for institutional change. They also influence the choices made among available options' (Olsen, 1998: 95).

In this book, political institutions are perceived as cross-national and inter-temporal variables influencing the possible behaviour of actors. In what follows, the role and function of political institutions will be considered as *empirical variables*, which will be investigated in terms of *patterned variations* of formal and informal rules of political decision-making. Institutions are thus conceived as conditions under which policy-making takes place, which set the limits to political and societal actors to act in a maximizing way, but which may well contribute to *optimal* types of policy-making and related performances. The formal and informal rules of a democratic polity define the *room to manoeuvre* for each actor involved in policy-making as an inter-dependent process – for example, the division of a party system and the organization of a system of interest representation direct the modes of behaviour and the interactions between relevant actors (see, for this in particular, Chapter 8 in this book). At the same time this approach allows for the investigation of political actions as mitigated forms of (rational) self-interest, since the rule configurations have been developed by most of the participating actors themselves in order to regulate and contain conflicts among them in such a way as to make manageable and viable agreements (or structure-induced equilibriums) feasible.

This interpretation and elaboration of new institutionalism allows for a different and fresh look at concepts such as democracy and interest intermediation in relation to policy efficacy and political efficiency in view of conflict resolution in societies that are characterized by political and socio-economic differences. The comparative analysis of democratic political systems presented in this book will assist us to answer the question to what extent the paradox between societal conflict and political consensus can indeed be solved by means of policy-making and can explain the cross-national variation in political performance.

1.5 THE POLITICAL CHAIN OF DEMOCRATIC COMMAND AND CONTROL

The analytical concepts that will be used throughout this book are – amongst other things – derived from the discussion of the 'political' and 'new institutionalism' in the previous sections. These discussions have served the purpose of introducing our theoretical perspective as well as outlining our principal concern, namely how to investigate the political process of policy formation and related performance in plural societies within an established system of representative democratic politics. These processes can be sketched

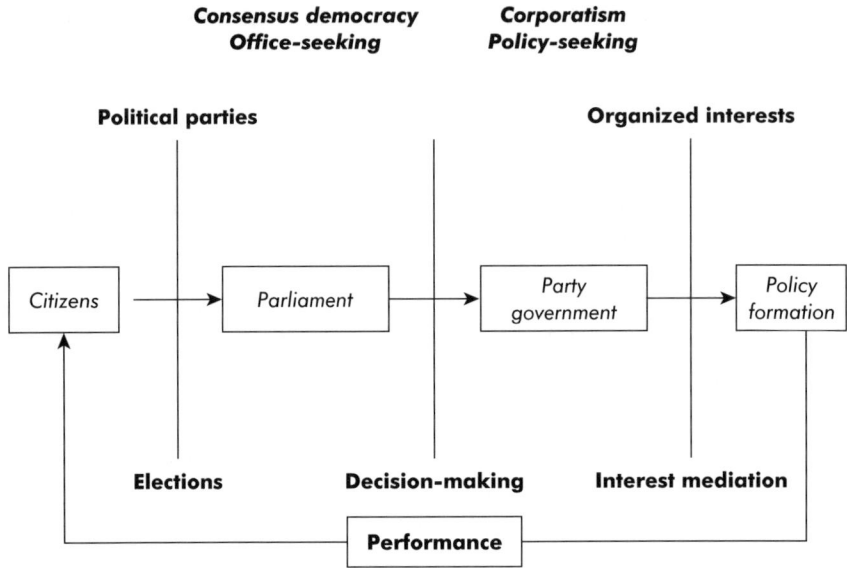

Figure 1.1 *Political chain of democratic control and command (adapted from:* Pennings et al., *1999: 224)*

as a sequence of interrelated institutions, indicating the various instances of democratic control and command (Keman, 1996; Pennings et al., 1999). Figure 1.1 shows this political chain as well as the stages at which political actors are involved in this process and the rule configurations that have con-currently emerged.[4]

The *political chain of democratic command and control* is a simple, descriptive model of representative democracy showing the relations between various relevant actors and political institutions, which – at the end of the day – results in some kind of policy-making and a related policy performance. The political and social actors that are supposed to play a central part in achieving a politi-cal order that is stable and beneficial to all, are political parties and organized interests. These actors are driven in this model by office-seeking motives (i.e. gaining seats in parliament and government), on the one hand, and by policy-seeking motives (i.e. the pursuit of public preferences in the decision-making process), on the other (see also: Strøm, 1990; Klingemann et al., 1994; Scharpf, 1997). This will be the focus of *Part Two* of this book. The extent to which actors get their own way, however, depends not only on their electoral strength, being in government, or their organizational size, but foremost on how strong and well-organized other actors are and how these power resources can be put to use. Hence, the way the political process is institutionalized will influence the relative weight and effectiveness of each actor.

These institutions – like the electoral system, the extant party system, modes of interest intermediation, or types of government – shape the room to manoeuvre of each actor involved as well as the patterns of interaction. In particular in plural societies with structural cleavages, political parties are important bearers of the related political conflicts, but more often than not are dependent on the co-operation of others to carry through their ideas and to translate them into public governance. Governments are also in part dependent on the co-operation of other actors, such as organized interests, in order to bring about adequate policy performances. In other words, each and every actor is *interdependent* and is therefore in need of each other's collaboration and co-operation to turn societal conflict into political consensus (Keman, 1999; Lijphart, 1999).

In this book this process and related outcomes will be examined by means of a cross-national comparative research design covering the contemporary democracies. This approach has been chosen for the simple reason that an empirical investigation of representative democracies would otherwise not be feasible. We need to compare this process on the level of national political systems as well as over time to be able to develop empirically-based theoretical perspectives. An additional, but by no means unimportant, reason is that the specific nature and developments of democracies has been a rather under-researched area in comparative politics so far (Landman, 2000). That is to say, there are few studies, which explicitly examine democratic politics in relation to its *policy-making* capacities, let alone relate it to its degree of survival (or: consolidation) of these democratic polities in terms of their *political performance*.

The structure of the book is two-dimensional: it follows by and large the sequential logic implied in the 'political chain of democratic command and control' which embodies the interactive pattern of actors and institutions in contemporary representative democracies that shapes the political *process*. This *systemic* approach is represented by the division of this book into Part Two, Part Three and Part Four. *In Part Two* the central focus is on political parties and their behaviour, in terms of competition and co-operation *vis-à-vis* other parties and with regard to the electorate. In *Part Three* we shift our focus to the way *political parties* operate in terms of interest mediation and representation in government. The role of institutions – the specific 'rules of the game' – is here examined with respect to public *policy formation*. Finally in *Part Four* we pay attention to the resulting *political performance* of democratic systems in terms of governance. This concerns the relationship between the organization of political rule, here representative democracy, as a regime and the population at large, i.e. the citizens of a country.

The second dimension structuring the ordering of the chapters concerns the way and extent to which the interactions between actors and institutions are cross-nationally patterned. For, as has been argued in this chapter, the analysis of theories of democracy requires a systematic comparative approach to assess the usefulness of existing theories (see: Guy Peters, 1998; Pennings et al., 1999; Landman, 2000). To this end each and every chapter pays full attention to theories that aim at explaining the role of actors (e.g. electorate, parties, government, etc.) given the institutional design of representative democracy within which they operate. Hence, in *Part One* we focus on the comparative analysis of democracy as a central topic within political science as well as on the comparative study of 'democraticness' of these systems. In *Part Two* the crucial and central role of political parties is considered and examined within the perspective of systems theory (Chapter 4). In Chapters 5 and 6 this role is analysed by means of the institutional approach of competition and co-operation between parties. *Part Three* explicitly discusses the political process of public policy formation by means of the 'new' institutionalism. First the focus is on the institutional design of 'negotiation democracy' as it has developed in comparative politics (Chapter 7). In Chapter 8 the interactive process between political actors and institutions is elaborated in terms of veto points. Part Three is closed by examining the development of the welfare state in contemporary representative democracies (Chapter 9). Finally in *Part Four* the focus is directed towards what one could call the production of democratic systems. This, all too often neglected, aspect of political systems is elaborated in Chapter 10 by discussing the present 'state of the art'. The other two chapters that make up this part of the book attempt to apply the institutional approach to representative democracy. Chapter 11 focuses on the working of and effects of institutions on the policy performance of democracies. This approach is extended in the final chapter, where the relationship between political process and systemic conditions is related to the topic of democratic performance in terms of public governance.

By presenting the study of contemporary democracy as a political process, we think to be able to analyse representative democracy not as a static system, but rather as a political regime in motion. For, although 'democracy' as a (continually contested) notion may well have existed throughout history, it must be understood as a *contemporary* political system that is in need of constant attention and discussion – not only in the so-called emerging democracies, but also in the established democracies of today's world.

NOTES

1 I leave aside the perennial problem of defining 'stability' as well as the, almost inevitable, inherent teleological bias of any such definition; but see Lane and Ersson, 1998: Chapter 4.
2 Note that the use of the term 'optimum' is different here from what is meant by a *Pareto-optimal* solution, i.e. the 'social welfare' function in Social Choice literature (see Mueller, 1989: 384 ff), nor the application of (economic) norms of 'efficiency' and 'effectivity' as employed by the Virginian school approach to problems of 'Public Choice' (see Lane, 1985: 150 ff). Essential to our understanding is the fact whether or not the actual outcome of the political process is acceptable to all concerned, rather than representing the perfect result one can theoretically construct, either on the micro-level (i.e. Social Choice) or on the macro-level (i.e. Public Choice). As far as 'choice' is involved we mean *political choices* shaping mandatory policies in a society by means of public goods. See: Keman, 1996.

3 It should be noted that both the informal and the formal 'rules of the game' depend on whether or not they are enforceable, i.e. whereas the 'Rule of Law' in a liberal democracy is in most instances accepted and adhered to by the public, this is less self-evident with the informal rules. Here the efficacy depends on whether or not the actors involved in the 'political game' are able to sanction each other for non-co-operation, defection or non-compliance. See also: Axelrod, 1984; Ostrom, 1990; Scharpf, 1997.

4 Of course, this is a gross abstraction from the actual history of most political systems and their sub-systems. Moreover, not all political actors became organized or gained access to the decision-making procedures simultaneously. Nevertheless, one may argue that all relevant actors are presently confronted by the existing sets of formal and informal rules simultaneously. Depending on their resources or their capacity to form coalitions they are always somehow, somewhat capable of either bending the rules or even altering them to allow for more room to manoeuvre. Essential to our understanding is the fact whether or not the actual outcome of the political process is acceptable to all concerned.

THE DEVELOPMENT OF THE STUDY
OF COMPARATIVE POLITICS[1]

Hans Daalder

'Comparative politics' existed long before it became a recognized subfield of the modern discipline of political science. A century or so ago, a knowledge of the variety of political systems formed part of the normal education of *literati* in different disciplines, such as law and philosophy, history and letters. There were classic writers on problems of modern government in different countries such as Mill, Bagehot, Bluntschli, Radbruch, Redslob, Duguit or Bryce. Their treatises contained many comparisons, over time as well between different societies. One might go back further in history. Political theory abounds with comparative discourse on both contrasts and commonalities in political life, as even a superficial survey of the writings of Aristotle and Polybius, of Dante and Machiavelli, of Bodin and Locke, of Montesquieu and De Tocqueville, not to speak of the authors of *The Federalist Papers*, immediately shows. Man has speculated comparatively on problems of government and society in both prescriptive and descriptive terms since times immemorial. If we nevertheless insist that modern comparative politics is somehow different, this is for three not unrelated reasons: *first*, modern comparative politics deals consciously with a political world which has changed drastically from the universe known to the great writers of the past; *second*, it has become the special terrain of a recognized subfield of contemporary political science; and *third*, as such it shares in both paradigmatic shifts and new developments in research techniques in that discipline.

2.1 THE ACADEMIC TRADITION

Several characteristics marked the understanding of government in Europe and the United States as it had developed by the beginning of this century.[2]

First, there was a strong normative overtone in discussions on government and democratic rule. Normative approaches were traditionally strong in fields like law, philosophy or theology in which problems of government were discussed at the time. Different ideological traditions, whether Conservative, Catholic or Protestant, Liberal, Radical or Socialist, inevitably had their impact on political discourse. So had more-specific traditions of political theory which nourished debates on crucial themes like sovereignty, community, authority, liberty, constitutionalism, rule of law and so forth.

Second, discussions of government often reflected particular conceptions of history. In the hands of some, this might lead to the elaboration of 'historical laws', often couched in terms of different 'stages' through which societies would develop. 'Diachronic' comparisons thus came naturally. Models of social change often showed a clear evolutionary or even teleological bias.

Third, there was generally a strong emphasis on political institutions, which were thought to be not only the results of past political strife, but also factors which could control present and future political developments.

Fourth, 'comparative' politics generally assumed specific country perspectives. Thus, in Britain 'cross-channel' dialogues easily developed into a contrast between (stable) British 'cabinet government' and (unstable) French 'gouvernement d'assemblée' (or for that matter British 'rule of law' versus French 'droit administratif'). Trans-Atlantic debates resulted in the conflicting typologies of a 'parliamentary' versus a 'presidential' system of democratic government. Perennial debates in France on the merits, or lack of merits, of the French revolution strongly coloured political discussions on problems of constitutionalism and popular sovereignty. Debates in what was to become Germany had a powerful impact on the analysis of state and nation, of the exercise of power, of 'organicist' versus 'liberal' modes of social and economic development, and of the comparative role of bureaucracies – subjects which were to become the concerns of future social science also outside German borders. Comparisons of European countries with the United States underscored the early nature of American democracy and stressed the importance of voluntary groups in a free society, but the United States could also be held up as a negative yardstick for alleged abuses, for its spoils system, the role of lobbies or a yellow press, or more generally the dangers of 'mass society'.

Typically, smaller European countries tended to be neglected in the reasoning of learned men outside the borders of the particular country itself. Linguistic frontiers may partly explain this. But probably more important was the assumption, typical of nineteenth and early twentieth century power politics, that small countries hardly mattered. At best they might be of little more than folkloristic interest, at worst they were seen as no more than transient players in a world in which the larger countries determined history.

'Comparative politics' then went generally not much beyond speculation and the study of 'foreign government'. Other states were generally seen as entities all on their own, or at most as possible yardsticks against which to measure developments in one's own society, and then often as negative yardsticks at that.

2.2 THE POLITICAL SHOCKS OF THE TWENTIETH CENTURY AND THE EROSION OF INSTITUTIONAL CERTAINTIES

All this was to change drastically in the wake of three fundamental twentieth century shocks: the breakdown of democracy in Weimar Germany, the rise of totalitarian systems and the turn towards authoritarianism of most of the new states which were established following the demise of European colonialism.

The formally legal '*Machtübernahme*' in Weimar Germany in 1933 shattered democratic hopes and self-confidence. The Weimar constitution had been heralded as the perfect model of democratic constitutionalism. Its fall destroyed the trust in political institutions as sufficient guarantees of democratic rule. Admittedly, some theoreticians attempted to retain 'institutionalist' explanations, singling out 'faulty' institutions such as proportional representation (e.g. Hermens, 1941), the presence of a directly elected President next to a 'normal' but thereby weakened *Kanzler*, or the absence of judicial review, as major factors in the destruction of democratic rule. But generally, institutionalist analyses stood discredited. A growing awareness of the patent discrepancy between the promises of the Soviet constitution of 1936 and the realities of naked power relations in the USSR reinforced this tendency, as did events in Italy since 1922 and in France in 1940.

The rise of totalitarian political systems massively changed the perceptions of politics. Their development, in some countries and not in others, raised new problems of comparative enquiry. Earlier beliefs about the 'natural' development of democracy foundered. 'Autocracy' had been a time-honoured category of political analysis, and 'absolutism' had been the natural counterpoint of constitutionalism and later of democracy. But totalitarianism seemed to represent an entirely new political phenomenon. Problems of power and leadership, of propaganda and mass publics, of repressive one-party systems and police rule, came to dominate political discussion. Sociological and psychological explanations seemed to offer better insights into the realities of totalitarian rule than did traditional political theory or institutional analysis.

The post-1945 world was soon to see also the rise of many new states from what had been colonial dependencies. Such states had generally been equipped with democratic constitutional arrangements, which in most cases proved ineffective to stem developments of authoritarian regimes, whether in the hands of traditional elites, military or bureaucratic governors, or revolutionary party leaders. Such developments further undermined a belief in institutional approaches, and called for alternative modes of analysis.

One effect of the great political shocks of the twentieth century was a massive migration of scholars, notably to the United States of America, but to a lesser extent also the United Kingdom. One needs only list prominent names such as Karl W. Deutsch, Henry W. Ehrmann, Otto Kirchheimer, Paul Lazarsfeld, Karl Loewenstein, Hans Morgenthau, Franz Neumann, Sigmund Neumann, and Joseph Schumpeter, to make clear the importance of this factor for new developments in the study of politics. That field was also to attract the progeny of European refugees who, as a typical 'second generation', turned to the analysis of comparative and international politics in great numbers. Exiles from Hitler were followed by migrants from Communist repression, and later still by a growing number of Third World scholars who opted to stay in the First World. A desire for the systematic study of comparative politics came naturally in such circumstances. It heightened concern with the realities of political power, both within and between states. It made for a characteristically ambivalent attitude about democracy: if anything the belief in democratic values became stronger, but expectations about its chances turned toward pessimism.

2.3 ACADEME AND A CHANGING POLITICAL UNIVERSE

If migrant scholars looked back naturally on developments in continents they had left, the world was changing, and so was the role of the United States in what was rapidly becoming global politics for policy-makers and students of politics alike. Although Europe remained a key area, other parts of the world, including notably the evolving Communist bloc, Japan and a rapidly growing number of new states, became matters of urgent political and intellectual concern. So did Latin America, long regarded as a backyard of a Monroe doctrine America. Comparative politics saw the number of its possible units of analysis grow beyond recognition. At the same time problems of political stability and legitimacy, of social and economic development, of competing political regimes and ideologies assumed an entirely new importance.

The need to understand this new world could be met in a variety of ways. It underscored the importance of experts on single countries, notably those which became the object of particular policy concern. It increased the relevance of traditional area studies which it released from their (sometimes almost museum-like) preoccupation with the unique features of 'other' civilizations; in the process cultural anthropology became a more central field in contemporary social science. At the same time, older beliefs about inevitable – and presumably static – differences gave way to concerns with political and social change – inter alia toward democracy – and beyond this: to discussions of the extent to which such changes could, and should, be engineered.

All this fitted in well with the traditional temper of American academics. The lure of 'science' had traditionally been strong and had expanded much beyond the 'natural sciences' into the social sciences and even the humanities. So had the assumption that 'science' could and should lead to practical policy results. There was a strong belief that the academic enterprise should centre on the elaboration of testable theories. At the same time, the idea of interdisciplinary study stood in high esteem. It was given a strong impetus within some of the great universities (the University of Chicago being a particularly important centre). Such interdisciplinarity was moreover reinforced by new agencies, including government research councils, the newly established (American) Social Science Research Council and a growing number of private foundations all becoming increasingly involved in sponsoring 'relevant' research. This in turn facilitated a massive expansion of graduate schools, and fostered collaborative research between senior and junior scholars, the latter being called upon to 'test' particular theories elaborated by the former through detailed empirical research. All this came to coincide with the development of new research tools, which helped to foster what was soon to become known as the 'behavioural revolution' (from which electoral and value studies have benefited). Next to library research and field work in a participatory setting, the survey became a powerful research tool.[3] Governments also began to develop more and more important statistical data to monitor the effects of new policies. A rapidly growing number of international organizations, whether global (such as the United Nations and its specialized agencies, the World Bank or the International Monetary Fund), or regional (the OECD growing from the efforts of the Marshall Plan, and the European Communities being particularly important), came to collect statistical data on many countries. To the extent that they were presented in standardized form, this facilitated comparative inquiry. More and more efforts also went into the construction of time-series data, necessary for the study of developments over time. This massively increased amount of quantitative data (initially developed mainly in the context of economic and social policies and used in particular by economists and experts in social policies) also found its way into data handbooks and data archives (see e.g. Banks et al., 1997; Mackie and Rose, 1991; Woldendorp et al., 2000). The computer revolution was concurrently to facilitate the storage, analysis and access to such data. The efforts of individual scholars first, research sponsoring agencies later, made the pooling and preservation of research data (including the products of survey research for secondary analysis) increasingly common practice. All this occurred at a time of a massive expansion of academic enrolment, which increased facilities not only for graduate research, but also for publishing research findings. Both university presses and specialized commercial publishers massively expanded. Journals proliferated. So did professional associations and the number and specialization of workshops and panels at academic conferences.

If both the mass, and the sophistication, of such developments in social science were taking place initially mainly in the United States, they soon became an international reality. Early in the post-1945 period deliberate efforts were made to foster international comparative research. One powerful stimulus came from UNESCO, which established its own International Social Science Research Council, and which provided a powerful stimulus for the establishment of international professional bodies such as the International Political Science Association (IPSA) or the International Sociological Association (ISA). Many national governments expanded their research councils. The idea of international exchange and research co-operation found increasing favour, with the fellowship programmes of a number of American Foundations, the Fulbright programme, and to a lesser extent agencies like the British Council setting a pattern. In the process English became increasingly the *lingua franca* of modern social science.

2.4 THE NEW COMPARATIVE POLITICS

Against this general background of political change on the one hand, and a massive expansion of international and national policy-making and research on the other hand, 'comparative politics' developed rapidly. The shift in terminology from the older term of 'comparative government' to 'comparative politics' was symbolic for what was in fact a conscious desire to move away from the traditional concern with political institutions towards a preoccupation with political and social developments generally and within democratic systems in particular.

There are some particular landmarks in the development of modern 'comparative politics'. One of these was the Evanston seminar at Northwestern University in 1952 which brought together a group of then-younger scholars including Samuel Beer, George Blanksten, Richard Cox, Karl W. Deutsch, Harry Eckstein, Kenneth Thompson and Robert E. Ward under the chairmanship of Roy Macridis. In a statement, published in the *American Political Science Review*, they branded the existing study of comparative government as parochial in being mainly concerned with Europe only, as being merely descriptive instead of analytical, as overly concerned with institutions rather than processes, and as being insufficiently comparative, wedded above all to case method approaches (Macridis and Cox, 1953). Some of the members of the Evanston group vigorously clashed with stalwart representatives of an older generation, including such luminaries as Carl J. Friedrich, Maurice Duverger, Dolf Sternberger and William A. Robson during a colloquium of IPSA in Florence in 1954 (Heckscher, 1957). Such older practitioners of comparative government were not readily persuaded by the new gospel. They were to note gleefully that the most irascible proponent of the new 'comparative politics', Roy Macridis, was soon to publish work on France and other countries along what seemed after all rather traditional lines. The continuing need to take account of specific country perspectives was also to become apparent in the work of other scholars of the group, who after all became editors and authors of influential textbooks organized on the basis of country studies (covering again mainly the larger countries; e.g. Beer and Ulam, 1958; Macridis and Ward, 1963).

In the meantime, a group of scholars (including some members of the Evanston Seminar) was being formed who as a group would have a lasting influence on the development of comparative politics. Many of them were, or would be, active in what was soon to become known as 'the Committee' (i.e. the Committee on Comparative Politics of the American Social Science Research Council). In the second half of the 1950s, this Committee deliberately brought together a number of leading area experts. With Gabriel A. Almond as its highly influential chairman, it set itself to recasting the analysis of comparative politics along mainly *structural-functionalist* lines. As Almond explicitly stated in the influential volume edited by himself and James S. Coleman, *The Politics of the Developing Areas* (1960), the ambition was to find 'a common framework and set of categories to be used in … area political analysis'; to this end Almond himself engaged in 'experiments in the application of sociological and anthropological concepts in the comparison of political systems', irrespective of time or area. This work was eventually to lead to the famous 'crises of political development' model, which sought to analyse political systems in terms of the character and sequence of six major processes: legitimacy, identity, penetration, integration, participation and distribution (see also: Pye, 1966). One manner in which to validate such approaches was to bring together members of the Committee with experts on areas, particular institutions or social processes for a series of books on different aspects of political development, including communications (Pye, 1963), bureaucracies (LaPalombara, 1963), political culture (Pye and Verba, 1965), education (Coleman, 1965), parties (LaPalombara and Weiner, 1966), and (belatedly) state-formation (Tilly, 1975). Two works were intended to cap the approach: a book offered mainly as a textbook (Almond and Powell, 1966), and a co-authored volume on *Crises and Sequences in Political Development* (Binder et al., 1971). Whereas the first seemed to proclaim certainty, the latter revealed considerable self-doubt and disagreement in the Committee. Clearly, its members did not see eye to eye on such fundamental matters as the existence or not of a linear development from tradition to modernity, and the possibility to engineer social change and democratization or not.

Of course, such debates were not restricted to members of the Committee. A great many scholars, in different disciplines, tried their hand at defining processes of political development and modernization.[4] For all their diversity and disagreement, such writings had in common an attempt to understand processes of social change, conceived as in principle comparable over different areas and time-periods, and tackled with instruments from whatever social science discipline seemed appropriate. Such approaches also led to a reconsideration of past patterns of political and social change in nations already seen as fully or mainly modernized, including the United States itself and Western Europe. Historians were asked to join in such efforts at comparative understanding (see for example: Black, 1966; Tilly, 1975, 1990; Grew, 1978).

The impact of these approaches on the discipline was substantial. All manner of Ph.D. candidates swarmed out to study processes of social and political modernization in countries all over the world. They did so with different interests and intent. Some became thoroughly intrigued with the persistent role of traditional structures and beliefs, making them eager novices in the ranks of area specialists and cultural anthropologists. Others concentrated rather on the other end of the presumed tradition–modernity continuum, identifying largely with the search of economists and experts on public administration for 'development'. Yet others felt happier with the work of various international organizations which sought to monitor and stimulate social and economic developments with the aid of statistical indicators, regarding the universe of nations, or some particular sample of it, as a laboratory in which to test particular development models (see: Przeworski and Teune, 1970).

2.5 INEVITABLE REACTIONS

For all its exhilaration the political development boom was to create its own reactions, in rather different ways.

One reaction consisted in the development of counter-models of development which treated the prosperous West not as the prototype of a modern society which others were naturally to attain at some later stage, but as the root cause of an inequitable distribution of the world's goods. Marxist theories of (neo)imperialism held capitalist development responsible for the exploitation of the Third World, and regarded the so-called 'independence' of former colonies as a thin guise for what was in practice 'neo-colonialism'. Notably from the background of Latin America, which had much older independent states than Africa and parts of Asia, developed the various brands of 'dependency' theory which emphasized the co-existence of traditional sectors of society and the economy with modern economic sectors which were in practice little more than the *emporia* of the advanced economies in the USA and Europe. Such models were given a more elaborate treatment in Wallerstein's *World System* approach, which became in many ways an academic industry of its own.

A second reaction came from those who had difficulty fitting Communist systems into the framework of general development theories. To many, such a problem did not seem particularly urgent: the comparative study of Communist societies was to a considerable extent a world unto itself, and many were happy to leave it at that. The idea of a possible convergence of systems in the West and the East seemed to most observers bereft of reality, perhaps a matter of speculation for economists, not for those who knew the patent differences in political life from direct physical experience or historical analogy. But developments of Communist states did yet enter the field of general comparative politics for at least two reasons. Communist models might and did serve as example and inspiration for Third World countries, notably in their Chinese and Cuban variety. And in a more theoretical vein, a debate arose on the issue to what degree totalitarian systems were themselves a product of modernity. This point had been strongly argued by Carl J. Friedrich, who saw in that characteristic the fundamental difference between older systems of autocracy and royal absolutism and modern totalitarian systems (Friedrich, 1954; Friedrich and Brzezinski, 1956), but was denied by scholars like Wittfogel who saw many common features between the systems described by him in his *Oriental Despotism* (1957) and systems of modern totalitarian rule. Nevertheless, whether seen as possible models of modernization, or as alternative expressions of modernity itself, the study of totalitarian systems remained on the whole outside the scope of general comparative politics writing. At least one reason for this was the tendency to equate political *modernity with democracy*, in systems already existing or as the natural end-product of political development.

A third reaction to the political development literature consisted in the allegation that it rode roughshod over the uniqueness of particular areas or countries. Such was the natural reaction of scholars nurtured in a tradition of 'configurative' studies, whether of a particular local culture, or a particular political system. Such scholars were not comfortable with what they regarded as overly general categories of analysis. They emphasized that the essence of political and social systems lay in the complicated interaction of many variables which could only be disentangled by destroying the uniqueness of the whole. And they tended to deny the possibility of real comparative study given the inability of scholars to really know more than one or two cases sufficiently well (but see: Ragin, 1987; Rueschemeyer et al., 1992 for recent attempts to remedy these differences between the case study approach and 'many cases, few variables' studies).

2.6 RETHINKING EUROPE

For a time Europe became a somewhat ambiguous area in the development of the new comparative politics. The Third World seemed to attract most of the theorizing and field research, as did to a lesser and more specialist sense the development of Communist systems. Europe seemed possibly somewhat old-fashioned, a world of staid democracies about which all was known and where little happened. The very concept of Europe had become somewhat hazy, moreover. The erection of the Iron Curtain had lopped off a number of countries which had formerly formed a natural part of the European universe. If one saw Western Europe as for all practical purposes identical with 'democratic Europe', then certain European countries (including some members of NATO, like Greece, or Portugal, not to speak of Spain) presumably did not belong. If democracy were the defining characteristic, why then not study all modern democracies together, thus abandoning the very existence of 'Europe' as a distinct area (a conclusion drawn for example by Lijphart, 1984)?

Whatever such qualms, 'Europe' was soon to figure prominently on the map of comparative politics again, through a variety of circumstances. The persistent concern about 'totalitarianism' naturally made for comparative enquiry into past events: what after all had caused the breakdown of democratic regimes in some countries, and not others (see notably the consciously comparative study of Linz and Stepan, 1978). When much later Greece, Spain and Portugal all returned to democratic rule, the reverse question arose: what were the causes for such transitions from authoritarian rule (see: O'Donnell et al., 1986; Diamond et al., 1988). The failure of imposed constitutional regimes in many former colonies raised the issue whether alternative models of democracy might have done better; where was one to find these but in Europe (the British dominions usually being regarded as mere offshoots of a British system)? The general concern with development posed many questions for which the history of different European countries might provide possible answers, whatever the dangers of historical analogies. There was a rich literature on European countries, and access to sources was relatively easy. Europe contained, moreover, a variety of cases vital for comparative analysis with a generalizing intent, provided one really knew the specific cases that made up Europe, and went beyond the exclusive concentration on a few larger countries only.

Much of the history of the development of comparative politics writing in and on Europe can in fact be written in terms of a desire to take account of the political experience of particular countries (for a fuller elaboration of this theme, see: Daalder, 1987). As a special subdiscipline, European comparative politics grew largely from the efforts of a new post-war generation of younger scholars who engaged in a massive trek, to some extent to the United Kingdom, but particularly to the United States. They found there an exhilarating world of scholarship, with all manner of theoretical speculation and rich empirical research. This was in strong contrast with the paucity of 'modern' social science literature in their own country, and led naturally to a desire to emulate and replicate studies on America with comparable studies at home. At the same time, a confrontation with Anglo-Saxon scholarship also provoked a natural reaction against what were often felt to be too specifically 'British' or 'American' theories, typologies or models, and fostered a desire to develop alternative theories and typologies which were more in line with the understanding of one's own country. At a minimum, more countries should be brought onto the map of European comparative politics, which somewhat ironically required 'translating' their experience into Anglo-American concepts.

Thus, some of the most innovative comparative politics writing by European scholars betrays, on closer analysis, a strong influence of particular country perspectives. This had been irritatingly clear from what purported to be a general study of political parties by Maurice Duverger (1954), which for all the help the author received in data collection from an early IPSA network of European political scientists, was shot through with French perspectives and prejudices. But one can also document the impact of Italian concerns in the much more sophisticated analyses of party systems by Giovanni Sartori (1976). There is the disappointment of a left-socialist German emigré-scholar about post-war developments in Germany and Austria in the work of Otto Kirchheimer (see the collection by: Burin and Shell, 1969; Krouwel, 1999), just as Scandinavia provided the undoubted background of the development of a centre–periphery model in the rich work of Stein Rokkan (1970). An even clearer example is the deliberate development of the con-sociationalist model against the background of The Netherlands, Belgium, Austria and Switzerland, to counter the massive impact of what seemed too easy an identification of Anglo-American models of government with democracy *per se*.[5]

From the mosaic of such parallel studies a much more sophisticated picture emerged of the diversities of European experience which could be studied both in a diachronic and a synchronic manner, culminating in what is as yet the most satisfactory attempt at understanding the complexities of European political developments contained in Stein Rokkan's so-called 'topological-typological' map, or 'macro-model' of Europe (Flora et al., 1999; Rokkan, 1970; Rokkan, 1975; Rokkan and Urwin, 1983; cf. Daalder, 1979).

2.7 DIFFERENT RESEARCH STRATEGIES FOR STUDYING DEMOCRACY

Taking developments in the study of 'Europe' as an example, the considerable variety of modes of comparative study becomes readily apparent.

A seeming paradox is provided by the country monograph. To the extent such a monograph is written to elucidate particular political experiences for a more general public, it may offer insights of comparative importance. This is much more true if the monograph seeks to prove, or disprove, specific theoretical propositions first developed with one or more other countries in mind. The most telling example, however, is the consciously theory-based analysis of a single country case (e.g. Eckstein, 1966; Lijphart, 1968). Moving to a somewhat higher level of abstraction are comparative analyses of two, or a few, particular countries.[6] Most 'comparativists' must confess that their real knowledge of different countries tapers off quickly beyond a rather limited number of cases. One obvious way to overcome such limitations is collaborative research, in which, for any given research question, experts on different countries are asked to join in a common research effort. Most books on (European) democratic comparative politics consist of edited volumes of this kind. Such volumes bring much needed information on different countries together and testify to the fruits of cross-fertilization. But most of them suffer the natural defects of group enterprises. The choice of countries is often a function of the availability, or even the reliability, of individual country experts. Even the most rigorous attempt at editorial guidance rarely results in an even quality, let alone genuine comparability, of country chapters. Introductory and concluding chapters very often are of a rather ad hoc and impressionistic nature (but see for impressive examples volumes of a lasting nature, such as Neumann, 1956; Dahl, 1966; Rose, 1974; Budge et al., 1987).

This strengthens the case for attempting individual syntheses after all. The difficulty of such an enterprise becomes readily apparent, however, if one seeks for post-war equivalents of the great comparative government treatises of the past (e.g. Friedrich, 1941; H. Finer, 1949; not to speak of earlier classics such as Lowell, 1896 or Bryce, 1929). These are very hard to find (e.g. Blondel, 1969; S.E. Finer, 1970; for later attempts to analyse 'European democracies' see Smith, 1972; Castles, 1982; Steiner, 1986; Pelassy, 1992; Keman, 1996; Lane and Errson, 1998; Gallagher et al., 2000), and encounter the obvious problem of an increased number of countries to be treated, with many more empirical research findings of potential relevance to be covered.

Rather than on analysis at the level of countries as a whole, work has tended to focus on particular institutions such as monarchy (e.g. Fusilier, 1960), heads of state (Kaltefleiter, 1970), the formation of cabinets (e.g. Bogdanor and

Butler, 1983; Pridham, 1986; Budge and Keman, 1990; Laver and Shepsle, 1994), parliaments (Wheare, 1963; von Beyme, 1970), electoral systems (Lijphart, 1993), parties in general (Sartori, 1976; von Beyme, 1985; Panebianco, 1988), particular party families, interest groups, bureaucratic structures, and so on. In studies focusing on particular institutions or groups, there is always real danger of analyses that are out of political and social context.

Alternatively, there is the massive growth of quantitative 'cross-national studies'. As stated before, both the quantity and the quality of data have increased massively in the last decades, through the efforts of governments, international organizations, the gallant work of those who prepare 'data hand-books'[7]), and organize data archives. Such data invite cross-national studies, in a large number of fields. Thus one need only inspect the guide to journal articles in 'Electoral Studies', not to speak of important collaborative volumes (ranging from Rose, 1974 to Franklin et al., 1992), to see the richness of studies on electoral behaviour, and of elections (cf. Bartolini and Mair, 1990). We have important studies on political participation (influenced notably by the works of Verba et al., 1978; and Barnes and Kaase, 1979) and on the impact of changing values (an area dominated by the highly debated analyses of Inglehart, 1977, 1990). The study of cabinet coalitions has offered a fertile testing-ground of formal theories (for a useful survey and discussion see Laver and Schofield, 1990). As we shall see presently, the data revolution has also had a great impact on the study of the development and problems of modern welfare states and public policy. Not all such cross-national studies are really comparative, however. Although they draw on data from many countries, they are often directed more to problems of general political sociology or psychology than to a systematic inspection of country variables. 'Contextual' knowledge is often neglected, and with it possibly the essence of comparative politics itself, which in the words of Sidney Verba presupposes that one tries to generalize – using that term loosely – about nations, or to generalize about subnational entities like bureaucracies, parties, armies and interests groups *in ways that use national variation as part of the explanation* (italics HD; Verba, 1986: 28). A lack of knowledge of the countries studied has made some such 'cross-national' analyses verge on what Stein Rokkan once dubbed mere 'numerological nonsense'.

2.8 NEW APPROACHES TO THE STUDY OF DEMOCRATIC POLITICS

Developments in modern comparative politics, then, were largely the result of a greater knowledge of individual countries on the one hand, and of a true revolution in data collection and analysis techniques on the other. But at the same time, new political problems appeared on the political agenda, which resulted in something like a paradigmatic shift. If comparative politics had concentrated thus far mainly on problems of regime change, political institutions, and what in systems theory one calls 'input' structures, a new concern developed with problems of public policy and political 'output' (see Chapter 10 of this book). Various factors contributed to this development.

One cause was the (renewed?) 'Left' revolution in social science in the 1960s and 1970s, which faced the question why 'capitalist' systems endured, once-confident prophesies to the contrary notwithstanding. This led to a new concern with the role of the state which seemed somewhat forgotten in otherwise rival approaches of systems theory and economic determinism.[8] A parallel debate arose on the extent to which political parties – notably Socialist ones (see Castles, 1978; Schmidt, 1982b; Keman, 1988, 1990) – did affect government policies or not (see Chapter 9 of this book). A major element in the discussion became the degree to which states differed in their dependence on external economic forces (e.g. Katzenstein, 1985), which could only be solved by comparative inquiry. Even when such studies related to European countries only, the obvious relevance of international economic structures and events brought scholars closer to those who had long been preoccupied with world economic realities (e.g. the proponents of a World Systems approach mentioned earlier).

A second major factor was the development of 'neo-corporatism'. Originating to some extent from a transposition of an approach found useful in the study of Latin America (e.g. Schmitter, 1974, reprinted in Schmitter and Lehmbruch, 1979), it won great acclaim in attempts to explain 'Europe', and possible differences within it. By emphasizing the close interaction between public and private actors, the neo-corporatist approach seemed successfully to bridge input and output structures, and to present a more realistic picture of power relations and policy-making than either those who had spoken uncritically of 'the' state, or those who had embraced a naive 'pluralism', had been able to provide (see Chapter 8 in this book). Neo-corporatism became in Schmitter's words 'something like a growth industry'. But the gap between 'general' theory and empirical validation remained substantial, to the detriment of the value of the approach as a tool for general comparative analyses as distinct from the study of specific policy areas.

A third major contribution came from those who set out to analyse the development of the welfare state in comparative terms. On the one hand, this work fitted in well with the concerns of older development theorists: one should note the link between state expansion, economic policies and processes of political development which had characterized the work of German *Kathedersozialisten* and *Nationaloekonomen*; (re)distribution had been one of the paramount concerns of the Committee on Comparative Politics; and the leading empirical scholar in this field, Peter Flora (1974, 1975; Flora and Heidenheimer, 1981; Flora, 1986) saw his work as filling a gap in Rokkan's macro-model of democratic politics in Europe. On the other hand, comparative work on the welfare state was to encounter what was soon to become the major debate on its 'fiscal crisis', and on possible limits of state intervention more generally (Castles et al., 1987; Keman et al., 1987; Lane and Ersson, 1990). The label 'political economy' was to cover a wide variety of concerns, ranging from rational choice paradigms based on individualist self-interest, to studies of specific policy areas, competing models of general economic and monetary and fiscal policy, and renewed debates on political legitimacy. The full weight of such new approaches on the study of comparative politics is discussed by other contributors in this volume.

2.9 THE GREAT NEW CHALLENGES

But such challenges would seem to pale before the momentous changes taking place in what had been thought of as the Communist world, and the attendant shifts in contemporary international relations. In addition, the progress of European integration, however halting, is affecting the very basis of independent states as the unit of analysis on which so much of comparative politics has rested.

The long-standing assumption of a natural division of labour between the study of international relations engaged in analysing the interaction of states, and comparative politics concerned with the study of processes within states, always rested on somewhat dubious ground. It left unclear how scholars were to handle the formation of (new) states; it glossed over the great influence of domestic political processes on the making of foreign policies; it belittled what became known in the international relations literature as 'transnational' politics; and it postulated a degree of political independence for 'sovereign' states which never completely fitted the realities of an interdependent world (as advocates of a World System approach, dependency theorists and other political economy theorists had long maintained).

The division of the world into rival blocs had arguably permitted a certain separation of international relations and comparative politics. The assumption that existing states within a bloc remained distinct units of analysis seemed tenable in a world of relatively stable alliances (the necessary *ceteris paribus* qualification being as easily forgotten as it was given). The much more fluid international scene of today makes such an assumption rather more questionable.

At the same time, developments within the European Union increasingly undermine the role of member states as independent units, even though international modes of decision-making remain juxtaposed to supranational ones. Powers of decision in vital matters are either shared or transferred to organs 'beyond the nation-state'; while at the same time states also lose formal or effective powers to regional or local units. The 'national' power to control citizens, groups and enterprises becomes more dubious in a world of increased mobility and communication, affecting the status of individual 'states' as realistic units for comparative analysis.

But the greatest, if generally unexpected, challenge to comparative politics comes from events in Central and Eastern Europe. We mentioned earlier that the study of Communist states had become mainly the concern of a specialist group of scholars. Experts on Communism have largely lost their 'subject', although they have retained their knowledge of language and area. Scholars who were mainly concerned with the study of the development and the working of democracies, on the other hand, stand before an entirely new universe. Their concern had generally been with the comparative treatment of *existing democratic states*, which is a far cry from the *making of new democracies* in societies which have not known democratic rule for two political generations or more. For all the words spoken by pundits at symposia, in newspaper columns or journal articles, the extent to which proven knowledge exists is unclear.

The future of democracy presupposes at a minimum the creation of new institutions, but the brunt of comparative politics teaching since Weimar has tended to discount the independent effect of political institutions. Seemingly abstract debates on the merits of presidential, semi-presidential or parliamentary systems of government, on unicameral or bicameral legislatures, on electoral systems and their effect on the politicization of cleavages and the formation of party systems, on the proper role of judicial bodies, have become suddenly matters of crucial importance again (see: Lijphart, 1994). But they must function in areas with all the remnants of a totalitarian past, rival claims for political control and citizenship, possibly severe disagreements on the nature of the political unit itself – and all this amidst economic ruin and change. It is as if all major issues in the study of comparative politics are chaotically thrown together: the formation of states, the working of institutions, the rivalry of parties and groups, competing ideologies, the provision of state services and their limits, issues of economic interdependence, international power politics, and what not. Against this, one must ruefully acknowledge that basic political phenomena such as civil war, terror, ethnic conflict or the shattering effects of ideological strife, have traditionally tended to fall in the interstices of the study of international relations, comparative politics and political theory, rather than forming their core.

Comparative politics, then, stands before its greatest challenge yet. Never before were so many fundamental questions raised at one and the same time about the development of democracy, democratic governance and related performances. In all honesty one should acknowledge that it provides few definite answers.

NOTES

1　This is a revised and updated version of a chapter published in Keman (ed.) (1993).
2　For a full and sophisticated treatment, see the introductory chapter by Eckstein in: Eckstein and Apter, 1963.
3　Most notably in the field of electoral research, but also in other comparative analyses, e.g. the influential work of Almond and Verba on political culture, 1963.
4　To mention only some of the more prominent ones: Lerner, 1958; Apter, 1965; Organski, 1965; Barrington Moore, 1966; Zolberg, 1966; Rustow, 1967; Huntington, 1968; Eisenstadt, 1973: see also useful readers such as Macridis and Brown, 1961, 1986; Eckstein and Apter, 1963; Finkle and Gable, 1966; Eisenstadt, 1971.
5　See: Almond, 1956 and contra Lijphart, 1975, 1977; for a review of Lijphart and the parallel work of other writers like Huyse, Lembruch and J. Steiner, see: Daalder, 1974.

6 The value of this strategy had not been lost on members of the Committee on Comparative Politics which sponsored as one of its first projects a comparison of Japan and Turkey, see: Ward and Rustow (eds), 1964.

7 See for more notable examples covering rather different variables and countries Taylor and Jodice, 1983; Flora, 1983; Mackie and Rose, 1991; Lane et al., 1995; Katz and Mair, 1992; Woldendorp et al., 1993, 2000.

8 In that light the famous title of Evans, Rueschemeyer and Skocpol, *Bringing the State Back In* (1985) would seem to testify as much to a new vision of those who had been strangely blind, as to the real record of political studies they criticized.

3 COMPARING DEMOCRACIES: THEORIES AND EVIDENCE

Hans Keman

3.1 INTRODUCTION

The field of comparative politics has been characterized by a volatile relationship between methodological issues and a focus on political development. In the previous chapter Hans Daalder has given an account of how these two elements are not only intertwined, but also show an interaction. This development and the interaction between substance and method delineates 'comparative politics' as a distinct field of (or within) political science. To be exact: the development and diffusion of 'democracy' as a political and societal regime has dominated the research agenda of political science since the 1950s. Hence, research into and the analysis of democracy has always been a central concern of political scientists and the 'core business' of comparative politics and remains so. In this chapter we shall therefore attempt to record the 'state of affairs' with respect to this development from the perspective of *positive theory* (i.e. the development of knowledge and insights based on empirically developed propositions and related inferences). This account is derived from the vast comparative literature on *democracy*, its occurrence and diffusion, on the one hand, and its political performance based on *comparative data-analysis*, on the other.

Yet, before discussing the comparative analysis of democracy it may be useful to make some general points as regards the relationship between substance and method in comparative politics (Section 3.2). The conclusion of Section 3.2 will be that democracy ought to be defined as a concept that can 'travel across time' without undue stretching or limitation. This exercise is the subject of Section 3.3 where a number of indicators and quantitative variables will be discussed in terms of their theoretical validity and empirical reliability. In Section 3.4, the focus will be on the various explanations of comparative 'democraticness' (or: the degree of democratic development as a regime and as a polity; see: Bingham Powell, 1982; Rueschemeyer et al., 1992; Keman, 1996; Potter et al., 1997; Landman, 2000; Schmidt, 2000). Finally, in Section 3.5 attention will be paid to the performance of democratic states in view of their 'age' as well as the impact of the (so-called) 'waves of democratization'.

3.2 DOING COMPARATIVE RESEARCH: SUBSTANCE AND METHOD

There have been several attempts to delineate the boundaries of comparative politics, yet there is little agreement at present on its distinctiveness. Essentially, one could argue that there exist four different ways of defining comparative politics: first, those who distinguish it from other approaches to political science by referring to certain concepts employed which can only be properly understood by means of comparative analysis; second, those who take as a point of departure the central features of the political process which can be analysed for all political systems; third, there are those who maintain that politics can only be understood by employing a macroscopic perspective; fourth, and finally, there are many who define comparative politics by means of its method, i.e. the art of comparing, and who justify this by referring to the famous quote of Kipling: What know they of England, who only England know?

Although the last way of delineating comparative politics is purely methodological, it is the most prevalent one. However, I do not wholly concur with this view, for it would mean that the domain of a discipline is defined by its method, rather than by either its *substance*, i.e. the study of politics, which is then, of course, still in want of a definition itself, or by its *mode of explanation* that is supposed to advance our knowledge of the core subject (Faure, 1994). In this section I shall focus on what comparative politics can add to political science by means of its *use of attributes of macro-social units in explanatory statements* (Ragin, 1987: 5). This calls for an elaboration of the substance matter in terms of an identifiable object of study – democracy – and how this relates to empirical analysis – comparing democratic regimes.

In general, comparative political *research* is defined in two ways: either on the basis of its supposed core subject, which is almost always defined at the level of political system (Kalleberg, 1966; Wallerstein, 1974; Almond and Powell, 1978; Mair, 1996), or by means of descriptive features that claim to enhance knowledge about politics as a process (Apter, 1965; Roberts, 1978; Bingham Powell, 1982; Dogan and Pelassy, 1990; Lane and Errson, 1994; Keman, 1993a). These descriptions are generally considered to differentiate comparative politics from other fields within political science. Although it is a useful starting point, it is not sufficient. Some authors are more specific in their description and add to this general point of departure that comparative politics concerns nations and their political systems (Wiarda, 1986; Lane and Ersson, 1994), or the study of geographic areas. Finally, some authors deliver a more or less exhaustive definition in which 'the comparative study of political phenomena against the background of cultural, sociological and economic features of different societies' is the focus of comparative politics (Macridis, 1986; Berg-Schlosser and Müller-Rommel, 1987; Dogan and Pelassy, 1990; see also: Mair, 1996).

All these descriptions may be useful up to a point, but they do not help to mark off the field, and they require greater specification. Comparative politics must be defined in terms of its theoretical design and its research strategy on the basis of a *goal-oriented* point of reference – what exactly is to be explained – as in this case, democracy. A way of accomplishing this is to argue for a more refined concept of 'politics' and develop concepts that 'travel' and can thus be related to the political process in various societies. In addition, a set of rules must be developed that direct the research strategy, aiming at explanations, rather than at a complete description of political phenomena, by comparing such phenomena across systems, through time, or cross-nationally. At this point most comparativists often stop elaborating their approach and start investigating – however, without realizing that theory and method are *interdependent* modes of activities.

Comparative politics should be seen as an approach that aims at explaining the political process in a society by means of a (meta-) theoretical framework of reference and where explanations are validated by comparing macro-societal units of analysis (see also: Roberts, 1978; Ragin, 1987; Przeworski, 1987; Castles, 1989b; Lane and Ersson, 1994). The goal of comparative politics is to explain those 'puzzles' which cannot be studied without comparing and whose explanations are derived from logical reasoning. Hence, there can be no comparative research without a thorough theoretical argument underlying it, nor without a methodologically adequate research design to undertake it (Pennings et al., 1999; Landman, 2000).

In most discussions of comparative politics theoretical and methodological aspects are divorced, or – at least – treated separately. For example, Ragin (1987) and Przeworski (1987) emphasize predominantly the methodological aspects of the art of comparison as a 'logic of inquiry', which is often underdeveloped or incompletely elaborated. Theoretical progress and explanatory value appear then to emanate from their 'logic' (see: Przeworski, 1987: 45ff; Ragin, 1987: 125ff). Yet, the comparative analysis of the political process must be founded *a priori* in theory and then related to the best fitting 'logic of inquiry'.[1] Hence, a theory of democracy – be it simple or encompassing – must first be developed before one starts pondering over the adequate research strategy.

Another example of separating theory and method can be found in the study of electoral behaviour. This vital part of the political process can be explained fairly well on the basis of deductive reasoning. To validate its micro-level-founded hypotheses a comparative research design is not necessary. It can be done, but it is only genuinely comparative if the explanatory concepts are analysed by examining the variation in the political properties on both the micro- and macro-level. Electoral behaviour or party behaviour that is explained by means of the working of electoral systems, features of a party system, or the existing rules of government formation are in need of a comparative analysis (see, for example, Lijphart, 1984, 1999; Sartori, 1976; von Beyme, 1985; Bogdanor and Butler, 1983; Budge and Keman, 1990; Vanhanen, 1997). However, studies which focus on intra-systemic variation or micro-level variation are, notwithstanding their quality *per se* and usefulness as sources of information, not genuinely comparative in nature (see also: Blondel, 1990; Guy Peters, 1998).

This conclusion seems to hold for other types of cross-national research too: since the 1970s the study of 'electoral volatility' in Western Europe gained momentum, when it appeared that the division of party systems and the structure of voting patterns was less stabilized than originally assumed (Daalder and Mair, 1983; Crewe and Denver, 1985). It is interesting to note (with the help of hindsight) that most analyses were, in fact, based on country-based analytical descriptions with little comparative information. What was lacking was a truly comparative set of theoretical references concerning – in this case – the *explicandum*, i.e. 'political stability', that at the same time is consciously linked to a comparable set of operational terms (see: Bartolini and Mair, 1990: 35–46).

The same observation can be made with respect to the study of government formation. On the one hand, there are collections of country-studies (often developed on a shared list of elements present in each case description, e.g. Pridham, 1986; Laver and Budge, 1992) that stress the idiosyncratic nature of a country's political process, rather than the commonality of the development under review. On the other hand, a development can be observed with respect to the politics of coalition-building in which an underlying theoretical argument has been developed that directs the research, where countries are not the principal focus but a collection of comparable cases that show variation concerning what is to be explained (e.g. Laver and Schofield, 1990; Budge and Keman, 1990; Laver and Shepsle, 1994). Other examples could be mentioned to support this point regarding the relation between theory and method in comparative politics. Yet, the principal message is that much of the research that is labelled as comparative, either lacks theoretical foundation or is based on a research design that is not truly comparative in substance. As a possible way to remedy this weak relationship between substance and method I propose to focus on the *'political'* as a multi-dimensional space that is apparent and visible in all present societies and is always closely related to debates on the 'democraticness' of a society (Dahl, 1971, 1989, 1998).

The 'political' in a society can be described on the basis of three dimensions: politics, polity and policy (Schmidt, 1993a; Keman, 1997b). Politics is then what I would like to call the *political process*. On this level actors (mostly aggregates of individuals organized in parties, movements, or groups) interact with each other when they have conflicting interests or views regarding societal issues that cannot be solved by themselves (i.e. deficiency of self-regulation). The process of solving those problems which make actors clash is more often than not visible through the *institutions* that have emerged in order to facilitate conflict resolution. Institutions help to develop coalescence and to achieve a consensus among conflicting actors through compromising alternative preferences. These institutions manifest themselves in the rules of the game in a society. This is what is meant by the 'polity'. In many cases this code of conduct is organized by means of a democratic polity and the related 'rule of law' (Keman, 1999; Schmidt, 2000). The options chosen or decided upon for political action to solve the problem is what we shall call *policy formation*. Hence, political action, the relation between politics and policy-making, requires a degree of autonomy in order to be feasible and effective. In short, a theory of the political process must assume that there exists a mutual and interdependent relation between politics and society, which is shaped by the existing as well as emerging 'rules of the political game'. The issue at hand is then to investigate to what extent and in what way this process can be observed and affects societal developments. That is to say that all those processes that can be defined by means of these three dimensions are worthy of our attention as long as the analysis requires comparison in order to explain the process. The next step therefore is to specify the *unit of analysis* for comparative purposes. This is in our vocabulary the 'core subject' (Pennings et al., 1999; Landman, 2000).

To give a concrete example: the study of the development of democracy as a political system is not by definition a subject of comparative research. Yet, arguably, no one will deny that it is part of the substance that is embodied in what we have called the 'political' and has a strong relation with societal development. The core subject is then not *democracy per se* but instead the extent to which politics, polity and policy can be identified as properties of the democratic process.

Although the core subject of comparative politics has been specified in relation to the 'political' in a society – here democracy – it does not imply that we have a *theory* too. Rather than looking for broad concepts or micro-based theories it appears to me that a theoretical approach in comparative politics should focus on the interaction between political actors and institutions, and seek to establish in which way this interaction influences a system's capacity to perform in accordance with the needs and demands of a society. A viable trajectory to follow is to take stock of the existing ideas and theories concerning the origins, development and consolidation of democracy – as Todd Landman (2000) does – and falsify and verify these ideas by means of comparative analysis. Another road to travel is: take a seminal theory – such as for instance Dahl's theory of polyarchy – and attempt to specify in a rigorous way how and to what extent this approach to democracy stands up to reality and explains democratic developments at present (Schmidt, 2000).

In this chapter we shall use both trajectories. In Section 3.3 the conceptualization of democracy by Robert Dahl, *polyarchy*, will be the point of departure (Dahl, 1971). In Section 3.4 a number of explanations of the development of democracy will be discussed and comparatively examined. Both trajectories, this will be obvious, require a comparative method based on data on a macroscopic level and measured on a system level (see further: Lane and Ersson, 1994; Guy Peters, 1998; Pennings et al., 1999; Landman, 2000).

In sum: the *theory-guided* question of comparative politics is to what extent the 'political', the core *substance* of comparative politics, can indeed account for, and is shaped by the political actions in one system compared with another. It is this process and the attempts to explain it by systematic comparison as a *method* that distinguishes comparative politics from other fields in political science and at the same time makes it a field within political science.

Arguably there is not a concept that is more central to the substance matter of the 'political' than *democracy*. Not only is it a contested concept in political science, but also a fertile ground for theory development. Finally, it goes almost without saying, democracy is a regime type that represents all dimensions of the 'political': politics, polity, policy. It is therefore a *systemic* element of society in general. The study of democracy, central in this book, is typical for comparative politics both in terms of substance and method.

3.3 THE CONCEPT OF DEMOCRACY AS A COMPARATIVE VARIABLE

One of the basic features of any democracy is that there is a (freely) elected government which can be held accountable for its actions. Hence elections are an essential element of democracy and of paramount interest to political scientists. The same observation can be made with respect to the formation and operation of parliament as well as regards the composition and termination of government. Political parties play a key role in both elections and governments, shaping the actual process of democratic decision-making. There is, however, little consistent and reliable information in the shape of standardized information on the actual organization and working of democracies. Before discussing the comparative information on democracy we shall therefore briefly elaborate what is meant by democratic governance.

In principle democratic governance entails, as Abraham Lincoln put it in 1861: 'Government by the people, for the people, of the people'. In fact elections play a major role in the relationship between people and their government. Hence, the most prevalent form of democracy is *indirect* (possibly, with certain features of direct democracy; Budge, 1996a). To put it differently, democratic governance is *basically representative government shaped by an institutional arrangement* (which is almost always constitutionally driven; Schumpeter, 1942: 265–8). In addition, representative government is seen as establishing the legitimate authority of the state within a democratic society (cf. Weber in: Schmidt, 2000: 180–2). Finally, this institutional arrangement provides the basis for the mutual obligations between the democratic leadership or government, and the population. These obligations ultimately define the conditions that have to be met in order to delineate the concept of democratic government. These are (Held, 1987; Beetham, 1994):

1. popular representation by means of elections (freely and regularly held);
2. fully guaranteed civil and political rights for all citizens (effectively);
3. supremacy of the rule of law (by means of a constitution or basic laws).

In Table 3.1 information is presented on how far these conditions are indeed met (see also: Schmidt, 2000: 264–92) across the universe of discourse – in

Table 3.1 *Features of democraticness around the world*

Indicators	Age	Democraticness	
		Polyarchy (%)	Other (%)
Electoral competition	New	27.8	72.2
	Recent	63.2	36.8
	Old	100.0	0.0
Effectiveness of political rights	New	8.1	91.9
	Recent	39.1	60.9
	Old	90.9	9.1
Effectiveness of civil rights	New	12.3	87.7
	Recent	39.1	60.9
	Old	96.0	4.0
Summary			
Electoral competition		59.4	40.6
Political rights		12.2	87.8
Civil rights		18.2	81.8
N = 197 states		66 (33.7)	131 (64.3)
N of old democracies = 19 (9.5%)			
N of recent democracies = 52 (26.8%)			
N of new democracies = 72 (36.3%)			
N of non-democracies = 54 (27.4%)			

Explanation: See the appendix to this chapter for a description of the variables. The percentages represent the number of cases that proportionally belong to 'democracies' or not on each indicator of democraticness.

Source: Vanhanen (1997), Schmidt (2000).

today's world. Table 3.1 demonstrates first of all – and this is important for using the comparative method – that there are indeed distinctive groups within the universe of discourse (i.e. 197 states) as well as that there is considerable variation among those polities that are considered as 'polyarchic' (33.7 per cent). In other words there is sufficient cross-national variation to warrant statistically relevant information about the degree of 'democraticness' in the polities under review here.

A second observation from Table 3.1 is that in many cases we may speak formally – or constitutionally – of democracy, but this appears not to be reflected in the three requirements listed. On the contrary: fully established democratic practices (which is indicated by degrees of 'democraticness') are mainly available in the 'old' democracies. In 'new' (i.e. representing the countries that are democratized after 1988) and 'recent' democracies (i.e. established after the Second World War) there is room for (much) improvement. This is especially true for effectively observing civil and political rights in many democracies. Thirdly, the concept of polyarchy (to which we shall return below), indicating a high degree of political participation, on the one hand, and of popular representation, on the other, is present in one-third of all states. Obviously, democratization not only takes time as a process, but also varies considerably in terms of indicators of electoral competition and the observance of civil and political rights (Huntington, 1991; Landman, 2000).

BOX 3.1 'POLYARCHY' – THE TERM AND ITS MEANING ACCORDING TO ROBERT A. DAHL

'"Polyarchy" is derived from Greek words meaning "many" and "rule", thus "rule by the many", as distinguished from rule by the one, or monarchy, and rule by the few, oligarchy or aristocracy. Although the term had been rarely used, a colleague and I introduced it in 1953 as a handy way of referring to a modern representative democracy with universal suffrage. Hereafter I shall use it in that sense. More precisely, a polyarchal democracy is a political system with the six democratic institutions listed below. Polyarchal democracy, then, is different from representative democracy with restricted suffrage, as in the nineteenth century. It is also different from older democracies and republics that not only had a restricted suffrage but lacked many of the other crucial characteristics of polyarchal democracy, such as political parties, rights to form political organizations to influence or oppose the existing government, organized interest groups, and so on. It is different, too, from the democratic practices in units so small that members can assemble directly and make (or recommend) policies or laws.

Briefly, the *political institutions* of modern representative democratic government are:

1. *Elected officials.* Control over government decisions about policy is constitutionally vested in officials elected by citizens. Thus modern, large-scale democratic governments are *representative*.
2. *Free, fair, and frequent elections.* Elected officials are chosen in frequent and fairly conducted elections in which coercion is comparatively uncommon.
3. *Freedom of expression.* Citizens have a right to express themselves without danger of punishment on political matters broadly defined, including criticism of officials, the government, the regime, the socio-economic order, and the prevailing ideology.
4. *Access to alternative sources of information.* Citizens have a right to seek out alternative and independent sources of information from other citizens, experts, newspapers, magazines, books, telecommunications, and the like. Moreover, alternative sources of information actually exist that are not under the control of the government or any other single political group attempting to influence public political beliefs and attitudes, and these alternative sources are effectively protected by law.
5. *Associational autonomy.* To achieve their various rights, including those required for the effective operation of democratic political institutions, citizens also have a right to form relatively independent associations or organizations, including independent political parties and interest groups.
6. *Inclusive citizenship.* No adult permanently residing in the country and subject to its laws can be denied the rights that are available to others and are necessary to the five political institutions just listed. These include the rights to vote in the election of officials in free and fair elections; to run for elective office: to free expression; to form and participate in independent political organizations; to have access to independent sources of information; and rights to other liberties and opportunities that may be necessary to the effective operation of the political institutions of large-scale democracy.'

Taken from: Dahl (1998: 86–7).

From the literature and related data, it is clear that electoral rights and elections more often than not precede the extension of political rights concerning participation in processes of decision-making. The concept of polyarchy is an attempt by Robert Dahl to operationalize the process of democratization as well as elaborating a set of criteria for deciding whether or not a political system can be counted as a 'democracy' (Dahl, 1971, 1984, 1989, 1998). The typology, presented by Dahl in 1971, is a process based on the development of a set of institutions that is close to what one could call the 'ideal type' of democracy (Dahl, 1971: Ch. 10). In his own words polyarchy is:

> … a kind of regime for governing nation-states in which power and authority over public matters are distributed among a plurality of organizations and associations that are relatively autonomous in relation to one another and in many cases to the government of the state as well. (cf. Dahl, 1984: 237)

From this definition it will be clear that central to the adequate functioning of polyarchy is not only the existence and working of institutions, but also the existence and actual room for manoeuvre of societal groups and their organization. The institutionalization of the democratic process of governance is a prerequisite (or: a *conditio sine qua non*), not yet the establishment of a regime as a fully fledged democracy. These necessary institutions are, according to Dahl (1998: 38ff; see also Box 3.1):

- universal suffrage and the right to run for public office;
- free and fairly conducted elections;
- availability and observance of the right to free speech and protection to do so;
- the existence and free access to alternative (and often competing) information (not controlled by government);
- the undisputed right to form and to join relatively autonomous organizations, in particular political parties (and crucially: parties in opposition);
- responsiveness of government (and parties) to voters and accountability of government (and parties) to election outcomes and parliament.

It is this set of institutions *taken together* that distinguish polyarchic regimes from other regime types. The coming about of these institutions can then be seen as the *process* toward democratization. The endured existence and observance of the whole set is the hallmark of an *established* democracy (see also: Schmidt, 2000: 393–5; Keman, 2000b). It should be noted that this elaboration of the concept of democracy mainly focuses on 'politics' (i.e. pluralism), on the one hand, and on the 'polity' (i.e. Rule of Law), on the other. The 'policy' dimension is not obvious in Dahl's conceptualization and appears to be considered as an inherent effect of decision making. This then ought to be evaluated in terms of the 'common good' and 'Public Welfare' as post hoc observations (see for this: Dahl, 1989; Saward, 1994; Keman, 2000b).

Dahl's concept of polyarchy is not only a seminal contribution to democratic theory, but has also been a powerful incentive for empirical analysis.

Table 3.2 *Increase in polyarchies over time*

Period	Total polyarchies in 1990	Percentage of total number of countries	Increment in percentage
1860–1900	6	13.9	11.2
1900–1920	15	29.4	15.7
1920–1950	25	33.0	3.6
1950–1980	37	30.6	−2.4
1980–2000	66	33.7	3.1

NB: Data for 2000 are based on the author's own computations.

Source: Dahl (1998: 8).

Almost by definition, this type of research has been of a comparative nature and has induced a great number of attempts to measure polyarchy.[2] It is this type of comparative politics that makes it distinctive from other fields within political science: substance and method are complementary.

It is important to distinguish between operationalizations of polyarchy that aim at the *process* of democratization and those that measure *level* of democratization. If the researcher is interested in elaborating the extent to which a democratic polity is more or less polyarchic, he/she can choose to measure the established fulfilment of the set of institutions (listed above). Dahl did so by distinguishing, among a number of established democracies, the universality of suffrage (Dahl, 1971). According to this criterion Switzerland, the USA, Canada and Australia were lagging behind the other established democracies. In Switzerland women gained the full right to vote only in 1971. In the USA the coloured population were in fact hindered from exercising this right (in particular in the Southern states), whereas in Australia and Canada minorities (Aboriginals and Eskimos) were excluded from full citizen rights until the 1960s. Likewise in a number of established democracies certain parties were forbidden (e.g. communist and fascist ones, mostly during the 1950s) and in a number of 'emergent' democracies parties and trade unions find it difficult to exist (e.g. in Chile, Columbia, Turkey, etc.). Hence, the process of democratization focuses on the degree of establishment (and actual working of) all six institutional requirements listed by Dahl. This process of establishing liberal democracy as a fully-fledged political system is presented in Table 3.2.

It immediately becomes clear that although the absolute number of polyarchic polities has increased, the relative number remains quite stable over time. The implication being, of course, that becoming a member of the established club takes a long time. This can also be made visible by inspecting the distribution by *age* of polyarchic democracies (Figure 3.1).

Of all cases involved it can be seen that 40.1 per cent are not democratic at all. If we define the waves of democratization (see for this also: Huntington, 1984, 1991; von Beyme, 1994; Schmidt, 2000: 463ff) as those originating before the Second World War, those after 1945 but before 1988, and those after 1988 (respectively: 'old', 'recent' and 'new') then it is clear that the most recent wave has produced most democratic cases in history (note, however, this

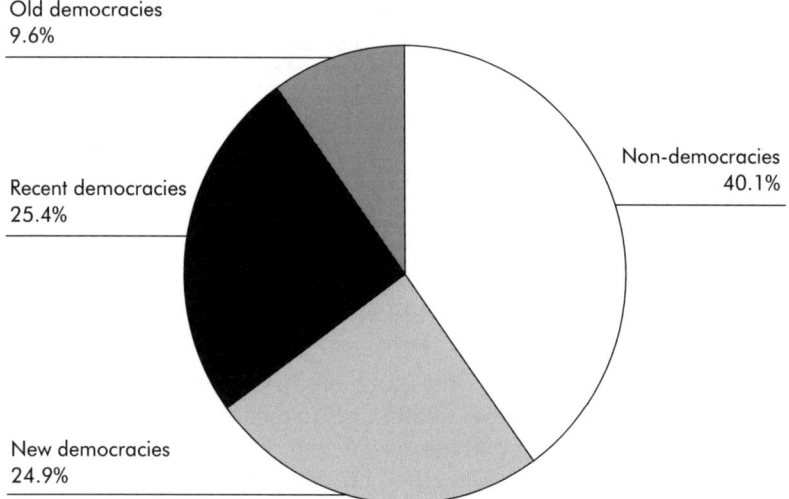

Old democracies
9.6%

Non-democracies
40.1%

Recent democracies
25.4%

New democracies
24.9%

Figure 3.1 *Distribution of polyarchy by age. Source: Vanhanen, 1997 (N = 172)*

does not mean they are fully polyarchic!). The first wave is characteristic of the countries which belong to the so-called OECD-world and are mainly found in Europe, North America, Australia and New Zealand. From these 'old' democracies a number became non-democratic during the 1920s and 1930s (e.g. Germany, Italy, Spain and Portugal). The second wave was produced in part by the victors of the Second World War, on the one hand, and as a result of the decolonization process, on the other. Although a number of these new states turned to non-democratic polities again, other states returned to a more democratic organization of state and society. This has been the case in Southern Europe (Spain and Portugal), Latin America (Uruguay) and the Far East (South Korea). Finally, the end of the Cold War as a consequence of the downfall of the Soviet Union as a world power has resulted in a strong increase of democratization in Central and Eastern Europe and elsewhere.

According to Schmidt it is difficult to assess what factors produced these waves. Yet, one may well suggest that certain shocks or crises have triggered off, at least in part, the sudden growth of democracies. Most commentators agree that the Great War (1914–18) has been a catalyst for the introduction of *universal suffrage* in most existing democracies and the adoption of democratic institutions in, until then, autocratic states. The second wave – the postwar era (after 1945) – conforms to this hypothesis, although at the same time the 'iron curtain' curtailed existing democracies in Central Europe. The third wave can be considered to have arisen in the wake of the collapse of the power of the Soviet Union. Hence, it can be posited that change in the international context is a powerful influence on the *process* of democratization.

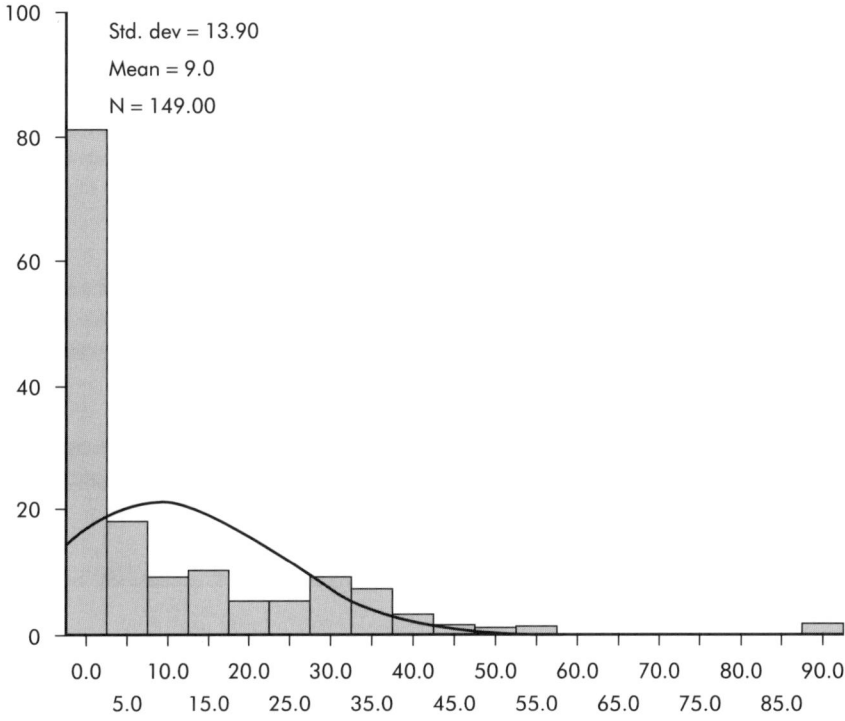

Figure 3.2 *Distribution of cases on the Index of Democratization (Vanhanen, 1990)*

Conversely, one may observe that internal forces have often been conducive to a degeneration or the downfall of democracy.

The waves of democratization that have occurred do paint only a rough picture of the development toward greater democraticness. The hypothesis sketched above is insufficient to explain fully the process of becoming a fully established democracy as defined in the concept of polyarchy. Among many comparativists Tatu Vanhanen can count as a prime example who has attempted to describe and analyse this very process (Vanhanen, 1990, 1997). Vanhanen's approach is both straightforward and encompassing. His aim is to develop an index of polyarchy, and therefore he has elaborated two measures representing 'participation' and 'competition' that together form an *Index of Democratization (ID)*.[3]

This index is measured over time and by means of regression analysis (see Appendix to Chapter 10 in this book). Vanhanen attempts to show the development of polyarchy by comparing the predicted level with the actually established level. From his analysis it appears that on average the countries score higher today than in the 1980s (1980 = 8.96; 1990 = 13.9) on the Index of Democratization (see Figures 3.2 and 3.3). Indeed, the world has changed

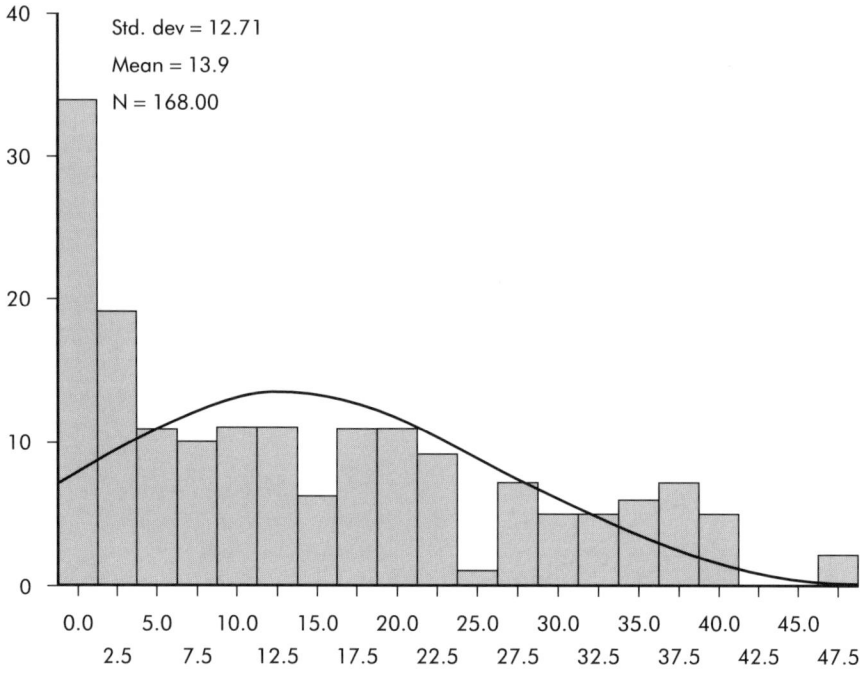

Figure 3.3 *Distribution of cases on the Index of Democratization (Vanhanen, 1990)*

towards more democratization and now contains a number of countries that have taken the road to greater polyarchy.

Even at first glance one can observe that the cross-national distribution has indeed moved towards higher values for more countries than in the 1980s. Without concluding that polyarchy is genuinely prevalent across the world in 2000, it is true that the majority of countries are more or less democratic and increasingly meeting the criteria defined by Dahl. Let us therefore turn now to an inspection of how far this process has indeed resulted in many cases where – in addition to the dimensions of Participation and Competition that are represented in Vanhanen's Index of Democratization – other indicators of polyarchy are available.

Most other indicators of democracy focus on the extant *level* and on either the *institutions* available or on the *quality* of democratic procedures. Coppedge and Reinicke (1990) have developed a scale that examines the available institutions that promote a pluralist organization of society. In addition to examining the requirements for free and fair elections, they have developed indicators to measure the degree of freedom of organization, of speech and information, and of access to government sources of information. This operationalization is quite close to Dahl's idea of polyarchy (see: Dahl, 1984, 1998: 85). Hence, Coppedge and Reinicke measure the extent to which

Table 3.3 *Distribution of levels of democracy according to regime type (N = 137)*

	Democracy		Non-democracy	
	Presidential	Parliamentary	Dictatorship	Autocracy
Coppedge and Reinicke	27.1%	22.1%	32.9%	17.9%
Jaggers and Gurr	32.8%	20.4%	31.4%	15.3%

groups in society can organize themselves and are capable of conducting a viable opposition. Yet, as Schmidt rightly observes, this kind of operationalization tends to ignore the formal institutions (i.e. Rule of Law) that restrict the powers of government and the state (Schmidt, 2000: 402; see also: Colomer, 1996; Lane and Errson, 2000). To some extent this defect has been solved by Jaggers and Gurr (1995). Within the research programme 'Polity III' (see also: Dahl, 1998: Appendix) these students of democracy have collected data across most nation-states on:

- those institutions that facilitate and promote political choice by citizens;
- availability of basic civil and political rights for all citizens;
- existence of constitutional requirements that limit the executive powers.

Jaggers and Gurr have developed a scale that enables them not only to differentiate between 'autocracy' and 'democracy', but also the level of democracy available (see for an explanation: Jaggers and Gurr, 1995; Schmidt, 2000: 404).[4] What do these cross-national variables tell us about the level of democratization?

First of all, as can be seen in Table 3.3, it appears that the method employed leads to different results. The number of *non*-democratic countries is proportionally twice as high according to Coppedge and Reinicke than found by Jagger and Gurr (the difference is 30 cases). This need not surprise us, since the latter rely mainly on formalized institutions, whereas the former much more focus on individual and group rights within a society. Secondly, Coppedge and Reinicke's survey was carried out in the 1980s and not during the 1990s. Hence, their results are representative of the situation before many of the communist states could transform their polity (see also Table 3.2). Finally, the method of Jaggers and Gurr is basically two-dimensional and allows for more differentiation *within* democracies and *between* non-democratic states. This difference is further highlighted by the fact that the bivariate relationship between the two scales is −0.62 ($R^2 = 38.7\%$). Yet, at the end of the day the differences are less if one controls their results for regime types developed by Alvarez et al. (1996). Alvarez has made a four-fold division of polities across the world into Presidentialism, Parliamentarism, Dictatorships and Autocracies (Table 3.4).

Controlling for these regime features, the differences are less and the values are even quite similar. At the same time it should be noted that on the

Table 3.4 *Distribution of political and civil rights worldwide (1999)*

	Civil rights	Political rights
Polyarchies		
Parliamentary	2.03 (11.9%)	1.39 (8.5%)
Presidential	2.87 (23.9%)	2.26 (19.7%)
Non-democracies		
Dictatorial	4.48 (39.6%)	4.80 (44.5%)
Autocratic	5.15 (24.6%)	5.44 (27.3%)
Total Mean	3.60 (100%)	3.43 (100%)
N	157	157
Correlations		
Civil rights	1.00	0.90
Polyarchy scale	−0.66	−0.70
Vanhanen Index	−0.70	−0.68
Jaggers and Gurr	−0.76	−0.83
Coppedge and Reinicke	0.69	0.67

Note: The lower the score the better the performance.
Source: Schmidt (2000); see also Appendix.

level of individual cases the differences are – again – not great, but certain cases appear to be odd or even out of place. This has been documented by Manfred Schmidt (2000: 405–7), who also shows that there are many countries considered democratic, whereas this seems rather counter-intuitive.[5]

Some of these results could well be contested because the data used are more often than not supplied by public authorities or derived from constitutional documents (see for this problem also: Woldendorp et al., 2000: Ch. 2). The researcher must take this information at face value if there is insufficient alternative information. Yet, this need not be the case, since the actual availability and observation of political and civil rights (Gastil, 1990; Freedom House, 1999) has been established since 1971. Contrary to the indicators and scales discussed here, this type of research focuses explicitly on the execution of individual rights not interfered with by the state (and its agencies). Secondly, the information is gathered by means of independently organized surveys polls (see: Gastil, 1990; Beetham, 1994; Freedom House, 1999: 547 ff; Schmidt, 2000: 409 ff).

For our presentation in this chapter, we have used two scales: Civil Rights and Political Rights. Both scales run from 1 to 7, where a low value implies actual availability and observation for these rights. Taken together these two scales provide information on the extent to which a nation is not only formally democratic, but can also be considered as truly liberal democratic in practice and therefore as close as can be to Dahl's polyarchy. As can be seen in Table 3.4, the prevalence and observance of political and civil rights do make a difference. What is striking is the marked difference between parliamentarism and presidentialism in this respect. The latter regime type consistently shows a worse record in observing civil and political rights, notwithstanding its rule of law. One may well wonder, with Linz (1990; but see also: Stepan and Skach, 1994), whether or not a presidential system is more prone to abuse. Alternatively, one could suggest that – although in parliamentary systems the executive and legislative powers are fused and governance appears more often than not volatile (see: Lijphart, 1992) – such a system appears to be associated with more persistent and effective 'checks and balances'.

All in all, it can be concluded that the indexes produced by *Freedom House* can be considered as proper indicators to compare the 'democraticness' of a society cross-nationally. The same conclusion applies to the regime types of Alvarez et al. (1996) as regards their distinction between democratic and non-democratic regimes. Yet, at the same time we also observe that the statistical relationship between regime types and civil and political rights is lower than those between the indexes of democracy and civil and political rights (Spearman's Rho between Regime Types and Civil and Political Rights is respectively: -0.52 and -0.58). In fact, none of the correlations between the indexes of Democracy and of Civil and Political Rights is extremely high (apart from Jaggers and Gurr, none of them is characterized by $R^2 \geq 50\%$). Nevertheless, we argue that the *concept* of polyarchy, as developed by Dahl, can indeed be measured to indicate the degree of 'democraticness' of a political system, and even within a society, whilst at the same time the cross-national variation remains sufficient. Hence, so we argue, although we have measured various dimensions of democracy as a system *and* its performance as a procedure, it is not yet satisfactory as a *truly* comparative variable. According to Bollen and Paxton (2000) this is mainly due to the (ab)use of 'subjective' measures (such as, for instance, those of Coppedge and Reinicke) or to the unreliability of the findings by Freedom House (1999) or Gastil (1998). An alternative line of enquiry could be to return to Dahl's original ideas and to combine the various measures (Bollen and Paxton, 2000: 78–9).

In our view the following procedure could be followed:

- combine *objective* measures with *subjective* ones;
- distinguish between conditions for *pluralism* and institutions of *polyarchy*.

To this end we collected a number of scales and indexes (see: Bollen, 1993; Bollen and Paxton, 2000; Schmidt, 2000) that have been developed both subjectively and objectively. Secondly, we have grouped these variables as being productive for creating pluralistic conditions or promoting polyarchic institutions (see the Appendix for the variables used). By combining subjective and objective measures we hope to improve the *reliability* of the data in use. By *ex ante* dividing the measures into more pluralistic and polyarchic we aim to improve the *validity* of the variables in use. The statistical procedure to carry this out is factor analysis (Table 3.5) – with one factor solution, Principal Axis Factoring (PAF) aiming at high levels of explained variance.[6]

By this means of data reduction, a number of indexes and scales – be they objective or subjective ones – have been dropped or appeared not to add much additional information. What we have found is – in our opinion – two valid *and* reliable variables indicating the extent of democracy and degree of democaticness across the world.[7]

Table 3.5 *Factor analysis of democracy scales and indexes*

	Pluralism		Polyarchy	
Variables used	• Political rights • Civil rights • Coppedge and Reinicke		• Vanhanen • Jaggers and Gurr	
Loadings	PCA	PAF	PCA	PAF
	0.946	0.502	0.926	0.585
	0.949	0.817	0.926	0.585
	0.856	0.821		
% of variance	84.28%	84.15%	85.79%	88.26%

PCA = Principal Component Analysis; PAF = Principal Axis Factoring.

In Table 3.6 we report the distribution of the level of pluralism and polyarchy and the related democraticness. Of the 127 nations that have positive scores on both dimensions – pluralism and polyarchy – about one-third (N = 43) of the countries included can be considered – according to this operationalization – as genuinely democratic (i.e. the score is ≥ 1.0). This is a relatively high number of countries.

Of course, what can be noticed from Table 3.6 is that the 'older' and the 'richer' the countries are the stronger their democraticness appears to be. In addition, the parliamentary types of democracy score consistently higher than any other type of regime, including presidentialism. Finally, it should be noticed that Latin-American countries do fare better than post-communist ones. This supports the idea that 'ageing' is an important factor in developing higher levels of democraticness. There are also some cases

Table 3.6 *Average scores of indicators of the level of democracy for type of countries, duration and regime type*

	Pluralism (N = 161)	Polyarchy (N = 145)	Democraticness (N = 127)
Type of countries			
OECD-members (N = 28)	1.06 (17.4%)	1.25 (20.0%)	2.29 (22.0%)
Post-communist (N = 23)	−0.67 (3.7%)	0.04 (15.9%)	−0.55 (4.7%)
Latin-American (N = 22)	0.59 (19.9%)	0.32 (15.2%)	0.73 (17.3%)
Other countries (N = 72)	−0.48 (59.6%)	−0.62 (49.7%)	−1.19 (56.7%)
Duration			
Old	1.23 (19.2%)	1.40 (18.6%)	2.66 (21.3%)
Recent	0.81 (46.5%)	0.75 (37.2%)	1.48 (42.7%)
New	−0.11 (34.3%)	0.20 (44.2%)	−0.04 (36%)
Regime type			
Presidential	0.45 (27.1%)	0.48 (34.1%)	0.89 (31.4%)
Parliamentary	0.94 (22.1%)	1.23 (20.5%)	2.16 (21.5%)
Dictatorial	−0.56 (32.9%)	−0.65 (30.3%)	−1.22 (32.2%)
Autocratic	−0.82 (17.9%)	−1.25 (15.2%)	−2.48 (14.9%)

NB: N = number of cases included for each indicator; percentages in parentheses are of total N (see headings).

where scores appear counter-intuitive or implausible. Examples are: Brazil (1.28), Papua New Guinea (2.07) and the Philippines (1.05), which seem to score unexpectedly highly. Conversely, other countries like South Africa and Mexico are scoring below par, which seems equally odd at this moment. Yet, overall we are convinced that this variable contains not only a lot of information but can also be considered as quite valid and reliable. Hence, in the remainder of this chapter we shall employ these three indexes of democracy to analyse not only its distribution across the universe of discourse, but also to (re)consider a number of associations with the other variables that can be seen as explaining the cross-national variation in democraticness as well as possibly accounting for certain societal performances (see also Chapter 11 by Lane and Ersson in this book).

Some of these possible and informative relationships have already been incorporated in Table 3.7. Looking at the values in more regional terms one can easily see that the OECD-world is the most democratic world at the moment. This need not surprise us as most of the nations included are 'old' and established polyarchies. It is more surprising that the post-communist countries score relatively low (but, in part, due to lack of data). Thus, duration appears to be strongly associated with the degree of democraticness, which is reflected in Table 3.1. Less straightforward is the association between 'democraticness and 'regime type': although the non-democratic types are indeed low in all respects, the differences between 'parliamentarism' and 'presidentialism' are noteworthy. The latter category has lower scores than one might expect. Part of the explanation, however, may well be the fact that the majority of presidential regimes were founded after the Second World War or even more recently. Second, most of the democracies are not (yet) wealthy (and, for instance, do therefore not belong yet to the OECD-world).

In summary in this section we have surveyed and discussed the various ways democracy can be conceptualized, measured and transformed into a valid and reliable cross-national variable:

- *pluralism* – representing the possibilities of organizing as a group on the societal level free from the state;
- *polyarchy* – indicating the positive conditions for the population to participate in national decision-making;
- *democraticness* – a combined measure of both these variables and thus presenting the degree of democraticness in a society from a comparative perspective.

3.4 EXPLAINING VARIATIONS OF DEMOCRACY

Most explanations of the development towards democracy and its vitality as a system have been characterized by a focus on *non*-political factors and, more often than not, on *functional* approaches (see for an excellent overview: Landman, 2000; Schmidt, 2000; also Dahl, 1998).

Secondly, the study of democratization and the working of democracy has been a continuous bone of contention regarding the application of the comparative method. On the one hand, it concerned a discussion with respect to the proper research design: the 'variable oriented' approach *versus* the 'case related' approach (cf. Przeworski and Teune, 1970; Lijphart, 1975; Ragin, 1987; Rueschemeyer et al., 1992; Keman, 1993a; Pennings et al., 1999). On the other hand, it concerned the choice and specification of the concept of democracy and its measurement (see the previous section).

In this section we shall employ the 'variable oriented' approach for a worldwide universe of discourse (see: Vanhanen, 1997; Bollen and Paxton, 2000). This is not done because we think that a 'case related' approach is wrong or inadequate. On the contrary. Yet, we hold the view that a cross-national analysis with a high number of cases and few variables is crucial for theory development. First, it induces the development of parsimonious models which can be used to verify general statements. Second, if certain explanations appear tenable they can (and should) be applied to well-defined sets of countries on the basis of a 'most similar systems design' (see: Janoski and Hicks, 1994; Pennings et al., 1999). Finally – as Rueschemeyer et al., have correctly pointed out – the two approaches need not be mutually exclusive but can be considered to be complementary. Hence, we view the development of explanatory models which are both parsimonious and plausible as a useful *and* necessary step for explaining essential phenomena within political science. Elsewhere this position is formulated as follows:

> There is no point in constructing a general explanation clogged up with minutiae of time and place. The purpose of a theory is to catch and specify general tendencies, even at the cost of not fitting *all* cases (hence one can check it only statistically, and it is no disproof to cite one or two counter-examples). The theory should, however, fit the majority of cases at least in a general way, and provide a sensible and above all an applicable starting-point for discussion of any particular situation, even one which in the end it turns out not to explain – here it can at any rate serve as the basis of a special analysis which shows which (presumably unique or idiosyncratic) factors prevent it from fitting. A general theory of this kind serves the historian by providing him with an entry point and starting-ideas. These, we would argue, he always brings to the case anyway; with a validated theory he knows they are reasonably founded and has a context within which he can make comparisons with greater confidence. As we suggested at the outset, there is no inherent conflict between historical analysis and general theory. Each can, indeed must, be informed by the other and supplement the other's efforts. Theory is therefore a *necessary* simplification and generalization of particular motives and influences, not simply a restatement of them, though complete loss of contact with historical reality will render it too abstract and ultimately irrelevant. (Budge and Keman, 1990: 194)

Surveying the literature on explaining democracy as a system and its development (i.e. the process) the following answers have been offered:

- *Economic development* and socio-economic *circumstances* influence both its development and working (see: Lipset, 1959; Cutright, 1965; Dahl, 1971;

Bollen, 1979; Przeworski, 1985, 1991; Burkhart and Lewis-Beck, 1994; Berg-Schlosser and De Meur, 1996).
- *Modernization* of society and the extension of *public welfare* are conducive to (further) democratization of the national state (see: Lerner, 1958; Lipset, 1959; Neubauer, 1967; Inglehart, 1977; Vanhanen, 1989, 1997; Dahl, 1998).
- *Institutionalization* of democracy as a regime in relation to its *viability* which over time enhances the level of democraticness (see: Moore, 1966; Linz, 1978, 1994; Dahl, 1984; Hadenius, 1992; Diamond and Plattner, 1994).
- *Organized political action* in terms of participation and opposition, which 'makes democracy work' (in whatever fashion or way) is an important and often neglected facet of *democratic politics* (see: Almond and Verba, 1963; Moore, 1966; Lepsius, 1978; Vanhanen, 1997; Putnam, 1993; Jaggers and Gurr, 1995; Norris, 1999).

It goes almost without saying that these tentative answers are quite broadly formulated and are difficult to answer properly in empirical terms. Nevertheless, most students of comparative democracy are in agreement that the factors mentioned here do matter.

The issue at hand, however, is to what extent do these factors *account* for the cross-national variation regarding the extent of pluralism, polyarchy and democraticness (as empirically developed in the previous section). In addition, one ought to examine *in what way* these factors matter. That is to say, is it possible to develop a valid and robust model that not only demonstrates the interdependence of the factors mentioned, but also their causal impact. In short, is it possible to develop a 'middle-range' theory regarding the democraticness of political systems (see: Lane and Ersson, 1994; Pennings et al., 1999).

As a first step we report in Table 3.7 the bivariate relations between conditions for pluralism, institutions of polyarchy and democraticness and a number of variables that are devised to represent economic and societal developments as well as features of politics. Even at first glance, it is obvious that in general the various tentative ideas concerning the societal and economic circumstances that promote democracy seem to be associated with the democracy variables. Apart from *Electoral turnout* and *Presidentialism* all statistical relations are significant. Yet, these exceptions are not too surprising since we examined *all* cases and in the majority of countries elections are not held at all. Presidentialism – although we only assigned those cases as presidential where there is a situation of limited exercise of powers only (see: Derbyshire and Derbyshire, 1996) – can be found in many countries where the civil and political rights are less developed or observed, and the institutionalization of democracy is apparently underdeveloped (see also Table 3.6). Hence, the idea of Linz and others that presidential systems are often less democratic than other (in particular: parliamentary) systems appears tenable. The general conclusion must be therefore that the other factors – social and economic – do contribute to the development and level of democraticness.

Table 3.7 *Bivariate relations between indicators of democracy and social, economic and political variables*

Variables	Indicator of democracy		
	Pluralism	Polyarchy	Democraticness
Pluralism	1.0	0.81	0.93
Polyarchy	0.81	1.00	0.95
Democraticness	0.93	0.95	1.00
Gnppc (1995)	0.64	0.59	0.65
Govexpc (1995)	0.32*	0.49	0.43
Central government exp.	0.45	0.58	0.54
Urbanization	0.50	0.59	0.56
Human development	0.65	0.67	0.69
Electoral turnout	0.11*	0.15*	0.08*
Presidentialism	0.05*	−0.04*	0.00*
Parliamentarism	0.50	0.63	0.59
N	161	145	127

Note: All results are Pearson product moment correlations; less significant results ($p \geq 0.01$) are flagged (*); see Appendix for an elaboration of the variables used.

Source: See Appendix.

Let us turn therefore to the question to what extent these factors matter for having and maintaining a democratic society. In Table 3.8 we report four regression models representing four equations that reflect the main answers to the question: how do we explain the occurrence and viability of democracy? The four models are all, but for two factors, statistically significant (the rate of urbanization and the size of the public sector appear irrelevant in this context) and thus all lend support to the answer as to why democracies are dependent on certain factors to develop and remain viable as democracies. Most of the results are unsurprising and underwrite extant knowledge (see: Beetham, 1994; Landman, 2000). Yet, it is also clear that none of the models is superior to the others: neither in terms of explained variance (adjusted R^2), nor in the magnitude of influence.

The first model, depicting the working of the market as well as the state, demonstrates that the 'wealth of a nation' is certainly an incentive for democratization. However, this is not the case for the size of the public sector. Yet, at the same time it is also clear that this is an insufficient condition *per se*. There are many outliers that prove the contrary. For example, many non-democratic nations have also considerable levels of public expenditure. Likewise a number of states with aggregated economic riches spring to mind that are close to dictatorship or autocracy (e.g. some of the Arabian countries). In short, we hold the view that economic wealth certainly can help to foster democracy and is more often than not associated with higher level of democraticness, but is not *the* driving force as many political scientists and economists in the period directly after the Second World War claimed (Lipset, 1959; Diamond and Marks, 1992; Castles, 1998).

The same can be said of the *societal forces* (the second model). Although much of the literature claims that the composition of society and its

Table 3.8 *Regression analysis of factors explaining democracy*

Independent variables		Dependent variables		
		Pluralism	Polyarchy	Democraticness
Economics	α	−14.1	−25.8	−3.6
Gnppc	β	0.45 (3.95)	0.42 (3.91)	0.51 (4.80)
Govexppc	β	0.12* (1.08)	0.25 (2.33)	0.17* (1.59)
	R^2	25.5%	33.1%	35.8%
Society	α	−17.7	−18.6	−3.7
Urbanization	β	−0.12* (−1.13)	0.07* (0.70)	0.01* (0.09)
HDI	β	0.66 (6.49)	0.56 (5.64)	0.61 (5.71)
	R^2	32.4%	36.9%	36.8%
Institutions	α	−7.3	−7.2	−1.5
Presidentialism	β	0.34 (4.48)	0.34 (4.51)	0.37 (4.79)
Parliamentarism	β	0.74 (10.49)	0.73 (9.76)	0.76 (9.78)
	R^2	40.3%	39.3%	42.6%
Politics	α	−16.5	−19.44	−3.9
Electoral turnout	β	0.35 (3.37)	0.38 (3.84)	0.38 (3.79)
Central gov. exp.	β	0.19 (1.81)	0.24 (2.39)	0.25 (2.54)
	R^2	16.8%	22.9%	23.5%

Note: OLS procedure has been employed; number of cases is 82 and 110; *t*-values are in parentheses; insignificant results are flagged:*.

consequences for inter-class rivalry are important for understanding the process of democratization as well as the stability of a democratic regime, this hypothesis is not supported by our analysis.

From our analysis it transpires that urbanization – used as a proxy for modernization – is unrelated to the indicators for democracy. Hence, it is either an invalid proxy indicator or the modernization thesis is not valid. We think both explanations are plausible (and this is supported in much of the literature; see: Rueschmeyer et al., 1992; Landman, 2000).

Conversely, the *quality of life* as expressed by the Human Development Index is an important asset for developing and sustaining democracy. Yet, again as with economic factors, we can only go along with this claim as far as it implies a necessary condition; but – judging by an explained variance of approximately 36.8 per cent – it is an insufficient condition for improving the level of democraticness of a nation. In addition, it should be noted that both explanations – the economy and society – tend to become functional ones. If so, and we think this is correct, the causality of the argument is weak if not absent. Rather we would go along with those who advocate a more 'case oriented' approach that enables researchers to disentangle the subtle variations within a society and to develop 'path dependent' explanations (e.g. Dahl, 1966; Rueschemeyer et al., 1992; Putnam, 1993).

The third model concerns the impact on the level of democraticness of the organization of the *democratic polity*. Too often the *institutional* fabric of democracy has been considered as the end-result of democratization. We think this view is biased if not wrong. The coming about of a democracy, whether it is 'old' (and now established, as in the OECD-world) or 'new' (hence recently established, as in Central and Eastern Europe) the struggle for more democracy is mainly fought out over institutions.

Democracy, no one denies that, is a process. This is especially true concerning the development and transformation of the 'rules of the game' and how the games can subsequently be played (Sartori, 1984; Lijphart, 1999). This was true in Europe in the eras before and after the Great War (1914–18) and it is still true today (and not only in 'new' democracies: one need only think of the recent debate and institutional changes in countries such as Belgium, Italy, Japan, New Zealand, etc.). In other words: institutions not only matter for organizing democracy, but – as the analysis shows – *how* it works. In the analysis reported in Table 3.8 we observe that both types of democracy are strongly related to pluralism, polyarchy and democraticness. Of course, this appears to be a blatant tautology, but this would be missing our point: both types of democracy are indeed consistently influencing the viability if not endurance of a democratic system (Jones, 1995). This is especially the case for 'parliamentarism' (again). If the model is correctly specified it predicts a more solid road to polyarchy than via 'presidentialism' (see for this also: Stepan and Skach, 1994; Linz, 1994; Keman, 2000b). We claim, therefore, that the stronger the polity, together with its 'rule of law', the more it upholds the democraticness of that nation and also improves its working. Whether or not this is also true in terms of its policy performance remains to be seen (but it will be discussed in Chapters 11 (Lane and Ersson) and 12 (Keman) in this book; but see also Lijphart, 1999, on this subject).

The last model reported in Table 3.8 concerns the active use of designated powers by the people and by the state. On the one hand, we examined the use of the ballot box, and on the other hand, we scrutinized the idea that central government is strongly associated with democraticness: a democratic state will be conducive to greater state intervention (by popular demand). Both contentions are only weakly supported, and – as was the case with economics and society – we can only repeat our observation that, although there is a relationship, it is not convincing and cannot be considered as a major factor for democratization and democraticness as such (see also: Bingham Powell, 1982; Schmidt, 1989b; Pinkey, 1993; Keman, 2000b).

In summary: the cross-national analysis of factors promoting pluralism, polyarchy and democraticness demonstrates (ceteris paribus) that favourable economic conditions and high(er) levels of human development are incentives for achieving higher levels of democraticness. However, like political factors, they are not crucial *per se*, nor functional under all circumstances. It appears rather that the interplay of these factors benefits further democratization and may well enhance the level of democraticness of a nation. Hence there is not a definitive set of factors, conditions or prerequisites (although their absence may certainly harm the level of democraticness attained!) that allows for a successful development and extension of democracy (although some, like Huntington, 1991, claim there are; cf. Schmidt, 2000: 483–7). Hence, there is no recipe nor an exhaustive causal model of

Table 3.9 *Multi-variate model of democraticness*

	Dependent variable = democraticness of nations		
Constant (α)	−4.872 (7.913)		
Independent variables	Beta	*t*-value	R^2
Human development	0.62	7.02	37.0%
Parliamentarism	0.58	6.52	48.9%
Presidentialism	0.40	4.99	60.6%
Economy	0.30	3.55	65.65%
Central government	0.20	2.78	68.35%
Electoral turnout	0.13	1.98	69.5%
Government (govpc)	−0.21	−2.25	71.1%

Note: OLS-regression stepwise analysis; N = between 72 and 84; see Appendix for variables.

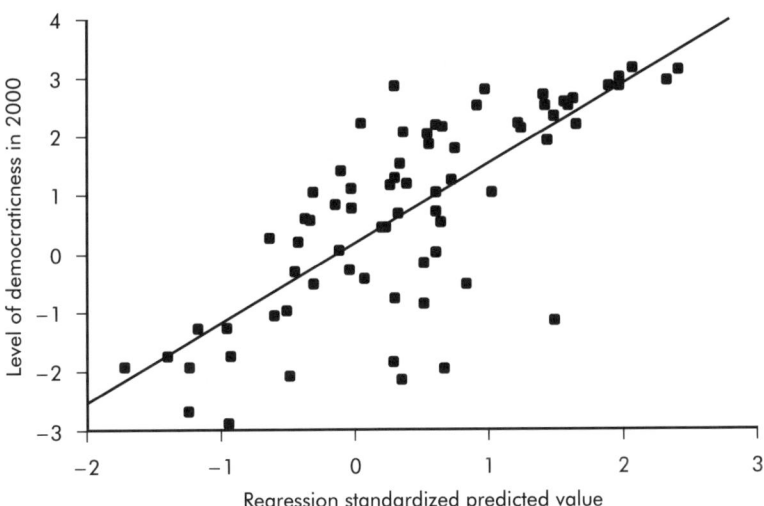

Figure 3.4 *Plot of democraticness against explanatory factors*

democracy. Nevertheless, our results show that a number of accepted theories have produced a set of factors that may well be more conducive to democratization and democraticness than others. Table 3.9 reports therefore the tenability of these factors in one equation. This is not done to claim a comprehensive model. On the contrary: the regression analysis is intended to explore the relative weight of the factors involved with respect to our dependent variable: *level of democraticness*.

This stepwise progressive regression analysis confirms our earlier findings. The level of social wellbeing and economic wealth, on the one hand, and the institutional organization of the democratic state, on the other, are the principal factors that distinguish nations in terms of their achieved level of democraticness. The other factors mentioned could and should be considered as important in terms of added value. To what extent this really makes a difference with regard to the viability and performance of democratic regimes will be subject of the next section.

3.5 DEMOCRACY AND DIFFUSION: THE VIABILITY AND PERFORMANCE OF DEMOCRATICNESS

In Section 3.2 we briefly discussed the emergence and diffusion of polyarchic democracies over time (see Table 3.2 and Figure 3.1). Although the absolute number of cases has increased, this is not so in proportional terms. Nevertheless, it goes almost without saying that the liberal format of democracy has been spreading across the world, in particular since 1945.

Students of democracy have observed that the diffusion and growth of democracies appears to occur in 'waves' (Huntington, 1991); Manfred Schmidt describes four waves (2000: 463ff). The first wave occurred around the turn of the last century (1900) and faded out after the Great War. The second occurred in the aftermath of the Second World War. The third wave is considered to have taken place during the 1970s and early 1980s, whereas the fourth wave coincides with the demise of the 'second world' of communism. It is immediately clear that the factors driving these waves are external (to the society concerned), on the one hand, and internal (or: domestic), on the other hand.

Three of the four waves can indeed be defined in connection with international affairs, the last one being the end of the so-called Cold War. The third wave (1973–88) is also driven by international factors: the catchword is here 'globalization' of social and economic relations and its impact on national circumstances (Przeworski, 1991). Hence, the argument for explaining waves of democratization is strongly based on (sudden and drastic) changes in international relations and a changing 'world order' (Kennedy, 1987).

This 'global' perspective, however convincing it may seem, is of course not the complete story. After the Great War, political rights were indeed extended in many West European countries, but not in all. In many countries it was a short-lived experience that developed into dictatorships again: Poland, Hungary, Italy, Spain, Portugal to name a few. And, as Therborn (1977) points out, the extension of democracy was mainly intended to integrate the working class population, who had suffered most from the Great War and were growing stronger as a result of the process of industrialization. This means that although universal (male) suffrage was accepted, it did not imply in most cases fully-fledged polyarchy (Jaggers and Gurr, 1995). In other words, it depended strongly on the internal *country-specific* situation whether or not democratization took place and became rooted in society (Rokkan, 1970).

Todd Landman (2000: Chapter 7) reviews the possible internal factors regarding regime change towards democracy, particularly in Latin America. Although there appears to be a lot of variation if one studies case-specific developments (see also: Rueschemeyer et al., 1992; Linz, 1994) the common

Table 3.10 *Cross tabulation of democraticness and waves of democratization* (N = 57)

Level of democraticness	Waves of democratization			
	First	Second	Third	Fourth
High (N = 14) 24.6%	68.8% (19.3%)	23.1% (5.3%)		
Medium (N = 15) 26.3%	25.0% (7.0%)	23.1% (5.3%)	36.4% (7.0%)	23.5% (7.0%)
Low (N = 14) 24.6%	6.3% (1.8%)	38.5% (8.8%)	18.2% (3.5%)	35.3% (10.5%)
Below par (N = 14) 24.6%		5.4% (3.5%)	45.8% (8.8%)	41.2% (12.3%)
N	16	13	11	17

$\chi^2 = 32.6$ (DF = 9); eta = 0.674

Note: Democraticness is the same variable as used earlier in this chapter (see Figure 3.3); waves of democratization are taken from Schmidt (2000: 467–8); the level of democratization is assigned by transforming the values into four categories of equal percentiles.

denominator is the extent to which political and social resources are concentrated in a few hands or not. Secondly, the capacity and necessity to forge coalitions that can replace the political and economic elites (or merge with them) is an important feature (as it was in Europe around the turn of the 19th century). Yet, again, this seems to be a part of the overall explanation and is not a secular trend of the transition to democracy. Another important factor is, for instance, the diffusion of 'models of democracy' (Lijphart, 1977; Pinkey, 1993). In particular during the 'second wave' the colonial powers and the United States served not only as an example, but also actively exported 'their' brand of democracy to the Third World or to the occupied countries (e.g. Italy and Japan). This resulted in an institutionalization of democracy which appears not all that viable and has been often conducive to a return to non-democratic politics or a halfway development toward a polyarchic type of democracy (see: Pinkey, 1993; von Beyme, 1994; Derbyshire and Derbyshire, 1996).

All in all we can conclude that both internal and external factors drive the diffusion of democraticness. Four waves of democratization can be distinguished which have produced – according to our operationalization of democraticness – at this moment 57 nations that are sufficiently pluralistic and polyarchic. In Table 3.10 we report a cross-tabulation of these democracies. Obviously, the longer a democracy exists the higher the level of democratization appears to be. There are, of course, some outliers, which are Germany, Finland and Japan. These countries were re-democratized after the war and apparently are still lagging behind the others. However, this cannot be true for Ireland and Switzerland or the USA. On the one hand, it may be argued that their low scores on democraticness have to do with their 'institutional sclerosis' (cf. Olson, 1982) that has impaired a full development in terms of polyarchy. On the other hand, it may well be an artefact resulting from the measurement of electoral turnout and party competition (see: Schmidt, 2000: 400). The largest cross-national variation is to be found in the countries that belong to the second and third wave of democratization. Certain economically less developed countries are in this category (like the Bahamas, Mauritius, etc.). Among the countries (re)democratized during the third wave one finds the South European countries (Portugal, Greece and Spain) as well as the Latin American ones. The latter category is slow in (re)developing civil and political rights for the individual citizen (in particular in Chile, but also in Argentina and Brazil). The final wave is dominated by Central and East European countries, for example, Romania and Bulgaria, but also by Latin American countries that are lagging behind in achieving a high(er) level of democraticness. We conclude, therefore, that although early democratization correlates with level of genuine democracy, it is not a rule that latecomers show an identical pace and pattern in developing a fully-fledged democracy. Hence, other factors must be taken into account to explain this observed cross-national variation of democraticness.

In the previous section we established that the differences in the level of democraticness could be ascribed to the institutionalization of the democratic polity. If this is tenable worldwide, so we argue, then these factors should also account for the viability and performance of democraticness. In other words, we expect that our indicators of democracy – pluralism and polyarchy – not only shape the level of democraticness, but are also related to higher levels of socio-economic development and government expenditure. In Table 3.7 we reported the relevant correlates for the indicators used to establish the level of democraticness.

From these results it appears that indeed socio-economic variables and the size of the public sector is strongly associated with democratization and democraticness. A replication of the stepwise regression of these factors on the level of democratization shows an (adjusted) R^2 of 79.3 per cent and a strong role for government, on the one hand, and the economy on the other.[8] Yet, the most striking feature is, that if we control this comprehensive model for the *age* of democracy (or the 'waves' of democratization) then this has a strong and negative effect on the level of democraticness that is reached. Hence, *time* is indeed an important factor for *being* a democracy.

In summary: we have demonstrated that the establishment and institutionalization of democracy is to a large extent a matter of time. By comparing the contemporary democracies by waves it appears that the older a democracy is the greater is its viability. Yet, this argument cannot be reversed: the variation in democraticness is larger across the polities that recently experienced their transition to democracy. Secondly, it transpired from our analysis that – as we had already observed – the more viable and comprehensively institutionalized a liberal democratic system is the more likely a positive socio-economic and governmental performance will be (this issue will be elaborated in Chapter 11 by Lane and Ersson). Hence, we conclude that – on the basis of a variable-oriented approach with a large N (= 57) – democracies need time to develop their viability, which expresses itself in high(er) levels of affluence and responsive governance.

3.6 CONCLUDING REMARKS

The study of democracy and democratization is one of the most contested topics in political science. In this chapter our point of departure has been to discuss this essential and crucial variable of political life worldwide from the perspective of the comparative approach to political science. The reasons to choose this perspective are twofold:

- Democracy, however it is conceptualized, is in our view essentially a *macroscopic* entity and needs therefore to be elaborated and researched on the *system level*.
- Theories of democracy, of whatever creed and level of abstraction, need to be discussed by relating hypotheses to *empirical* reality and therefore must be elaborated and researched *comparatively*.

This is what this chapter set out to do. *First*, we have argued that the comparative approach always should make clear what its 'core subject' is and thus what its substantial point of departure implies. The triad: politics–polity–policy has been our point of departure and it has been subsequently applied to the phenomenon 'democracy'.

Second, we set out to develop an empirically driven conceptualization of democracy making use of much of the existing literature. We employed especially the seminal contribution of Robert Dahl to the debate in elaborating empirically the concept of 'polyarchy'. This led to an empirical measure consisting of 'pluralism' and 'polyarchy' which has served as dimensions of what we have called level of *democraticness*. In this way both the system as well as the process can be properly analysed. It appeared in the course of this chapter that these truly comparative variables could travel well without undue conceptual stretching (Sartori, 1984; Dogan and Pelassy, 1990).

Third, we attempted to make more sense of the many and diverse explanations of the process of democratization by carrying out a cross-national regression analysis of the influence of their various factors on the levels of democraticness. We found that many explanations fit the data used. At the same time it also became clear that certain factors are rather conditional (like socio-economic development and government expenditures), whereas others can be considered as more or less effect-productive (like the age of a democracy, parliamentarism and presidentialism) or are less relevant than is often thought (like electoral turnout).

Overall, this chapter served the purpose of demonstrating the usefulness of the comparative approach to the study of democracy as a systemic 'whole'. In the parts to follow, this holistic perspective is abandoned. The chapters of Parts Two and Three, in particular, will focus on specific and essential parts of established democratic systems at work.

NOTES

1 It should be noted that the work of Adam Przeworski, when focusing on a 'core matter' is not guilty of the charges made here; see: Przeworski, 1985; Przeworski and Sprague, 1986. It remains a remarkable feature, however, that his and Ragin's methodological work appears to be divorced from actual empirical analysis. Ragin's replication of Rokkan's mapping of nation-building in Europe, or his case-related ideas on intra-national developments (Ragin, 1991) are hardly convincing in relating theory and method. See also: Landman, 2000.

2 Dahl himself has become more ambivalent about attempts to measure the democraticness of a society. Nevertheless, he has stimulated this type of research himself (see: Dahl, 1971: 238ff). In his latest book he states that collecting data on the availability of the set of institutions may be possible, but that deciding whether or not these institutions function properly is another matter. See: Dahl, 1998: 196–9.

3 $P = $ votes/population $\times 100$. $C = 100 - $ Vote share largest party (per cent). The Index of Democratization is then:

$$ID = (P \times C)/100 \text{ [see: Vanhanen, 1997: 35–6]}$$

Obviously the larger the voter turnout, and the less oligopolistic the party system is, the higher the ID score will be. Conversely the lower the turnout and the more oligopolistic the structure of the party system, the lower is the ID score. To some extent this is a weakness, if not a bias, of this index since if produces certain counter-intuitive results (see: Schmidt, 2000: 400–1; also: Bollen, 1993; Dunleavy and Margetts, 1994).

4 In this chapter the focus will be exclusively on the Democracy-dimension of their scale.

5 Examples are Argentina, Brazil, Fiji, Papua New Guinea, Peru, the Dominican Republic, Pakistan, Russia, Albania, just to mention a few; the exclusion of democracies like Spain and Mexico, for instance, is also odd.

6 Instead of employing Principal Components Analysis – which is usually done – Principal Axis Factoring is selected. The advantage is that the communality is not derived from a fixed eigenvalue (1.0) but directly from the correlation-matrix itself. This reduces the inherent error-terms. In this case it means that the R^2 is lower (79.9% versus 87.3%) but it does not affect the distinctiveness of both factors ($r = -0.70$). See also: Pennings et al., 1999: 101–4.

7 For the purpose of comparability both variables have been transformed into z-scores. In addition a single variable was constructed combining the values of both variables which represent an index of democraticness. The basic variables are:

Name	N	Range	Mode
Pluralism	161	3.15	1.36
Polyarchy	145	3.35	−1.36
Democracy	127	6.30	−3.15

8   The equation yields the following results:

Constant (α)	= 1.33
• Affluence	= 0.37 (3.23)
• Human development	= 0.41 (3.35)
• Central government	= 0.10 (2.54)
• Parliamentarism	= 0.10 (1.76)
• Presidentialism	= −0.40 (−2.74)
• General government	= −0.28 (−2.13)
Adjusted R^2	= 79.3%

Note: *t*-values in brackets. Independent variables are presented in standardized values.

APPENDIX TO CHAPTER 3: VARIABLES AND SOURCES

Variables	*Sources/computations*
Central government expenditures	World development indicators at *www.worldbank.org/data/*
Civil rights	Freedom House 1999 (Schmidt, 2000)
Coppedge and Reinicke	Coppedge and Reinicke (Schmidt, 2000)
Democraticness	Computed as the standardized sum of polyarchy and pluralism
Duration of democracy	Adapted from Derbyshire and Derbyshire (1996) and Banks (1998)
	1 = new democracy established after 1988
	2 = recent democracy, established after 1945
	3 = old democracy, established before 1945
	When disturbed the score lessens by 0.5.
Electoral competition	Vanhanen (1997), Schmidt (2000)
Electoral turnout	IDEA: www.idea.int/voter_turnout
Government expenditures	World development indicators at www.worldbank.org/data/
HDI	UNDP Human Development Report 1998
Jaggers and Gurr	Jaggers and Gurr (Schmidt, 2000)
Parliamentarism	Derbyshire and Derbyshire (1996)
Pluralism	Factor score of the indexes of political rights, civil rights and Coppedge and Reinicke
Political rights	Freedom House 1999 (Schmidt, 2000)
Polyarchy	Factor score of the indexes of Jaggers and Gurr and Vanhanen (1997)
Presidentialism	Derbyshire and Derbyshire (1996)
Regime type	Alvarez (1995) (Schmidt, 2000)
Urbanization	Vanhanen (1997)
Vanhanen Index 1993	Vanhanen (1993) (Schmidt, 2000)
Vanhanen Index 1997	Vanhanen (1997) (Schmidt, 2000)
Waves of democratization	Schmidt (2000)

PART TWO

PARTIES AND GOVERNMENT IN DEMOCRACIES

An essential feature of *representative* democracy is, of course, its *indirect* nature. Although in modern parlance the citizen is still the 'principal' and the executive and legislative branches of constitutional government are then the 'agents', it is obvious that both government and parliament are the crucial actors in modern democracy. The citizen is important at the time of election, but then he/she must wait and see until the next election in what way and to what extent parties in parliament and in government have indeed translated the citizens' preferences into policy. Conversely, parties are to a large extent dependent on how the electorate chooses.

In *Chapter 4* Ian Budge et al. examine this relationship between parties and electorate from the perspective known as systems analysis of political life. Two concepts are introduced to assess the actual working and functioning of representative democracy: *Responsiveness and Accountability*. The former concept indicates the extent to which citizens' preferences are indeed translated into policy priorities of political parties. The latter concept is intended to measure whether or not parties fulfil their programmatic promises in terms of policy measures.

From this perspective an empirical analysis is presented, which demonstrates cross-nationally that this is more often the case than not. In addition Budge et al. claim that not only parties – in or out of government – can be held responsible, but also that indeed public policy formation is actually moving toward accountable performances. This seems good news, but at the same time it becomes also clear that on average the public policy performance of representative democracies is often characterized by inertia and incremental change.

In *Chapter 5* an analysis is presented which examines in more detail the role of ideology – considered as offering discrete choices to electorates – in relation to party behaviour. It appears that the differentiation in electoral systems and the existence of strong cleavages together, produce strong effects in terms of voters' participation and voting behaviour. Pennings' analyses reinforce contemporary findings that the citizen is willing to participate in elections, if and when the issues at stake are clear and the impact of voting is considered to be meaningful. Hence, elections do matter for the citizen as well as for the competing parties. This conclusion obviously runs counter to the ideas that 'politics is dead' and 'parties are all the same'. On the contrary.

The effects of electoral change and party choice, however, do appear to affect patterns of co-operation between parties. Mair argues in *Chapter 6* that stable patterns of electoral behaviour and thus of party positions are changing, albeit gradually. His analysis shows that during the last five decades of the twentieth century the mode of *party competition* has changed. Especially during the 1990s it became more clear that 'new' parties develop into strong actors, partly due to increased volatile voting behaviour within national systems, partly because of socio-cultural shifts within society. Arguably, new patterns of party co-operation and party competition are developing. What kind of effect this development has on representative government it is too early to tell. Nevertheless, it goes without saying that 'party politics' still matters: for the individual to safeguard his or her interests with respect to the 'public domain'; for the political party it implies that it must be flexible and persevering in order to remain a stable actor within the political system.

4

COMPARATIVE GOVERNMENT AND DEMOCRACY: MODELLING PARTY DEMOCRACY ACROSS 16 COUNTRIES[1]

Ian Budge, Richard Hofferbert, Hans Keman, Michael McDonald, Paul Pennings

4.1 STUDYING DEMOCRACY COMPARATIVELY

Previous chapters have discussed the concerns and methods of comparative politics as applied to the study of democracy. This chapter offers a first application of these approaches to the practical task of comparing political systems. It focuses on *democratic* systems for a number of reasons. First, democracy is the most widely diffused way of organizing polities in the contemporary world. Many countries which term themselves democracies of course fall considerably short of the ideal. Nevertheless they do follow practices (such as holding regular elections) which are recognizably democratic (see also: Derbyshire and Derbyshire, 1996; Chapters 3 and 12 in this book).

A second reason for studying democracy empirically is paradoxically normative and moral. It is the political system preferred both by ourselves and probably our readers. Our reasons for preferring it are partly evaluative – beliefs in equality and liberty and so on. But they are also based on factual assumptions about the way democracy actually works. For example, we assume that democratic arrangements *do* make governments more responsive to voters. As the argument for supporting democracy depends on such factual assertions just as much as on normative beliefs, it is as well to check them out to make sure they are correct.

From both an empirical and a normative point of view therefore it makes sense to concentrate on comparing democracies if one is studying comparative politics – just as economists concentrate on the free market rather than the different examples of command economies. The parallel goes further. Just as firms and consumers are central to the free market whatever country it functions in, so political parties and voters are central to democracy whatever its national context.

There is little dispute nowadays that modern democracy is essentially party democracy. That is, it depends on political parties to present alternatives for electoral choice and to organize government afterwards so as to bring electorally preferred policies into effect. Much research on individual parties and national party systems, as on particular aspects of political parties, has been carried out within the framework of this assumption – studies of party structure and organization, relations between leaders and members, strategies of electoral competition and of coalition formation, policies and performance of parties in government.

This list of the party characteristics and behaviours which have been studied, is already long and could be extended. Our aim is to put all these aspects of party activity together systematically in order to form an overall picture of how parties behave and what they do within the everyday workings of democracy.

Democracy is considered here as a set of institutional and political processes operating in similar ways across different countries. If the processes were not similar we could not talk about democracy as such without a country qualifier ('American democracy' as compared with 'Dutch democracy' for example). But we *do* talk about democracy as a general system with common characteristics wherever it operates. Each national setting may add certain political idiosyncrasies and deck out the fundamental underlying processes in a different guise. But the common essentials must be there underneath – otherwise we would not know that the country was democratic in the first place (Dogan and Pelassy, 1990).

Our aim is to identify the shared, defining processes of democracy and specify theoretically how they work. We then go on, using comparable statistics from 16 democratic countries, to see if the theoretical formulation *does* adequately describe their political processes. We thus move from formulating to testing *a priori* theory in our analysis below and build on the validated theory to produce a quantified description (simulation) of the processes at work.

4.2 COMPARATIVE EVIDENCE ON DEMOCRACY AS A PROCESS

Both testing and even – paradoxically – formulating relevant theory depends on having evidence to fit into it. For a systematic and comprehensive theory one needs systematic and comprehensive evidence – statistical in form, as it is only through statistical analysis that we can extract information from large quantities of data extending over 40 years across 16 countries. There is an inevitable interaction between evidence and theory. The theory specifies the kind of data which is necessary in order for it to apply to the real world i.e. to operationalize it. However, the nature of the data which are available forces adaptations in the operationalization which often lead one to revise the original theory in significant ways. Just thinking about the way the theory needs to be applied often reveals inconsistencies or a lack of relevance in its assumptions. Lacking this discipline – owing to the dearth of relevant evidence at the time – made early attempts at comparative modelling of politics far too abstract and general, to an extent which called their relevance to comparative analysis into severe doubt.

The evidence now available 30 years later to check and fill in our model of democratic processes is much more extensive. One use of our model in fact is to organize and focus the large comparative data sets now available, even in areas not previously considered accessible to quantitative analysis, such as the declarations and programmes of political parties. These are key elements in any attempt to link government responses to contextual developments and electoral expectations. Estimates of party policy-stands are now available in the massive data collection brought together by the ECPR's Manifesto Research Group, which includes codings and statistics for election (and government) programmes for 25 democracies over the whole post-war period (Budge et al., 1987; Klingemann et al., 1994). Specially collected for this analysis are indicators of social and economic developments, voting behaviour, government composition and expenditures for 16 countries over the same time-period (Woldendorp et al., 2000; see also Chapter 12 in this book). These statistics are deliberately designed to be comparable across countries, so they facilitate the type of pooled comparative investigation described below in Section 4.4.

Before coming to the data we need to specify our theoretical model. As noted above this has its roots in the 'systems analysis' of the 1950s (Easton, 1953, 1965). The models developed within this framework were at once too comprehensive and too simple to be easily researchable. But they did create habits of thinking about national politics as particular examples of general underlying processes, and provided an overall framework within which to relate them.

The 'systems model' shown in Figure 4.1 illustrates these generalizing and simplifying tendencies very well. It conceives of politics rather like the developing computers of the time, receiving 'inputs' from the environment and processing them into 'outputs' which then 'feed back' into the environment to modify the 'inputs' coming into the system in the next sequence. The 'political system' is thus autonomous and to a considerable extent in self-regulating equilibrium. That is, it can under normal circumstances adjust its outputs so as to produce manageable inputs, which do not over-tax its ability to process them. However its 'feedback' only affects 'inputs' to some extent. They may also be affected by other changes in the environment stemming from actions of other political systems (war and invasion for example), from changes in the socio-economic context (globalization) or in the world of states (internationalization). Any such change may be too much for the 'processing' capacity of an individual system and may cause 'breakdown'. This may also be provoked, however, by the unintended or unanticipated consequences of the political outputs themselves. These are mostly government policies and expenditures. An example of unintended consequences would be the series of health and social security measures we describe in general terms as the Welfare State. Besides resolving problems of health and welfare these also create 'big government' – for example in terms of excessive regulation of ordinary life and an overblown bureaucracy – which in turn may create 'government overload' and 'system breakdown' (see for this: Chapters 9 and 10 in this book).

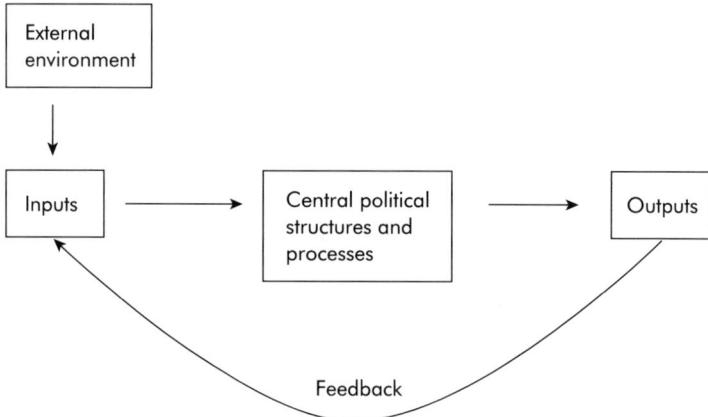

Figure 4.1 *A systems model of political processes. Source: Adapted from David Easton (1965)*

To some extent therefore even when processing internal 'inputs' – individual and group demands and expectations – the system may 'overload' and break down. However, another set of inputs may give it extra resilience. These consist of the diffuse support given to a legitimate system by its citizens, which induces them to demonstrate, act, fight and even die on its behalf. Such loyalties are not necessarily traded in return for specific benefits received from the system. They are positive orientations formed primarily in childhood towards an important object in the environment. This emphasis encouraged much research on childhood 'socialization' to politics, an area currently almost wholly passed over by 'rational choice' approaches which take preferences and tastes as given (Easton and Dennis, 1969; Budge, 1993; Conover and Searing, 1994). In seeking to model all political systems anywhere at any point in time, the 'systems model' raises vast questions. Being so abstract and general it can also accommodate practically any answers. It does not specify what inputs and outputs are central and which are peripheral to the polity, so welfare is as relevant as dog-ownership. It does not define either 'support' or 'breakdown', so it is difficult to relate them to each other. Most famously, the central political processes and structures are left as an opaque 'black box' into which inputs come and outputs go without any inkling as to how one produces the other, or how the political processes transform them.

Such information, in a concise easily operationalized form, is however provided by another 'model' of the 1960s – Miller and Stokes' seminal analysis of representative-constituent relationships (Miller and Stokes, 1963). While focused on the US House of Representatives, the model can obviously apply anywhere constituency-based politicians make voting decisions reasonably autonomously. The model (Figure 4.2) sketches possible relationships between majority constituency preferences (Box A) and the final vote cast by

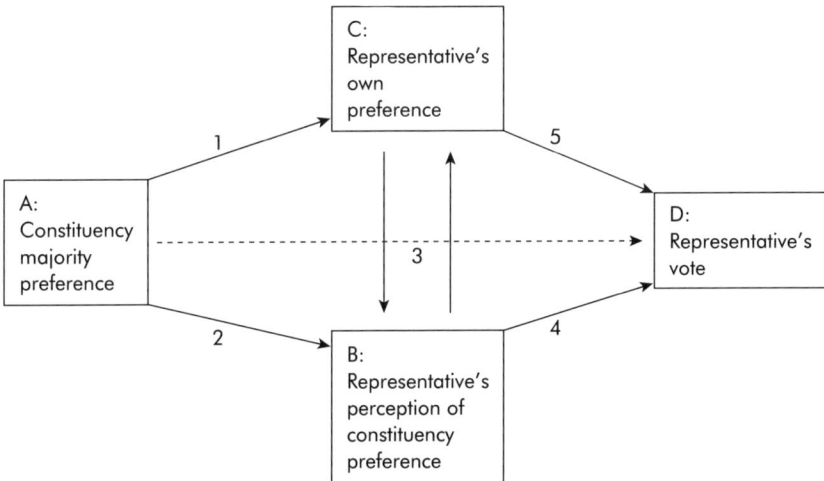

Figure 4.2 *A model of representative-constituency relationship.*
Source: Adapted from W.E. Miller and D.E. Stokes (1963)

the Representative in the Assembly (Box D). Presumably the two are going to be reasonably congruent – if they are totally unrelated the model becomes irrelevant as it is designed to explain the congruence which is assumed to exist. Assuming congruence there are two alternative ways this might come about. Either the representative acts as a 'delegate', voting for what he perceives to be the option favoured by the constituency majority (link 4 in Figure 4.2), without reference to his own preference. Or the representative acts as a classical 'representative' voting for his own preference (link 5) without reference to his perception of majority preferences. In that case the only way for the constituency to influence votes is to choose a representative whose preferences coincide with voters' (link 1).

Of course the 'Delegate' style of linkage where the representative feels bound to vote according to his constituents' preferences without regard to his own, only works if (s)he correctly identifies what the constituency opinion is (link 2). Thus we can envisage two pathways of constituency influence on the representative's vote: 2–4 as opposed to 1–5 of this model.

Once we set out the possibilities systematically, however, we can see another possibility. The representative's preferences and perceptions may interact (link 3 in Figure 4.2). Either his preferences colour his perceptions, so (s)he sees the constituency majority as supporting his or her own opinion whatever it may be. Or, (s)he may constantly tailor his/her own preferences to his or her perception of constituency ones. Thus we might see constituency influence on vote working through links 1–3–4 or through links 2–3–5 of the Representative-Constituency model.

Of course, constituency influence might work in other ways. Perhaps party influence might make the representative vote the same way as the constituency majority wishes even though it is neither his own preference nor perception (the dotted line in Figure 4.2). Or party influences might make her/him ignore both her/his own perceptions and preferences and those of the constituency altogether. In that case no link in Figure 4.2 would exist at all and the model is wrong in focusing on these relationships without including parties and their organizational features (Katz and Mair, 1992; Krouwel, 1999).

The nice thing about the Miller–Stokes model is that most of the linkages could be checked out against the parallel surveys of constituents and legislators, which the authors had conducted. These were cross-sectional (relating to only one point in time). So which version of link 3 was operative was not clear. All conceivable patterns of relationships were found between individual legislators and constituents, But the majority of cases conformed clearly to one or other of the linkage patterns identified in the model – varying, however, with the policy area involved (warfare versus welfare, for example: Keman, 1987).

This example of a theoretical model closely linked to data and capable therefore of being operationalized and measured, has been continuously influential over the last 30 years. Primarily used in research on US politics, it is capable of supporting comparative generalizations provided its assumption of autonomous legislative voting is met. Looking at the way this model has been applied indicates also now such theoretical constructions should be handled:

1. The model is not a precisely specified theory of the representative process. Rather it accommodates at least three hypotheses about the way this works – 'delegate', 'representative' and 'mixed'. Whichever of these modes predominates is compatible with the model, as is also a whole range of numerical values for them. What we end up with after the data-analysis may be, however, a more refined and specified model with some of the linkages shown not to exist in certain areas.
2. As a result the model cannot be 'disproved' by testing in any conventional sense. It can however be 'improved'. That is, knowing whether some of the links do not exist, or whether some operate in certain policy areas and others in others, enables us to specify it further and apply it more precisely. This is particularly so as the various linkages 1–5 can be expressed as equations linking one component of the model (e.g. constituency majority preferences) to another (assembly vote). Thus the whole diagram can be turned into equations with specified numeric values after it has been operationalized and analysed. This in effect is what we do with our own model below.
3. If the model cannot be disproved by showing that *some* of the conceivable linkages do not exist in practice anywhere, it could however be shown up as irrelevant if *none* of its linkages appears to be important. If for example only the dotted line in Figure 4.2 describes the relationship between constituency preferences and representative vote, there is not

much point in including the personal preferences and perceptions of representatives. This would be even truer if representatives followed their party line regardless of constituency preferences, when none of the linkages in Figure 4.2 would hold. Such a result would lead us to seek alternative models in which *party* preferences and perceptions figured as the main components. It is in this sense that we will check out our model of the central democratic processes below, moving from a specification of the likely main components of such processes to linkages between them: operationalization of these for comparative data, elimination of some conceivable linkages which do not appear in practice, and quantification of those that do. Once we can express the model as a series of equations with parameter values based on the data, we can also demonstrate how a change in one of the parameters works through to the others.

Quantification thus enables us to pass from a theoretical to a working model of democratic processes, generating predictions from the interactions of the model as a whole which can then be further tested to supplement the partial checks of each link on its own. In Section 4.7 we will illustrate the functioning of such simulations, through which the specified model becomes more like a real theory. At the current stage of our research we have to stop there.

4.3 MODELLING PARTY DEMOCRACY

Figure 4.2 is obviously much more focused on a particular political process than Figure 4.1. As a result it is more easily specified, operationalized and tested. The price paid for specificity and concreteness is its limitation to democracies with a constituency-based electoral system and loose party discipline (possibly only the United States). We seek to make our own model of democratic processes more generalizable in line with the 'systems model' of Figure 4.1, while avoiding its excessive abstraction. We hope that this will produce an overview which can be fitted to comparative data in a broader and more flexible manner.

As we have seen, the first step in model building is to specify the essential elements in the democratic process. Only then can we go on to describe relationships between them. Usually we think of these elements as *actors* – voters, parties, and governments. These appear in our model. Its starting point, however, is with developments in the environment surrounding the democracy (analogous to 'inputs' in the systems model of Figure 4.l). This is because democracies, like all states and polities, have to cope with a continuing stream of events, if not problems. Some of these to be sure are produced by other actors – a threat of war by another state for example. But others emerge from impersonal forces which are hard to identify with any one actor – unemployment, inflation, international tensions, environmental degradation are all examples of such 'unattributable' pressures on the democracy.

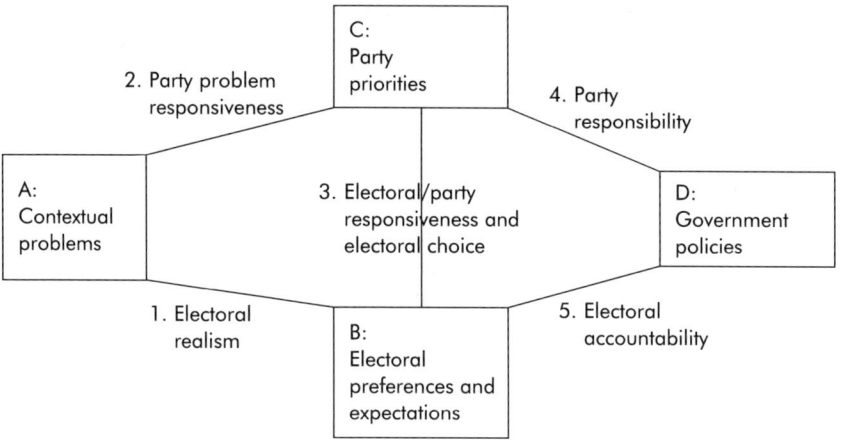

Figure 4.3 *Central democratic relationships in the functioning of democracy*

Contextual problems, electoral concerns, party priorities and government policies are the four components of our model pictured in Figure 4.3. Our model therefore is problem-driven. Given that some development has taken place with likely effects on societal well-being, the model asks – what response (if any) do voters make to it? What response (if any) do parties make?[2] What response (if any) do governments make? How do contextual developments get translated into a (electoral, party, government) response? And how does all this affect voting for a government, the characteristic and defining democratic process of election? These questions are specified in Figure 4.3, which details and labels the primary relationships of interest for democratic functioning. Relationship 1 of the model for example is concerned with how far voters correctly perceive the 'objective' problems that confront democracy.

It is interesting to see that an empirical analysis can confront a normative problem often raised in discussions of democracy: how far can ordinary people be trusted to have a correct sense of political priorities? The model puts this question directly because it is central to a process that relies on elections. How far in responding to voters (link 3 in Figure 4.3) do parties as a result ignore real problems, so that link 2 does not really exist? Or do parties directly respond to problems and ignore voters' preferences as 'elite' theorists have argued (Schumpeter, 1942; Plamenatz, 1973; Lively, 1978)?

All these are central questions of traditional democratic theory. Naturally they have to be raised and answered – even in a descriptive model of democracy – precisely because they *are* so central. The same is true for other links in the model – like party responsibility (link 4 in Figure 4.3) – how far do parties in government actually carry through the policies on which they won the election? Elitist theories, again, query the existence of such a relationship, while 'mandate' theories of democracy depend on it. And how far and in what way (if any) do voters hold government parties to account for what they have done in government (link 5 of the model).

Investigating these relationships already raises many fundamental questions, which we would like to concentrate upon. Even a parsimonious and stripped-down model however has to take account of at least two other factors:

1. *Institutional constraints*: For example, in a Federation the central government may respond less to problems (or may even be constitutionally prohibited from action) as there are state governments which may have a monopoly of the necessary powers. This implies that institutions may not only affect the speed and type of response to problems but also exert a direct effect on what is done (see: Schmidt, 1996a; Lane and Ersson, 1997; Braun, 2000).
2. *Bureaucracy*: Governments are composed not only of parties but also of bureaucrats who may implement party programmes but will also pick up and act on problems directly. The fact that most of our statistical measures of societal developments are devised and recorded by bureaucrats is significant. They want to keep an eye on problems in order to respond directly themselves (see: Lehmbruch, 1999; Olsen, 1998).

In Figure 4.4 a direct link (7) between problems and government response is incorporated, which it labels 'Governmental problem responsiveness'. This supplements the indirect links (2 and 4) between problems and policies, through the priorities set out by parties in their programmes – which if elected they are supposed to translate into public policy (according to standard democratic theory, at any rate; Keman, 1997a; Lijphart, 1977, 1999).

Figure 4.4 notes, however, that link 2 (also link 3) – party responses to problems on the one hand and to electoral concerns on the other – can be affected by party ideology. Socialist parties could be more sensitive to unemployment as a problem than parties of the Right and the opposite could be true of inflation. Centre parties are often regarded as more sensitive and responsive to voters than the ideology-bound Socialists or Liberals. A final possibility allowed for in the figure is that governments may not simply follow policies laid out by their constituent parties at the preceding election. They may also respond directly to voters' concerns, modifying their positions to come closer to those of the median voter (link 6). Taken as a whole then, Figure 4.4 presents a simplified but not unrealistic picture of the central democratic process, as it emerges from conventional descriptions and theories of democracy.[3] Hopefully therefore it is not too controversial as a basis for comparative statistical investigation. Before we go on to that investigation, however, we have to examine the comparative data, which are used to specify the model.

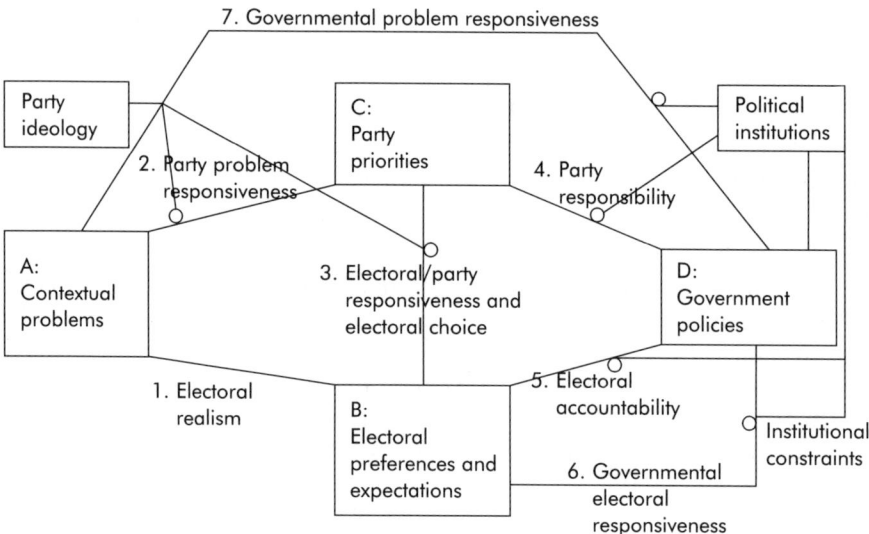

Figure 4.4 *Additional relationships and constraints in democratic processes.*
NB: O *indicates an interaction effect*

4.4 COMPARATIVE DATA SETS

The NIAS Research Group has measured all factors included in Figure 4.4 for 16 OECD-countries. OECD-countries were chosen because, from 1972, under the influence of the International Monetary Fund (IMF), they have been recording government expenditures in exactly the same way. Public expenditures in different policy areas are used as indicators of government policy precisely because they are available in the same form for all countries. The areas covered are shown in Table 4.1. Data generally cover the period 1945–94 but analyses covering government expenditure only run from 1972 because of comparability considerations.

Having data in the same form across countries is absolutely crucial for a comparative investigation like this and applies also to the indicators we have chosen for contextual problems, electoral concerns and party programmes. We want to describe how democracy works, not British democracy, American democracy, Italian democracy, etc. This implies at some stages pooling our data across countries and time, and even where country by country checks have been done, we made sure this is done with comparable categories – eliminating at least methodological variation between national units. Making data truly comparable involves sacrifices (Sartori, 1970; Pennings et al., 1999). Where indicators are not available for all countries they have been left out. Often a simpler index has to be preferred to a more valid one – simply because the latter is not available everywhere or is not reliable. For example, the measure of 'welfare needs' we use is the percentage of the whole population aged 65 and over, which requires most servicing.

Table 4.1 *Major data-based measures of contextual problems, electoral concerns, party priorities and government policies*

Contextual problems	Electoral concerns	Party priorities	Government policies
	Most important problem is:		
Unemployment	unemployment and inflation	Left–Right ideology	Size of central government (% of GDP spent)
Per cent of population aged over 65	Welfare	Per cent welfare emphasis	Expenditure on welfare (% of GDP)
Per cent of population aged 5–15	Education, youth	Per cent education emphasis	Expenditure on education (% of GDP)
State involvement in militarized inter-state disputes (MIDS)	Foreign affairs and war	Per cent peace emphasis	Expenditure on the military (% of GDP)
	Alternatively: Estimates of median voter position on: Left–Right ideology welfare emphasis education expansion peace emphasis		

The same can be said of government expenditures themselves. They do not represent the whole of a policy. Had we comparative measures of legislation or of administrative measures in the various policy areas we would use them. But we do not have them. Expenditures are very important in effecting policies, however, and are capable of telling us a lot about what governments actually do, as opposed to what they say they do (see also: Klingemann et al., 1994; Castles, 1998).

Fortunately, electoral programmes have been coded into a fairly refined range of 56 categories (most recently reported in Budge et al., 2001). These can be combined into specific measures of the priority given by parties in elections to, for example, welfare and defence, as well as into a general measure of Left–Right ideology (ibid.: 22). Measures are based on the percentage of sentences in each programme given to a particular topic, or to 'Left-wing' minus 'Right-wing' topics. These seem good measures of the policy priorities parties say they have and which can be compared with the relative amount of resources they actually devote to them in government (see also: Keman, 1997a; van Kersbergen, 1997).

Really comparable public opinion data over our 16 countries – needed to measure electoral preferences and expectations in our model – are hard to find, however. Instead we have used estimates of the median voter positions[4] derived from votes and party programmes, on the assumption that voters vote for the parties whose policy positions are closest to their own. Assuming also an even spread of voters on each side of party positions on the policy continuum, the proportion of voters sharing each party's policy positions can be calculated and the position of the middle elector – the one associated with the majority position – estimated from the overall distribution (Kim and Fording, 1998; see also: Pennings and Lane, 1998; Budge et al., 2001).

Our major indicators for policy expenditures are summarized in Table 4.1. We investigated many more policy areas than these reported in this table.[5] However, only those involving total (government) expenditure and expenditure on welfare and defence appeared as significant at all levels of the data-based equations linking problems, electoral concerns, party priorities and government policy. Education expenditure is included below for comparison, as expenditures here seem – like those in most policy areas – to be purely problem-driven and not responsive to either party or electoral priorities. Many of the indicators in Table 4.1 relate to more than one policy-area. Inflation and unemployment for example might have effects both on the general amount spent by government and on the amount spent, particularly, on welfare. Similarly a party's or voter's position to the Left or Right might in theory have consequences for all the policy-areas, as it has a general relevance for party priorities in a variety of specific areas.

The data we generate using these indicators have two major characteristics:

1. They do not change much over time. Stability and persistence are their main characteristics, even in terms of party policy priorities.
2. Partly as a result they do show great differences between countries. This is because countries start off from very different levels of welfare or inflation in the first place. Any changes that then occur over time trend in the same direction, however, suggesting that there are common international influences at work, despite initial national differences. This indicates that there is scope for a pooled, aggregate analysis of our data as well as a need to check every result statistically at an individual country level to make sure it does not misrepresent national cases. The results we now report were found at both levels.

4.5 AN OVERVIEW OF RESULTS FROM COMPARATIVE STATISTICAL INVESTIGATION

Are the direct impacts of problems on governments more or less important than those mediated by parties and voters in a democracy? We can certainly say that direct impacts of problems on governments are more important in most policy areas. In most, relationships 4 and 6 – i.e. *party responsibility* (translating policy priorities into government policies) and *government responsiveness* (adapting policy-making to the relevant constituencies) – do not consistently hold. This may be because we do not have adequate data. Out of the policies we *can* investigate, only welfare, defence and general government activity show a pattern of relationships conforming to those labelled 4 and 6 in our model (Figure 4.4). In other areas, education being an obvious example, the bureaucracy seems to react directly to contextual pressures without prompting from either parties or voters. These policy areas are described by link 7 (Government problem responsiveness) in Figure 4.4. Political institutions (federalism, centralization) also affect patterns of policy expenditure greatly, making a major contribution to national differences in the areas we investigated. Obviously whether a country is Federal or Unitary makes a great difference to the amount central government spends, and the policies it undertakes (Keman, 2000a). Quantitatively therefore, one can say that party-mediated links between problems, electoral concerns and government policies emerge as much less numerous than the direct links.

However, we should qualify this finding in two ways:

1. The two areas where we have found party priorities to affect government targets[6] – welfare and defence – are the areas to which most money is directed. They are also central to Left–Right conflicts between parties and thus to the major political confrontation in most democracies (Keman, 1984).
2. Our findings relate to expenditure targets for the various policy areas, not to the direct formulation of policy goals through legislation or administrative decrees. For obvious reasons neither of these types of policy-enactment have been quantified in a manner suitable for comparative investigation. In the one case where they have been quantified, even for investigation within a single country (the USA) we have found a very strong, even causal relationship, between Left–Right priorities enunciated in party programmes and the general 'liberalism' of presidential actions (McDonald et al., 1999).

This suggests – if we had comparable information for other countries – that many policy areas would show significant party influence in legislative terms even though much legislation and administrative action would still be technical and non-partisan in character. However, slow-moving policy expenditures, constrained by pre-existing plans, legal contracts, long-term programmes and so on – constitute the toughest test of party influence over policy. In education, for example, it is harder to get new schools built than to change the curriculum. Thus the finding that party priorities do influence the crucial welfare and defence budgets is a stronger affirmation of the importance of parties than it appears at first sight.

The general picture that we form of party democracy is thus one where parties focus on the points central to their (Left–Right) *ideology*. They compete on these for votes and concern themselves with setting targets for them in government. Other matters they leave to the bureaucracy and routine government action (e.g. if the birth-rate rises, new schools need to be planned in five years' time).

Of course, if routine action is botched or not taken, the question will spill over into day-to-day politics and involve party confrontations. However, such issues do not have the staying power of ones related to long-standing differences (above all, of those related to Left–Right stands). Remedial action can be taken on such 'occasional' issues and they will fade away. Only if they occur at the height of an election will they affect voting. Otherwise attention turns back at elections to mainstream questions lining the Right up against the Left – 'guns' versus 'butter', or: defence versus welfare.

Turning now to the responsiveness of parties to real problems (link 2 in Figure 4.4) and to electoral concerns (link 3) we have a very definite finding. Parties appear *not* to be responsive! They do not change priorities, neither as new problems emerge nor as electoral concerns change. These two are in fact bound together, as our public-opinion data show voters to be quite realistic about problems currently facing the democracy (link 1). During the post-war boom and the Cold War (1950–72) they overwhelmingly thought foreign affairs and war were the most important problems. After 1972 they become predominantly concerned with the domestic problems of unemployment and inflation. Which of the two is regarded as most important is closely related to the actual situation in the country at the time, as measured by such indicators as percentage of unemployed and rates of inflation (Castles, 1999).

In spite of 'objective' problems often being reinforced by electoral concerns, parties hardly take any notice of them. The reasons for this are rooted in their domination by a fixed ideology. Leftwing parties *always* emphasize the problem of (present or future) unemployment very heavily. Thus they do not concentrate on it more when it is high than when it is low. The same applies to Rightwing parties with regard to inflation or defence. Thus links 2 and 3 in Figure 4.3 do not exist in reality. Nor are party responsiveness and responsibility affected by the nature of the party ideology. All parties are the same in this regard.

Does this mean that in general parties are inflexible and unresponsive? Yes! But we must draw a distinction between individual parties and the party *system*, which they make up. The *system* offers voters both policy choice and a means of responding flexibly as circumstances change. If you think unemployment is important at the time of an election you can vote for a Leftwing party who are always concerned about it. If at the next election unemployment has gone down but inflation is rising, you can vote for Rightwing parties who are permanently obsessed with inflation. Parties themselves do not respond but the *party system* offers a range of policy options out of which voters can vote for the most appropriate one. Party systems appear thus to function as a 'window' of opportunities, rather than delineation of the voters' choice (Mair, 1997; Pennings and Lane, 1998).

Party inflexibility and lack of responsiveness can even be seen, paradoxically, as *beneficial* for democracy in two ways:

1. They generally ensure that voters have a clear-cut choice between different policy alternatives. Parties are generally distinguishable both in terms of current policy and by their record. Indeed current policy and record are often interchangeable – for example only 13 out of a total of

57 parties in the study significantly changed their Left–Right positions before and after 1970, which appears as a 'watershed' in post-war economic development.

2. This degree of commitment to certain policies also gives voters a guarantee that parties will actually seek to carry out their promises in government. That is they will be 'responsible' in the sense of Figure 4.4 (link 4). They will try to carry out their promises not because voters will punish them if they do not (it is in fact hard for voters to know whether or not parties have tried to carry out promises, in a situation of great uncertainty). Parties will however try to carry out policies because they *want* to, and their ideology pushes them into it in the policy areas where they take a stand. This is probably a better guarantee for fulfilment of the mandate than any external mode of enforcement.

Parties may want to carry through their policies in government but are they able to? The idea that they are, has been challenged both by 'policy output' studies (e.g. Hofferbert, 1966; Wilensky, 1975), that found social and economic factors determined expenditures; and theories such as 'incrementalism' (Davis et al., 1966) that find that bureaucratic inertia and stand-offs overwhelm party influences for change (for counter evidence, however, see Castles, 1982: Schmidt, 1989a; Keman, 1993b; Stimson et al., 1995).

The lack of change from year to year in the data, on which we have already commented, certainly favours an incrementalist view. Current government expenditure on most policy areas looks very like last year's. However, this could be because this year's problems also look much like last year's and party commitments also do not change much. However, it goes almost without saying that there are many constraints on altering policy, especially spending policy, even for a party which has an electoral mandate. Interest groups and bureaucracies, contracts already signed, work already done – as well as general economic constraints – may all have to be overcome before spending can change. And everything may be put back to square one by the (premature) fall of the government.

Once we turn our attention from immediate changes in spending totals to the way parties try to alter expenditure *targets*, we can however see more scope for party intervention. Spending aggregates do change substantially over time (both welfare and defence over the post-war period) even if change from one year to another is limited. The questions are: How is the direction of change being affected? How are the ultimate spending targets being altered?

The findings, both from an immediate and long-term point of view, are that party commitments do have an effect on spending priorities, in some specific policy areas (welfare and defence). On the general size of central government expenditure, direct party influences are, however, displaced by the preferences of the median voter. In this area, in other words, the government responds directly to electoral preferences (link 6 in Figure 4.4): here government is sensitive and responsive to the electorate, even if parties, as we have seen, are not.

On welfare and defence, party priorities substitute for directly expressed electoral preferences in setting targets. If voters want to change spending patterns in these specific areas they need to vote for another party. It is significant that these policy areas are highly ideological – one central to the Left, the other to the Right. Within a general budget constrained by popular preferences and other factors, there seems indeed a direct trade-off between the two areas which makes political contrasts even more intense (Keman, 1987). However, change towards target levels of expenditure moves very slowly. Only 5 per cent of the desired change is realized each year. An average government life of three years means that parties can cover only 15 per cent of the distance between present levels of expenditure and their target level in any one government. The slow rate of change perhaps accounts for the pervasive cynicism about parties' ability to effect any policy-change at all in government.

Of course, we must also qualify this by the consideration that it is often easier to legislate or regulate others than to alter one's own spending. For the reasons stated above, this study is confined to expenditures. But we have already noted single-country evidence that legislative measures may respond quite quickly to party (and electoral) priorities (Stimson et al., 1995; McDonald et al., 1999). One also has to take into account the other factors allowed for in Figure 4.4. Institutional constraints such as federalism and centralization are very important in accounting for differences in spending outside defence – between countries but not of course over time. Such institutional arrangements do not change much over time. They exert a direct effect, not an interactive one, as was envisaged in Figure 4.4. The development of problems has both cross-national and dynamic effects. Even in policy areas central to the parties or swayed by electoral preferences therefore, governments and bureaucracies do also respond directly to problems. Thus link 7 in Figure 4.4 is always present, even when party-mediated relationships also hold (see also: Braun, 2000; Wachendorfer-Schmidt, 2000).

With some modifications therefore the theoretical expectations of the model are upheld in three central policy areas. Here there is always some political input either from voters or parties. But this operates within constraints imposed by institutions (like the state format and the extant party system), prior commitments made by party government and the impact of problems themselves – all as expected.

The last link in the model (5: Electoral accountability of parties) is one of considerable interest to party specialists. It is the 'feedback' element in our model (Figure 4.1). How does party management of government affect voting? Are parties rewarded for governmental success and punished for government failure? Or is their electoral fate divorced from what they do in government? – A disquieting possibility for theories which see democracy as a way to hold governments to account.

In fact the answers to these questions are mixed (see: Tufte, 1978; Budge and Keman, 1990; Pennings et al., 1999). Government parties *do* seem to be held to account by voters – but in terms of an overall reaction to their (economic) success, not in terms of a detailed appraisal of what they have actually done or attempted to do in the way of policy. So it is not whether a government intervened extensively in society and economy that counts, nor whether it reduced government intervention and activity. Rather it is judged on whether employment and inflation are better or worse than expected over a fairly short time-span of up to five years. Voters do, however, discriminate between the kinds of parties which form the government, in order to refine their judgement about how to direct their vote. Parties get punished more severely for failing to fulfil their own policy priorities – employment for a Leftwing government and inflation for a Rightwing one – than they do for failing on 'opposition' priorities.

Both 'prospective' and 'retrospective' judgements appear to enter into voters' appraisals of government performance and their subsequent vote. They are concerned not just to punish or reward the existing government but also to indicate which party should have the future direction of policy. Thus, if a Leftwing party has been associated in government with rising unemployment, it can hardly be judged capable of confronting it in the future, even though it continues to emphasize it as a problem. In the election it may well be voted out in favour of a Rightist alternative which at least could not do any worse on unemployment and will probably do better on inflation (Hibbs, 1992; Cusack, 1997). Such reactions also depend, however, on the party system's being able to offer distinct Left and Right ideological alternatives which can form clearly differentiated governments. In many multi-party democracies they cannot, because parties of both tendencies are associated in coalition governments which form without much reference to the election results. In such situations it is always unclear in advance what government will form, even if a clearly Left or Right wing one does actually emerge eventually.

The extreme case where the party system offers no possibility to voters of influencing government composition and policy are the 'Grand Coalitions' in 'consensus democracies' like Switzerland and Austria, where all significant parties whatever their ideological complexion join to form the government. In this case voters can neither reward nor punish nor influence the future direction of the government since this will remain the same however they cast their votes. They can only vote therefore on non-policy grounds. As a result the votes for parties in the current election closely resemble those they got in the last election, subject to some long-term secular erosion.

In contrast the Anglo-Saxon countries offer voters a choice between ideological types of majority party government, clearly Left and clearly Right. Thus the aggregate party vote in the current election fluctuates a lot and can clearly be explained as a reaction to how well the government has met economic expectations (Tufte, 1978).

The type of party system, and whether or not this offers a choice to voters for establishing an alternative government, thus clearly has to be taken into a fully specified and validated model. How we have revised the initial possibilities we sketched in Figure 4.4 in the light of these findings is discussed in the next section.

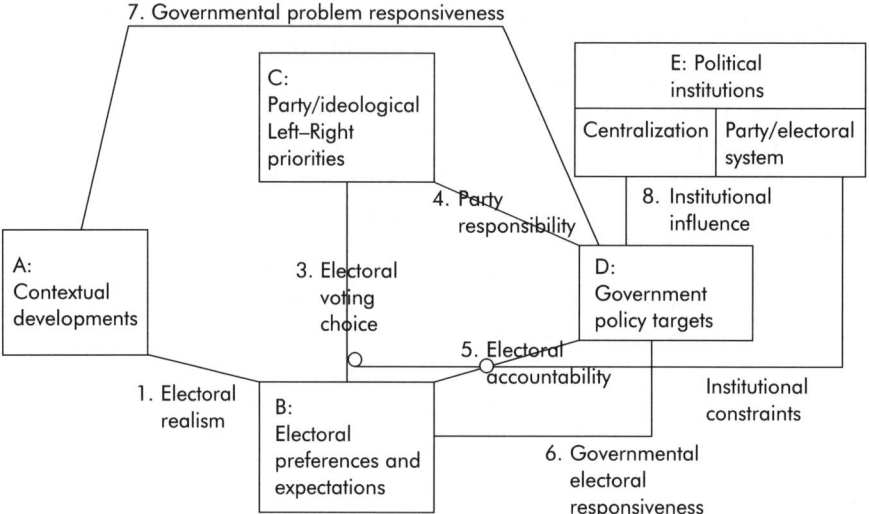

Figure 4.5 *The validated general model of democratic processes*

4.6 A VALIDATED AND SPECIFIED MODEL OF DEMOCRATIC PROCESSES

Our full model – revised in the light of the comparative findings – is illustrated in Figure 4.5.

It is a simplified and modified version of Figure 4.4, owing to the discovery that some hypothetical relationships appear not to exist in reality. Thus parties have been found rather unresponsive both to 'objective' societal developments and electoral concerns, so link 2 of Figure 4.3 – party responsiveness – is eliminated. Link 3, between voters and parties, is simplified to voters choosing, by their votes, between fixed party programmes, with a new interactive effect deriving from the fact that choices appear to have an impact only where the party system allows for clear-cut government alternatives of Left and Right. This also affects the possibility of party governments being held accountable by voters in terms of their economic policies (link 5). Again this can only happen when a clearly distinguishable party alternative can be voted in to replace the existing one in government.

A further simplification derives from the fact that Left–Right ideology is so closely related to the parties' policy-stances that it cannot really be regarded as a separate factor. In Figure 4.5 it is moved into the party priorities box (C). The Left–Right position of a party is closely related to the specific stands (e.g. on welfare and defence) which affect government policy (D). The pervasive importance of this central dimension of party competition is indeed a major finding of our research. It is supported by the similar recognition of its primacy made in other comparative research (e.g. Bartolini and Mair, 1990; Keman and Pennings, 1995). However, its influence over expenditures has to compete with the structural impact of institutions, for which a new link (8) is added to Figure 4.5. This link represents the organizational context within which government must operate.

What then is the picture of *party democracy* that we can draw from Figure 4.5? The process is, as we surmised initially, driven by the emergence and development of domestic and international problems which democracies face. Most of these are handled by bureaucratic processes inside government ministries (link 7), though they may spill over momentarily into everyday politics if something goes wrong. If such issues involve voters at all, these will be found to be organized in distinct social constituencies and will probably be involved in interest group activity rather than direct party activity. The issues that concern the electorate as a whole are highly selective and concentrated on four policy areas – peace and war, inflation, unemployment and welfare (link 1, Figure 4.4). These relate closely to Left–Right divisions – not coincidentally. The reason this particular form of ideological contestation is so important and universal is that it *does* channel and focus the issues most voters are most concerned with and can translate into voting choices.

For the same reasons parties are also concerned with them. But they react in a different way. Instead of responding to immediate circumstances they formulate a long-term prospective and diagnosis of societal problems. Having worked it out and thought it over, they find it – their ideology – difficult to change, except in detail. This fixed ideological basis explains the relative stability of party positions, which emerges so strongly in the empirical analysis so far (see also: Castles, 1998, and Schmidt in Chapter 8 in this book).

By adopting different diagnoses and solutions to the same set of issues, the parties help organize a one-dimensional Left–Right policy-space for elections, which simplifies *electoral choice* (link 3, Figure 4.5). Their strong ideological commitments also give a guarantee that they will actually try to implement the policy they say they will adopt if they go into government, thus underpinning *party responsibility* (link 4; see also: Keman, 1997b; Pennings, 1998).

We have found party responsibility to operate in the central policy areas of welfare and defence. On the overall size and activities of government – the range and extent of its intervention in society – governments seem to react directly to voters (link 6, Figure 4.5). Popular influence on government thus does not stop with voting for parties but forms an input into this major policy area. In a sense it guarantees that this area of influence is relevant, regardless of the specific features of the party system (Scharpf, 1997). As government parties are evaluated by voters on the basis of what they have done to alleviate the main problems they are concerned with, they are held accountable by the voters (link 5). Since the 1970s these problems have been mainly inflation and unemployment. However, the extent to which a clear-cut judgement on government performance can be expressed depends also on the degree of choice offered to voters by the party system. If there are no clear-cut choices available between programmes for future action, this may diminish tendencies to vote for a non-governmental alternative or render it difficult to make clear which coalition is to be preferred (link 3, Figure 4.5).

This takes us back into the question of the policy alternatives offered by the parties, and the importance of Left-Right ideology in distinguishing these (i.e. Box C in Figure 4.5). At each election this circular process starts again. The new element in the election is not, as Downs (1957) would make us believe, change of position by parties. It is the development of 'objective' problems and how these change electoral concerns and voting choices (Electoral Realism, link 1, Figure 4.5). *Voters, not parties, are the dynamic elements for change in democratic processes.* Parties, from soon after their initial emergence, take a fixed ideological position. The only way in which new policies will be offered is from a new, electorally significant, party. But their emergence has been a relatively rare phenomenon until the 1990s (see Chapter 6). This may indicate that existing party systems offer a reasonable range of approaches to major problems and are capable of adapting their point of view to the existing problems in a convincing fashion (Pennings and Lane, 1998).

4.7 SPECIFYING MODELS FOR PARTICULAR POLICY AREAS

Figure 4.5 gives a general picture of democratic processes, which applies quite well to the 16 countries we examined. However, it is very generalized in the sense that these processes differ within particular policy areas. In most areas, only links 7 and 8 operate – that is, the central bureaucracy responds to problems directly without either party or electoral mediation. On the overall extent of government activity voters exert an additional influence through link 6 – governments seem to respond to what the public think is appropriate in terms of their extension or reduction of activities. On welfare and defence, party priorities are important (link 4), as are contextual and structural influences. Where ideological alternatives exist, government priorities may additionally change in response to election results which transfer power from one party to another.

Each of these situations can be represented by a specific model which isolates those elements and processes in the generalized one and which holds for a specific area. Doing so also allows us to specify the processes quantitatively in the form of equations which can be used predictively.[7] Four areas will be elaborated below. First of all the case of spending on education. This area is characterized by the 'routinization' of government involvement. This is not the case with the second example: 'big government'. The growth of public expenditures has been disputed ever since the 1970s. Third, we focus on the trade-off between 'butter and guns' which is a constant issue of post-war development. Finally the situations where electoral choice and party positions do matter are discussed.

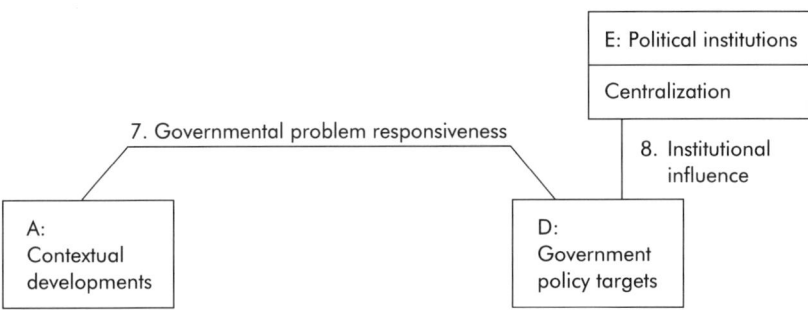

Figure 4.6 *Democratic policy processes in the field of education*

4.7.1 Non-mediated Processes: Education

We start with the simplest case where government decisions about policy expenditure respond only to contextual developments (A) and political institutions (E). Education is a good example of such an area, which we shall use as an illustration.

Only two influences seem to act on decisions about education expenditure: increases in the school-age population, and the degree of government centralization. This makes for a very simplified model compared with the general one in Figure 4.5. However, it is the one which is representative for most areas of government expenditure.

As an equation the 'education' model is:

$$EDEXP\%GDP_t = 0 + 0.9\ EDEXP\%GDP_{t-1} + 0.08\ \%POPSA_t + 0.1\ CENT_t$$

What the equation says is that Education expenditure in the current year (t), expressed as a percent of Gross Domestic Product, will be closely related to expenditure last year (t – 1). This is natural as commitments will not change drastically over one year. At the same time, however, current expenditures will also be affected by the increase or decrease in the number of people eligible for school – the per cent of the population aged 5–15 (POPSA = school age population). Finally, CENT-ralization refers to the influence on expenditure of institutional arrangements – whether the country is Federal (scored –1), moderately centralized (scored 0) or very centralized (scored +1). The baseline expressed by the intercept of zero shows that in the absence of any school pupils expenditure would of course tend towards zero.

In practice, given the constraints on and stability of the factors governing expenditure, actual outlays do not differ a great deal from one year to another. The real interest, as explained in the appendix on expenditure targeting, is how medium-term spending targets are affected by the influences at work, and how quickly they can be attained. Were education expenditures left to drift on their own, independent from school age population or centralization, they would move from their average level of 5 per cent of

GDP in the 1970s downwards at a rate of 10 per cent a year till they reached zero. However, given any substantial numbers in the school-age population at all, expenditures will gradually increase by 10 per cent per year to a target value which can be calculated. The effect of the school-age population on target expenditures, from the equation above, is:

$$\frac{\text{Coefficient } (0.08) \times \text{value } (10\% \text{ are of school age})}{1.0 - 0.9 \text{ (coefficient of lagged dependent variable)}}$$

This gives: (0.8% of GDP)/(1.0 – 0.9). The *target value* for education expenditure is thus *8% of GDP*

Assuming that we are dealing with a moderately centralized country where the centralization variable takes a value of zero and can be discounted, we can make predictions on this basis as to how expenditures would move given a certain percentage in the school-age population. Even in this simple case, however insulated it may be from purely political change, targets would not be stable as school attendees would fluctuate in number each year. Actual expenditures would vary even less, as progress towards the target is only 10 per cent of the gap to be covered each year. Thus it would take around ten years to attain the target even if numbers of school attendees remained the same, which is unlikely. In other words, if and when democratic politics is not relevant for policy-making in a certain area, this formula is capable of measuring how long it will take to reach a 'natural' equilibrium. Often this is considered as a manifestation of 'incrementalism' (Tarschys, 1985; Keman, 1993b) but then used in a pejorative meaning with reference to the ill-effects of democratic polities. Yet, as the equation clarifies, even if external influences and demographic change are met it requires time to achieve an (societally) acceptable balance.

4.7.2 Popular Influence on the Overall Size of Government

Fluctuations in spending targets, even amounting to reversals of direction, are even more likely when directly political influences intrude. The simplest case is where public opinion makes itself felt on the type of role government ought to play in society or economy – expansive or restrictive. The processes operating in this central policy area are sketched in Figure 4.7.

Even though governments are supposed to respond to public opinion in this instance, they also have to respond directly to societal developments and operate within the structural constraints (degree of centralization) already identified. The model gives us an equation which can be expressed as follows:

$$\text{GOVEXP\%GDP}_t = 0.07 + 0.85 \text{ GOVEXP\%GDP}_{t-1} + 1.31 \text{ CENT}_t + 0.04$$
$$\text{Median-Voter-LR}_t + 0.08 \text{ UNEMP}_t + 0.11 \text{ INF}_t$$
$$+ 0.22 \text{ \%POP65}_t + 0.02 \text{ OPENECON}_t$$

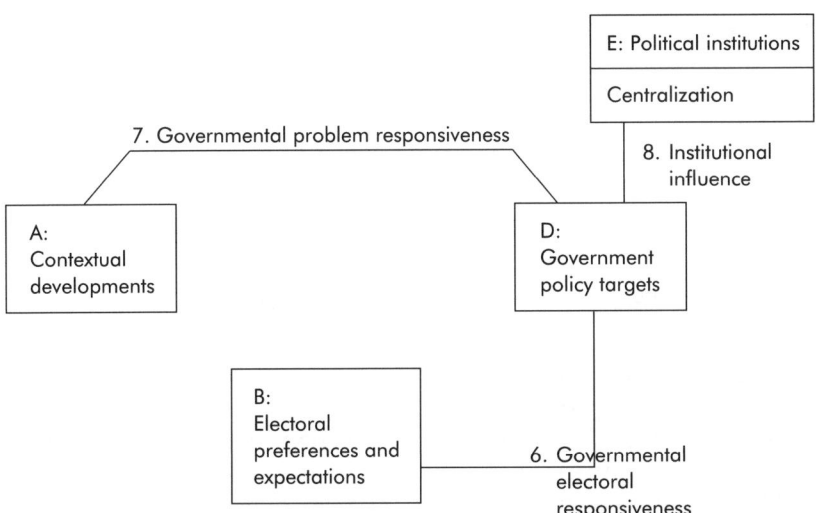

Figure 4.7 *Democratic policy processes affecting government size*

Again government expenditure this year is closely related to expenditure last year because of legal and structural requirements (contracts, continuing commitments, etc.). However, external and political influences also enter into the equation. The central government will do more where there are no state or local governments with their own competences. Governments will intervene more when unemployment ($UNEMP_t$) rises, and when more elderly people need social services ($POP65+_t$). The more the national economy depends on trade ($OPENECON_t$ – i.e. imports plus exports as a per cent of GDP) the more governments seem forced to do domestically in order to mitigate the effects of world developments. Rising inflation (INF_t) necessarily increases government spending.

Besides these direct impacts on government, shifts in public opinion about how active government should be have a relatively small but still significant impact (Median-Voter-LRt). A shift in median opinion of one unit along the Left–Right scale is associated with a quarter per cent change in the target value of spending. A change of opinion from very Left (12, as in Denmark in 1973) to very Right (–15, Denmark in 1974) would change the target by 6.75 per cent of GDP, in relation to an overall current expenditure of 40 per cent of GDP. This is quite impressive. It represents the most extreme change in public opinion observed in any of our democracies and it has strong effects on the viability of governmental action. These effects are tempered, however, by the slowness with which current expenditures adjust to the target – only at a rate of 5 per cent of previous expenditure each year. Thus it would take about 8 years to get from current to targeted expenditure, assuming nothing changed in the interval. But of course everything changes. Apart from 'objective' pressures on the government from contextual developments, opinion itself switches – back to the Left (+4) in Denmark by 1977. As a result Danish government expenditure did go down over the 1970s only from 40 per cent to around 38 per cent of GDP, where it stayed till the 1990s. Obviously, it is hard to predict the actual long-term consequences of popular changes of opinion, even though governments do adjust targets in response to them. Both contextual developments and popular moods bring about influences that tend to outweigh each other.

4.7.3 Party Priorities in Welfare and Defence

The same conclusions hold for the two policy areas where party priorities exert the political effects rather than public opinion acting directly. Although these constitute only two out of the ten policy areas examined for the study, they are major areas which take up in combination about half the government budget in most countries under review. The central issue of the post-war period has usually been how much should be spent on defence as opposed to welfare – the classic 'guns versus butter' argument. As we shall see, spending decisions in the two areas seem to mirror each other – when one goes up the other goes down – and to move at the same speed towards their targets (Domke et al., 1983; Keman and van Dijk, 1987). They seem to reflect the outcomes of a general party struggle between Leftwing and Rightwing priorities.

Of course expenditures are also driven, as always, directly by contextual problems and institutional imperatives. Figure 4.8 illustrates how party policy priorities operate within the context of these. Although voters' preferences and expectations are not shown as entering into this decision process, they may, of course, influence which party or parties form the government and thus determine what priorities prevail – only under certain circumstances however, which we will go into in our next section (see Figure 4.9). The equations which operationalize these relationships are, for welfare:

$$\text{WELFEXP\%GDP}_t = -0.88 + 0.95 \text{ WELFEXP\%GDP}_{t-1} + 0.01$$
$$\text{GOVPty WELFEM}_t + 0.32 \text{ CENT}_t + 0.09$$
$$\text{\%POP65} +_t + 0.03 \text{ INF}_t$$

As before, but even more so, current welfare expenditure is closely related to the previous year's expenditure (i.e. 0.95) – also to the degree of centralization of services in terms of the dominance of the central state (CENT_t). Spending is pushed up by inflation and also rises in response to the number of people in need, as measured by the percentage of the population over 65 (POP65+). The coefficient for the emphasis given to welfare by the party in government (GOVPtyWELFEM) implies that a unit difference in emphasis (1 per cent more of the election programme devoted to welfare) shifts the long-term target for welfare spending up by a fifth of 1 per cent of GDP. A 5 per cent increase in emphasis between *outgoing* parties and *incoming* parties, which occurs relatively often in the countries under review, will shift targeted welfare spending up by slightly more than 1 per cent – a significant sum given its proportion of overall public expenditure. However, movement

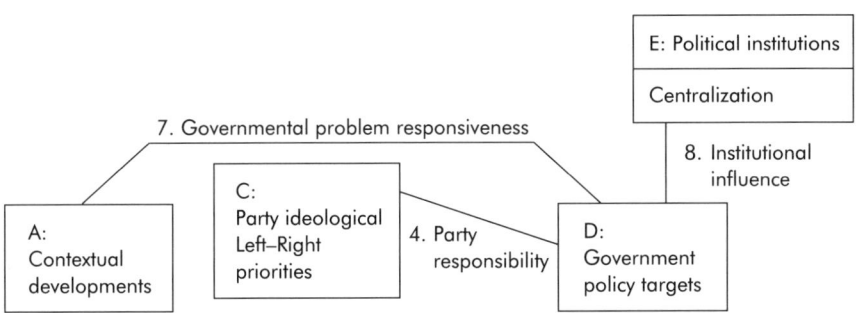

Figure 4.8 *Democratic policy processes in the fields of welfare and defence*

towards targets is slow, no more than 5 per cent of last year's expenditure is moved in their direction. Thus it would take 15–20 years to achieve desired goals. Changes in governments and contextual conditions render the target unlikely to be achieved therefore.

The corresponding equation for defence spending is:

$$\text{DEFEXP\%GDP}_t = 0.06 + 0.96 \ \text{DEFEXP\%GDP}_{t-1} - 0.01$$
$$\text{GOVPtyPEACEM}_t + 0.01 \ \text{INF}_t + 0.03 \ \text{MIDS}_t$$

As with welfare, current defence spending is closely related to what it was last year (96 per cent) – commitments and contracts for military hardware are even more determining here. It is increased by inflation, of course, and even more by involvement in violent disputes (MIDS). Naturally, military spending goes up if the country is involved in a war. However, what the government says about peace generally has an effect of reducing targeted spending by around a fifth of one per cent of GDP – almost the same as for welfare. Again movement towards the target is slow (4 per cent) and is likely to be interrupted by the cyclical movement of the other factors involved.

Both the magnitude and speed of spending changes in welfare and defence resemble each other (Keman and van Dijk, 1987). One can see this as a reflection of party conflicts, fought out in the electoral arena and resulting in changes of government and in its priorities. One can well envisage a Rightwing government which de-emphasized *both* welfare and peace being replaced by a Leftwing government emphasizing *both*. Thereafter the new government would trade increased welfare spending for decreased defence spending, almost dollar for dollar.

4.7.4. Electoral Choices between Government Priorities – Where there is a Choice

However, this party-mediated relationship between electoral wishes and government policy depends very much on the election results being reflected in the composition of the government and hence in its priorities. If

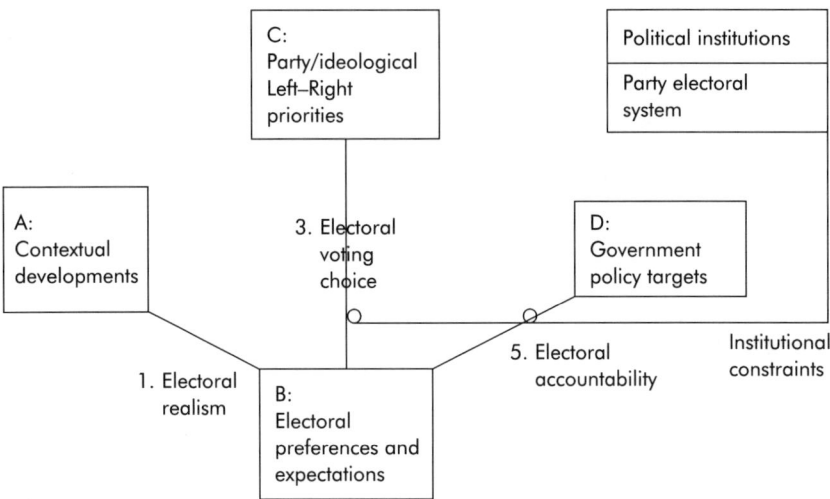

Figure 4.9 *Electoral choice between government priorities*

the same government continues in office whatever the election result (as in Switzerland), the same party policy priorities will prevail and links 3 and 5 (electoral choice and accountability) do not operate. This is shown graphically in Figure 4.9 as the constraint which the party system puts on these relationships.

Multi-party systems, commonly associated with proportional representation, normally ensure that no single party can get a majority and form a government on its own. In this case the government that forms depends on post-election negotiations, and only indirectly on the election results.

This consideration tends to inhibit the electorate from voting on grounds of current policy. It means that little change in the balance of government and opposition votes may be expected. Thus in the majority of democracies with PR and multi-party systems, little party-mediated representation of voters' wishes takes place in government. Links 3 and 5 of Figure 4.9 only operate indirectly, even through a direct influence of opinion over the overall size of government will be relevant (see Figure 4.7). Where voters *can* select between party priorities is where their votes contribute to one party or coalition alternative or the other actually winning and bringing in their particular policy priorities to government. This takes place in particular where votes are aggregated in small constituencies, in which candidates with a plurality win – Australia, New Zealand (till 1993), Canada, the United States, Britain and Ireland (and to some extent in France). In these democracies the government is formed by the plurality party, or party combination (e.g. in Australia) in the election. Voters respond by switching their votes between the parties, and voting for or against government in terms of both record and ability to confront immediate challenges.

The equation which expresses these tendencies is:

$$\text{INC VOTE\%}_t = 51.89 + 0.55 \text{ GDP GROWTH DEV}_t - 2.3 \text{ ECONEXP}_t - 0.19 \text{ TIME} - 6.67 \text{ CANADA} + 6.30 \text{ US}$$

The expressions for Canada and the US simply reflect the fact that incumbent parties (INC VOTE) receive lower votes in Canada, with its frequent minority governments, and more in the US with its strict two-party system, than is the norm elsewhere (about 45 per cent of the vote). TIME records the long-term decline in the vote of the large parties who form governments which has occurred in all democracies during the post-war period (see: Woldendorp et al., 2000).

The really interesting elements in the equation are the ones which reflect voters' evaluations of government performance (link 5 in Figure 4.9) and promise (link 3). These include voters' judgements on whether the government has pushed general economic growth above the post-war average (GDP GROWTH DEV = GDP growth deviation). If it has done it will be rewarded with about half a per cent of votes for each per cent GDP has grown above average and vice versa if it has fallen. The economic expectations variable (ECONEXPt) relates government performance on inflation and unemployment, the two key issues so far as voters are concerned, to whether Right or Left form the government. If all is going well on both issues, the government can expect to retain its votes. If it is doing worse than expected on the issue it is less concerned about – unemployment for a Rightwing government, inflation for the Left – it will lose 2.37 per cent of the vote. If it is doing worse than expected on its issue of main concern it will lose almost 5 per cent of its vote.[8] This equation then lends support to the theory of the 'Political Business Cycle' (Tufte, 1978; Lessmann, 1987). At the same time it is clear that a major criticism is involved: only if specific institutional conditions are met (i.e. those shaping 'majoritarian democracy') then the model specified here can and will produce results as predicted.

Taking this caveat into account, the equation representing Figure 4.9 enables us to make predictions about what would happen if, for example, unemployment increased from 5 to 10 per cent, and inflation from 2 to 7 per cent as happened in many countries with the oil shock of the 1970s. One key point that emerges when we fill in the values in the equation is that unemployment meets popular expectations about what it should be, more slowly than inflation. As employment is the key issue on which parties of the Left are judged, this implies that Rightwing parties have a general electoral advantage which should keep them longer in government than parties of the Left. In fact, for four out of the five countries where this equation holds, Rightwing parties have been in office longer over the period from 1945 to 1995 (the exception is Canada; see: Woldendorp et al., 2000).

Answering such 'what if' questions gives us a better insight into the actual political workings of democracies. It also enables us to check out holistic predictions based on our model as a whole rather than examining its relationships separately, link by link. If such predictions work out, as the one outlined above seems to do, we can be more confident about the extent to which our model describes the actual working and development of democracy in the contemporary world.

4.8 GENERAL LESSONS FROM MODELLING DEMOCRATIC PROCESSES

The uses of such a description go beyond the predictive potential, however. They provide a specification of how democracy works which is capable of qualifying or modifying many of the more sweeping assertions made about it, without much evidence, in general or normative discussions. Key points which emerge from the general model are as follows (see Figures 4.3 and 4.4).

1. In most policy areas the bureaucracy reacts to problems without much direct input from voters or parties. This is understandable where problems are 'technical' or 'de-politicized', such as accommodating increasing numbers of schoolchildren in school, or road construction where traffic grows. But how technical is 'technical'? Parents may have views on the appropriate size of classes, for example, which then affect the provision of accommodation. It is true that bureaucracies do not confront problems and social developments on their own: politicians who head ministries and agencies have an interest in meeting public demand so far as they can. Bureaucrats may even anticipate political reactions to their actions and try to bring policies into line with them. Nevertheless in many areas appointed and not elected officials seem to make the actual decisions rather than elected parties or public opinion. These considerations are, of course, not new. Public Administration literature discusses these themes more often than not (Wildavsky, 1980; Lane 1985; March and Olsen, 1989). Yet, the issue here is that much of 'routine' politics is quite devoid of democratic control and appears hardly to 'matter'. By analysing this from the viewpoint of an elaborated model of 'democratic politics', we are now in a position to judge this as an established conclusion. The finding that most decisions on public expenditures are taken by non-democratic bodies must surely modify easy optimism about the possibility of full popular control in a democracy, even through political parties.
2. Reinforcing this discovery is the finding – even where public opinion or median voters' positions and party priorities have an influence – that these are not necessarily the most important factors shaping decisions. Objective problems and structural constraints appear to have a big direct impact on what government does.
3. Moreover, political influences affect long-term targets rather than expenditures next year. Spending changes are very slow, so that by the time they are halfway to consummation new political priorities, let alone

changing objective circumstances, will probably have dictated a new set of targets. Thus political objectives are rarely fully attained, and from a short-term perspective may even seem to have been abandoned – a fact which makes for widespread cynicism about the extent to which parties keep their promises.The typical scenario is where party activists and voters have been keyed up for a campaign to put the opposition party in power. Buoyed up by enthusiasm on election day they expect the 'promised land' to be ushered in next year. Then they find that policies look much the same and they are being urged by suddenly moderate leaders to face realities and show patience. No wonder they then feel betrayed and leave the established parties to switch to a 'new' messenger of a promised land.

4. Besides constraints on policy, there are also constraints on voters' expression of their own political will. Public opinion does make itself directly felt on the appropriate size of government. Where opinion is mediated by the parties, as implied by our opening remarks about 'party democracy', it can express itself where these offer clear programmatic alternatives of Left and Right. In most cases, however, institutional devices and socio-cultural cleavages play an intermediary, if not an intervening role. Hence the voters' choice is *indirectly* relevant and depends on the working of a party system and the leverage of different parties (especially those in opposition) in parliament and government. Hence, part of the democratic quality of parliamentary government is in dispute, endangering, if not depriving voters of the opportunity to shape government spending priorities in the direction that they see as fitting the 'contextual problems'.

5. Where voters do have the opportunity of selecting a government to conform to current needs, they do so with a good appreciation of the real problems and of the credentials of the party needed to confront them. Perhaps of necessity their evaluation is broad and approximate. They are not interested in the details of what current or future governments may decide – spending more on welfare as opposed to defence for example. Rather they are concerned with the objectives, particularly the economic objectives, they have attained. A Leftwing government is elected because it is particularly good at tackling unemployment. If it becomes associated with high unemployment (regardless of how far its policies may have actually ameliorated it) it will be changed for a Rightwing government (and vice versa with inflation) if unemployment (and inflation) develop negatively (Cusack, 1997).

As experts themselves disagree about the effects of policy on problems, a broad evaluation is probably the only one that voters or anyone else could make if they have to decide and vote. Its broad nature rather cuts across elaborate discussions of the political information needed by voters: they clearly do not need to know much about politics in detail to make sensible evaluations. (Budge, 1996a; Lupia and McCubbins, 1998). Parties also seem in practice to act in a simpler and more direct fashion than is often attributed to them. Far from being office-seekers who fine-tune policy in pursuit of votes, they seem ideologically embedded entities incapable of responding quickly or sensitively either to problems or public concerns of the moment.

Ideological steadfastness has advantages not usually recognized in normative theory. It gives parties a clear and distinct image rooted in their basic concerns and past record. This makes it feasible for voters to make incisive evaluations of whether they have succeeded or failed in their own terms – the Left with employment and welfare, the Right with inflation and warfare – and thus to decide on their vote with little need for elaborate information-processing, which they probably could not undertake anyway. When all is said and done therefore our validated model does uphold the most basic assertion of all – that democracy enables citizens to influence the central areas of government policy and bring government actions more into line with their own preferences. This is after all the major claim of democracy and it is upheld by our investigations. If there remain many policy areas where, broadly speaking, improvements could be made, our model also points to how this could be done – primarily by consolidating and clarifying the party alternatives available for governing, taking into account the time horizon and institutional context that directs policy-making and its targets in a liberal democracy.

NOTES

1 This chapter is the result of a collaboration that took shape during our stay at the *Netherlands Institute of Advanced Studies* in 1996.

2 Assuming that parties rather than individual representatives are the major actors. (See for this: Laver and Schofield, 1990; Keman, 1996).

3 Important collective actors in democracy not included in our simplified representation are the media (TV and newspapers) and interest groups. We know that parties often get their ideas about what voters are thinking and what the problems are from the media – whose reports could diverge from the 'reality' in some respects, making them important independent influences on action. We also know that interest groups may be as important as institutions in constraining or influencing what governments do. The reason we do not include media or interest groups in our model is twofold. First, including two more components would vastly multiply the number of linkages we have to take into account, making it harder to specify and check the model – which is after all a *simplified* representation of reality. Secondly it is much harder to assemble comparative data on groups and media than on the factors we do include. What we can say in defence of our decision is that the four elements included in the model do seem central to *more* democratic processes than either groups or media. Important though they are, groups may be aligned with particular parties and thus their impact is likely captured to a considerable extent by party priorities. The media have to reflect what is going on around them or lose credibility. Thus the indicators included (e.g. on socio-economic developments) probably capture media effects indirectly.

4 The importance of the median voter in representing public opinion can be expressed in terms of voters' choices. If electoral preferences can be arranged along a left–right policy spectrum then the median voter is the one who pushes the count over 50 per cent, going from either left or right. A simplified illustration of this is given below for an electorate of five voters.

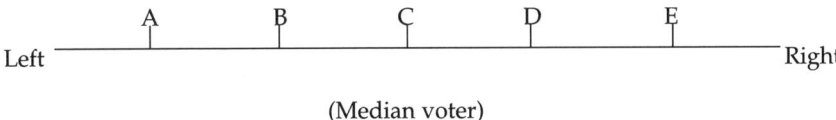

(Median voter)

On this dimension, voters are placed in terms of their policy preferences from left to right. C is the middle (or 'median') voter. For a policy to have a majority it must get C's support. On this argument, policy will always move towards C (the median) position. This is very nice for C of course who will always get his or her way under ideal democratic conditions. But it is also a reasonable outcome for the other voters, indeed the best they can hope for. A and B would much prefer to have C's policies adopted rather than those of D and E. Similarly D and E prefer C to A and B. Thus the power of the median voter and the adoption of that voter's preference by government is the best way of meeting everybody's preferences under the existing distribution of opinion. The other voters do not get all they want but they get more than if the opposing wing could simply impose their preferences. The median position is thus in a sense the 'average' or 'majority' position and can be used to sum up the preferences of voters as a whole.

5 Not all the areas on which we collected information are reported there, however, because many of those investigated revealed only a context–government link (link 7 in Figure 4.4) and some influence from institutions. These policy areas are represented by education in Figure 4.4 and Table 4.1. We are more interested for the purposes of the model in those which show the influence of party mediation (welfare and defence) and of public opinion (size of government). The other policy-areas investigated were roads, transport and communications, agriculture, health, public order and money supply. In many of these, technical considerations predominate, so it is perhaps not surprising that levels of expenditure neither enter into party competition nor are directly influenced by public opinion.

6 For a discussion of why we take expenditure targets rather than annual changes in policy expenditures as our dependent variable see the Appendix to this chapter.

7 The following elaboration of the overall model as represented in Figure 4.4. is based on our investigations. The information therefore represents the outcomes of our data-analysis.

8 Voters are expected to generate expectations about each of the main economic trends as follows:

- GDP growth – expected growth is the post-war mean national growth.
- Unemployment – the expected rate is a two-year moving average for each country weighted as $\frac{2}{3}$ for year t–1 and $\frac{1}{3}$ for year t–2.
- Inflation – the expected level is a three-year moving average with weights assigned as $\frac{1}{2}$ for year t–1, $\frac{1}{3}$ for year t–2, and $\frac{1}{6}$ for year t–3.

These expectations are modelled to reflect the media's presentation of statistics on these trends. Various alternative scorings were experimented with but these scores gave the most plausible results in terms of gains and losses of votes.

APPENDIX TO CHAPTER 4: TARGETING POLICY PRIORITIES: A PURPOSIVE STATISTICAL MODEL

Our model of democratic decision-making firmly links government policy to contextual developments, party ideology and public concern. We could be wrong about these relationships but, if we are, it is a matter for grave disquiet. The whole quality of democracy depends upon their existing in some form or another.

This consideration makes it odd that many attempts to model governmental policy-making statistically have ignored external influences altogether. Rather they have viewed decision-making as bound by past decisions, modified 'incrementally' by the results of bargaining in governmental circles and among the bureaucracy. No allowance has been made for the possibility that external factors might have an effect.

The way these assumptions have been expressed statistically is in the form of an adaptive expectations model (Davis et al., 1966). Essentially, processes of internal bargaining and mutual adaptation are expected to limit change, which will tend toward a long-run equilibrium position fixed by the internal balance of power in the bureaucracy. The process is seen as dominated by decisions which have been made in the past, so that the most important determinant of present expenditure is past expenditure. Thus the equation takes on this form:

$$EDUCEXP_t = 0.7 + 0.9 \, EDUCEXP_{t-1} \tag{1}$$

That is, the level of expenditure on Education this year, at time t, is related closely to the level of Expenditure last year (time t–1).

A simple but not terribly informative interpretation of the detailed equation is that from a base of 7/10th of a per cent on Education (the intercept), spending in year t is 9/10th of spending in year t–1. A more useful way to view it is with an eye to the long run. For instance, one can calculate that a nation spending 5 per cent on Education in year t–1 is expected to move to 5.2 in year t; from 5.2 the system then continues to 5.38 in year t + 1. This sort of growth continues until the country reaches 7 per cent spending. Once the 7 per cent target is reached the system stabilizes: $[0.7 + 0.9(7)] = [0.7 + 6.3] = 7.0$. The movement toward the 7 per cent equilibrium also results when the expenditure at t–1 is above 7 per cent – e.g. starting at 9 per cent at t–1, the spending at t is 8.8, and at t + 1 it is 8.62. Fortunately, the equilibrium value can be calculated directly from the coefficients themselves. It is equal to the intercept divided by one minus the slope = $0.7/(1 - 0.9) = 0.7/0.1 = 7$.

The equation has another interesting aspect. This is the ability to estimate the speed with which the country moves toward its spending equilibrium. The denominator in the equilibrium calculation (i.e. one minus the slope) estimates the speed and it records the rate of change in the difference between where the country is currently and where it can be expected to stabilize. Given that $1 - 0.9$ equals 0.1, we have a 10 per cent movement per year. In the example above, a country at 5 per cent Education spending in year t–1 and heading for 7 per cent moves to 5.2 at year t, a 10 per cent closing of the 2 unit gap between 5 per cent and 7 per cent. From year t to t + 1 the country closes the 1.8 gap by another 10 per cent from 5.2 to 5.38.

These processes are described by the equation above as driven by the internal dynamics of administration, since no external factor, either contextual or political, is related to them. Now, we can certainly agree that institutional effects could be very powerful. The bureaucracy and its associated interest groups may have strong views, resources may be limited to an extent that keeps expenditure close to current levels, or other matters may arise which distract decision-makers from their 'external' commitments.

However, we find it frankly incredible that external influences can be totally ignored. As it stands, the equation states that the same decisions will be made about education regardless of whether 0 or 50 per cent of the population are of school age. This is just not credible.

The solution is to build on the insight that there are severe constraints on what parties might do to set policy in government, while allowing realistically for the influence of external factors – in the first place contextual problems and party commitments. At the technical level we can build on the idea that there is a point towards which policy moves – only this is a target set in response to circumstances, not a mechanical long-term equilibrium produced by a balance of internal government processes. The relative speed with which policy will be adjusted towards the target might also be subject to the purposes and intentions of parties – perhaps in terms of the perceived seriousness of problems or perhaps in order to placate opposition groups.

We can easily adjust the existing equation to reflect the influence of parties. The introduction of party policy stands into the statistical model is a simple matter of expanding the bivariate equation so that it becomes multivariate. The equation that captures the direct influence of the parties is:

$$\text{EDUCEXP}_{t-1} = 0.6 + 0.9\ \text{EDUCEXP}_{t-1} + 0.02\ \text{PtyEDUCEM}_t \qquad (2)$$

where PtyEDUCEM is the percentage of sentences in a party's programme devoted to Education. This equation estimates, in the absence of the programme's saying anything about Education, that the target value for the Education proportion of the budget is 6 per cent $[-0.6/(1 - 0.9) = 6]$. For each 1 per cent of the platform devoted to Education, the target value is expected to increase by 0.2, i.e. $(0.02/(1 - 0.9) = 0.2$. Thus when a party devotes 10 per cent of its programme to Education, it is saying the target is to be increased by 2 per cent, i.e. $(0.02 \times 10)/(1 - 0.9) = 2$. Overall, then, the party that gives 10 per cent emphasis to Education has a target of 8 per cent, the 6 per cent plus the 2 per cent. Viewed across nations the equation describes the typical kind of multiple forces at work. Viewed across time, a switch from a party with zero emphasis to one with 10 per cent of its emphasis on education will move the target eventually to spending 8 per cent of GDP on Education. But because the new spending will be approached gradually at a rate of 10 per cent movement, from old to new target, per year, the party switch will have moved Education spending from the old 6 per cent target to just over 7 per cent in the course of eight years after the switch. In general, given the constraints on spending, party retargeting is limited and affects the long-term outcomes only slowly. It is also always subject to a change in government, which might reverse the targets. Slow change in expenditure priorities is what often leads fervent supporters to feel they have been betrayed by a government. It also contrasts with the rapid changes that can be made in legislation (McDonald et al., 1999). However, one may wonder how effective the legislation is going to be if corresponding expenditures are not in place to effect the policy.

We can allow for the effects of contextual developments just as we have done for parties. Allowing for an increase in the size of the school-age population we get:

$$\text{EDUCEXP}_t = 0 + 0.9\ \text{EDUCEXP}_{t-1} + 0.08\%\text{SA}_t \qquad (3)$$

where SA is the percentage of the population aged 5–15. This says that in the absence of persons of that age in the population, the target for spending is zero. This is recorded by the intercept divided by one minus the slope: $0(1 - 0.9)$. The target is adjusted in accordance with the school-age population. For every 1 per cent of the population school-aged, the target is increased by eight-tenths of 1 per cent. Thus the target is 16 per cent when the school-aged make up 20 per cent of the population.

Putting party and contextual effects together in the same equation then gives us equations similar to those in Section 4.7, the basis for our simulations. As it happens the party effect on education expenditure is not a significant one, leaving contextual developments as the main influence on policy.

5 VOTERS, ELECTIONS AND IDEOLOGY IN EUROPEAN DEMOCRACIES

Paul Pennings

5.1 INTRODUCTION

Two central concepts which structure the behaviour of parties and voters are ideology and institutions.

Ideology can be defined as a relatively stable body of assumptions about the world which produces plausible reasons for public action (Budge, 1994). In fact, this type of ideology often takes the form of a plan or programme which is part of a *famille spirituelle* (von Beyme, 1985). Ideology in this sense is not static, but it may evolve over time (for example the evolution of Marxism into several ideological streams like Socialism and Social Democracy, or Liberalism into a progressive and conservative type).

Institutions are the rules which structure the behavioural pattern of the actors involved (Shepsle, 1997). Institutions such as the structure of party competition and electoral laws are important to understand the cross-national variations in electoral behaviour. We need the concept of institutions in order to understand how democratic actors use the existing formal and informal rules of the political game and accompanying arrangements (here: party systemic) in order to achieve their electoral goals.

Ideology and political institutions have in common that they limit the room to manoeuvre for policy choices (Keman, 1997c). The effect is that, although democracy offers an unlimited freedom of choice by means of elections, the outcomes of the democratic process are mostly stable over time. This paradox of modern democracies, namely that they offer the possibility of an unlimited range of choices ending up with a very confined and often limited pattern of policy options, can best be explained by the role of ideology and institutions in the democratic process.

This chapter gives an overview of the differences between democratic institutions, in particular electoral systems, and their effects on electoral behaviour of citizens. At first glance, the functioning of contemporary democracies suggests that these democracies are highly similar. For 'liberal' democracies are characterized by electoral and political institutions which structure democratic politics. However, a closer look shows many variations between democratic systems (LeDuc et al., 1996; Woldendorp et al., 2000). Some of them are also highly significant for the outcomes of the democratic process. For example, differences between electoral systems (the way votes are translated into seats) and party systems (the way parties interact given their numbers and distances of policy preferences) are decisive for the election outcomes and their consequences. These variations are the core of electoral politics, i.e. how citizen preferences get on the political agenda through elections. Elections give citizens agenda-control. The normative meaning of elections (i.e. what they should accomplish) is that they are considered to legitimize the power of rulers, to exert electoral control over these rulers and to represent groups of citizens in order to ensure that policy-making is truly public and democratic.

How and to what extent these normative goals are achieved is an empirical matter and may vary significantly (Bingham Powell, 2000). This chapter seeks to describe and explain these differences and their consequences. A 'most similar' approach is used in order to limit the number of variables explaining the differences between democracies (Pennings et al., 1999). A comparable set of countries is arrived at by restricting the universe of discourse to European countries with a long-standing democratic tradition. As Europe is more than just a collection of countries, but also developing into an overarching polity with very diverse member states, electoral politics is discussed both at the country level and at the European level.

5.2 THE STATE OF THE ART: THEORIES OF ELECTORAL BEHAVIOUR

The central role of ideology in electoral politics does not imply, of course, that this is the only determinant of electoral behaviour. This is exemplified in the long-lasting debate on the determinants of party choice: how and why do voters chose for one particular party? The range of different theories accounting for party choice can be grouped into three categories: the *sociological, psychological* and *economic* approach (Barry, 1978; Dalton and Wattenberg, 1993; Van der Eijk and Franklin, 1996; Heywood, 1997). Ideology is the central concept in the economic approach which has become dominant since the 1970s.

5.2.1 The Sociological Approach

The sociological approach focuses on group-related variables, such as class and religion, as main determinants of voting behaviour. This approach stems from the period when parties still had a stable group base. Social group-base voting means that voters feel attached to parties that historically have supported the social group to which a voter belongs. The two main examples of social cleavage voting are *class voting* (the working class supports the Left, and the middle class the liberal and conservative parties) and *religious voting* (religious groups vote for parties that adhere to their religion).

One of the best-known sociological theories on voting behaviour is the *social cleavage theory* which originated from the work of Lipset and Rokkan (1967). Cleavages are lasting societal divisions between social or political groups which may give rise to open conflict if and when 'politicized'. The type of party system depends on these divisions. The main distinction is between party systems which are based on one cleavage and those with more cleavages (Kitschelt, 1997; Pennings, 1998). *Unidimensional systems* in which the class cleavage is most salient are found in the UK, Scandinavia and in several Mediterranean countries, like Spain and Portugal (Lane and Ersson, 1998). *Multidimensional systems* combine two varieties of cleavages (class and religion), e.g. in Austria, France, Germany, Italy, the Netherlands and Switzerland (and in Belgium, where a language cleavage exists). When one cleavage internally divides the group of another cleavage (the so-called *cross-cutting cleavages*) we obtain a two-dimensional party competition (Lijphart, 1999).

The basic assumption underlying the sociological approach is that party choice results from group membership. Lipset and Rokkan proposed that the party systems were 'frozen' since they originated in the 1920s (their so-called 'freezing hypothesis'). Especially the introduction of universal suffrage proved the crucial catalyst which froze the cleavage structures into place. The reason is that democratization went hand in hand with the rise of closed ideological shops, so that 'the party systems of the 1960s reflect, with few but significant exceptions, the cleavage structures of the 1920s' (Lipset and Rokkan, 1967: 50). This closure of the electoral market left little room for new cleavages to develop.

As long as party systems are stable, the sociological explanation is a strong one. But, since the mid-1960s, empirical research has shown quite univocally that the old social cleavages have weakened. As a consequence, the bond between parties and voters has also weakened in Western Europe (the so-called *party dealignment*), but only if old cleavages have not been replaced by new ones (*realignment*: see Dalton et al., 1984; Franklin et al., 1992; Pennings and Lane, 1998; Lane and Ersson, 1998). The old cleavages dissolved because of major shifts in the social structure, such as the embourgeoisement of the working class, the growth of the welfare state, increasing education, mobility and urbanization. These changes eroded the social class, and the religious and community bases of social structures. This does not mean that the traditional cleavages have completely disappeared. Class and religion are still important in Western Europe, be it that their impact is less obvious than before 1970 (Bartolini and Mair, 1990). These cleavages have to some extent been replaced by other ones (such as the environmental one) and the rising importance of 'issues' (salient issues, often of a temporary nature).

The weakening of cleavages has far-reaching consequences for the functioning of party systems and democracies as a whole. First of all, parties transform from representative bodies to office seekers (i.e. Cartel parties; Katz and Mair, 1992) competing for power for themselves and seeking electoral support in more or less homogeneous societies in which cleavages have more or less vanished. Second, new cleavages and new parties emerge as a response to new lines of division in society, such as the 'post-materialist' and 'lifestyle' issues (see also Chapter 6, by Mair). Partly this has already happened, but these new parties, such as the Green parties, do not seem to be able to take over the position of the established parties (although some of them are gaining ground, such as in Germany and Belgium). Many established parties managed to integrate new issues into their traditional vocabulary and were able to maintain their electoral shares in doing so, but there are notable exceptions (such as Christian Democratic parties in the Netherlands and Italy). In order to survive, established parties have to develop new lines of division to obtain power. Parties are involved in 'cleavage politics', which comes down to 'exploiting' cleavages by means of redefinitions of cleavages as a reaction to changes in the social structure. An example is immigration, which is used by Right extremist parties to gain electoral support by sharpening the division lines between natives and immigrants (e.g. the *Vlaams Blok* in Belgium and the FPÖ in Austria; Mudde, 2000).

Since the old cleavages are declining and sociological cues have become less important determinants of party choice, the psychological theories have gained influence. A classical example in this field is *The American Voter* (Campbell et al., 1960) which links party choice to *party identification*: voters are inclined to support their preferred party. Here it is not the group, but the individual who is guided by long-term psychological dispositions. The key term in the psychological group is 'partisanship' or party attachment: the psychological identification with a party. The rationale behind party identification is that it reduces the complexity of politics and increases the efficiency in determining one's choice (Budge et al., 1976). Presently, most electoral studies are critical about the applicability of party identification to European voters because it is hard to separate party attachment from vote intention. But, as far as equivalents for party identification have been found in European contexts, the findings for the USA and Europe are the same: there has been an erosion of the long-term partisan loyalties, which is called *partisan dealignment*. When party dealignment is not accompanied by party realignment, political competition becomes more and more personalized with a minor role of political parties. It may lead to political apathy, but also to a rise in non-partisan political activities by so-called *apartisans*: politically active citizens who remain unattached to political parties. The so-called 'Catch-all party' can to some extent be seen as a manifestation of this trend because this type of party seeks electoral support among all citizens without relying on strong bonds with particular groups by means of ideology or cleavage (Krouwel, 1999).

The new politics theories have proposed alternative explanations for party choice now that social cleavages and party attachments have weakened (Kriesi, 1997). The best-known new distinction was formulated by Ronald Inglehart, namely that between *materialism* (centring upon material well-being) and *postmaterialism* (centring upon quality of life and self-actualization), which may be abbreviated as MPM (Inglehart, 1977, 1997). The focus of MPM is on new value orientations and life styles of individuals which are hardly organized compared with for example 'new social movements' which often have at least some attachment to one or more particular political parties

(Kriesi et al., 1995). In most countries, the old cleavages (religion and class) are still more important than the MPM-dimension. Its significance is increasing, but this also depends on the economic situation, as MPM appears to move up and down with the economic tide (Lane and Ersson, 1999: 122–3). Table 5.1 shows the cross-national relationships between party choice and old and new values. The old values are represented by the religious–secular and Left–Right cleavages, the new values by materialism–postmaterialism. In all countries, except in Germany, the old cleavages correlate more strongly with party choice than does MPM. In most countries the salience of the old cleavages is stable. However, when interpreting these figures, one should realize that the meaning of the old values has changed over time (i.e. have tended to become less orthodox) which is one of the reasons why they are still quite significant.

This finding is confirmed by the *Beliefs in Government*-project (Kaase and Newton, 1995). This project tested hypotheses based on the premise that a large gap between citizens and the state is arising which distorts the 'democraticness' of established democracies (i.e. the degree to which voters can influence the decision-making process). But the data (mainly Eurobarometer and European Values Survey) suggest that the postulated fundamental change does not occur. The project did find, however, more modest changes which suggest that the role of parties within the democratic process is diminishing. First, there is a clear increase in *non*-institutionalized forms of participation which are characterized by the bypassing of elections and parties. This is supported by the second change, namely the decline in attachment to political parties. However, these changes are not caused by a profound dissatisfaction among citizens, but by a greater capacity for criticism and a greater willingness to do so (Fuchs and Klingemann, 1995). According to this research, there is no decline in generalized support for democracy among the citizens in Western Europe. Instead, this project signals the rise of new demands, issues and collective actors and changes to the party systems in order to adapt to these developments. This ongoing democratic transformation produces greater responsiveness towards the demands of citizens and larger citizen involvement in the political process. The remarkable conclusion, contrary to the initial assumptions, is that the democraticness of Western societies has not been in decline since the 1960s, but rather appears to be stronger, albeit in a different way. This conclusion is strongly based on how voters perceive the democratic process and how they seek to take part in it. The introduction of institutional variables into the analysis, as is discussed below, indicates however a less optimistic conclusion regarding democraticness.

The *economic approach* to voting behaviour has become well known since Anthony Downs' seminal book *An Economic Theory of Democracy* (1957). It is often referred to as the spatial theory of elections (Ferejohn, 1997). The main assumption here is that voters are rational, meaning that they make voting decisions in a calculating manner by choosing the party that will provide more benefits than any other. According to Downs, voters do not make decisions on the basis of long-term social or psychological dispositions but make their

Table 5.1 *Old and new cleavages and party choice in Western Europe, 1970–90*

Country	Cleavages	1970 1975	1975 1980	1976 1985	1986 1990	1990
Belgium	Religious-secular	0.54	0.51	0.54	0.44	0.44
	Left-Right materialism	–	0.23	0.25	0.36	0.36
	Materialism-postmaterialism	0.23	0.13	–	0.31	0.24
Denmark	Religious-secular	0.30	0.40	0.37	0.35	0.35
	Left-Right materialism	0.49	0.48	0.56	0.61	0.55
	Materialism-postmaterialism	0.34	0.51	–	0.47	0.46
France	Religious-secular	0.39	0.37	0.34	0.37	0.37
	Left-Right materialism	–	0.40	0.49	0.42	0.42
	Materialism-postmaterialism	0.38	0.38	–	0.31	0.28
Germany	Religious-secular	0.35	0.22	0.30	0.34	0.34
	Left-Right materialism	–	0.13	0.24	0.30	0.30
	Materialism-postmaterialism	0.24	0.22	–	0.45	0.41
Ireland	Religious-secular	0.21	0.23	0.21	0.25	0.25
	Left-Right materialism	–	0.15	–	0.21	0.21
	Materialism-postmaterialism	0.19	0.19	–	0.13	0.20
Italy	Religious-secular	0.47	0.48	0.34	0.46	0.46
	Left-Right materialism	–	0.45	0.28	0.30	0.30
	Materialism-postmaterialism	0.34	0.38	–	0.30	0.28
Netherlands	Religious-secular	0.65	0.57	0.58	0.51	0.51
	Left-Right materialism	0.55	0.52	0.52	0.56	0.45
	Materialism-postmaterialism	0.36	0.40	–	0.42	0.44
Norway	Religious-secular	0.47	0.32	0.35	0.41	0.41
	Left-Right materialism	–	0.66	0.63	0.51	0.44
	Materialism-postmaterialism	–	–	0.47	0.36	0.34
Sweden	Religious-secular	–	–	0.36	0.34	0.28
	Left-Right materialism	–	0.66	0.64	0.64	0.47
	Materialism-postmaterialism	–	–	–	0.27	0.28
UK	Religious-secular	0.14	0.14	0.09	0.16	0.16
	Left-Right materialism	0.53	0.49	0.53	0.54	0.46
	Materialism-postmaterialism	0.23	0.17	–	0.45	0.38

The entries are correlation coefficients (eta) between party choice and value orientations. The higher the score, the stronger is the impact of a cleavage on party choice. '–' means that a score is not available.

Source: Knutsen (1995b: 488–9).

judgement about parties by evaluating current policy positions of parties and candidates.

In case of both cleavages and social movements there is not always a clear link between choice and outcome. The choice is mainly based on group loyalties irrespective of the specific goals which are formulated by the parties. The *rational choice theories*, however, state that voters chose between alternative sets of policy proposals which are put forward by parties and candidates. The choice of the voters is based on a comparison between their own ideological position and that of the political parties. Most voters will chose the party which is closest to their own position on an ideological dimension, mostly the Left–Right scale. This theory is also known as *the smallest distance hypothesis or the proximity theory*. The preferences of voters are assumed to be a function of proximity: the smaller the ideological distance, the stronger the preference. Parties are expected to move towards the position of *the median voter* which cannot be defeated by any other in a majority vote. In doing so, the potential number of voters is maximized. When a party is successful with this strategy it may become *a pivot party* which occupies a position on the middle of the ideological spectrum (policy-seeking capacity), yet simultaneously has sufficient weight (office-seeking potential) to influence the behaviour of other parties (Keman, 1997a: 87).

If Downs' assumption on party behaviour is correct, we can expect *party system convergence*, meaning that established parties tend to move to moderate ideological positions. This tendency may enhance an electoral strategy of parties which is often called *catch-allism*: parties seek to accomplish a wide electoral appeal aimed at vote maximization (Kirchheimer, 1966a). The catch-all party is characterized by an indistinct ideological profile and a loose connection with the electorate (Krouwel, 1999). According to Krouwel, there is no general tendency towards catch-allism in Europe: ideology remains, amongst other factors, an important tool for most parties to profile themselves. But, as far as convergence does occur, it enhances electoral volatility since it becomes easier for voters to switch between parties given the reduced distances between the competitors.

One theory which challenges Down's assumptions about voting behaviour and party competition is *the issue-ownership theory* of Budge and Farlie (1983). This theory discusses voting behaviour in direct relation to party behaviour. Party competition is seen as the process in which parties distinguish themselves from each other by emphasizing particular issues which fit best into their ideological profile. Parties manage to make themselves visible and reliable to voters by owning certain issues. Contrary to Downs, the prediction of this theory is that parties will *not* converge. Parties will stick to their ideological profile and keep it as distinct as possible because this makes them recognizable and credible to voters.

Another, more complicated, challenge to the smallest-distance hypothesis comes from *the theory of directional voting*, pioneered by Rabinowitz and MacDonald (1989). The focus is on the intensity with which ideological positions (issues) are held. This theory can therefore be seen as a psychological model. Instead of ideological distance, the directional theory assumes that the directional fit between party and voter is decisive for the party choice. This theory is related to the broader category of theories on *issue voting* that assume that voters are not primarily oriented towards an enduring ideology but towards short-term issues. The increased attention for issue voting is understandable, given the decline in long-term forces shaping the vote.

The intensity of an issue for the voter is calculated by the directional model as the product of his/her own intensity and the party-intensity toward this issue (Rabinowitz and MacDonald, 1989). In the directional model extreme parties would have an electoral advantage over moderate parties because of the importance of the intensity. This problem is incorporated into the directional model by assigning negative weighting factors to parties that are extremist on one or more issues. As a result, it is assumed that the voter will be most attracted to the non-extremist party which is intense on issues which are important to the voter and also takes the same position as the voter (either for or against). Contrary to the proximity theory, the directional theory would predict that parties are not convergent but divergent. In the proximity theory, the winning party will be moderate under the assumption of a normal distribution of the voters on one dimension. In the directional model, the party will be more extreme (but not extremist) on one or more issues. Which intensity will be decisive will depend on the exact preferences of voters for issues which change from election to election. A party with an intense position on an issue which is also felt to be important by a majority of the voters may win now, but lose during the next elections when another intense issue catches the attention of voters. The directional model is clearly better equipped to analyse and explain electoral change than most other theories, as the latter often assume that positions of voters and parties are more of less fixed and do not change radically over time.

Another theory on ideological voting focuses on *performance voting*: voters pay more attention to results (government performance) than to promises (ideology). Government parties which perform badly will be punished by voters, even by voters who do support the views of these parties. A similar interpretation of party choice stems from the theory of *Political Business Cycles* (Tufte, 1978; Schneider and Frey, 1988). The basic assumption is that the electorate's voting decision depends on the state of the economy. The government may attempt to influence its re-election prospects by altering the state of the economy. This is done, for example, by a synchronization of expenditures in electorally appealing areas (like social spending) with the timing of general elections. However, most studies of the Political Business Cycle show that it is not a structural and dominant feature of modern democratic politics (Whiteley, 1980; Pennings et al., 1999). As far as it does exist, it is most likely to appear in Anglo-Saxon countries because majoritarian systems enable the voter to judge the achievements of a single party on government, which is not more difficult or even impossible in case of multi-party coalition governments (Whiteley, 1980; Tufte, 1978).

As the democraticness of political systems is the degree to which voters can influence the decision-making process and its outcomes, it depends highly on the *choices* or setoff policy-options which are offered to voters. Most theories on voter and party behaviour suggest that the possibilities of voters to make choices which matter are severely limited. During the period of frozen cleavages the choices were fixed by the cleavage structure. During the period of dealignment, choices are (to varying degrees) limited by the convergence between parties. And in multiparty systems it is almost impossible for voters to make choices which directly affect the composition of government and public policy-making (Budge and Keman, 1990). In systems with a pivot party, important choices regarding government composition and policy-making are made by this party (Keman, 1994). This party seeks to maintain the status quo, which leaves little room for alternative choices.

In sum: the institutional arrangements of democratic systems may in various ways narrow down the choices offered to voters and therefore limit the 'democraticness' of these systems. Hence, not only 'institutions matter' as such, but influence the electoral patterns of voting behaviour across European democracies. Below, this hypothesis will be examined cross-nationally.

5.3 INSTITUTIONS AND THE ELECTORAL DIVERSITY OF EUROPEAN ESTABLISHED DEMOCRACIES

The established European countries are in many respects 'most similar': they share more characteristics regarding the political-institutional organization of their democracies than not. They are alike in terms of rule of law, democratic rights, regular elections, etc. Yet, in some respects there are significant differences that affect the functioning and performance of the established democracies. The electoral and party systems, both crucial for the functioning of democracies, do differ across countries and time periods (Lijphart, 1994).

Electoral systems are sets of rules which define how votes are cast and seats are allocated. The electoral system is part of the electoral law which encompasses a broader family of rules governing the process of elections. The variety of electoral systems stems from at least four differences which can be summarized as follows (Blais and Massicotte, 1996: 50; Farrell, 1997; Gallagher, 1997; Jesse, 1994; Lane and Ersson, 1998: 201; Lijphart, 1999):

1. The *electoral formula* or counting rules (i.e. how are votes to be counted to allocate seats) can be subdivided into *majority* (a candidate requires an overall majority; i.e. First-Past-the Post = FPTP), *plurality* (a candidate requires an absolute majority of votes to be elected) and *proportionality or list systems*. The latter category is divided into largest remainder and highest average systems. The *largest remainder* system translates the votes into seats in two stages: (a) those parties with votes exceeding the quota are rewarded seats and the quota is subtracted from their total vote; (b) those parties left with the greatest number of votes (= the largest remainder) are rewarded the remaining seats in order of vote size. The *highest average system* is more common and operates by two alternative divisors: *d'Hondt* (most common) and *modified Sainte-Laguë* (MSL).[1] This system tends to produce more proportional results than the d'Hondt divisor. However, in proportional systems, the degree of electoral disproportionality is low, irrespective of the divisor which is used.

2. *The constituency structure*, its nature (whole constituency or districts) and district magnitude (i.e. the number of seats per district).[2] Countries with many constituencies may increase proportionality by means of *two-tier districting*: a certain number of seats are allocated in a second-tier such as across the nation as a whole. All remaining seats from the first-tier are pooled and their distribution is determined by the second-tier. In case of an imbalance between the population densities of constituencies some

parties may be favoured over others (the so-called *malapportionment*). The practice of redrawing constituency boundaries with the intention to favour the governing party, is called *gerrymandering*. This form of political manipulation was most likely to occur in non-proportional systems like the UK, but nowadays constitutional safeguards make manipulation more difficult.

3. Variations in the *ballot structure* (how voters express their choice) concern the number of votes and the type of vote. The basic distinction is between a categoric ballot structure where the voter can declare a preference for just one candidate or party (e.g. FPTP) and an ordinal ballot structure where the voter can rank-order candidates in order of preference (e.g. the preferential systems). The most open form of ballot structure in list systems is *Panachage* which operates in Luxembourg and Switzerland: the ballot paper allows voters to give preferences to candidates from more than one party.

4. The outcome: the degree of *disproportionality* (i.e. the disparity between the votes received and seats allocated). Both the district magnitude and the electoral formula have an important bearing on overall proportionality. The more districts in a country the less proportional the outcomes of the electoral system are. Electoral disproportionality will also be higher in countries with single member districts (such as in the United Kingdom). An *electoral threshold*, which a party must pass in order to be granted any seats in the parliament, is used to minimize the risk of too many (even extremist) parties which is one of the drawbacks of proportional systems (it is used in Germany and Sweden, for instance). The electoral threshold is a built-in distortion of the translation of votes into seats.

The different combinations of these four features discussed here lead to different electoral systems. An overview of these systems is presented in Table 5.2. The five main European systems are discussed below (see also: Farrell, 1997; Heywood, 1997).

The First Past the Post System (FPTP-system) is a 'simple plurality system' in which the country is divided into single-member constituencies and where voters select a single candidate who needs to achieve a *plurality* of votes (which is not the same as a majority!). The main European example is the UK. This system offers voters a clear link between representatives and constituencies and a clear choice of potential parties in government. It also makes for a strong, stable and effective government in that one single party has majority control of the assembly. The major disadvantage of this system is the *'wasted votes'*, namely the votes cast for losing candidates and those cast for winning ones over the plurality mark. The awareness of the possibility that their votes are wasted will push many voters into *tactical voting*: they do not vote for the party that is closest to them, because their vote might be wasted. The high disproportionality of FPTP-systems implies that small parties are under-represented. Winning candidates who have less than

Table 5.2 *Electoral systems in Western Europe*

Country	Ballot	Tiers	Formulas (electoral system)	1980s	1990s	1980s	1990s
			Electoral formula 1990s	District disproportionality magnitude			
Austria	One	2	PR: Hare + d'Hondt (party list)	20.3	20.3	2.2	2.8
Belgium	One	2	PR: Hare + d'Hondt (party list)	7.0	7.5	6.0	8.0
Denmark	One	2	PR: MSL + Hare (party list)	7.3	10.5	3.3	4.5
Finland	One	1	PR: d'Hondt (party list)	13.2	13.3	5.1	7.0
France	One	1	MAJ + PLUR (majoritarian)	1.0	1.0	18.7	40.3
Germany	Two	2	PLUR + PR: Hare (two-vote)	1.0	1.9	1.4	5.8
Ireland	One	1	PR: STV (single transferable vote)	3.8	4.0	5.2	6.4
Italy	Two	2	PLUR + PR (Semi-PR): Hamilton (party list)	19.5	1.3	4.7	13.6
The Netherlands	One	1	PR: d'Hondt (party list)	150.0	150.0	3.0	2.9
Norway	One	2	PR: MSL + MSL (party list)	8.3	8.7	5.1	6.3
Sweden	One	2	PR: MSL + MSL (party list)	11.1	11.6	2.6	3.3
Switzerland	One	1	PR: d'Hondt (party list)	8.2	7.7	5.1	7.5
United Kingdom	One	1	PLUR (First past the post)	1.0	1.0	12.9	17.6

Source: Lane and Ersson (1998: 200). Ballot refers to the number of ballots used by an elector at the election. Tiers refers to whether there is a higher-level reallocation of votes. The electoral systems refer to PR (proportional representation), MAJ (majoritarian), PLUR (plurality of vote).

50% of the votes, can still represent the whole of the district at the national level (by means of the so-called 'manufactured majority'). This feature causes FPTP-systems to score low on 'democraticness' because of the absence of the *'One Member, One Vote' principle*: some votes count more than others. In addition, the choices which are offered to the voters are mainly between the two main parties. Alternative choices are formally possible, but can hardly be a threat to the status quo (see: Budge, 1996b).

In *majoritarian electoral systems* candidates can only win with majority support (i.e. more than 50 per cent of the votes). The main European variant is the second ballot system, which is used in France. There are single-candidate constituencies and also single-choice voting. To win the first ballot, a candidate needs an overall majority of the votes cast. If no candidate gains a first-ballot majority, a second ballot is held between the two leading candidates. The main advantage is that the system broadens electoral choice (because there are two ballots), but the disadvantage is that it is little more proportional than FPTP-systems.

The *party list systems* are proportional systems which are found in countries throughout Europe. The entire country is treated as a single constituency (only in The Netherlands) or there are a number of large multi-member constituencies. Parties compile lists of candidates in descending order of preference (mostly based more on the preferences of the party elites than of the party members, see: Pennings and Hazan, 2001). Parties are allocated seats in direct proportion to the votes they gain in the election. The obvious advantage compared with FPTP-systems is the high degree of proportionality and fairness, which is also reflected in low *electoral thresholds* for smaller and new parties. The main disadvantage is that the link between representatives and constituencies is broken, which might hamper the democraticness of PR-systems compared with FPTP-systems because it is more difficult for voters to reach and influence their representatives.

The *two-vote system* or *additional member system* (AMS) is a proportional system which is used in Germany. A proportion of seats (50%) is filled by the FPTP system using single-member constituencies. The remaining seats are filled using a party list. Voters cast two votes: one for a candidate in the constituency election and one for a party. The advantage is that the system balances the need for constituency representation (i.e. regional) against the need for electoral fairness. On the other hand, the single-member constituencies are not conducive to high levels of proportionality, because of the resulting 'wasted votes'. The size of the constituencies is also higher than in FPTP-systems, which also decreases proportionality.[3] Nonetheless, the democraticness is enhanced by a two-vote system, because it enlarges the number of choices which can be made, both at the constituency level and at the national level.

The *Single Tranferable Vote System* (STVS) is used in Ireland. There are multimember constituencies, each of which returns up to five members. There is *preferential voting*, meaning that voters rank the candidates in order of preference. Candidates are elected if they achieve a quota, which is the minimum number of votes needed to elect the stipulated number of candidates. The votes are counted according to the first preferences. If not all seats are filled, the bottom candidate is eliminated and his or her votes are redistributed according to second preferences, and so on. One of the advantages of this system is that it allows for competition amongst candidates from the same party. One disadvantage is that an STV election count can take a long time, so that it is only suited to small countries. Obviously, STV enhances the democraticness compared with FPTP-systems. In fact, STV is the Anglo-Saxon way to secure proportional representation (Gallagher et al., 2000).

This overview of electoral systems clarifies that electoral behaviour involves far more than just casting a vote. The type and number of choices which are offered to voters differ per system, and in that sense some systems are more 'democratic' than others. Once votes have been cast, a wide range of electoral institutions determines what happens with these votes. The comparison of electoral systems indicates that all of them have both advantages and disadvantages: there appears to be no ideal system. In most systems electoral reforms have been proposed in order to compensate for these disadvantages. But, until recently, most electoral systems did not change radically, regardless of their faults, because changes in these systems would directly affect the status quo. But, in 1993/94, three established democracies – Italy, Japan and New Zealand – radically changed their voting systems. These changes were possible because of factors like electoral dealignments, political crises and the use of referendums. We may conclude therefore that democratic electoral systems survive as long as they do not suffer from a serious lack of democratic legitimacy.

The discussed features of electoral systems have consequences for the *policy outcomes* of political systems. In particular, they determine the impact of vote change for the complexion of party government. For example, a small change in the votes for the two-main parties in two-party systems may determine which party will govern and hence will affect the colour of party government and the subsequent policy decisions regarding the type and degree of state intervention. In multiparty systems these effects are mitigated by coalition governments which might incorporate both winners and losers of elections. The occurrence of abrupt policy shifts and effective policy-making are thus more likely in two-party systems. Hence, electoral systems are not merely worth studying for those interested in elections. These systems are central institutional devices which affect the functioning of polities as a whole, including the outcomes of these systems.

5.4 THE ROLE OF IDEOLOGY IN ELECTIONS

Ideology is a set of ideas which provides a guideline for political action. It is essential for the understanding of voting behaviour, as it is the main tool which voters use in order to detect the differences between parties and to determine their preference for parties. Ideology in electoral politics often refers to the *Left–Right dimension* which presents a juxtaposition of state intervention on the one hand (the Left) and state abstention or restrictiveness on the other (the Right). Left–Right ideological orientations serve as a basic reference point for voters' choices. It is also the main vehicle for parties to differentiate themselves from each other. This explains the enduring importance of the Left–Right distinction as a determinant of party choice. As a consequence, the theory of Anthony Downs, stating that parties will in the long run converge in order to increase their vote share, is questionable because it implies an 'end of ideology' or a least a severe weakening of the ideological identities of parties. Although party ideology remains an important vehicle for party competition, there are numerous examples of *convergence* between parties. But convergence has not been so persistent that it has become a dominant feature of all party systems. Furthermore, the degree of convergence varies over time. Clearly, convergence decreases the democraticness of a system because it reduces the scope of choice and its consequences for policy-making. Convergence makes politics matter less for citizens.

When parties are close to each other on the Left–Right scale this will increase the number of *floating voters* (i.e. voters who do not decide the candidates and parties they might vote for till the last moment) and also the *electoral volatility* (i.e. the degree to which votes switch among parties between subsequent elections) because small distances between parties make it easier for voters to switch between them (see also Chapter 6). This statement sounds simple and plausible, but the problem which has been discussed for many years now is how ideology can be measured in a way that is comparable across time and across countries (Budge et al., 1987; Budge and Keman, 1990; Kim and Fording, 1998). This topic is discussed here in more detail in order to demonstrate that one should not consider ideological positions as absolute and given entities but as strategic positions which are taken by political competitors. These positions of parties and voters are not given but estimated by political scientists. There are several ways to estimate these positions, and it clearly matters which method is chosen. For this reason there is an ongoing academic debate on how to measure the ideological positions which are taken by parties and voters. In general, we can distinguish three types of Left–Right scales (Laver, 2001):

- scales based on the coding of *party manifestos* (Klingemann et al., 1994);
- scales based on the placements of parties by *experts* (Castles and Mair, 1984);
- scales based on the *self-placement* of voters (Inglehart and Klingemann, 1976; Van Deth and Scarbrough, 1995).

The manifesto scales and the expert scales are primarily party scales: they are used to compare party positions in several policy dimensions in order to be able to determine the policy distances between parties. This information is important to determine the competitive space of party systems. Next to party scales, there are voter scales which measure the ideological position of voters. The best-known scale is the Left–Right self-placement scale on which voters position themselves. One limitation of this type of scale is that it is limited by the number of countries and the period of time in which it can be studied. A second problem is that it cannot be used in comparative research because the location of the middle (which is the central reference point for any Left–Right placement) is not the same in European countries. Hence, aggregate country measures based on Left–Right placement are mostly not very adequate for comparative research (Budge, 2000).

Another measure of ideological positions is *the median voter position* which indicates the central tendency among voters. One measure of this position, introduced by Kim and Fording, combines party manifesto data and election return data (Kim and Fording, 1998). It can be used to compare voter ideology across different countries and time periods and to establish the distance between party positions and voter positions (Pennings et al., 1999). Figure 5.1 shows the ideology scores averaged across 13 European democracies over the period 1968–88 (see for the calculation of these scores: Note 3 in Chapter 4 in this book). The 1970s turn out to be the period in which voters were on average most inclined towards the Left. The 1980s, on the other hand, are characterized by a swing to the Right. However, countries differ significantly on the degree to which these changes have taken place. By combining these data with data on the ideological positions of parties, it is possible to determine the degree of *party responsiveness*, i.e. the extent to which party policy positions correspond with median voter positions (Keman, 1997b; Pennings, 1998).

The theory of issue saliency argues that parties will not jump from the one side of the Left–Right scale to the other (so-called *leapfrogging*) in order to

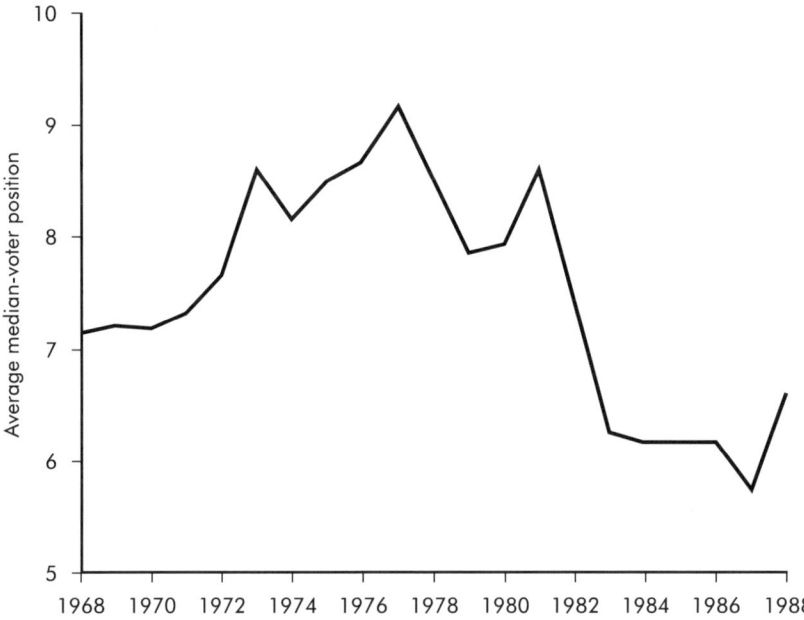

Figure 5.1 *Voter ideology in Western Europe*

attract votes, because parties would lose their credibility were they to move
suddenly to opposite positions. This makes the ideological party positions
more or less fixed. This has been demonstrated, for example, by Budge et al.
(1987) who analysed the movement of party positions over time using factor
analysis on coded party manifestos. Figure 5.2 presents the UK party positions between 1945 and 1992 in a *two-dimensional space of party competition*
which is based on factor analysis on a selection of issues. This example confirms the expectation that parties are ideologically fixed. There is hardly any
leapfrogging between the conservatives and the social democrats (Labour
Party) in the UK. At the same time, both parties are adapting their positions
within certain boundaries in order to be able to react to external and internal
pressures (i.e. public debates and party debates) which push the party in a
certain direction (either moving to the Right or the Left). However, these
movements are clearly limited. Any movement to the Right is sooner or later
reversed, and vice versa. This pattern makes parties look dynamic and adaptive in the short run without losing their credibility and also fixed and stable
in the long run. The effects on the 'democraticness' are positive. Ideological
rigidity makes parties reliable for voters. They can be sure that parties will
not change their policy positions overnight, which is a prerequisite for
voters to determine whether promises are actually fulfilled.

The research of party movements in liberal democracies has shown that
party positions are, within certain boundaries, more or less stable. Radical
changes in the ideology of parties are possible and do occur, but they are

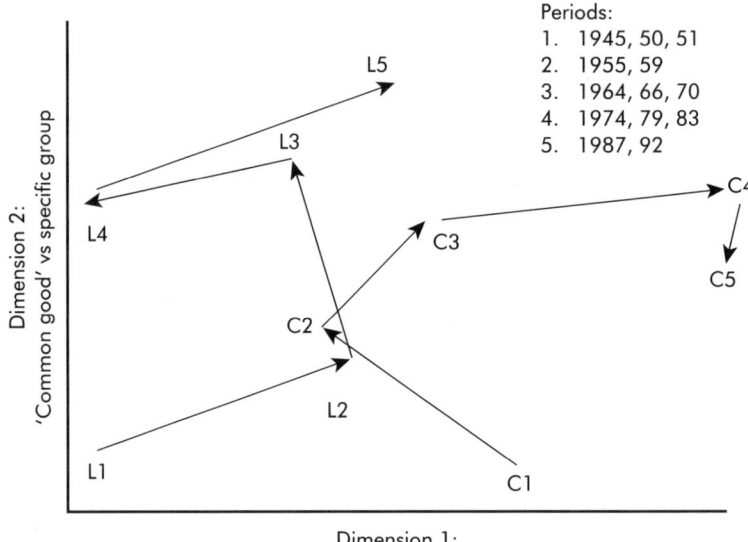

Figure 5.2 *UK party positions 1945–92. Source: own computations based on Budge et al. (1987: 71)*

exceptional (see, for example, the Austrian FPÖ, as reported in: Budge et al., 1987: 289). Individual voters, on the other hand, are not restricted in any sense. They can move into any direction they want to, albeit that these movements are also restricted because otherwise ideology would loose its meaning as a tool that enables voters to differentiate between parties and to make a choice. But sometimes movements of voters are so massive and intense that they lead to *earthquake elections*, such as in Italy in 1992 and the Netherlands in 1994 when the Christian Democrats lost the main part of their vote share.

The fixed ideological positions of parties enable them to bind certain groups in the electorate, which gives parties a stable electoral support. Trends in the electoral support for large and small party families in Europe are summarized in Figures 5.3 and 5.4. Among the large party families we see a moderate loss of the Christian democrats and the social democrats since the 1970s, whereas the liberals and the conservatives manage to uphold their vote shares or even increase them slightly.

The first two groups have in common that they propagate a collectivist ideology, based on group values (Christianity or solidarity). The electoral losses of the established collectivist parties do not necessarily benefit parties with a non-collectivist ideology, such as liberal parties. Within the group of small party families there are both winners and losers. The communist and agrarian parties are losing votes (these are also collectivist), whereas the others are winning votes. These are interesting trends which indicate that the

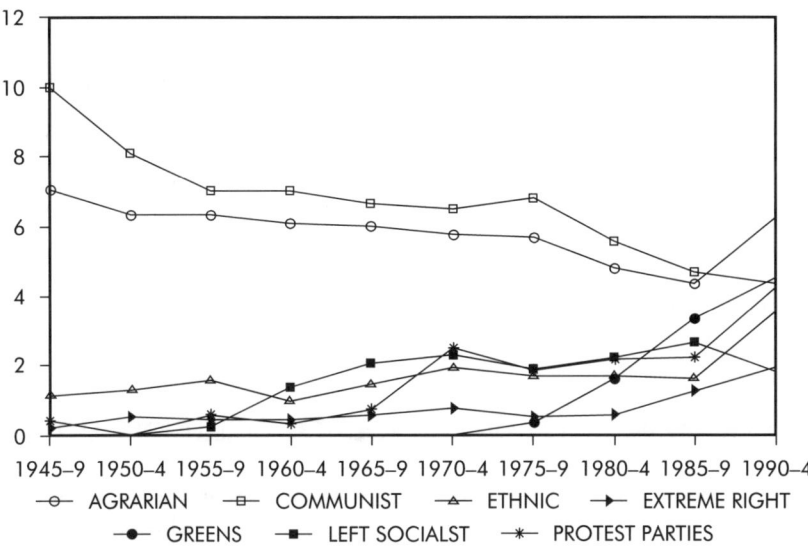

Figure 5.3 *Mean vote shares of small-party families*

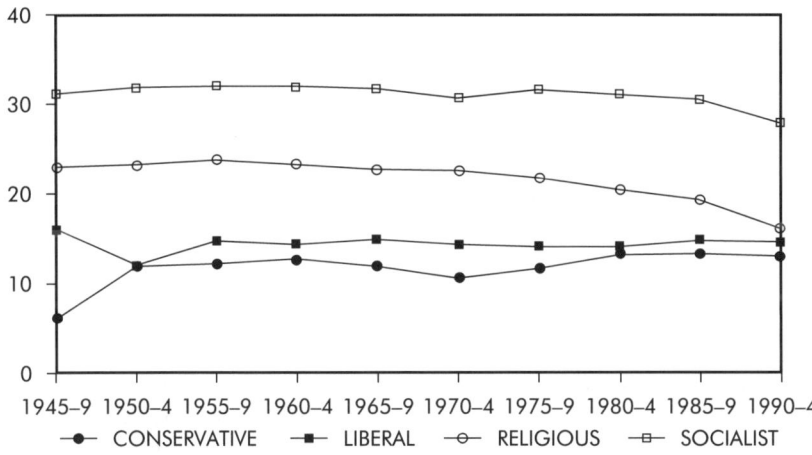

Figure 5.4 *Mean vote shares of large-party families*

political arena is becoming more scattered into smaller party groups, such as green parties and regionalist parties. Whereas the vote share of the established European parties in 1960 was around 92 per cent, this decreased to 78 per cent in the early 1990s (Kitschelt, 1997: 147). It has become more difficult for all parties to maintain a core group of supporters. The heartland of parties is becoming smaller and the political battlefield is becoming larger.

The changing vote shares of party families seem, at an aggregate level, moderate. But as the figures are presenting mean scores, they are hiding actual changes at the country level. The general tendency, however, is that in most countries the established parties (and their dominant ideologies) have been confronted with varying degrees of electoral losses since the 1970s. The reasons for this are similar to the causes of the rise of electoral volatility: the bond between voters and parties becomes weaker and it appears easier for voters to switch between parties. One reason is apparently the decline in *sociologically* driven voting. Another reason might well be the increase in *economically* driven voting behaviour. A different explanation may well be a perceived decline in *democraticness*.

5.5 ELECTORAL PARTICIPATION AND POLITICAL DISILLUSIONMENT

A representative democracy is not a direct democracy in the sense of popular self-government in which there is a direct and continuous impact of citizens on public decision-making. Given the institutional devices of liberal democracies, a gap between citizens and decision-makers is unavoidable (Dahl, 1989). On the other hand, this gap should not become too wide, because this could lead to distrust and disillusionment and might well in the long run undermine the legitimacy of any democracy.

One sign of mistrust and disillusionment is a decrease in voter turnout. For many decennia this phenomenon was hidden in several established democracies because *compulsory voting* made citizens vote, whether they liked it or not. Since the abolishment of compulsory voting in several European democracies (it still applies to Austria, Belgium, Greece, Liechtenstein, Luxembourg and to Switzerland in some cantons), there has been a moderate tendency towards lowering of turnout. But there are more reasons for this. Turnout is only weakly related to perceptions of voters and their trust in politicians. As Table 5.3 shows, the individual determinants are much weaker than the institutional determinants of turnout.

Voting participation is mainly determined by institutional setting (Budge and Farlie, 1976, Bingham Powell, 1982; Franklin, 1996; Hague et al., 1998). The most obvious institutional factor is compulsory voting, which boosts turnout significantly. In other systems, a low voting age will often coincide with a low turnout because of a weak propensity of younger voters to vote. The higher the salience of elections is, the higher the turnout. In PR electoral systems the turnout is only slightly higher than in non-PR systems. This is because PR is fairer, it presents the electorate with more parties to vote for, and PR is more competitive because many parties have a chance to win at least one seat and will therefore attempt to mobilize voters (Blais and Dobrzynska, 1998). However, in two-party systems the turnout is slightly higher than in multi-party systems, because in the former case voters are more directly able to chose the party that will form the government. A vote is more easily cast when it matters. Hence, PR has both negative and

Table 5.3 *Factors which increase turnout*

Features of the electoral system	Features of individuals
(Explained variance = 0.87)	(Explained variance = 0.06)
Compulsory voting	Middle age
Proportional representation	Strong party loyalty
Postal voting permitted	High education
Weekend polling	Goes to church
Electoral salience (elections decide who governs)	Belongs to a union
	Higher income

The explained variance refers to a regression analysis performed by Franklin (1996) and is based on data for the OECD (N = 22).

Source: Hague et al. (1998: 101).

Table 5.4 *Trends in electoral participation, 1986–99*

	National elections			European elections
	1986–88	1992–94	1998–99	1999
Austria	90.5	82.5	–	49 (–18)
Belgium	93.4	–	90.8	93 (+3)
Denmark	84.0	84.3	86	50 (2)
Finland	72.1	–	65.3	30 (–28)
France	66.2	69.3	–	45 (–7)
Germany	84.3	79	82.2	45 (–15)
Ireland	–	68.5	–	50 (+6)
Italy	88.9	87.4	–	70 (–5)
The Netherlands	85.8	78.3	73	30 (–5.7)
Norway	84	75.8	–	–
Sweden	86	88.1	81.4	38 (–3)
Switzerland	47.5	–	–	–
UK	75.4	77.8	71.4	23 (–13)

Note: Percentages are total votes cast as a percentage of eligible votes. In parentheses is the change between 1994 and 1999 for the European elections.

positive effects, with the overall impact being a slightly positive one (Blais and Dobrzynska, 1998). Finally, the turnout will increase when the polling allows for postal or weekend voting (see also: van der Eijk et al., 1996).

Many commentators assume that there is a decline in electoral participation, indicating that voters are becoming less willing to cast their votes during elections which is often seen as an indication of declining legitimacy. Table 5.4 shows that there is no *general* decline in turnout. This is not to deny that in some countries there is a consistent decline in turnout rates. Some political scientists and commentators interpret these changes as rather small and insignificant (Andeweg, 1996), while others see in it a clear sign of an increasing political apathy (Lane and Ersson, 1998: 142). On the level of European elections, however, political scientists agree that there is a trend toward lower turnout. The next section will explain why this development occurs.

5.6 EUROPEAN PARLIAMENTARY ELECTIONS

European democracies are not only a group of independent countries, which have in common that they belong to the same continent. Since the 1950s the economic integration has also stimulated integration and co-operation within Europe. Since the early 1980s there have been attempts to achieve forms of *political* integration. The installation and elections for the European Parliament was the first major step in this direction.

The first Europe-wide elections were held in June 1979. From the very beginning, European elections have been perceived as *second-order* elections because no actual executive power is at stake (Oppenhuis, 1995; Hix, 1999). The complexion of the Council of Ministers and the European Commission is not affected by these elections (Marsh and Franklin, 1996). There are several consequences of this. First, the electoral behaviour in European elections is partly driven by the *first-order* arena and therefore by national concerns. Voters may, for example, use the European elections to disapprove of national government performance to date. Second, many citizens may be less inclined to turn out and vote. Finally, voters may prefer smaller parties in European elections because there is no real danger of wasted votes for gaining power in European elections. This is called *quasi-switching*: voting for a different party in the European election than would have been supported in a national election held at the same time (Marsh and Franklin, 1996: 13; Oppenhuis et al., 1996: 289).

At the European level the role of elections is clearly not as decisive as at the national level. This is often referred to as the *democratic deficit*, but there are also differences in how this problem is defined. Members of the European Parliament define the democratic deficit in terms of a lack of power on the part of the European Parliament to assert itself in relation to the Commission and the Council of Ministers. Others, for example Van der Eijk and Franklin (1996), claim that the problem is not that the European Parliament lacks power, but that it lacks a *mandate* to use the power. The main reason is that national states are reluctant to engage in power sharing at the European level. European politics is played as a *zero-sum game* between member-states who are determined to protect their national interests. As a consequence, European elections are heavily fought on the basis of national instead of European political concerns, which undermines the European democratic process.

Does the democratic deficit mean that there is a crisis of political legitimacy in the European Union? There are arguments for and against this statement. One argument for this statement stems from Van der Eijk and Franklin (1996). In their view, European elections are second-order elections, not because they are necessarily less important than national elections, but because they do not meet the standard conditions of democratic elections. Elections are considered to legitimize power, to exert electoral control and to represent groups of citizens. These conditions imply that voters have some awareness of the political stance and record of candidates and parties by means of an adequate media coverage. These conditions are lacking in the

European Union. The main reason is that national affairs and issues dominate both the national and European elections. There is no proper electoral connection between the citizens of the European Union and its leaders, or there is no organized democratic choice in Europe (see also Chapter 4 in this book). In this view, the lack of European content to European elections and the lack of electoral representation is endemic and can only be changed by means of a totally new European structure.

In contrast to this view is the statement that the current crisis of representation is not the result of defects in the structure of the European Union, but of a lack of legitimacy. It appears that representatives in the European Union are in favour of more European integration, whereas many voters are more reluctant is this respect. This indicates that there is a fundamental disagreement between voters and European politicians on issues such as the European Monetary Union (Thomassen and Schmitt, 1997; Schmitt and Thomassen, 1999).

Finally, there is the view that the democratic deficit is not a problem of legitimacy, but arises from a crisis of political parties (Andeweg, 1996). There is a general demise of political parties because they lost a part of their credibility as the sole and main representatives of the people. This crisis is strongest at the European level because weakly organized parties with low ideological profiles are confronted by well-organized competitors. A range of alternative groups (pressure groups, social movements) has taken over a part of the representative role of parties. As a consequence, voters and pressure groups no longer see political parties and elections as the main vehicles of democratic influence, as there are alternative routes to achieve goals.

The present lack of 'democraticness' in the EU should not be interpreted as a fundamental and irreparable flaw of European politics. This chapter has shown that 'democraticness' is also problematic at national levels, due to institutional and ideological rigidities which narrow down the choices of both parties and voters (see also: Pennings, 1998). On the EU-level there is an additional cause which is unique to that level, namely the reluctance of member states to give up power. Despite this difference, the conclusion for both the national and European levels is the same: in representative democracies policies are formulated by *actors with bargaining power* and not directly by voters. This is the reality of representative democracy in general.

Whatever the differences between European and national elections may be, one common element prevails: the central role of *ideology*. Van der Eijk et al. (1996) claim that, despite significant differences between the various political systems in Europe, in all systems voters arrive at their party choice in a similar manner. In that respect, the mechanisms that drive party choice are not influenced by national contexts. In this sense the European electorate can be considered as driven by the same motivations. The relative effects of cleavages, issues, ideology, and approval of government on party choice are similar in European democracies. Of all factors which are discerned by Van der Eijk et al., the ideological factor (i.e. the Left–Right distinction) is the most important explanation of party choice.

It would be wrong, however, to conclude from this that the only thing that matters is ideology. Explaining party choice is not the same as explaining variations in democraticness. For that we need to take into account institutional variables. The previous discussion of electoral systems has shown that institutional rigidities narrow down the number of choices and, more importantly, the outcomes of these choices. Both ideology and institutions enable *and* restrict democraticness at the same time. They enable it by structuring the element of choice within the democratic process. Ideology enables parties to present choices which are recognized by voters. Institutions ensure that these choices are translated into policies. They restrict it by means of barriers and thresholds to newcomers and alternative ideas. Perhaps this paradox is one of the most fundamental problems of representative democracy: the elements that make it work also impair its working and thus demonstrate the limitations of making democracy work under variable circumstances.

5.7 CONCLUSIONS

The role of ideology (and especially the Left–Right distinction) is crucial for the functioning of European democracies. It gives both voters and parties a tool to distinguish between policy positions in an efficient way. This does not mean, however, that the Left–Right dimension is the only basis of electoral politics nor that its role is static. 'Left' and 'Right' are not theoretical dogmas for voters, but a tool for interpreting party positions. The meaning of Left and Right changes over time. Whereas ideology was once fixed to dogmatic principles on how to perceive the world (for example communist or Christian values), now ideology – defined as party manifestos – has become more flexible and is constantly being adapted to the needs of both voters and parties for reasons of competition in terms of office and policy-seeking behaviour.

Whereas ideology affects party choice, institutions determine how votes are transformed in seats (and hence into political power). Ideology and institutions are both important. How parties compete and how voters do affect the election outcomes is highly determined by political institutions. Institutions structure the behaviour of parties and voters alike in their room to manoeuvre and limit the number of choices that can be made, but at the same time offer stability over time. On the one hand institutions facilitate the transformation of individual preferences (i.e. votes) in collective choice by means of laws and rules in various ways. On the other hand, the stabilizing effect of institutions does not guarantee electoral choice at all times and places. The opening up of cultural and social horizons makes voters more inclined to change their vote from election to election. This is a relatively new form of electoral behaviour which can alter the functioning of party systems, party competition and the role of pivotal parties. Electoral institutions themselves, however, are not easily affected by electoral volatility or even instability. Instead, they remain a stable force in modern established democracies even in times of electoral turmoil. Hence institutions matter regarding the way the people's will is expressed, and parties, representing the population, are capable of contributing to the democraticness of a political system.

NOTES

1   In this system, each party's votes are divided by a series of divisors to produce an average vote. The party with the 'highest average' vote after each stage of the process wins a seat, and its vote is then divided by the next divisor. This process continues after all seats have been filled.
2   Only The Netherlands consist of only *one* nation-wide constituency containing all seats that are distributed (N = 150).
3   The two-vote system has also recently been introduced in New Zealand and Italy. The former country had a FPTP-electoral system, whereas the latter had a PR-electoral system.

6

IN THE AGGREGATE: MASS ELECTORAL BEHAVIOUR IN WESTERN EUROPE, 1950–2000

Peter Mair

6.1 INTRODUCTION

During the 1990s, in each of four west European polities, governments were formed which were without precedent in post-war democratic history. The first of these occurred in Ireland in 1993, when the long-dominant Fianna Fáil party forged a coalition with the Labour Party, whose experience in office up to then had been confined to partnerships with Fianna Fáil's traditional opponent, Fine Gael. One year later in The Netherlands the three major secular parties, the Liberals, Labour and Democrats 66, formed the so-called 'purple coalition', the first government to be established in Dutch democratic history which did not also include the Catholic or Christian Democratic mainstream. The third case occurred in Italy in 1996, when the new coalition which then won office was the first of more than 50 post-war governments to include the principal party of the left – the former communist Democratic Party of the Left. Finally, in 1998 in Germany, a 'red–green' alliance won office for the first time, a change of government which not only marked the first entry into the German cabinet of the small Green party, but which also represented the first time in post-war Germany that an incumbent government was replaced in its entirety by opposition parties.

These four examples are important, not only because they represent changes in party composition of government, which is a reasonably common and a regular occurrence in most parliamentary democracies, but rather because they each reflected a major change in what had been up to then the prevailing patterns of government formation and alternation. In Ireland, through at least five decades of party competition, voters had become accustomed to confronting two principal governing choices: on the one hand, there was the single-party alternative of Fianna Fáil, which had always publicly refused to enter a coalition with any of the other parties in the system; on the other hand, there was the coalition alternative that was usually formed by Fine Gael and Labour on their own, but that occasionally also involved other minor parties. In fact, the first break with this pattern had occurred in 1989, when Fianna Fáil had finally abandoned its stand-alone strategy, and had formed a coalition with the Progressive Democrats, a new party which had been mobilized principally by dissenting Fianna Fáil elites in the late 1980s.

But it was the second break, occurring in 1993, that was more important, for then the party entered a coalition with one of its traditional opponents, Labour, and thus opened up a wholly new set of strategic alternatives not just for itself, but also for Labour, whose options in the past had always been restricted to building an alliance with Fine Gael. The changes in The Netherlands in 1994 were no less important. Although the government formation process in The Netherlands has often proved both lengthy and relatively open, no single government since 1917 had been formed without the presence of either the Catholic People's Party or its pan-Christian successor, the Christian Democratic Appeal. The secular coalition which took office following the record electoral losses of the CDA in 1994 was therefore wholly novel in character, as was CDA's dismissal to the opposition benches.

In Italy, the change was even more striking and was certainly also signalled as such. Despite participating in the 'emergency' reconstruction governments of 1946 and 1947, the Italian Communist Party had been systematically excluded from office thereafter, with the subsequent governments being consistently dominated by the centrist Christian Democrats. The eventual collapse of the DC in the wake of the *mani pulite* scandals, as well as the dramatic rise of the new centre-Right Forza Italia and the rapid growth of the neo-fascist Social Movement, later the National Alliance, forced a sea-change in Italian party politics in the 1994 elections, eventually leading to the much-heralded *alternanza* of 1996, in which a centre-Left alliance dominated by the Democratic Party of the Left, the successor to the Communist Party, managed to form its first ever government.

Finally, the alternation in Germany in 1998, in which the centre-Right Kohl government was displaced by a new Leftwing coalition, not only ushered the Greens into office for the first time, but also represented the first time that Germany had experienced a total alternation in government: up to that point, voters had become accustomed to partial changes in government composition, with either the SPD (in 1969) or the FDP (in 1982) remaining in office while changing their coalition partner (from the Christian Democrats and Social Democrats respectively). In 1998, by contrast, the turnover was wholesale.

These four cases constitute examples of quite fundamental shifts in the traditional patterns of government formation in their respective polities in European democracies. But they were far from being isolated examples during this politically turbulent decade. In France in 1997, for instance, a government had also been formed which, by virtue of its inclusion of the Greens for the first time, was also without precedent. Greens had also been included for the first time in the new Finnish coalition which took office in 1998, and both Green parties were included for the first time in the Belgian coalition which took office in 1999. In both Finland and Belgium, therefore, as well as in France, Germany, Italy, The Netherlands and Ireland, the 1990s have witnessed the introduction of quite innovative governing formulae. Even the United Kingdom, where the conventional patterns of single-party government formation and alternation had remained essentially unchallenged since 1945, seemed at least partially affected by this new wave of innovation, with the opposition Liberal Democrats being invited to participate with the newly incumbent Labour administration of 1997 in a key cabinet committee, thereby bringing the British case closer to the experience of coalition government than had ever been the case in the past half-century.

Innovation and novelty in processes of government formation are always interesting in themselves and may well be taken to indicate the emergence of far-reaching changes in the traditional structures of competition which define the party systems concerned (Mair, 1997: 199–223). Indeed, it is at this level that one might best search for the most meaningful evidence of party system change. For the purposes of this present analysis, however, it is even more interesting to reflect on the possibility that these sometimes dramatic shifts in prevailing patterns of party interaction within the legislative and governing arenas might be symptomatic of more fundamental changes occurring at the mass electoral level. In other words, by opting for new modes of interaction at the elite level, as it were, party leaderships might well be attempting to respond to a growing uncertainty regarding mass electoral preferences and behaviour. In this sense, an expansion of the options available for cross-party co-operation, collusion or competition within the legislative and governing arenas may well signal yet another means of coping with new electoral challenges – and opportunities – on the ground (Mair et al., 1999)

6.2 AGGREGATE ELECTORAL CHANGE

For more than two decades now, students of party politics in western Europe have been debating the extent to which there exists real evidence of change in mass electoral alignments, as well as the implications of that change. These debates and the arguments are now well enough known (see also Chapter 5). Basically two approaches are involved here. On the one hand, there are those approaches which have a primary focus on analyses at the individual level, and which marshal substantial evidence regarding the declining impact of social-structural factors on the formation of electoral preferences, and which also present reasonably robust and convincing data documenting quite important shifts in value orientations (e.g. Franklin et al., 1992; Van Deth and Scarbrough, 1995; Inglehart, 1997). Within this approach, the emphasis rests on the waning of traditional cleavages and hence on the 'de-freezing' of both long-standing alignments and long-standing party systems. On the other hand, there are those approaches which focus mainly on aggregate electoral patterns as well as on the overall balance of party support, and which draw evidence from these patterns in order to emphasize continuity rather than change, and persistence and survival rather than transformation (e.g. Bartolini and Mair, 1990; Mair, 1997: 19–90; Pennings and Lane, 1998). In fact, these two apparently conflicting interpretations may be seen to be quite compatible with one another, in that party and party system adaptation has been such that, however different the logic of individual voting choice has become, it has nevertheless proved possible for many parties to maintain their broad aggregate patterns of support (Mair, 2001). Moreover, despite the obvious sea changes at the level of the individual voter, it has been quite remarkable to observe the extent to which this did not appear to be translated into fundamental shifts at the aggregate level. Voter choice may be differently grounded than before, but, at least in the aggregate, and at least through to the end of the 1980s, it has often tended to reproduce quite conventional and historically familiar outcomes.

That, at least, is what could be concluded from the aggregate electoral evidence that was accumulated through to the end of the 1980s. Since then, of course, the story might be different. Indeed, the 1990s already look quite different. As noted above, for example, the party leaderships now often appear to be adopting quite innovative strategies in building governing coalitions, and this may well reflect their own sense of shifts in their aggregate support patterns. In addition, and within the European Union area in particular, we have witnessed quite a rapid hollowing out of party competition, with the various national governments, and the parties which make up these governments, being increasingly constrained to operate within a relatively narrow policy consensus. This too might be expected to have implications for aggregate voter preferences. Moreover, at mass level, it is also clear that a new element has been introduced into the equation through the increasing and often compelling evidence of popular distrust of, and disengagement from, conventional politics (e.g. Norris, 1999), a development which itself is probably related to the depoliticization of policy making. Even apart from any argument that might suggest that it is only in the most recent elections, in the 1990s, that the evident changes charted at the level of the individual voter will finally have begun to feed through to changes in the overall balance of party support, these other key changes might in themselves be expected to find a reflection in the aggregate.

Whether this is the result of the more or less lagged impact of individual level change, therefore, or as part of the environment created by new patterns of party competition and collusion, it might therefore reasonably be hypothesized that real evidence of change could now also be visible at the aggregate level. In other words, and in contrast to the picture available at the end of the 1980s, we might now reasonably hypothesize that patterns of aggregate electoral support in western Europe at the end of the 1990s will reveal increased evidence of flux, volatility and perhaps even realignment.

The following sections of this chapter will be devoted to a test of this hypothesis by means of the presentation and analysis of four key indicators of mass electoral behaviour, each being aggregated by decade and by country. This mode of analysis enjoys two particular advantages as far as cross-national comparative research is concerned. First, and most simply, it affords an opportunity to explore any insights that might be derived from the analysis of aggregate data on electoral behaviour. Unlike most survey data, these aggregate data are remarkably easy to access and are perfectly suited to standardized cross-national analysis. Nevertheless, whether for reasons of a sociological or psychological bias, they are often neglected by many students of electoral behaviour, who tend instead to rely primarily on individual-level data. Aggregate data cannot easily be used to make individual-level inferences, of course, and in this sense they remain quite limited. As against this, however, it can be argued that it is of major theoretical importance to recognize that the patterns derived from individual-level analyses may not necessarily be reflected at the aggregate level – and hence both sorts of data are required in order to appreciate the full complexity of electoral behaviour – while it is also important to study the aggregate patterns in order to properly identify the questions which need to be addressed at the individual level (see for this: Pennings et al., 1999: Chs 3 and 7).

The second advantage of these data is that they allow us, for the first time, to draw a broad and, in my view, telling picture of how aggregate patterns of mass electoral behaviour have unfolded through the five decades from the 1950s to the 1990s, that is, through what is now an unprecedented and completed half-century of peaceful and stable democratic development in western Europe. In effect, therefore, aggregate data afford a particularly valuable sense of perspective. That said, this particular perspective is indeed a very broad one, in that, partly in an attempt to even out the effect of one-off disturbances, the data are not presented or analysed on an election-by-election basis, but rather in terms of decade-by-decade averages.

The four key indicators which will be discussed in this paper are all derived from the results of national parliamentary elections, and comprise (i) levels of participation or turnout, (ii) levels of electoral volatility, (iii) levels of support for new parties, and (iv) levels of support for two new party families in particular: ecology parties or green parties, on the one hand, and parties of the extreme right, on the other hand. For two of these indicators, turnout and electoral volatility, I present summary figures of the mean value by decade, for each country, from the 1950s to the 1990s. Similar summary figures for the total new party vote are presented for each decade from the 1960s to the 1990s, new parties being here simply defined as those which began contesting elections no earlier than 1960. Finally, for both the ecology parties and extreme right parties, I present the decade averages only from the 1980s and 1990s, since prior to the 1980s both of these party families were relatively insignificant in cross-national terms.

The data presented here refer only to western Europe, and are limited even within that area (N = 15). Since I am concerned with patterns which can be traced back to the 1950s, I deal only with those polities which have experienced an uninterrupted period of stable democratic rule across the past

Table 6.1 *Number of elections, by country and by decade**

Country	1950s	1960s	1970s	1980s	1990s
Austria	3	2	4	2	4
Belgium	3	3	4	3	3
Denmark	4	4	5	4	3
Finland	3	2	4	2	3
France	3	3	2	3	2
Germany	2	3	2	3	3
Iceland	4	2	4	2	3
Ireland	3	3	2	5	2
Italy	2	2	3	2	3
Luxembourg	3	2	2	2	2
Netherlands	3	2	3	4	2
Norway	2	3	2	3	2
Sweden	3	3	4	3	3
Switzerland	3	2	3	2	3
UK	3	2	4	2	2
TOTAL	44	38	48	42	40

*Unless otherwise stated, the electoral data used in this analysis and relevant to each of the Tables refer to national parliamentary (lower house) elections only, and are drawn from Thomas T. Mackie and Richard Rose, *The International Almanac of Electoral History*, 3rd edn (Basingstoke: Macmillan, 1991); Tom Mackie and Richard Rose, *A Decade of Election Results: Updating the International Almanac* (Glasgow: CSSP, 1997); and various issues of the *Political Data Yearbook*, published annually as part of the *European Journal of Political Research*. In addition, various web-sites have been used for data on the most recent elections in 1998 and 1999, up to and includ-ing the Swiss election in October 1999 – the last parliamentary election to be held in any of these fifteen countries in the twentieth century.

half-century. This means that I have excluded the cases of Greece, Portugal and Spain, despite the insights which these cases can provide for the comparative analysis of electoral participation and volatility in particular (e.g. Morlino, 1998). For obvious similar reasons, I have also excluded the cases of the new post-communist democracies. A list of the countries for which data have been included, together with the number of elections in each country during each of the five decades, is shown in Table 6.1. This overview tells us that, on average, in every polity 14 elections were held, i.e. roughly every 3.5 years.

I should finally emphasize that the analysis which follows is markedly plain: for the most part, I simply present the data as aggregated by decade and by country, and comment on the patterns which are evident and the implications which these suggest. The figures tell their own story, and part of the value of presenting them is that we can now begin to identify with reasonable precision what has been happening to electoral behaviour in the aggregate across each of the five post-war decades (see also Gallagher et al., 2000: 257–67). Moreover, although certain conclusions are drawn from the patterns which become evident through this particular presentation of the data, these conclusions might well be challenged and qualified by more sophisticated time-series analyses, or by comparable studies that might be carried out at the level of the individual voter.

6.3 MASS ELECTORAL PARTICIPATION

The first indicator to be dealt with here concerns levels of electoral participation or turnout. Given the widespread attention that has recently been devoted to the increasing evidence of what Robert Putnam has defined as 'civic dis-engagement' (e.g. Putnam, 1995), as well as to the apparently more generalized growth of distrust in, and indifference to, traditional politics and political leaderships (e.g. Hayward, 1996; Norris, 1999), it is perhaps through this measure that some of the most striking changes in aggregate electoral behaviour might be identified. At the same time, however, while expectations regarding the possible decline in levels of electoral participation have been current for some years, they appear to have found little backing as yet in the aggregate empirical data. Reviewing the evidence from the 1960s through to the end of the 1980s, for example, Andeweg (1996: 150–1) noted that most countries in Europe were exhibiting a more or less trendless fluctuation in turnout levels: although participation had indeed declined slightly in some countries in this thirty-year period, it had increased in others, resulting in what was in fact just a very small decline in Europe as a whole across this period.

This pattern – at least as far as the period through to the 1980s is concerned – is also more or less confirmed by the mean levels of turnout summarized in Table 6.2. Indeed, through each of the four decades from the 1950s to the 1980s, average turnout levels across all the long-established democracies in western Europe scarcely altered, increasing marginally from 84.3 per cent in the 1950s to 84.9 per cent in the 1960s, and then falling slightly to 83.9 per cent in the 1970s and to 81.7 per cent in the 1980s. That said, this fall-off from the 1970s to the 1980s, while small, was reasonably consistent, with only two of the fifteen countries included here bucking the general trend: Belgium, where voting is compulsory, and where actual turnout increased slightly from 92.9 to 93.9 per cent from the 1970s to the 1980s, and Norway, where turnout increased from 81.6 to 83.1 per cent. In The Netherlands, mean turnout remained the same in both decades. In each of the other twelve countries, however, mean levels did in fact decline in the 1980s, whether marginally, as in Austria, which recorded a fall of less than 1 per cent, or more substantially, as in France, which recorded a fall of more than 10 per cent.

But this is not the most important pattern to be revealed by these data. In fact, now that the complete figures for the 1990s can be included, we can witness what may well prove to be a major shift in the pattern, with the small overall decline in turnout recorded in the 1980s being succeeded by a more dramatic decline in the 1990s, and with average turnout across western Europe falling from 81.7 per cent to 77.6 per cent. To be sure, even at this level, which is the lowest recorded in any of the post-war decades, turnout remains relatively high, with an average of slightly more than three-quarters of national electorates casting a ballot in the elections held during the 1990s, a figure that remains substantially higher than that recorded in nation-wide

Table 6.2 *Mean levels of electoral participation, by country and by decade (% of electorate)*

Country	1950s	1960s	1970s	1980s	1990s	Change 1950s–1990s
Austria	95.3	93.8	92.3	91.6	83.8	−11.5
Belgium	93.1	91.3	92.9	93.9	92.5	−0.6
Denmark	81.8	87.3	87.5	85.6	84.4	2.6
Finland*	76.5	85.0	81.1	78.7	70.8	−5.7
France	80.0	76.6	82.3	71.9	68.9	−11.1
Germany	86.8	87.1	90.9	87.1	79.7	−7.1
Iceland	90.8	91.3	90.4	89.4	86.4	−4.4
Ireland	74.3	74.2	76.5	72.9	67.2	−7.1
Italy	93.6	92.9	92.6	89.0	85.5	−8.1
Luxembourg	91.9	89.6	89.5	88.1	87.1	−4.8
Netherlands**	95.4	95.0	83.5	83.5	76.0	−19.4
Norway	78.8	82.8	81.6	83.1	77.1	−1.7
Sweden	78.7	86.4	90.4	89.1	85.0	6.3
Switzerland	69.0	64.2	52.3	48.2	43.8	−25.2
UK	79.1	76.6	75.1	74.1	75.4	−3.7
Mean (N = 15)	84.3	84.9	83.9	81.7	77.6	−6.7

*From 1975 onwards, Finnish citizens living abroad were also given the right to vote in Finnish elections, but the proportion doing so has been substantially smaller than those resident in Finland itself. Figures reported here refer only to turnout levels among Finnish residents.
**From 1971 onwards, it was no longer compulsory for Dutch citizens to attend at the polls.

elections in the United States (see Franklin, 1996). Even allowing for this, however, and even allowing for the fact that the most recent drop from the 1980s to the 1990s is less than 5 per cent, it is nevertheless striking to see the overall figure now dipping below the 80 per cent level for the first time in five decades. Moreover, this drop is also more or less consistent across countries, with as many as 11 of the 15 democracies also recording their lowest ever decade averages in the 1990s. The exceptions to this pattern include Belgium, where the decade averages are almost invariant, but where the lowest level was recorded in the 1960s, and Denmark and Sweden, which both recorded their lowest levels in the 1950s. Even in these three cases, however, it should be noted that turnout levels in the 1990s were lower than in the 1980s. The fourth exception is the United Kingdom, which recorded its lowest level in the 1980s. Indeed, the United Kingdom is the only one of these fifteen countries which recorded even a marginally higher level of turnout in the 1990s than in the 1980s. In 2001, however, this new upward shift was dramatically reversed, with turnout in that particular election falling to a record low of just 59.4 per cent.

This general pattern is very striking, and all the more so when account is taken of the sheer extent of the decline in particular countries. In Austria, for example, where turnout had remained safely above the 90 per cent level in each of the preceding four decades, the drop in the 1990s was almost 8 per cent. Similarly sharp declines were recorded in Finland, in Germany, which had absorbed the new voters of the former Democratic Republic during this period, and in The Netherlands and Norway. Even more striking, albeit across the longer term, is the case of Switzerland, where the then exclusively male electorate recorded an average of 69 per cent turnout in the 1950s, but which now records an average of less than 44 per cent.[1] More generally, while an average turnout level across Europe in the 1990s of more than 75 per cent appears to belie any notion of substantial levels of mass disengagement, these new figures do tend to sustain the notion of a gradual erosion in popular commitment to conventional politics. As Table 6.2 demonstrates, the decrease in turnout of voters between the 1980s and 1990s was 4.1 per cent, whereas this is only 6.7 per cent for the whole period under review. In this sense, the increasing concern with declining participation which is being voiced by governments and political observers throughout western Europe seems not to be misplaced. In the 1990s, at least, the figures are beginning to bear this out.

6.4 AGGREGATE ELECTORAL VOLATILITY

The second indicator to be dealt with here concerns aggregate electoral volatility, a simple summary measure of election-to-election shifts in the balance of party support across the whole party system. As was the case with turnout, expectations about increasing shifts in the balance of party support in national party systems have also been current for a number of years. Here too, however, the empirical record at the aggregate level has so far failed fully to confirm these expectations. Thus while party systems in some countries did indeed experience a substantial increase in their levels of electoral flux through the 1970s and 1980s, others appeared to become even more stable than before, resulting in what was generally a 'stable' and relatively low level of aggregate electoral change across western Europe as a whole (Bartolini and Mair, 1990; Mair, 1997: 76–90). In fact, the asymmetry that was to be found among the various national developments had already been highlighted by Pedersen (1979), whose article charting patterns of aggregate electoral change across western Europe from the late 1940s through to the 1970s is often seen as having presented the first real evidence of mass electoral 'de-freezing'. Prior to Pedersen's path-breaking article, the conventional wisdom had tended to accept at face value the famous freezing hypothesis of Lipset and Rokkan (1967), particularly since this had been so strongly underpinned by Rose and Urwin's (1970) evidence of persistence in the long-term patterns of individual party support. Since the end of the 1970s, however, this image has tended to be turned on its head, with the evidence from survey data in particular suggesting that the western democracies in general were experiencing a breakdown in their electoral alignments and cleavage voting patterns, and that these were being replaced by more short-term and essentially unpredictable dynamics (Dalton et al., 1984; Franklin et al., 1992). As noted above, however, these undeniable individual-level changes did not seem to translate very extensively into shifts at the

Table 6.3 *Mean total volatility, by country and by decade*

Country	1950s	1960s	1970s	1980s	1990s	Change 1950s–1990s
Austria	4.1	3.3	2.7	5.5	9.4	5.3
Belgium	7.6	10.2	5.3	10.0	10.8	3.2
Denmark	5.5	8.7	15.5	9.7	12.4	6.9
Finland	4.4	7.0	7.9	8.7	11.0	6.6
France	22.3	11.5	8.8	13.4	15.4	−6.9
Germany	15.2	8.4	5.0	6.3	9.0	−6.2
Iceland	9.2	4.3	12.2	11.6	13.7	4.5
Ireland	10.3	7.0	5.7	8.1	11.7	1.4
Italy	9.7	8.2	9.9	8.6	22.9	13.2
Luxembourg	10.8	8.8	12.5	14.8	6.2	−4.6
Netherlands	5.1	7.9	12.3	8.3	19.1	14.0
Norway	3.4	5.3	15.3	10.7	15.9	12.5
Sweden	4.8	4.0	6.3	7.6	13.8	9.0
Switzerland	2.5	3.5	6.0	6.4	8.0	5.5
UK	4.3	5.2	8.3	3.3	9.3	5.0
Mean (N = 15)	7.9	6.9	8.9	8.9	12.6	4.7

Note: Data on volatility levels through to 1985 are drawn from Bartolini and Mair (1990); thereafter, I have made my own calculations based on the electoral results as reported in the sources listed in the footnote to Table 6.1. The rules for the calculation of volatility levels are those listed in Bartolini and Mair (1990: 311–12).

aggregate level. Indeed, even by the end of the 1980s, aggregate electoral volatility on a European-wide basis still remained relatively muted, while many of the traditional parties which had dominated electoral competition in the 1950s or even earlier continued to be serious contenders. These older parties certainly had seen some of their aggregate support slipping away to the benefit of new formations (see also below), but it nevertheless remained striking to see how much of their vote share they had managed to retain even through to the end of the 1980s.

As is the case with levels of electoral participation, these earlier impressions are now also confirmed by the mean levels of aggregate electoral volatility across the different decades from the 1950s to the 1980s, as summarized in Table 6.3. The indicator reported in this Table is that originally proposed by Pedersen, whereby total (or aggregate) electoral volatility is defined as 'the net change within the electoral party system resulting from individual vote transfers' (Pedersen, 1979: 3), and is measured as the cumulated (aggregate) electoral gains of all winning parties in a given election, or, which is the same thing, as the cumulated (aggregate) electoral losses of all losing parties in that election.[2] As can be seen in Table 6.3, levels of this measure of aggregate electoral volatility across the fifteen countries as a whole scarcely changed between the 1950s and the 1980s, with the west-European-wide national average falling from 7.9 per cent in the 1950s to 6.9 per cent in the 1960s, and then rising slightly to 8.9 per cent in the two subsequent decades. This was hardly the stuff of electoral earthquakes. That said, these overall averages conceal quite a bit of flux within the individual party systems. Thus we see Denmark, The Netherlands and Norway moving from a remarkably quiescent 1950s to a relatively unstable 1970s, before falling back again in the 1980s. Conversely, both France and Germany begin the post-war period with relatively substantial flux, before then settling down in the 1960s and 1970s. In other words, while the average level of aggregate electoral volatility in western Europe as a whole tends to remain quite stable, this is partly due to contradictory patterns of development among the different polities (see Bartolini and Mair, 1990).

Here again, however, as with the evidence of turnout, the more important observation is that this picture appears to change significantly across the fifteen polities now that the recent figures for the 1990s have become available. Indeed, across western Europe as a whole, as can be seen from Table 6.3, the 1990s becomes the peak decade for electoral volatility, with an average of 12.6 per cent, almost 4 points greater than that recorded in the 1970s and 1980s. Not too much should be made of this, of course. On a scale which has a theoretical range running from 0 to 100, and which even here has a range of decade averages that run in practice from 2.5 (1950s Switzerland) to 22.9 (1990s Italy), a mean value of 12.6 still probably reflects more (short-term) continuity than change. On the other hand, this is the first of the five post-war decades in which the overall mean breaches the 10 per cent threshold, while it is also the first decade to record such a major shift from the previous mean value.

The significance of the 1990s can also be underlined by reference to the individual national experiences. Thus, in all but four of the countries (the exceptions are Denmark, France, Germany and Luxembourg), the 1990s also constitute a national peak, which, in the majority of cases, exceeds 10 per cent: Belgium (10.8), Finland (11.0), Iceland (13.7), Ireland (11.7), Italy (22.9), Netherlands (19.1), Norway (15.8) and Sweden (13.8).[3] As noted above, this increased volatility may be explained in a variety of ways, whether by suggesting the possibility of lagged effects which are eventually working through from the level of the individual voter to the aggregate percentages, or by focusing more directly on the 1990s experience itself, including the influence of changes which have taken place at the level of party competition, or of those wrought by the end of the Cold War, or by deepening European integration. Whatever the source or sources of change, however, the aggregate evidence of change in the 1990s is undeniable. In this sense, as was the case with levels of electoral participation, the end of the century seems different.

In sum, and thus far, the inclusion of aggregate data from the 1990s appears to present quite a radical shift from the patterns visible through to the end of the 1980s. Fewer voters than previously seem willing to participate in elections, although turnout levels in themselves still remain reasonably high; and among those who do participate there is greater evidence of preference switching between parties from one election to the next. Moreover, not only do both of these indicators reach a relative extreme in the 1990s (whether recording troughs in the case of turnout, or peaks in the case of volatility) across western Europe as a whole, but they are also at their most extreme in a small majority of the individual polities. That is, *both* extreme lows in turnout and extreme peaks in volatility were recorded in the 1990s in Austria, Finland, Iceland, Ireland, Italy, The Netherlands, Norway and Switzerland. Moreover, it is only in the single case of Denmark that there is neither a trough in turnout nor a peak in volatility during the 1990s. In this sense, the evidence of 1990s exceptionalism is not only striking, but it is also reasonably consistent when looked at cross-nationally.

6.5 ELECTORAL SUPPORT FOR NEW POLITICAL PARTIES

Amidst the flurry of expectations released by the literature on party and party system change during the late 1970s and 1980s, a reasonably consistent emphasis has been placed on the potential challenge posed to more traditional parties by the emergence of new alternative organizations (e.g. Lawson and Merkl, 1988). To some degree, this emphasis derived simply from the shock of the new, with particular attention being paid to the quite pervasive rise of new Green parties, and, somewhat later, to the more uneven development of various parties of the extreme right (see below; see also: Müller-Rommel, 1998). Even beyond the appeal of these two particular party families, however, there was a general sense that voters were turning their backs on the older parties and were beginning to seek out new alternatives. In part, these new parties were seen to appeal to more-specific or sectoral interests, capable of filling specific niches in the party system which were being neglected by the broad aggregative appeals of their traditional opponents (e.g. Lane and Ersson, 1994). In part also, they were seen to have a greater organizational appeal, in that the older parties tended to remain tied to a mass party model in which the role of the individual member or supporter was often downgraded. New parties were also therefore seen to be in a position to take advantage of processes of cognitive mobilization, and of the wider dispersal of political and civic skills (e.g. Dalton, 1984).

The evidence of new party success in national elections in Europe, which is the third indicator to be dealt with here, is certainly unequivocal (see Table 6.4). Moreover, in contrast to the evidence regarding levels of participation and electoral volatility, we can also witness a general upward trend through the decades rather than simply a sudden shift in the 1990s in particular. For the purposes of this analysis, new parties are simply defined as those which first began to contest elections no earlier than 1960. Hence any party that began to contest elections in the 1950s or earlier is for these purposes an 'old' party. It follows from this that the decade averages reported in Table 6.4 do not include the 1950s: by (my) definition, the values in this first decade were 0. It should also be emphasized that this simple operational definition takes no account of the origins of the new party in question, in that a new party is regarded as new even when it was created simply through the merger (in the 1960s or later) of two or more pre-existing 'old' parties. My concern is with

Table 6.4 *Mean total vote for new parties, by country and by decade (percentage)*

Country	1960s	1970s	1980s	1990s	Growth 1960s–1990s
Austria	1.7	0.1	4.1	11.5	9.8
Belgium	2.8	11.4	12.9	23.7	20.9
Denmark	8.7	26.9	30.7	24.9	16.2
Finland	1.6	8.2	13.7	22.3	20.7
France*	16.3	29.1	27.1	41.7	25.4
Germany	4.3	0.5	7.5	13.9	9.6
Iceland	2.4	4.7	19.3	21.6	19.2
Ireland	0.3	1.4	7.9	10.0	9.7
Italy**	9.5	3.3	7.1	66.8	57.3
Luxembourg	3.1	12.0	11.5	22.4	19.3
Netherlands	2.3	26.6	44.5	45.9	43.6
Norway	3.9	13.6	15.1	19.7	15.8
Sweden	1.1	1.6	4.5	14.5	13.4
Switzerland	0.4	5.3	12.2	14.9	14.5
UK	0	0.8	11.6	2.3	2.3
Mean (N = 15)	3.9	9.7	15.3	23.7	19.8

*French data exclude 'general' categories listed in elections results as 'other left', 'other right', and so on.

**Italian data in 1994 and 1996 refer to results in the PR districts only.

new parties as such, rather than with new politics in particular (but see below). Finally, the figures summarized in Table 6.4 refer to the total vote accumulated by all such parties in each election (averaged by decade) rather than to the mean support won by each.[4]

As can be seen from Table 6.4, new party success across western Europe as a whole has grown from an initial national mean of 3.9 per cent in the 1960s, to 9.7 per cent in the 1970s, to 15.3 per cent in the 1980s, and finally to 23.7 per cent in the 1990s. In effect, therefore, by the 1990s, an average of almost one voter in four was supporting parties which had not contested elections prior to 1960. From one perspective, this can be seen as reflecting a relatively sizeable shift in partisan preferences over time, and as marking a substantial move away from the older party alternatives. On the other hand, it needs also to be borne in mind that the period from the 1960s to the 1990s encompasses 40 years of electoral competition, thus affording ample time for new parties to emerge and develop. Moreover, although the growth in mean support for new parties across western Europe as a whole is reasonably steady through the different decades, the variation at national level is here quite pronounced. Some systems seem remarkably inhospitable to new parties, for example, while in others such parties have grown to command very substantial support. In the United Kingdom, for instance, new parties have made virtually no headway apart from the brief surge of the new Social Democratic party in the 1980s.[5] New parties also seem to face reasonably strong obstacles in Ireland and Austria, as well as in Germany and Sweden – at least prior to the 1990s. In both France and The Netherlands, by contrast, new parties have come close to winning a majority of the vote in the 1990s, while in Italy the dramatic changes wrought by the so-called Second Republic have given new parties an average of two-thirds of the vote in the 1990s as a whole, including more than 80 per cent of the vote in the election of 1996.[6] Even allowing for these national differences, however, it is still striking to note that it is precisely in the 1990s that total support for new parties in many of the west European countries reaches its post-war peak. Indeed, it is only Denmark and the UK which run counter to this trend, with both peaking in the 1980s and then falling back – quite markedly – in the 1990s. Interestingly, Denmark was also the only country which failed to record extreme levels for either the turnout or volatility indicators during the 1990s, while the United Kingdom was the only country recording an increased level of participation during this final decade. In both countries, therefore, it seems that the trends which appear more or less common to all other west European polities are effectively countered – at least for now. Elsewhere, as is also the case for new party support, the differences marked by the 1990s tend to be both pronounced and consistent.

6.6 ELECTORAL SUPPORT FOR THE GREENS AND THE EXTREME RIGHT

The final indicator to be included within the broad overview of mass electoral behaviour follows immediately from this discussion of new parties, and concerns the levels of support won by two of the most important new party families to have emerged in European politics in the last twenty years – Green parties, on the one hand, and extreme right parties, on the other. Both of these families are important because they may be seen as offering the basis for a new realignment in traditional party systems. Their approach to politics and political style fall intentionally outwith the conventional remits of the traditional parties, and unlike, for instance, the Dutch Christian Democratic Appeal or the Italian Left Democrats, they both offer examples of new parties which constitute more than simply a fresh organizational packaging of pre-existing concerns and commitments. In this sense, they are rightly grouped together as 'challenger' parties (Müller-Rommel, 1998), and they are particularly important because of that. Moreover, as Ignazi (1992) suggests, they may also be linked to one another as counterparts in a newly divisive conflict between the winners and losers of post-industrialism, and, as such, any major growth in their support might well suggest the onset of processes of realignment.

Table 6.5 summarizes the aggregate support for both of these party families in the 1980s and 1990s (see also Gallagher et al., 2000: 202–33). In this case, only these last two decades' averages are summarized, since, in the large majority of countries, these parties scarcely figured in electoral terms during the earlier post-war decades. One major problem involved here is that of determining which parties are to be included within the extreme right category. While the Green party category is easily specified – more often than not the parties themselves adopt a label involving the words green, ecology or environment, and they have almost all been established explicitly to promote Green issues – the meaning of the extreme right category, as well as the label itself, is subject to substantial debate (e.g. Mudde, 2000; Betz, 1994). Moreover, precisely because there is a confusion within definitions of the extreme right between the promotion of a particular ideology, on the one hand, and the adoption of particular issue-positions, on the other, it is often difficult to specify when particular parties might be seen as moving in or out of the category itself. In any case, for the purposes of this analysis I have identified a group of some 23 parties (listed in Table 6.5) which I have categorized as extreme right. And while some of these might be borderline cases, and while other parties not included here might well be regarded as being better suited to the category, it is unlikely that an alternative categorization would make that much difference to the overall levels of electoral support summarized in Table 6.5.

A number of observations can be made about these summary data. As far as Green parties are concerned, for example, it is striking to note from Table 6.5 how relatively unsuccessful they are. Although Green parties have begun to contest the 1990s elections in all 15 countries, albeit not all 1990s elections in all countries, together they have polled an average of just 5 per cent of the vote across western Europe as a whole. This is not a substantial figure, although it does represent a doubling of their average share of the vote in the 1980s, and also reflects a growth in support in every country other than the UK. Moreover, even though there is a reasonable amount of cross-national variation in Green party support in the 1990s, there is only one country – Belgium – where the average vote during the 1990s has reached double figures. All of this suggests that the Green electoral challenge has proved relatively weak. Nevertheless, this should not be taken to imply that Green parties can be dismissed as wholly irrelevant. As noted above, they have now broken through the threshold of executive power in three of the four major European states – France, Germany and Italy – as well as in Belgium and Finland. In addition, and as most studies of Green parties are keen to attest, they have also played a very influential role in shaping the overall policy agenda. Notwithstanding such successes, however, their electoral record is not very impressive, and in this sense they still remain relatively marginal actors.

The pattern presented by extreme right support is different in a number of respects. As can be seen from Table 6.5, extreme right support is far less evenly spread throughout Europe, with highs of 22 and almost 21 per cent of the vote in Austria and Italy in the 1990s, for example, and with no presence at all in any of the most recent elections in Iceland, Ireland, or the UK. Indeed, what we see here are two quite heterogeneous clusters of countries in the 1990s: those where the extreme right either does not figure or polls very badly (Finland, Germany, Iceland, Ireland, Luxembourg, The Netherlands,

Table 6.5 *Mean vote for Green parties and extreme right parties, by country and by decade (%)*

Country	Green parties			Extreme right*		
	1980s	1990s	Change 1980s–1990s	1980s	1990s	Change 1980s–1990s
Austria	4.1	7.6	3.5	7.4	22.0	14.6
Belgium	6.0	10.9	4.9	1.5	9.7	8.2
Denmark	0.7	2.2	1.5	6.6	7.5	0.9
Finland	2.7	7.0	4.3	0	0.3	0.3
France	0.9	8.4	7.5	6.7	14.2	7.5
Germany	5.1	6.4	1.3	0.3	2.5	2.2
Iceland	0	3.1	3.1	0	0	0
Ireland	0.4	2.1	1.7	0	0	0
Italy	1.3	2.7	1.4	6.6	20.9	14.3
Luxembourg	6.4	9.3	2.9	1.2	1.2	0
Netherlands	1.1	5.6	4.5	0.6	1.8	1.2
Norway	0.1	0.1	0	7.1	10.8	3.7
Sweden	2.9	4.3	1.4	0	2.6	2.6
Switzerland	5.0	6.3	1.3	4.3	7.6	3.3
UK	0.3	0.3	0	0.1	0	−0.1
Mean (N = 15)	2.5	5.0	2.5	2.8	6.7	3.9

*Parties included: Austria (Freedom Party of Austria); Belgium (National Front & Flemish Block); Denmark (Progress & Danish People's Party); Finland (True Finns); France (National Front & 'other extreme right'); Germany (National Democratic Party, The Republicans & German People's Union); Italy (Italian Social Movement/National Alliance, Northern League & Fiamma); Luxembourg (Luxembourg for the Luxembourgeois); Netherlands (Centre Party & Centre Democrats); Norway (Progress); Sweden (New Democracy); Switzerland (National Action/Swiss Democrats, Freedom Party & Lega); UK (National Front). Note that not all elections in all countries were contested by these extreme right parties in the 1980s and 1990s.

Sweden and the UK), and those where it polls upwards of 7.5 per cent (Austria, Belgium, Denmark, France, Italy, Norway and Switzerland). Putting these contrasting patterns together yields a less than meaningful cross-European average of 6.7 per cent, which is more than double that recorded in the 1980s, and which is also quite substantially above that recorded by the more evenly spread Green parties. These figures alone would suggest that it is the challenge from the extreme right which is now the more important of the two. Indeed, this impression is compounded by the sheer unevenness of extreme right support across Europe – at least as yet. That is, and at least in certain systems, we appear to witness a very substantial challenge from this new right.

That said, there is also another important and perhaps more telling conclusion that might be drawn from these last data. Taken together, both Green and extreme right parties account for an average of just under 12 per cent of the vote in 1990s western Europe. At the same time, however, and as has already been seen above, new parties as a whole account for almost 24 per cent of the vote. What this implies, in other words, is that at least half of the new party vote across western Europe as a whole is being taken by parties which are more or less likely to be categorized as belonging to one of the more conventional party families, whether socialist, new Left, Christian, liberal, or whatever. And what this may imply, in turn, is that a large part of the apparent shift away from the traditional parties (defined here as being those founded before 1960) is simply being transferred across to repackaged – and perhaps smaller and more specialized – versions of these traditional alternatives rather than being won over to a wholly alternative politics.

6.7 CONCLUSION

The data as crudely presented here do not allow us to draw any hard and fast conclusions regarding the particular development that has just been signalled above, and to derive such conclusions would probably require more disaggregated party-by-party data, as well as a more nuanced country-by-country analysis. Should this conclusion prove valid, however, then it can be made to fit quite well with the impressions gained by the data on electoral participation and volatility. In brief, fewer voters have seemed willing to participate in elections during the 1990s than during previous decades (Table 6.2). At the same time, those voters who do participate seem substantially more willing to transfer their preferences between parties than was the case even in the 1980s (Table 6.3). Moreover, in the 1990s, support for new parties has grown apace, continuing, and even exacerbating slightly, the steady upward trend in new party support that can be seen to begin in the 1960s (Table 6.4). What we have seen with these last data, however, is that a large part of this move towards new parties might well prove to be contained within the conventional party families. And what this then would suggest, above all, is further evidence of disengagement: increased disengagement from conventional politics, on the one hand, as evidenced by the more or less consistent decline in levels of participation; and increased disengagement from traditional party organizations, as evidenced by the upward shift in volatility levels in the 1990s, as well as by the observed shift towards potentially *non-realigning* new parties, on the other hand.

The 1990s have proved to be different. But what is driving that difference? Had the declining levels of turnout and increasing levels of volatility that were recorded in the 1990s been accompanied by a major shift to one or other of the two important new party families, the Greens or the extreme right, then it might have proved possible to speak of the beginnings of a realigning change in mass electoral behaviour. As of now, however, the impression that comes across from these data is not one that points to realignment, but rather to increasing detachment and disengagement. Pending closer analysis, therefore, it seems more likely to be indifference rather than resentment that is beginning to guide mass electoral behaviour in western Europe at the end of the century. Yet, simultaneously we observe the reactions of the party elites that are apparently seeking a re-establishment of their electoral constituency, *inter alia* through new alliances. It remains to be seen therefore whether the increasingly innovative processes of co-operation and competition practised by the governing elites will eventually serve to challenge this growing indifference, or whether it will fuel changes in mass electoral behaviour even further.

NOTES

1   Indeed, unless overlaid with a gender perspective, these long-term Swiss data appear to confirm the lack of plausibility of cultural explanations of differential turnout levels (see: Jackman and Miller, 1995): in the 1950s, Switzerland recorded a mean level of turnout which actually exceeded that recorded in the 1990s by either France or Ireland, and which was only marginally less than that recorded in Finland.

2   In practice, and as is also the case here, since the rounding of the figures can lead to anomalies, aggregate volatility is usually calculated by summing the absolute values of cumulated gains and cumulated losses and dividing by two. This is not necessarily the best or most comprehensive of electoral change, of course. Like all aggregate measures it is likely to underestimate the extent of individual-level switches between parties, and since it measures only the change recorded from one election to the next, it also fails to take account of long-term changes in voting patterns. Nonetheless, as a simple and intuitively meaningful measure, it does offer a clear and cross-nationally comparable indicator of short-term electoral instability, and for this reason it is also often employed in tests of the mass electoral implications of the Lipset–Rokkan freezing hypothesis.

3   Another way of underlining the exceptionality of the 1990s, albeit at the level of the individual elections which are not separately dealt with in this paper, is by noting the percentage of national elections per decade in which total aggregate volatility exceeds 10 per cent. These are as follows: 1950s (N = 44): 25.0%; 1960s (N = 38): 21.1%; 1970s (N = 48): 35.4%; 1980s (N = 42): 35.7%; 1990s (N = 40): 62.5%.

4   For the sake of clarity, it should be noted that the new parties and electoral alliances included in this analysis are first, as noted above, those which emerge as the result of a merger between two or more pre-existing parties, one of the most obvious examples being the Dutch Christian Democratic Appeal (CDA); second, those which emerge as the result of a split in an existing party, where in some cases I regard all of the parties emerging from the split as new (e.g., in the cases of the former communist Democratic Party of the Left and Communist Refoundation parties in Italy), and where in other cases I regard the split as creating one new party that then runs alongside the now rump existing party (e.g. in the case of the Social Democratic split from Labour in the UK in the 1980s); and third, those genuinely new parties, such as the Green parties. Note also that I do not regard the splits which gave rise to separate linguistic versions of the Belgian Christian, Socialist and Liberal Parties as having created new parties as such, since the two wings of each of these parties had already maintained separate electoral constituencies for some time prior to the formalized division. For the more detailed analysis of these data (through to the end of 1998), see: Mair (1999).

5   It should be noted, of course, that the short-lived success of the SDP was remarkable in itself, given that the electoral system (FPTP) is a strong institutional barrier for 'newcomers' on the electoral market. See also Chapter 5.

6   This exceptional Italian figure inevitably contributes quite a lot to raising the
    overall European mean in the 1990s; without Italy, the decade average for the
    remaining 14 countries falls to 20.7 per cent. Excluding the Dutch figures would
    result in 21.1 per cent.

PART THREE

DEMOCRATIC INSTITUTIONS AND POLITICAL ACTION

A recent debate in contemporary political theory is about the role and working of institutions. Institutions can be defined as the formal and informal 'rules of the political game'. Almost every democracy is organized by means of a set of basic laws that describe how the 'game' must be played. At the same time it is generally acknowledged that the *application* of the rules varies from country to country.

In this Part the issue at hand is how (organized) societal interests can be effectively represented. In other words: whether or not citizens' preferences are, literally, better or worse handled by government and parliament given the institutional organization of the democratic system.

According Armingeon, one ought to analyse the institutional design of different democracies in terms of their *systemic* coherence. His point of departure is the recent work of Arend Lijphart, 'Patterns of Democracy'. The central concepts to be discussed are the institutional models of democracy and interest-mediation: *consensus democracy and corporatism*. Armingeon demonstrates, both conceptually and empirically, that Lijphart's ideas are tenable and relevant. They are particularly relevant as regards the policy formation that is realized in consensus democracies and are (in part) implemented successfully in a corporatist environment. Yet, it is also shown that this 'success story' strongly depends on *where and when* it happens. In other words: Chapter 7 shows that the institutional design of consensus democracy can be beneficial for the functioning of representative government, but not always nor everywhere. It is not a universal model of democracy, nor always feasible in reality.

This point is taken up by Schmidt in *Chapter 8*. His comparative analysis re-assesses not only the issue of 'Do Parties Matter', but also focuses on the institutional room for manoeuvre political parties actually have to pursue their goals in terms of *policy-making*. It appears that parties do play their role as mediators, or: representatives of the population, but are more or less constrained in their actions due to the division of party systems, the extant type of government (for example the kind of coalition) and constitutional devices that limit policy formation and implementation. Hence, an important lesson to be drawn from Schmidt's treatise is that the 'parties do matter' hypothesis strongly depends on the institutional design of the democratic polity in which they operate. Particularly important are – so it is argued – the existence of *veto-players*, who appear to be crucial for explaining the course of political action.

The importance of Schmidt's conclusion becomes evident in *Chapter 9*. Here the focus is on the development of the contemporary welfare state. The welfare state is considered as one of the main achievements of modern democracy. Yet, as Becker and Van Kersbergen demonstrate, it has also come under threat recently. The tendency towards retrenchment is discussed in relation to changing ideas of the parties that helped it on its way, on the one hand, and the impact of changing socio-economic circumstances, on the other hand. Although slowly and in varying ways, so it appears, the institutionalisation of *public welfare* within contemporary democracies is not irreversible. Hence, institutions matter, but circumstances as well, and for that matter new ideologies too. In sum, the contemporary welfare state, made possible by political action in representative democracy, is a vulnerable institutional fabric of society.

7

INTEREST INTERMEDIATION: THE CASES OF CONSOCIATIONAL DEMOCRACY AND CORPORATISM

Klaus Armingeon

7.1 INTRODUCTION: WHAT IS CORPORATISM AND CONSOCIATIONAL DEMOCRACY ABOUT?

In a democratic system societal interests are articulated, aggregated and transformed into political decisions, a process called interest intermediation. Consociational democracy and corporatism denote styles of decision-making of various actors in a democracy. Both styles share the element that decisions are usually not reached by plurality of votes or other power resources. Rather the actors seek to integrate a large number of actors or societal groups into a decision by negotiations and mutual concessions, respecting the autonomy of the various actors and their groups. Hence corporatism and consociational democracy are the major empirical instances of 'negotiation democracies'.

Both styles differ with regard to the actors involved: corporatist systems are made up of interest organizations – for instance trade unions – and the state; members of the consociational system are political actors like political parties, parliamentary groups, public administration and other elites, often from different levels of the state, i.e. local, regional or central level. Corporatism denotes the 'institutionalized pattern of policy formation in which large interest organizations co-operate with each other and with public authorities … in the authoritative allocation of values and in the implementation of such policies' (Lehmbruch, 1979: 150). Consociational democracies refer to a political style according to which political parties and governments regulate conflict by compromise and mutual concessions.

In contrast to negotiation democracies, democratic systems using the plurality of votes or resources as the dominant technique arrive at different modes of interest representation. With regard to the relation between voluntary associations and state, this mode is called 'pluralism'. Societal interests are articulated by organizations based on voluntary membership, and these organizations seek to influence the political system. In exerting pressure on government, parliament and public administration, they do not co-ordinate their policies with other associations or the state. In addition, they are not incorporated into the implementation of public policies. In majoritarian

	Negotiation	Plurality of votes or resources
Parties, elite & bureaucracy	Consociational democracy	Competitive democracy*
Interest organizations and the state	Corporatism**	Interest group pluralism

*Synonym: Westminster democracy or majoritarian democracy
**In some countries (such as Austria and The Netherlands) this is called social partnership

Figure 7.1 *Negotiation democracies vs non-negotiation democracies*

democracies, often labelled also as competitive or Westminster democracies (Lijphart, 1977), those who have – even a slight – majority decide; in the most extreme case the interests of the remaining 49.9 per cent of the population or members can be disregarded, and hence minorities and even large minorities are ignored. The basic argument states that each minority has a (fair) chance to become a majority and hence can at that time realize its interests and visions. Pluralism emphasizes strongly the building of temporary coalitions to influence a particular decision or to control a certain policy area. Corporatism and consociational democracy can thus be considered as empirical alternatives of interest group pluralism and Westminster democracy. Figure 7.1 shows the two views on how democracies work.

7.2 WHO DISCOVERED IT WHEN?

Both consociational democracy and corporatism stand in stark contrast to the classical model of Western democracy, being majoritarian and pluralist. In the 1950s and 1960s most Western political scientists assumed that there is only one type of democracy, the model being the political systems of Britain and the United States of America. John Stuart Mill once declared that it is 'next to impossible' to have democracy in multiethnic countries and 'impossible' in linguistically divided countries (quoted after Lijphart, 1996: 258). However, in the late-1960s some continental researchers claimed that some democratic continental political systems in fragmented societies are far apart from the majoritarian model without being less democratic. The Dutchman Arend Lijphart (1968) and the German Gerhard Lehmbruch (1967) pointed to the Dutch, Swiss and Austrian experiences. In The Netherlands and in Austria, it was argued, societies were deeply split due to socio-cultural cleavages. In The Netherlands a catholic, a Calvinist and a socialist segment co-existed without much contact among each other. For example, Catholics were born in catholic hospitals, brought up in catholic schools, attended catholic universities, married a catholic partner, spent their leisure time in catholic clubs and societies, were organized in catholic trade unions or employers' organizations and were buried by catholic funeral societies. These groups became separated pillars of society and it was only at the elite level that mutual contacts existed with members of other pillars. The same phenomenon had developed in Austria, although there were only two pillars or – in the Austrian term – 'Lager': a catholic 'Lager' represented by a catholic-centrist political party, the Österreichische Volkspartei, strongly supported by farmers and the middle classes, and the socialist-secular Lager, represented by the Socialist Party, which collected its votes particularly among the blue collar workers, mostly being members of the trade union movement under the leadership of the Austrian Trades Union Confederation. Switzerland has been different, since this society has been less pillarized. However, Lehmbruch (1967) contended that the rifts in society manifested themselves in regional units and were functionally similar. They represent different linguistic groups, denominations and economic systems. The latter range from agricultural economies in the mountainous regions to manu-facturing industries in the regions between the Jura and the Alps. Whatever the structure and the basis of the fragmentation of these societies have been, they share the common characteristic that in all these countries majority government by one 'pillar' or 'Lager' has not been a feasible strategy for the political parties and their elites. Neither single 'pillar' could gain the major-ity. And where a 'Lager' or a coalition of 'pillars' was able to reach majority, the size of the minority would be so large that its interests could not be ignored if one wished to exclude the risk of instability of the democratic system. Apart from Lehmbruch and Lijphart, major contributions in the development of the concept of consociational democracy have been made by Jürg Steiner (1974), Hans Daalder (1974) and the authors of a collected volume, edited by Kenneth McRae (1974).

Corporatism entered the scientific literature during the 1970s, about ten years after consociational democracy. Whilst Lijphart and Lehmbruch questioned the view that a true democracy has to be modelled after the majoritarian Anglo-Saxon systems, the debate on corporatism challenged the assump-tions that in a democracy the relation between interest associations and elites in parliament and public administration ought to be pluralistic. In this perspective of the group theory of politics (Truman, 1962), societal interests become organized and exert pressure on parliament and government, which reacts by delivering policies corresponding to strength and direction of the pressures by the interest organizations. Obviously this did not correspond to the actual way of co-operation between interest organizations and the state in many European countries. Government did not only react to pressures but actively intervened in economic processes; trade unions and employers' organizations participated in the Keynesian macro-economic steering in the 1960s and 1970s. These observations – reported for example by Andrew Shonfield (1965) – fuelled research in non-pluralistic but nevertheless demo-cratic systems of interest intermediation. A major contribution was made by the North-American Philippe C. Schmitter. He worked on interest groups in Brazil and other Latin American countries, using analytic concepts developed by a Romanian, M. Manoilesco. Manoilesco has termed the twentieth century the century of corporatism (Schmitter, 1979; Schmitter and Lehmbruch, 1979). In the authoritarian Latin American countries and Portugal, interest organizations were compulsorily built into the policy making and administration of the authoritarian state. This clearly did not apply to European nations, where interest groups co-operate voluntarily with the state and are not only parts of the executive branch but also represent societal interests. In an autobiographical note Schmitter has told how – in one day – he transferred the concept to Europe: He was at the time professor at the University of Geneva in Switzerland and received a letter asking him to write an article about Latin American corporatism – whilst having all his books on that theme in the USA. 'In my consternation, I happened to look down at that day's issue of the Tribune de Genève. It was open at the business section and there was an article about the annual price-fixing mechanism for milk and the role that the Association Suisse des Producteurs de Lait had played on it. I thought: How corporatist! … I had the central theme for my article: corporat(iv)ism … was alive and well within some advanced democracies – only it was societal and voluntary in its origins, not statist and compulsory as it was in Brazil and Portugal' (Schmitter, 1997: 292).

At the same time, Gerhard Lehmbruch (1979) published some articles, in particular starting from observations of the close co-operation between Austrian interest organizations and the state. In contrast to Schmitter, he defined his concept less in terms of structural characteristics of the system of interest groups. He rather put emphasis on the mutual co-ordination of private and public policies. Examples were wages policies concerted with price policies and social policies. Lehmbruch and Schmitter edited two volumes, which are – by now – the classic analysis of corporatism (Schmitter and Lehmbruch, 1979; Lehmbruch and Schmitter, 1982). At the beginning of the debate, the term liberal- or neo-corporatism denoted co-operation of interest associations and the state in democracies, as compared with authoritarian regimes (state corporatism or simply corporatism). However, in the course of scientific discussion, it became clear that state and liberal corporatism have little in common. Structures and outcomes of neo-corporatism turned out to be substantially different from corporatism in authoritarian systems. Hence there was no risk of confusion, if the co-operation of associations and state in democratic policy development and implementation was labelled, for the sake of simplicity, corporatism. More important has been a widening of the focus of analyses on corporatism. In the 1970s and early 1980s, the concertation of trade union wage policy with price policy of employers and tax and public welfare policy has been considered as the major example of corporatism. Later, corporatism has been found in other policy fields and among other associations (e.g. health policy and the relevant interest groups). Hence bargained incomes policies and macroeconomic policy co-ordination are no longer the paradigmatic cases of corporatism (Lehmbruch, 2000). The debate on forms and types of 'negation democracy' has, however, not been confined to conceptual discussion. At the same time a growing number of political scientists have attempted to develop these concepts empirically.

BOX 7.1 NEGOTIATION DEMOCRACY: THREE EMINENT SCHOLARS

Arend Lijphart (born in 1936 in Apeldoorn, The Netherlands) described the political system of The Netherlands as a consociational democracy. In his book *The Politics of Accommodation: Pluralism and Democracy in The Netherlands* (Berkeley/Los Angeles: University of California Press, 1968) he gave an in-depth portrait of a classical case of consociationalism. In 1984, in his book *Democracies* he developed the concept of consensus democracy, and in 1999 he published his *Patterns of Democracy* (New Haven/London: Yale University Press), systematizing and enlarging his analyses on consensus democracy. Arend Lijphart is Research Professor of Political Science at the University of California, San Diego.

In 1967, Gerhard Lehmbruch (born in 1928), a German political scientist, published 'Proporzdemokratie. Politisches System und politische Kultur in der Schweiz und Österreich', applying the concept of 'Konkordanz-' or 'Proporzdemokratie' (the Swiss and Austrian term for consociational democracy) to these two countries. A paper in English relating to the findings of 'Proporzdemokratie', 'A Non-Competitive Pattern of Conflict Management in Liberal democracies: The Case of Switzerland, Austria and Lebanon', was originally presented at a conference in 1967 and reprinted in Kenneth McRae (ed.): *Consociational Democracy: Conflict Accommodation in Segmented Societies* (Toronto: McClelland & Stewart, 1974). In addition to the debate on consociational democracy, Lehmbruch has contributed to the discovery of corporatism, too. The seminal papers 'Consociational Democracy, Class Conflict and the New Corporatism' and 'Liberal Corporatism and Party Government' have been published in an edited volume *Trends Towards Corporatist Intermediation* (Philippe C. Schmitter and Gerhard Lehmbruch, eds. Beverly Hills/London: Sage, 1979). Before retiring, Lehmbruch was Professor of Political Science at the University of Constance.

Together with Lehmbruch, Philippe C. Schmitter (born in 1936), working at universities in the USA, has been among the first to analyse corporatism in the OECD world. His articles 'Still the Century of Corporatism' and 'Modes of Interest Intermediation and Models of Societal Change in Western Europe' are milestones in the debate on corporatism. Both essays can be found in *Trends Towards Corporatist Intermediation*. More policy-orientated, another major volume on corporatism, edited by Schmitter and Lehmbruch, appeared in 1982: *Patterns of Corporatist Policy-Making*. Currently Schmitter works at the European University Institute in Florence.

7.3 CONSOCIATIONAL AND CONSENSUS DEMOCRACIES: DEFINITIONS AND DATA

Gerhard Lehmbruch defined consociational democracy as a non-competitive pattern of conflict management in liberal democracies (Lehmbruch, 1974), major examples being Austria, Switzerland and The Netherlands. In contrast, the political systems of the United States of America and of the United Kingdom correspond to the model of a competitive or majoritarian democracy (see Figure 7.1). According to Lijphart (Lijphart, 1968, 1997; cf. Bogaards, 1998) a consociational democracy is marked by four major characteristics, with grand coalition and autonomy of the segments (i.e. pillars, lager, etc.) being the major elements. The rule of proportionality and veto rights of the minorities are the other two, albeit secondary elements. The implications of these characteristics are rules of the consociational game, guiding according to Arend Lijphart (1968: 122–38) the behaviour of Dutch elites:

1. Politics is a serious business, doctrinal disputes should not stand in the way of getting the work done. It is actually not a game – with tactics of delay, equivocation and avoidance of responsibility, regardless of the consequences for the nation.
2. Pragmatic acceptance of ideological differences as basic realities which cannot and should not be contested.
3. Government by the elites of the various pillars facilitating compromises.
4. Proportional distribution of resources and power to the various societal segments.
5. Potentially divisive political disputes have to be neutralized but the compromises have to be justified *vis-à-vis* the rank and file. This is brought about by means of 'depoliticization'. For instance, governments rely on expert judgements in economic affairs or the resort to legal and constitutional principles.
6. In order to have a high degree of flexibility in the elite bargains, secrecy is a major precondition. Secrecy allows for moves in negotiations and compromises even if religious or ideological values are at stake.
7. In order to have the job done, the cabinet must have the right to govern and the parties involved are not expected to conduct a rigorous opposition in parliament. This does not exclude critique or challenge, but only with decent and polite restraints, not upsetting the delicate balance of power.

Using the criteria of Lehmbruch and Lijphart, The Netherlands, Belgium, Switzerland, Luxembourg and Austria have been examples of consociational democracies in Europe; Germany, Denmark, Finland and Italy can be classified as being a mixture of consociational and competitive systems, while the other Western European countries, Japan and the Anglo-Saxon countries belong to the group of Westminster democracies (Schmidt, 1997: 235; see also Table 8.2 in this book). However, in most consociational democracies changes have occurred which put into doubt their classification at present. The major example is The Netherlands. During the mid-1960s the pillars gradually lost their societal foothold and 'roots' (Daalder, 1995). Denomination and ideology ceased to be impermeable boundaries between the various groups of Dutch society. Hence The Netherlands moved away from the consociational pattern without having yet become a typical majoritarian democracy. In international comparison, for example with New Zealand, the persisting difference in style clearly remains obvious. On these grounds, another operationalization – or a changed concept amenable to operationalization – has been sought, which allows more precise measurement for international and intertemporal comparisons. In his book on Democracies, Arend Lijphart (1984) replaced the term consociational democracy by *consensus democracy*. In his analysis of *Patterns of Democracy. Government Forms and Performance in Thirty-Six Countries* (Lijphart, 1999) the analysis was substantially revised and extended to 36 democracies.

Consensus democracy can be measured more rigorously than consociational democracy. However, consensus democracy is not the same as consociational democracy. It is rather focusing on the *preconditions* of consociational democracy. Once these preconditions are met, the style of politics is not yet necessarily consociational. The major advantage of Lijphart's recent procedure is the more precise and transparent measurement. The major disadvantage is the addition of various important aspects into one indicator. Depending on the aspects selected and their operationalization, the results vary considerably. To give an example: Austria has been classified as a majoritarian democracy according to the former operationalization (Lijphart, 1984); the recent re-calculation moved it into the group of consensus democracies (Lijphart, 1999). In addition the question comes up, whether or not there are too many different aspects combined into one single index, ranging from the number of parties to the type of the relationship of voluntary associations and state or ranging from central bank independence to an index of federalism (Schmidt, 1997: 249). According to Lijphart consensus democracy consists of two dimensions: an *executive-parties and a federal-unitary* dimension. In Table 7.1, items 1–5, make up the executive-parties dimension, items 6–10 the federal-unitary dimension. The former dimension might be labelled the dimension of sharing power or of joint responsibility and joint power. The latter dimension concerns the division or temperance of power due to the distribution of power to various institutions; i.e. divided power (Lijphart, 1999: 5).

Empirically the most important challenge is to what extent the relationship between the executive-parties dimension and the federal-unitary dimension is apparent or not. For, being two separate dimensions, they are in principle unrelated. The first dimension (shared power/responsibility) is closer to the concept of consociational democracy than is the second. The index on the 'division of power' has more resemblance to the idea of number of veto points (Immergut, 1992), of checks and balances, or to the index of constitutional structures (Huber et al., 1993) or the index of constraints of central state government that is discussed in Chapter 8 of this book.

Table 7.1 *Majoritarian and consensus democracy – concepts and indicators*

Majoritarian democracy	Consensus democracy	Indicator
Dimension 1: Joint power/responsibility or 'executive-parties'		
1. Concentration of executive power: one-party and bare-majority cabinets	1. Executive power-sharing: grand coalitions	1. Proportion of time during which minimal winning cabinets and one-party cabinets were in power
2. Dominance of executive over legislative	2. Balance of executive and legislative	2. Executive dominance: average cabinet durability
3. Two-party system	3. Multiparty system	3. Effective number of parties: Laakso/ Taagepera-index
4. Majoritarian and disproportional electoral system	4. Proportional representation	4. Difference between vote and seat shares of parties, aggregated according to Gallagher's index of disproportionality
5. Pluralist interest group system with free-for-all competition among groups	5. Co-ordinated and 'corporatist' interest group system aimed at compromise and concentration	5. Extent of interest group pluralism. Siaroff index
Dimension 2: Divided power or federal-unitary dimension		
6. Unitary and centralized government	6. Federal and decentralized government	6. Index of degree of federalism and decentralization
7. Concentration of legislative power in a unicameral legislature	7. Division of legislative power between two equally strong but differently constituted houses	7. Index of bicameralism
8. Flexible constitutions that can be amended by simple majorities	8. Constitutions that can be changed only by extraordinary majorities	8. Index of constitutional rigidity
9. Systems in which legislatures have the final word on the constitutionality of their own legislation	9. Systems in which laws are subject to a judicial review of their constitutionality by supreme or constitutional courts	9. Index of the strength of judicial review
10. Central banks that are dependent on the executive	10. Independent central banks	10. Mean of three indices of central bank independence

Source: Lijphart (1999).

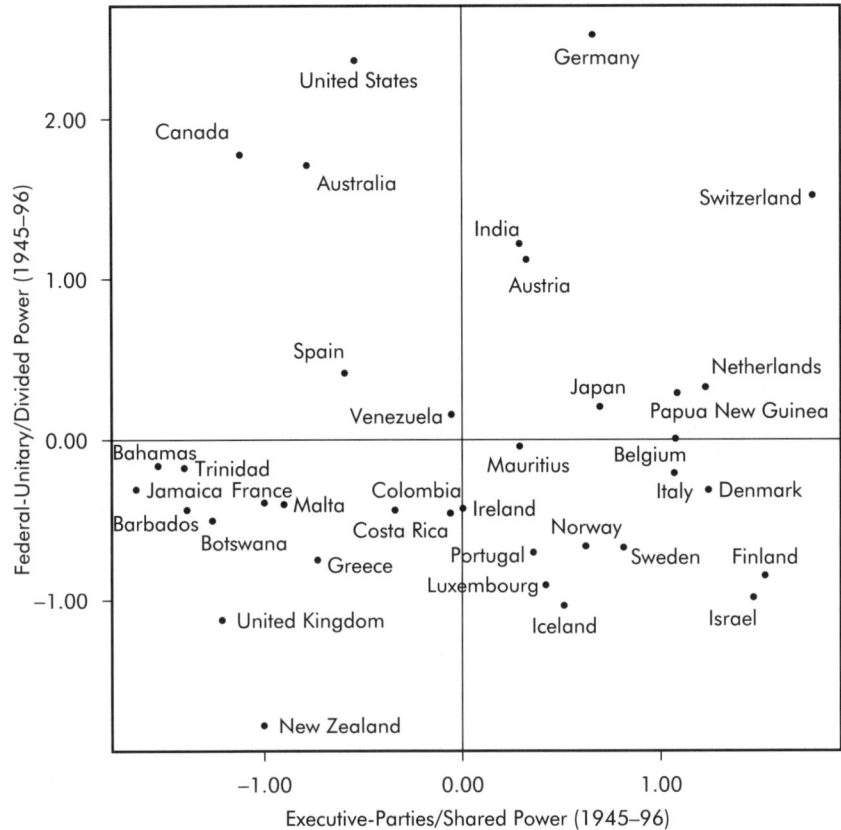

Figure 7.2 *Empirical location of 36 countries according to Lijphart's dimensions of consensus democracy. Source: Lijphart (1999)*

Lijphart (1999) calculated an index for each of the dimensions, representing the sum of the values of the variables in each dimension[1] listed in Table 7.1. The distribution of the 36 countries for 1945–96 over the two dimensions is shown in Figure 7.2. This demonstrates that indeed the countries originally classified as consociational democracies are clustered in the upper right-hand cell, which denotes strong preconditions for consensus formation and institutional devices promoting a division of power within the polity. The other countries in this cell are either federal systems (where powers are constitutionally divided) or 'new' democracies. Apart from France, Greece and the UK there are no European democracies in the cells on the left. Hence, apart from some 'new' democracies, almost all 'negotiation democracies' appear to be geographically located in Europe. Let us now turn to the empirical classifications of corporatism.

7.4 CORPORATISM CLASSIFIED: DEFINITIONS AND DATA

The debate on corporatism started with two different definitions focusing either on dimensions of policy-making or on institutional structures. Lehmbruch (1979) pointed to the concerted behaviour of private and public actors. For him corporatism is the voluntary co-operation of large interest groups and the state in formulating and implementing private and public policies. Schmitter however – like Lijphart in the case of consensus democracy – has been concerned with certain institutional characteristics, which differentiate pluralism and corporatism. His well-known definitions stated (Schmitter, 1979: 13, 15):

> *Corporatism* can be defined as a system of interest representation in which the constituent units are organized into a limited number of singular, compulsory, noncompetitive, hierarchically ordered and functionally differentiated categories, recognized or licensed (if not created) by the state and granted a deliberate representational monopoly within their respective categories in exchange for observing certain controls on their selection of leaders and articulation of demands and supports.
> *Pluralism* can be defined as a system of interest representation in which the constituent units are organized into an unspecified number of multiple, voluntary, competitive, nonhierarchically ordered and self-determined (as to type or scope of interest) categories which are not specially licensed, recognized, subsidized, created or otherwise controlled in leadership selection or interest articulation by the state and which do not exercise a monopoly of representational activity within their respective categories.

The underlying rationale for the institutional definition of corporatism and pluralism were constraints of both sides of the corporatist agreement. The state needs to have a limited number of private actors with which it will come to terms. And in order to make the agreement work, these private actors must be able to oblige their members to adhere to the agreement. Seen from the point of interest associations, the main problem is that they are at the same time representatives of a societal interest and of the state. Hence they are intermediaries which need organizational securities since they deliver collective goods and cannot attract members purely on the basis of collective-egoistic strategies. From this point of view, centralized, encompassing interest organizations with a large number of organizational securities (e.g. closed shop rules) or incentives (e.g. tax deductibility of membership fees) are a crucial pre-condition for corporatism (Olson, 1965).

In a seminal study book Peter Katzenstein (1985) introduced another differentiation. He made the point that small, economically open European states have to cope with the challenges created by the world market. Corporatism is a major means of achieving this adjustment to external change. It is based on the ideology of *social partnership*, a highly centralized system of interest representation made up a few large associations and a voluntary and informal co-ordination of these private actors and the state.

Although in some countries trade unions are weak, employers' associations are strong and the state is rather reluctant to be involved in settling societal conflicts and redistributing resources, there is a strong tradition of social partnership and co-operation. Switzerland is a good example. These are cases of liberal corporatism. In contrast, social corporatism denotes a system of interest representation with strong unions, weak employers' organizations and a redistributing state, as for example in Austria.

Finally, various corporatisms have been identified. The beginning of the debate of corporatism took place at a time when most governments have used techniques of macro-economic steering for some years. Hence the major examples for corporatist concertation stemmed from macro-economic policy making, in particular the co-ordination of trade union wage policy, employers' pricing policy and employment strategies and governmental fiscal policy, including tax and social policy (Armingeon, 1983). The main question therefore is related to the conditions under which trade unions were willing to restrain wages in the context of Keynesian demand management. This made the initial discussion blind for two aspects. The first concerns the level of co-ordination. Focusing on the macro-level, co-ordination at the meso-(branch) or micro-level (meso-corporatism) has been neglected to a large extent (cf. Williamson, 1989). Secondly, rather early in the debate it seemed as if trade unions were the Achilles' heel in the context of co-ordinating wage, price stability and social policy. This, however, did not apply once more under conditions of high levels of unemployment and economic policies oriented more towards the supply side. In these circumstances employers appear to become the crucial variable to understand the viability of corporatist bargaining (Streeck, 1984).

Apart from these caveats different meanings given to corporatism led to different operationalizations. For a recent survey and assessment see Kenworthy, 2000. Some considered the institutional make-up of the system of interest intermediation following the definition by Schmitter. Others focused more on the extent of concertation, like Lehmbruch. While for a long time all the indexes have been time invariant, Hugh Compston (1994, 1995a, 1995b, 1997) created an index which was calculated on an annual basis for 1970–93. It measured the extent of union participation in economic policy-making, thereby excluding the co-ordination of wage policy. Armingeon (1999b) and Traxler (1999) classified countries by periods. Lijphart and Crépaz (1991) proposed a pragmatic summary measure of all corporatism-indexes by simply adding up the standardized values of 12 separate indexes. Alan Siaroff (1999) repeated this procedure on the basis of 23 indices found in the literature. Like Lijphart and Crepaz he identified a group of countries which are considered to be highly corporatist (Austria, Norway, Sweden), a moderately corporatist group (Netherlands, Denmark, West Germany) and a group of non-corporatist countries (USA, Canada, New Zealand, Australia, United Kingdom, Italy, Ireland). A fourth group could not be classified at all, because the variation between the scores by different researchers is very high: Switzerland, France and Japan. The deviation is caused by classifying

Switzerland and Japan as 'strong corporatism' in the sense of co-operation between government and business without labour. Other researchers focus on membership strength and organizational structure of the labour movements in these countries. Consequently they arrive at the conclusion that in Switzerland and Japan there is no corporatism, because of missing institutional preconditions.

Siaroff (1999) tried to solve the problem by calculating an indicator of 'integration'. This would imply a long-term co-operative pattern of shared economic management involving the social partners and existing at various levels such as plant-level management, sectoral wage bargaining, and joint sharing of national policies in competitiveness-related matters (education, social policy etc.). This definition is not too far away from that of corporatism in the sense of concertation, although the actual operationalization includes institutional characteristics as well. Siaroff's additive measure is composed of eight variables belonging to three groups:

1. indicators of social partnership (strike level, nature and goals of trade unions, legal and state support for unions and union power);
2. indicators of industry-level co-ordination (nature of economic ties and outlook of firms; extent of co-determination in the workplace);
3. indicators of overall national policy-making patterns (nature of conflict resolution in national industrial adjustment and wage policy; extent of generalized political exchange in industrial relations and national policy making and general nature of public–private interaction).

The major weakness of Siaroff's approach is the apparent random selection of some items and their addition, i.e. giving each item the same weight. Yet, his index makes sense with regard to corporatism defined as concertation. In addition there is a substantial overlap of Siaroff's results with those of experts in the field, and finally the author is able to produce a time series of the extent of integration. This last point is quite important since most other indexes reflect the extent of corporatism in a country at a given point of time. Research has shown in the meantime that different periods produce quite different statistical evidence regarding the impact of corporatism (see: Keman, 1993b).

What immediately strikes the eye in Table 7.2 is that – notwithstanding the different operationalizations – most students of corporatism are in agreement. Actually – as has been shown by Keman and Pennings (1995) – most indices of corporatism are highly inter-correlated. Another observation to make is – as with consensus democracy – that there appears to be a geographic, if not regional, concentration of democracies that show corporatist features of interest intermediation: continental North Western Europe. Logically this brings up the question to what extent these two types of 'negotiation democracy' are perhaps – as Lijphart (1999) argues – two sides of the same coin?

Table 7.2 *Indices of corporatism*

Country	Schmitter's corporatism scale	Lehmbruch's corporatism scale	Corporatism scores (scale, combining the measures of 23 separate scales) combined measure		Integration scores (Siaroff's scale)			
			mean	std dev.	late 1960s	late 1970s	late 1980s	late 1990s
Austria	5	5	5.000	0.000	4.625	4.625	4.625	4.625
Norway	5	5	4.864	– 0.351	4.625	4.625	4.625	4.625
Sweden	4	5	4.674	– 0.556	4.750	4.750	4.625	4.625
Netherlands	4	5	4.000	– 0.989	4.250	3.875	4.000	4.000
Denmark	4	3	3.545	– 0.999	4.375	4.375	3.875	4.250
(West) Germany	3	3	3.543	– 0.940	4.125	4.125	4.125	4.125
Switzerland	3	2.5	3.375	– 1.286	4.125	4.125	4.125	4.125
Finland	4	3	3.295	– 1.043	3.500	4.250	4.250	4.375
Iceland	–	–	3.000	0.000	2.750	2.750	2.750	2.875
Israel	–	–	3.000	0.000	4.500	4.250	3.500	3.500
Luxembourg	–	–	3.000	0.000	4.000	4.250	4.125	4.125
Japan	–	Corporatism without labour	2.912	– 1.603	3.375	3.375	3.625	3.625
Belgium	3	3	2.841	– 0.793	4.125	4.125	3.625	3.750
Ireland	2	3	2.000	– 1.015	2.250	2.250	2.375	2.625
New Zealand	–	1	1.955	– 0.907	2.375	2.375	2.125	2.375
Australia	–	1	1.680	– 0.873	2.500	2.500	3.375	3.000
France	1	Corporatism without labour	1.674	– 0.792	1.875	1.875	2.250	2.250
United Kingdom	1	2	1.652	– 0.818	2.000	2.125	1.750	2.000
Portugal	–	–	1.500	– 1.000	NA	NA	2.375	2.375
Italy	1	2	1.477	– 0.748	2.000	2.125	2.750	3.000
Spain	–	–	1.250	– 0.500	NA	NA	1.875	2.000
Canada	2	1	1.150	– 0.489	1.625	1.625	1.750	1.875
United States	2	1	1.150	– 0.489	1.750	1.750	2.125	2.125
Greece	–	–	1.000	0.000	NA	NA	1.625	2.000
Mean			2.648		3.321	3.351	3.188	3.271
Std dev.			1.234		1.133	1.122	1.048	0.995

Note: Schmitter's corporatism scale: Social corporatism ranking compressed into a five-point scale (5: strong corporatism) (Schmitter, 1981: 294).

Lehmbruch's corporatism scale: A cumulative scale of corporatism: 5 = strong, 3 = medium, 2 = weak, 1 = pluralism, with Japan and France separately listed as corporatism without labour (Lehmbruch, 1984: 66).

Combined scale: Calculated by Alan Siaroff (1999: 184–5) as the arithmetic mean of stan-dardized scores of 23 corporatism scales of different researchers and research groups. The standard deviation indicates the extent to which the judgements and rankings by scholars vary. For example, Austria is unanimously classified as a case of strong corporatism, whilst in the case of Japan different scholars reach very different conclusions about the strength of corporatism in that country.

Siaroff's scale. Developed by Allan Siaroff (1999: 190–4). It is the arithemtic mean of the standardized scores of eight separate indicators: (1) Annual average level of strike volume, (2) nature and goals of trade unions, running from reformist to revolutionary-confrontational,

(Continued)

Table 7.2 *Continued*

(3) legal and state support for unions and union power, running from full support to only the basic rights of existence, (4) nature of economic ties and outlooks of firms, running from co-ordinated market economy to non-co-ordinated market economy, (5) extent of co-determination in the workplace, (6) nature of conflict resolution in national industrial adjustment and wage setting, running from bargained or networked to statist, with the state often imposing policies, (7) extent of generalized political exchange in industrial relations and national policy-making, running from extensive, both at the sectoral and the national level to none, (8) general nature of public–private interaction, running from concordance to pluralism.

Source: Siaroff (1999); NA = not available (during these periods).
5 = strong corporatism; 1 = no corporatism.
NB: the countries are rank-ordered.

7.5 CORPORATISM AND CONSOCIATIONALISM: IS IT NEARLY THE SAME?

The national values in Table 7.3 and Figure 7.2 are clustered: Consociational democracies tend to be corporatist (cf. Austria or The Netherlands), and Westminster democracies tend not to have corporatist structures (UK, USA, New Zealand). Lijphart and Crepaz (1991) argue therefore that corporatism is an element in the set of characteristics that make up consensus democracy, because of the conceptual affinity of corporatism with the executive-parties dimension of consensus democracy. Hence Lijphart (1999) has included corporatism (measured in the sense of integrated economies) as part of consensual democracy. Several criticisms were launched against this conceptual fusion. Lane and Ersson (1997) marshalled data and correlations demonstrating that the link is weak; Keman and Pennings (1995) pointed to missing correlations and, probably more important, to a missing theoretical link: the heartland of corporatism is Scandinavian, where strong left-wing parties and strong trade unions were conducive to trade union incorporation; while the heartland of consensus-democracy comprises politically-fragmented countries with weak or organizationally fragmented trade unions and relatively weak social democratic parties – for example The Netherlands, Belgium or Switzerland.

Obviously there are different ways of integrating interest organizations and political groups: in half of the countries under consideration majority rule dominates in the horizontal dimension (executive-parties) with concertation and compromise also missing in the vertical dimensions (state-interest groups). In Scandinavia and Japan, co-ordination among interest groups and state is much stronger than among political parties. Finally, in the continental countries – particularly in the smaller ones – accommodation is dominant in both dimensions. Gerhard Lehmbruch (1993, 1996, 1999) made the point that the common occurrence of corporatism and consociational democracy in West European countries has long historical roots, going back to the settlement of the denominational wars in the seventeenth century, e.g. the peace treaty of Westphalia in 1648 (see also: Daalder, 1995). This treaty established

Table 7.3 *Cross-tabulation of pluralism/corporatism with majoritarian/ consociational democracy*

	Pluralist	Corporatist
Majoritarian democracy	Australia, France, Greece, United Kingdom, Ireland, Iceland, Canada, New Zealand, Portugal, Spain, USA	Japan, Norway, Sweden
Hybrid cases of majoritarian and consociational democracy		(West) Germany, Denmark, Finland
Consociational democracy		Austria, Belgium, Luxembourg, Netherlands, Switzerland

Note: Pluralist/corporatist: Siaroff (1999); Integration scores mid–late-1990s, dichotomized by the arithmetic mean. Majoritarian, hybrid, consociational democracy: Schmidt (1997: 235).

the idea of avoiding majority rule in cases of deep societal cleavages, such as those created by denominational difference. It was in Western Europe that this notion of parity and negotiated agreement instead of majority decision became established as the dominant technique of conflict regulation. Thereafter, political elites extended this technique, acquired in their political socialization, to other fields where conflicts have to be regulated. In contrast, one could add, following Lehmbruch, that in Scandinavia the inclusion of unions into the political system is not due to a political culture of accommodation but to the strength and power of the Left in parliament and in working life, making union incorporation one strategy to pursue class interests (without much intention to compromise) in the political field (cf. Korpi, 1983). In some countries – the United States of America being a prime example – neither do the political elites use parity and compromise as the established routine procedure of conflict regulation nor is the Left strong enough to be successful in the democratic class struggle. In summary: corporatism and consociationalism are *not* nearly the same. They occur together under specific structural and historical circumstances.

7.6 RISE AND DECLINE OF CONSOCIATIONALISM AND CORPORATISM

Arend Lijphart described the rise of Dutch consociational democracy in his book on accommodation in The Netherlands (Lijphart, 1968). Seven years later, he declared Dutch consociational democracy dead, and another 13 years later he discovered that changes has been limited and that Dutch consensus democracy was still alive (Lijphart, 1989). In a similar vein, Philippe Schmitter declared the rise of European corporatism in the mid 1970s, its death in the late 1980s, and discovered its viability in 1997 (Schmitter and

Grote, 1997). Both authors point to substantial modifications which occurred over the past decades, though. However, recent quantitative analyses arrive at the conclusion of considerable stability, both with regard to consociational democracy as well as with regard to corporatism (see in addition to Siaroff, 1999; Lijphart, 1989, 1999; Schmidt, 1996a; Pennings, 1997a: 35; Traxler, 1992, 1995, 1998, 1999; for a dissenting view on the endurance of consociational democracy, see Kriesi, 1995: 311–32). This raises the questions as to the explanations which have been proposed for explaining rise, decline and resurgence of these institutions of interest intermediation.

The first explanation for the rise of consociational democracy is *functional*: in deeply fragmented societies a stable democratic order can only be established if majority rule is replaced by compromise, including all the major minorities. Applying the majority rule leads either to non-decision (since there is no majority at all) or to the suppression of minorities. These groups never have the chance to become a majority but they are large enough or geographically concentrated in such a way that they can challenge the continuation of the present system by internal strife. Basically it was that constellation of problems which led John Stuart Mill (cf. Lijphart, 1996: 258) to assume that democracy is not possible in segmented societies. Seen in that perspective, 'negotiation democracy' best fits segmented societies which do not have an alternative and reasonable choice but to introduce and sustain the rule of compromise. This leaves the question unanswered, why in some nations existing cleavages did not lead to consociational democracy. Why could, for example, multilingual Canada or Finland afford not to be fully consensual and why is there no consociational democracy in Norway with its strong regional conflicts? What type and strength of conflicts make consociational democracy uncircumventable? Obviously the functional needs are not too powerful, considering the cases of Switzerland or The Netherlands, where consociationalism was upheld although ever since the 1920s denominational conflicts were far from being in danger of escalating into civil war or devolution.

In addition to this functional argument, Lijphart (1968) put forward a *voluntaristic* explanation. At a certain point of time, a critical juncture, elites in segmented societies decided to set up the new consociational mode. However, this raises the question why other elites in comparable circumstances did not make that decision. Lehmbruch (1996) argues that the road to compromise can be taken more easily if elites have acquired techniques of compromise before – for example after historical settlements of denominational conflicts (see also: Daalder, 1966). The major question in this regard relates to the problem of how to prove the existence and strength of this chain from historical conflicts to standard operating procedures and then to the full institutionalization of consociational democracy.

A third argument points to institutions. For example the introduction of direct democracy – that is, referendums – forces elites to compromise if they do not want to risk being defeated in a popular vote due to mobilization of a neglected minority (Neidhart, 1970; Linder, 1994: Ch. 3).

Finally one could argue that elites have made a strategic choice since accommodation was the best rational solution to keep the peace and the power. A critical argument reverses the temporal connection: the elites have decided to introduce the system of compromise and consequentially they formed society in a pillarized way (Keman, 1999). Another critical argument assumes that indeed power corrupts: the leaders of the suppressed minorities become integrated into the governing circles and since they want to stay in the privileged position, they are willing to sacrifice the interests of their constituencies.

The explanations for the *decline* of consociational democracy mostly argue that the reasons for its rise have ceased to exist. Either the former conflicts have disappeared due to the process of secularization and modernization – like denominational conflicts – or the long-run effects of consociational regimes reduce the felt conflicts between the segments of theory (Steiner, 1999, pursuing an idea suggested by Philippe Schmitter). In this perspective consensus democracy loses its basis and it is only a question of time until the institutions fade away. At present it is hardly controversial to put forward that the constitutive conflicts of consociational democracies have to a large extent indeed vanished and that at the same time the institutional superstructure continues to exist. This can be explained by (a) institutional inertia, (b) non-conflictual political culture of elites, which persists although its historic basis has ceased to exist and (c) the replacement of old cleavages (e.g. denomination) by new or stronger cleavages (e.g. the regional-linguistic conflicts in Belgium or Switzerland).

The rise of *corporatism* has also been linked to various factors. On the one hand, it is argued that small economies exposed to the world market are vulnerable and cannot afford internal industrial conflict, and thus compromise is sought (Katzenstein, 1985). A second explanation points to the change from the regulatory role of the state to increased fiscal public intervention in order to steer the economy and to redistribute resources in the framework of the welfare state. Thirdly, the rise of corporatism is interwoven with the rise of Keynesian demand management, which makes government dependent on co-ordinated wage and price movements. Fourthly, corporatism correlates with left power. Trade unions are willing to join the round table once they trust that government will keep its promises. Alternatively, trade unions gain access to the state if the government institutionalizes this type of incorporation. A fifth reason might be an economic calculus. Labour unions trade off wage moderation to organizational securities and social and tax policies. This presupposes that government is capable of making such policies. In addition, it is argued that trade unions have to be strong and centralized so that their incorporation and their pacification induces a positive spill-over effect, and, in return, can assume that the union elites will implement their part of the bi- or trilateral agreement (Keman, 1999). Finally, as in the case of consociational democracy, corruption by power is assumed. Trade union leaders become alienated from their members and corrupted by the contacts with other economic and political elites. Since they want to stay in the centre of power they are willing to compromise on the interests of their members. However, for this latter hypothesis and its analogy in the literature on consociational democracy there is little empirical evidence.

The assumed decline of corporatism since the mid-1970s has been explained by changed circumstances or dysfunctionalities (Armingeon, 1997; Lijphart, 1999: Ch. 9; Schmitter and Grote, 1997): Ironically, globalization which once was considered a major impetus for corporatism has now become its danger. Increased international economic competition forces national governments onto a path of convergences of economic policy making (cf. Cerny, 1999). Apparently nothing is left to them but neo-liberal policies. These are detrimental to corporatism, since they include deregulation and austerity. In addition, the rise of neo-liberalism leads to a different role of the state in economy and society, therewith lowering its need for assistance by interest groups. Whereas Keynesian demand management relied on trade union wage co-ordination, this idea increased international competition, and the change of paradigm of economic policy caused decline of corporatism. In addition, the Left has been on the retreat after the mid-1970s, implying reduced access of trade unions to the political system. Furthermore employers became less dependent on trade union co-operation since worsening labour market conditions caused wage moderation without making a 'quid pro quo' feasible. For trade unions an incentive for co-operation has disappeared because governments ceased to reward wage restraint by, for example, social and tax policies. Finally, the attachment of individuals to collective organizations has tended to erode, and trade unions suffered a major crisis of membership combined with a successful attack of employers on central or branch-level bargaining (Visser, 1990).

Notwithstanding these plausible arguments, corporatism did not fully disappear, and if it retreated in the 1980s it was on the way back again in the 1990s. This might be due to globalization enhancing the willingness to co-operate on the domestic level and a biased idea about the change from Keynesian to neo-liberal policy-making (Garrett, 1998; Armingeon, 1999b; Oatley, 1999). In addition, the thesis of the decline of Social Democracy has been falsified, and the trade union membership crisis has been most severe in countries where union density already has been low. In contrast, in the Scandinavian countries the organizational resources of trade unions hardly changed. In addition the demise of Keynes co-ordination did not necessarily mean a decline of corporatism. Rather the actors chose another mode of co-operation (see, for instance, the Dutch example, Visser and Hemerijck, 1997) or they shifted concertation to other policy fields (Traxler, 1995; Traxler et al., 2001). Taking into account that corporatism has contributed to rising public debts and deficits and – sometimes – to price increases, this restructuring can be interpreted as an adjustment due to the dysfunctionalities of the former mode of co-operation. It was hardly a retreat of interest associations from their former power position. On the contrary, experiences from Dutch and German economic policy-making indicate a persisting need for public/private actor co-operation which the modified welfare state at the end of the twentieth century continues to have.

7.7 THE PERSISTENCE AND EFFECTS OF NEGOTIATION DEMOCRACY

From our survey it follows that not only does negotiation democracy have a long history, but also that it is quite resilient, having a remarkable resistance to challenges.

1. In most consociational countries, conflict regulation by negotiation and inclusion of all relevant societal interest emerged long ago. In Switzerland the introduction of the legislative referendum in 1874 and the inclusion of a representative of the major contending party in the government in 1891 marked the consolidation of negotiation as the dominant means of conflict regulation. Historically however, negotiation instead of majority decision had already been implemented for a long time in a number of cantons (states) which were later united in the Swiss Federation, that was founded in 1848. In The Netherlands in 1917 an agreement on major political issues was reached, labelled 'pacificatie' (peaceful settlement), leading to the institutionalization of the politics of accommodation, which can be seen as the apex of a long development (Daalder, 1995). Belgium and Luxembourg have a long experience of co-operation between the elites of the various societal segments, whilst in Austria 'Proporzregierung' – the Austrian term for consociational democracy – was established only after the Second World War. The seeds of European corporatism have been laid – according to Colin Crouch (1993) and Gerhard Lehmbruch (1996) – during the transition to the modern state in the period between 1789 and 1918. In most Western countries major institutional steps towards corporatist regulation have been taken in the time span between the end of the First World War and the Second World War (Armingeon, 1994). A surge of corporatist practices happened in economic policy-making in the 1960s and 1970s.
2. Although 'negotiation democracy' has been challenged in numerous ways, it seems to be resilient. Longitudinal analyses by Pennings (1997a: 35) and by Lijphart (1999: 255) do not support the view of a general decline of consensus democracy. And time series data collected by Compston (1994, 1995a,b), Siaroff (1999), Armingeon (1999b) and Traxler (1999) point to a remarkable stability of corporatism – also in the 1990s. Hence in countries where 'negotiation democracy' emerged long ago and appears to continue to exist or – at least – leave its traits on the mode of policy-making in these countries in the years to come (see also: Steinmo et al., 1992; Woldendorp, 1997).

If our contention holds, one may well ask: *Does it matter?* What difference do consociational democracy and corporatism make? A naive liberal view would arrive at the conclusion that both modes of interest intermediation are inferior to majoritarian or pluralist regimes. In this perspective the Achilles heel of negotiation democracy is the large number of actors involved whose interests have to be respected. This should lead to political systems with locked decision-making when government action is urgently needed and it should lead to over-regulated (labour) markets incapable of performing as well as free markets supposedly do.

Empirical research, however, cast serious doubts on these assumptions, although they do not arrive at the conclusion that negotiation democracy is undoubtedly the superior system.[2] On average consociational democracies produce indeed certain disadvantages. The costs of decision-making are high, in particular in terms of time: building compromise takes time. Sometimes, it may not even be possible to reach agreement. In this case consociational systems may be struck. If compromise is reached, consistent or coherent policy concertation is often absent. Rather policies are a pragmatic combination of divergent strategies. These compromises usually are reached behind closed doors. This makes the whole decision process hardly transparent and can create democratic deficits. Minorities often have the option to veto certain policies, which may block a development which all the remaining actors consider to be necessary for the common good. Hence there is the danger of the *tyranny of minorities*. In addition, consociational democracies are often charaterized by an economy with limited dynamics and thus low growth rates.

The Swiss case is instructive. The political programme of a co-ordinated traffic policy took 22 years to be negotiated between the various actors – and in the final popular vote in 1988 it failed to be accepted (Hirter, 1988). 150 years after its inception, the federal state still lacks a constitutional basis for its fiscal capacities: the regulation of federal taxes still being temporary. Both examples indicate how policy-making in a consociational democracy can take up a great deal of time. The 'tyranny of the minority' is based – inter alia – on a rule applying to larger (constitutional) reforms. In order to warrant the interests of the population of small cantons, a double majority by the people and by the states ('Ständemehr') is needed. Under this rule, theoretically, 9 per cent of the population (the majorities in the smallest cantons) can veto a positive decision of the remaining 91 per cent. Empirically this has not occurred yet, but there have been cases when a fifth of the Swiss voters vetoed the affirmative decision of the other 80 per cent (Linder, 1994: 180–1). Although Switzerland is one of the wealthiest countries in the world (measured in GDP per capita), its productivity and economic growth lags behind. This supports the assumption that consociational democracy can be an impediment to economic growth (Armingeon, 1999a).

On the other hand, on average consociational democracies are politically stable democratic regimes in fragmented societies – a non-feasible combination according to John Stuart Mill. As assumed, they protect minorities, and political participation is often strong. Quality of democracy – measured in terms of comparative ratings – is better (see Chapter 3). Inequality between women and men and between high and low income groups is lower. More is spent on social security if compared with the whole OECD-world. Bargaining often leads to non-zero-sum games, i.e. solutions which are better than a simple redistribution. Also, these political systems are nevertheless capable of major political reform. This is independent of the electoral cycle, since electoral results do not change much in the composition and structure of the system of decision-making and politicians do not have to present policies in order to increase their chances of re-election. Whilst consociational democracies take much longer to reach a decision, they appear to be much better in policy implementation. This is by and large due to the inclusion of the relevant groups in the process of policy formulation. Hence the potential opposition in the course of implementation is taken into account and pacified in a rather early stage of policy development. Lengthy negotiations and discussions often lead to improvements and thorough policy formation. A 'tyranny of the majority' is not possible in negotiation democracies. The difference in political satisfaction between voters of losing and winning parties in national elections is lower in consociational democracies than in majoritarian regimes (Anderson and Guillory, 1997).

Of course, some of these findings are contested. For example although satisfaction with democracy is high in Switzerland – as expected – political participation is not comparatively high and equality of income is medium by international standards. Some findings reported by Lijphart (1999) for the sample of 36 consensus democracies might be influenced by the distribution of economically most advanced nations in the dimension of shared power and responsibility: 15 of the 23 OECD countries under consideration belong to the group of consensus democracies (measured in terms of the shared power/responsibility dimension). Hence among the 19 consensus democracies the rich OECD nations are strongly over-represented. However, in an earlier study he was able to show that the positive correlation between consensus democracy and income and gender equality also holds in the OECD group (Lijphart, 1994; Birchfield and Crépaz, 1998). In his large sample (N = 36), Lijphart could not find systematic and significant correlation among economic variables such as inflation, unemployment and economic growth. In fact, for the OECD nations statistical evidence points to the ability of consociational democracies to hold down unemployment and inflation, while they seem to exert a negative impact on economic growth. In addition in this group of countries, consensus democracies tend to have higher level of public expenditures (see also Chapter 10 in this book) and higher levels of social security expenditures (Armingeon, 1996; Crépaz, 1996a; Pennings, 1997b; Schmidt, 2000: 239; Birchfield and Crépaz, 1998). For the most recent findings, see Lijphart and Armingeon, 2002.

The irony is that probably the strength of consensus democracy is the weakness of its majoritarian counterpart. In contrast to the smooth working of such an ideal-type political system, empirical cases of Westminster democracy often suffer from short-term orientation of politicians, superficial reactions to emerging problems, and a reduced capacity to solve problems and design encompassing policies with a time horizon longer than an electoral cycle. In that sense consociational democracy leads to more continuity and less disruption by means of electoral agendas regarding policy development (Pennings et al., 1999; Keman, 1993b).

Corporatist or integrated economies are in general superior to pluralist economies with regard to low unemployment, price stability, more income equality and industrial peace. No positive impact is discernible with regard to economic growth. In a recent study, the ability of national systems to cope with unemployment crises has been analysed. It turned out that corporatist and consociational systems are better in keeping the rise of unemployment under control in times when labour market conditions generally are worsening (Armingeon, 1999b; Woldendorp, 1995).

A particular strength of corporatism is the implementation of a policy package once it is agreed upon. This does not mean that no deviations from the initial plans occur. Rather, major opposition against a certain policy is tackled already when the strategies are designed. However, corporatism is not the undisputed mode of economic regulation. Some studies argue that its success is highly dependent on favourable circumstances – like a strong social democratic party in government (Woldendorp, 1997); others are not able to replicate the positive effects of the structure of collective bargaining on economic variables (OECD, 1997; Lane and Ersson, 1997: 23) or doubt the precision of the concept and the causal links between corporatist institutions and economic outcomes (Therborn, 1987b, 1992).

7.8 CONCLUSIONS

Democratic politics is the politics of government and opposition. And it is the result of interest group pressure on government. These are the notions of majoritarian democracy and of the group theory of politics. Both notions depend on preconditions which cannot be taken for granted. They presuppose a society which is so homogenous that two political parties are sufficient to represent the interests of the people. However, the populations of many nations are split along several lines of conflict such as religion, class, language and region and divided into a larger number of distinct groups. In most cases, none of these societal segments is able to build a majority in the political system. In all cases, minorities are too large to ignore their interests. In addition, the notion of competitive and pluralist democracy presupposes that government does not incorporate private organizations for public goals. However, governments are inclined or often are dependent on support of interest groups when, in the process of policy-making, expertise is needed and when, in the process of policy-making, co-operation and compliance are needed. In turn interest associations can take advantage of public support in the consolidation of membership and organization. *Negotiation democracy* is an institutional response to the non-fulfilment of the requirements of competitive and pluralist democracy. Negotiation democracy is characterized in the realm of the state in relation to interest representation by means of corporatism. With respect to political actors and related organizations it exemplifies consociational democracy. Finally, *consensus democracy* denotes an institutional set-up, being a precondition for consociational democracy without being necessarily identical with it. The conclusion must therefore be that negotiation democracy has a number of advantages. It appears not to be inferior to majoritarian democracy in governing the economy or in creating a society where women and minorities get a fair share. On the other hand, negotiation democracy has a number of disadvantages. Frequently it is slow and cumbersome, prone to deadlock and joint decision traps. Often the democratic process is not transparent and has an 'elitist' flavour. But even if the political elite, frustrated by experiences from the given system, were to opt for the alternative model of democracy/state-interest-group relation, this is hardly feasible. Nations are on a historic-institutional path which they cannot leave ad libitum. This might be one reason why the hypothesis of the decline of negotiation democracy is premature. It seems more likely therefore that it will stay with us in the years to come.

NOTES

1 Technically this is the standardized sum of the standardized values of each variable. This has to be done since variables were measured on quite different scales.
2 The following results are drawn from Keman (1997); Lijphart (1994, 1999: Chs 15 and 16); Schmidt (1997: 229–52; Birchfield and Crépaz, 1998); Armingeon (1996, 1999a, 1999b); Traxler (1998); OECD (1997); Pekkarinen and Pohjola (1992); Höpner (1997); Crépaz (1996a, 1996b); Siaroff (1999).

8

THE IMPACT OF POLITICAL PARTIES, CONSTITUTIONAL STRUCTURES AND VETO PLAYERS ON PUBLIC POLICY

Manfred G. Schmidt

8.1 DEMOCRATIC POLICY-MAKING

Democracy has been rightly praised for its comparative advantage over non-democratic political systems. But the worship must be qualified. It is not democracy *per se* which outperforms all other forms of government. It is 'established' or 'secure' democracy together with rule of law, effective protection of civic rights and a high level of welfare, such as in most democratic member countries of the Organization of Economic Co-operation and Development (OECD), which makes the major difference between relatively good government and all other forms of government (Schmidt, 2000: Part IV).

Take, for example, political equality or the guarantee of political and civic rights, such as political participation, accountability of political leaders and safeguarding of civil liberties (Freedom House, 1999), or legitimacy of a political order (Norris, 1999). In all these matters, established democracies are superior to 'fragile democracies' (Casper, 1995) and, even more so, to non-democratic regimes (Merkel, 1999; Schmidt, 2000). For example, established democracies offer more channels for political participation of their adult population than other regimes. Participation in 'secure' democracies comprises the election of political leaders (or of representative assemblies which choose the leaders) by the people and includes the possibility to vote incumbents out of office. Thus, it provides for change in government without shedding blood. The right of the citizens in a democracy to choose their political leaders generates, generally speaking, more accountability of the leaders *vis-à-vis* the public. Moreover, most established democracies outperform most non-democracies in most problem-solving activities. For example, the political process and policy-making in established democracies are more predictable than elsewhere. More predictability, or conversely, less uncertainty facilitates social and economic life of the citizens and reduces transaction costs for the economy. In other words: the extent of 'democraticness' of a society and the transparency of the relations between the democratic state and society enhances its public welfare (North, 1990; Keman, 1997a; Lijphart, 1999).

Why do established democracies outperform other political regimes? Theories of democracy suggest that four links between those who govern and those who are governed have been central. First, the right to vote of the adult population, including the have-nots, and a strategic position of the multitude on the electoral market, make its imperative to process the demand for political goods and services from majorities of the politically active population. Both institutions, democratic theory argues, have created a democratic market, in which preferences and votes are traded by political entrepreneurs and collective actors, such as parties and governments (Downs, 1957). Strong viable intermediating institutions between *demos* and government, which provide for interest articulation and interest aggregation, such as mass media, political parties and interest associations, are a second constituent part of the better performance of established democracies. Office seeking, policy pursuit and the effort to maintain political power on the part of political entrepreneurs is a third factor (Strøm, 1990; Pennings et al., 1999: Part III). A fourth mechanism resides in the discipline which the law, the constitution and judicial review impose upon legislators and the executive in a constitutional democracy. These institutions and their interaction have been conducive to a political process and a type of policy-making which resemble more than others the criteria of democracy defined in terms of 'government of the people, by the people [or representatives of the people – Manfred Schmidt] and for the people', to quote Abraham Lincoln's famous definition of 1863.

This chapter focuses attention on two of the mechanisms which have been central to the functioning of modern established democracies. First, it explores the role of parties in intermediating between *demos* and government through analysing the impact of political parties on public policy. Second, this chapter reports on the policy impact of the institutional context of incumbent and opposition parties, by focusing attention mainly on 'constitutional structures' (Huber et al., 1993) and 'veto players' (Tsebelis, 1995, 1999).

8.2 THE PARTIES-DO-MATTER HYPOTHESIS

According to the parties-do-matter hypothesis, or 'partisan theory' (Hibbs, 1992: 316), policy choices and policy outputs in constitutional democracies can be attributed to a sizeable extent to the party composition of government. According to this view, policy choices and policy outputs of a social democratic government, for example, differ from those of a liberal or conservative government. This hypothesis has been developed mainly in research on partisan effects in economic and social policy.[1] The parties-do-matter hypothesis is a stylized empirical theory of a democratic political market. Its proponents conceive of politics mainly as a market in which politicians and governments deliver policies in exchange for specific or generalized political demand and support from the voters. However, in contrast to most market theories, partisan theory is premised on the assumption that the nature of the democratic market varies from country to country due to the institutionalization of the democratic process. Therefore, the parties-do-matter hypothesis emphasizes a comparative approach to the study of political markets.

The major research field of partisan theory has been differences in public policy in economically advanced constitutional democracies in Europe, North America, Japan, Australia and New Zealand. In explaining these differences, the proponents of the parties-do-matter view have converged on seven key propositions on linkages between social constituencies, parties and policy:

1. Social constituencies of political parties in constitutional democracies have *distinctive preferences* and successfully feed the process of policy formation with these preferences.
2. Policy orientations of political parties broadly *mirror* the preferences of their *social constituencies*.
3. Political parties are *multi-goal* organizations. Their major goals are office-seeking as well as policy-pursuit.
4. Incumbent parties choose policies that are broadly *compatible* with office-seeking, policy-pursuit ambitions and the preferences of their social constituencies.
5. Governments are *capable* of implementing the policies that were chosen by the incumbent parties.
6. Regarding policy outputs, there exists a law-like tendency of partisan differences in public policy: cross-national variation, and within-nations differences, in public policy are significantly associated with – and, by inference, depend upon – *differences in the party composition of government*. Hence, a change in the party composition of government is associated with – and, by inference, causally related to – changes in policy choices and policy outputs.
7. Advanced partisan theory predicts partisan influence on policy in bivariate and multivariate *explanatory models of public policy differences,* controlling for alternative explanations, such as the distribution of power in parliament and in extra-parliamentary arenas, institutional arrangements, adaptation to changing environments, socio-economic circumstances and international interdependence, to mention only some of the variables.

8.3 MEASURING PARTY COMPOSITION OF GOVERNMENT AND FINDINGS FROM PARTIES-DO-MATTER THEORY

The proponents of the parties-do-matter hypothesis insist on precise operational definitions of their key variables. A prominent example is the measurement of partisan composition of government by the extent to which a particular party (or a specific family of parties) has participated in government (measured for example by the average percentage share of cabinet seats held over a specified period). Following this tradition, Table 8.1 arrays data on the long-term participation in office of four major families of parties in the

Table 8.1 *Participation of conservative, liberal, centre and social democratic parties in office in 23 OECD nations, 1950–2000*

Country	Conservative parties	Liberal parties	Centre parties	Social democratic parties	Others
Australia	68.75	0	0	31.25	0
Austria	0	1.42	36.73	56.62	5.23
Belgium	0	16.99	50.23	30.17	2.61
Canada	30.80	0	69.20	0	0
Denmark	13.80	26.10	3.53	54.52	2.05
Finland	10.32	11.80	32.66	29.96	15.26
France	27.33	17.73	13.07	18.83	23.04
Germany	0	17.40	53.43	24.74	4.43
Great Britain	67.98	0	0	30.25	1.77
Greece	42.72	10.02	0.83	29.37	17.06
Iceland	0	40.19	29.59	21.69	8.53
Ireland	67.10	0	19.88	10.80	2.22
Italy	0	7.09	63.29	21.61	8.01
Japan	96.92	0	0.08	1.90	1.10
Luxembourg	0	20.77	49.48	29.75	0
Netherlands	0	22.68	53.97	21.34	2.01
New Zealand	72.93	0	0.91	25.74	0.42
Norway	12.29	3.95	12.25	71.51	0
Portugal	0.30	22.88	2.23	13.10	61.49
Spain	7.51	0	11.15	24.10	57.24
Sweden	3.90	6.84	9.86	76.83	2.57
Switzerland	14.29	31.65	29.97	24.09	0
USA	54.90	0	45.10	0	0
Mean	26.4	11.2	25.6	27.8	9.0

Notes: Figures are cabinet seat shares in the period from 1 January, 1950 to 31 December, 2000. The data were collected on a daily basis. Classification of the political parties is based mainly on 'families' of parties (von Beyme, 1985), party programmes and policy orientations of the parties (see, for example, Kirchner, 1988; Schmidt, 1992a; Katz and Mair, 1992; Laver and Hunt, 1992; Ware, 1996). Data on cabinet seats were taken from various sources. Among these, the *Archiv der Gegewart* and Woldendoorp et al. (2000) deserve to receive first mention.
Column 1: name of country.
Column 2 ('Conservatives'): total share of cabinet seats of secular conservative parties, such as the British Conservative Party.
Column 3 ('Liberal'): parties of the tradition of West European political and economic liberalism. Classification is based mainly on Kirchner (1988: Appendix, pp. 479–503). The Canadian Liberal Party, though formally a member of the Liberal International, has been classified, following von Beyme (1985) and the data in Laver and Hunt (1992, Appendix B), as a centre-oriented party.
Column 4 ('Centre'): centre and centre-right parties (mainly Christian democratic parties or other members of the European People's Party (EPP), i.e. the Federation of Christian Democratic Parties in the European Community). Centre parties are parties of moderate social amelioration in a location to the left of conservative or conservative-neoliberal parties. See, for example, Veen (1983–94); Hanley (1994).
Column 5 ('Left'): social democratic parties (operationalized in terms of membership in Socialist International) and other leftist parties.
Column 6: Residual category.

second half of the twentieth century: secular conservative parties (such as the British Conservative Party), liberal parties (such as the German Free Democrats), religious centre parties (such as the Christian democratic parties) and social democratic parties as the major leftist tendency.

The data in Table 8.1 indicate a wide range of variation in the party composition of government in democratic OECD-nations. Three families of parties can pride themselves on a cabinet seats share of 25 per cent or more. These are the families of social democratic, secular conservative and Christian democratic (here classified as 'centre') parties. Significantly smaller is the proportion of cabinet seats gained by liberal parties, although the latter have held the reigns of power to an extent which exceeds their electoral strength by lengths.

Table 8.1 also reveals striking differences in the party composition of government across countries. Secular conservative parties, for example, have commanded a dominant position in government in Anglo-American democracies and Japan. In contrast to this, the Social Democratic parties' effort to gain portfolios has been most successful in some of the smaller states, above all in Sweden, Norway, Denmark and Austria. Large countries have mainly been governed by non-socialist political tendencies. Among these, centre or centre-right parties mainly of Christian democratic persuasion have been the major parties in office in continental Europe, for example in Germany, the Benelux countries and until 1993/94 also in Italy. In contrast to this, participation in government of the liberal family of parties is comparatively strong in the Benelux countries, Denmark, Germany, Iceland, Portugal and Switzerland.

The data in Table 8.1 indicate dramatic cross-national differences in the partisan composition of national governments. To what extent do these differences spill over to policy-making and policy outputs? This question has been controversially debated. According to one view, the room to manoeuvre available to incumbent parties is fairly small. In constitutional democracies the role of political parties in shaping public policy is typically severely defined by constitutional rules and constrained by the relative autonomy of social and economic life from political intervention. Thus, many areas of social and economic life in democratic states are not directly amenable to political manipulation. It is therefore unlikely that a political party, when in office, would be able to effectively control economic outcomes, such as rates of economic growth or rates of unemployment and inflation (Castles et al., 1987).

According to the parties-do-matter view, however, the leeway for political action in a democracy is sufficiently large to allow for significant policy differences between parties. A substantial body of scholarly work indeed shows that the hypothesis of partisan effects on public policy deserves to be extolled for its empirical quality. For example, partisan influence on public policy has been identified in cross-national studies. According to Edward Tufte (1978), for example, who follows closely the path created by Douglas Hibbs (1977), one needs basically two variables to explain a sizeable proportion of variation in policy outputs. The first is a left–right indicator of the party composition of government. According to Tufte, leftist parties are more inclined to spend more on social policy, equality and employment. The second key variable resides in the electoral calendar, which determines election-oriented policy-making. Add to this the evidence accumulated in Douglas Hibbs's studies (Hibbs, 1987a, 1987b, 1992, 1994). Hibbs argues that economic policy and also macroeconomic outcomes, such as the rate of unemployment and the rate of inflation, can largely be attributed to left–right differences in the party composition of government and choices of these governments. He further argues that leftist governments opt for, and achieve, full employment (albeit at the expense of higher inflation rates), while non-leftist governments emphasize the control of inflationary pressure (although at the expense of higher rates of unemployment). Consider also Cameron (1978), Sharpe and Newton (1984), Keman (1988), Castles (1982a, 1999), Schmidt (1998), who argue that leftist governments have been among the major determinants of the growth of big government. Add to this Budge and Keman (1990), Borchert (1995), and studies on the impact of the political-ideological centre of gravity on macroeconomic performance (Cusack, 1995), to cite a few examples. All these contributions are compatible with the hypothesis of partisan influence on public policy.

Evidence in support for this hypothesis can also be derived from comparing extreme cases, such as Sweden in periods of a national government led by the Swedish Social Democratic party, and market-oriented countries, such as the United States, where neither leftist nor Christian-democratic–centrist parties have played a major role (Pempel, 1982; Castles, 1989b; Olsson, 1990; Castles, 1993; Gould, 1993). The difference between Sweden's welfare statism and the more market- and company-led political economy in the USA, or Japan, exemplifies a broader pattern: large cross-national differences in the party composition of government are associated with very large differences in policy outputs (see also Castles, 1982b).

Furthermore, empirical studies of partisan effects on public policy have identified circumstances in which a large potential for radical policy change either in support of the right or in support of the left exists. There are, of course, facilitating circumstances for both political tendencies, such as high economic growth, low vulnerability of the economy, political stability, stable majority status, a divided opposition and a small number of veto players. Likewise, both rightist or leftist governments face difficult times if they find themselves confronted with an economic recession, high economic vulnerability, political instability, fragile majority status, a unified opposition and a large number of veto players. Moreover, parties of the right are faced with almost ideal circumstances if they act within the context of a centralized unitary state and if trade unions as well as the opposition parties are ideologically divided. Control over a centralized unitary state appears to be another central requirement of leftist governments. But in order to be successful in delivering the preferred policy, a leftist party in office also needs support from unions and quiescence of labour (Cameron, 1984). Moreover, leftist governments are faced with the requisite of successful concertation of economic policy, wage policy and monetary policy of the central bank in order to generate the desired macroeconomic outcomes, such as economic growth and employment growth (see, for example, Schmidt, 1982a; Cameron, 1984; Alvarez et al., 1991; Keman, 1993b). However, this requires a lower level of internationalization of finance markets and product markets than that of the late 1980s and 1990s (Scharpf, 1991, 1999; see, however, the dissenting position in Garrett, 1998).

A further finding in support of partisan theory deserves to be mentioned in this context. The dividing line between political parties differs from one policy area to the other. A classical division is the left–right difference in employment and labour market policy. It is to this difference that Hibbs' 'partisan theory' has focused attention. Employment in the public sector is also largely shaped by the difference between leftist and non-leftist parties. Government as an employer of last resort is typical for leftist parties, while it is opposed by centre, liberal and conservative parties. That these preferences have influenced policy on public employment, has been established in comparative studies on labour market policy (see, for example, Schmidt, 1987; Esping-Andersen, 1990; Sainsbury, 1994). Examples include the difference between the dramatic increase in public employment in Sweden in the 1960s and 1970s and the muted expansion, stagnation or even decrease of public employment in conservative- or liberal-dominated countries, such as Japan, Switzerland and the USA (OECD, 1997, 1999).

However, in countries in which the class cleavage coexists with religious or ethnic cleavages, the left–right difference does not dominate the party systems and voter alignments. For example, in most European nations the dividing line between supporters and opponents of the welfare state is more complex than the left–right difference. True: liberal and conservative parties are, in general, proponents of a 'lean welfare state'. But social democratic parties do not stand alone in supporting a strong welfare state. A pronounced pro-welfare state policy stance has also been adopted by Christian democratic parties (Van Kersbergen, 1995). It is largely for this reason that a major difference exists in social policy between nations in which Christian democratic parties and social democratic parties alternate in office, and nations in which liberal or conservative political tendencies hold the reigns of power (Esping-Andersen, 1990; Schmidt, 1998).

In contrast to the domain of social security issues, the dividing line in gender issues separates chiefly conservative and Christian democratic tendencies from social democratic, liberal and ecological parties. The latter group of parties demands higher levels of equality and strives for universal 'égalité des conditions' (de Tocqueville, 1990), including egalitarian gender relations. Conservative and Christian democratic parties, however, prefer more traditional family roles or more cautious moves away from gendered distributions of labour (Norris, 1987; Therborn, 1993; Schmidt, 1993b; Bussemaker and van Kersberger, 1999).

A fourth class of issues divides leftist parties and rightist ones alike, such as the issue of European integration in most Nordic countries and in the UK. This recent 'cleavage' tends to split parties that were dominant players and thus weakens their original relations with their social constituencies.

A fifth class of issues is marked by a dividing line between leftist parties on the one hand and centre and conservative parties on the other. Relevant examples include the public debt and budget deficits. For example, Wagschal's study of public debt ratios and budget deficits in OECD-nations in the 1960–92 period shows, that leftist parties in office opt for higher taxation and lower deficits, while non-leftist parties, in particular parties of centre and centre-rightist persuasion as well as some of the conservative parties, have tended to choose lower taxation loads, possibly at the cost of higher deficits (Wagschal, 1996).

Support for a moderate version of the parties-do-matter hypothesis comes also from studies in a wide variety of policy areas in Germany (Schmidt, 1980, 1992b). Without downgrading the impact of other political and economic determinants, it can be concluded from these studies that the hypothesis of partisan influence on public policy passes the empirical test reasonably well. Public policy inheritance may be statistically more important than policy choices at timepoint t (Rose and Davies, 1984). Yet, policy inheritance itself is largely a product of decisions taken in the past. Furthermore, acceptance or rejection of the inheritance is the product of political choices at timepoint t. Among the determinants of these choices, the party composition of government must be counted as a major variable.

8.4 INCUMBENT PARTIES, CONSTITUTIONAL STRUCTURE AND VETO PLAYERS

The hypothesis of partisan influences is an important analytical tool for a better understanding of public policy commonalities and differences over time and between democratic nations. Compared with many other hypotheses in the public policy literature, it can be regarded as a relatively successful candidate, notwithstanding the caveats that must be mentioned.

The *first* caveat resides in the truism that the political composition of government is only one variable among a wide variety of determinants of public policy. The parties-do-matter view is, thus, just one approach to the comparative study of policy outputs among other theories. Five alternative approaches have frequently been applied to the comparative study of public policy. The first of these approaches directs attention on economic and socio-economic variables, such as Wagner's law of the expansion of public expenditure (Wagner, 1893, 1911). A second family of theories explains public policy differences mainly in terms of power resources of social classes, such as market power and political power of labour relative to capital and the middle classes (for example, Esping-Andersen, 1990). According to a third school of thought, mainly neo-institutionalist in character, policy differences largely mirror differences in political and economic institutions as well as differences in the strategies adopted by collective actors (for example Hall, 1986; Scharpf, 1987; Armingeon, 1994). A fourth school of thought, focusing on the impact of policy inheritance, explains policy choices and outcomes largely on the basis of the feedback coming from policy choices and outcomes in the past (Rose and Davies, 1984; Pierson, 1991). International or transnational factors are in the centre of the fifth school. According to this view, political choices at the level of the nation state are largely constrained or determined by the impact of international interdependence and transnational organizations (see, for example, Scharpf, 1999; Kurzer, 1993). In order to arrive at a full understanding of the determinants of public policy, it is therefore mandatory to take these key variables also into account.

The *second caveat* concerns differences in the room to manoeuvre available to political manipulation. Although the hypothesis of partisan influence can be regarded as a law-like regularity, many areas of social and economic life in a constitutional democracy are not directly amenable to political manipulation (see for instance: Lane, 1985; Whiteley, 1986, Janovski and Hicks, 1994).

The *third caveat* on the parties-do-matter view relates to the veto player theorem (Tsebelis, 1995, 1999). A veto player is 'an individual or collective actor whose agreement (by majority rule for collective actors) is required for a change in policy' (Tsebelis, 1995: 301). The veto player concept stems from the idea of 'checks and balances' in the American Constitution and the classic constitutional texts of the eighteenth century and later. According to the latest version of the veto player theorem (Tsebelis, 1999), significant policy change is contingent upon five factors. The potential for policy change varies inversely with the total number of veto players, their cohesiveness and the ideological distance between veto players. Furthermore, the potential for policy change varies directly with the duration of a government and with an increase in the ideological difference between current and previous government. The latest version of the veto player thus incorporates one central element of the parties-do-matter hypothesis (see also: Birchfield and Crépaz, 1998).

The Federal Republic of Germany is an instructive example for the usefulness of the veto player concept. A large number of veto players co-govern in Germany (see Table 8.2). According to the logic of the veto player theorem, the room to manoeuvre for incumbent parties in federal government therefore tends to be narrowly circumscribed by powerful checks and balances, other things being equal. The checks and balances include above all federalism, local self-government, regulatory capacities of associations, and co-governing institutions such as the *Bundesverfassungsgericht* (Federal Constitutional Court) and the *Deutsche Bundesbank,* or more recently *the European Central Bank,* as well as co-administrative institutions, such as the social insurance institutions and welfare associations (*Wohlfahrtsverbände*). The Federal Republic of Germany insofar resembles a 'moderate' or 'semisovereign' democracy, in which the margin for political choices of incumbent parties is considerably smaller than the room to manoeuvre available to governments in majoritarian democracies. This nourishes the hypothesis that the partisan influence on public policy is more pronounced in majoritarian democracies and weaker in a non-majoritarian democracy, such as in Germany – unless one or more of the other variables of the veto player theorem, i.e. ideological distance, duration of government and size of the change in power, point in the opposite direction (Schmidt, 1996b).

The extent to which social and economic life is amenable to partisan influences varies thus from nation to nation and also from period to period. A larger proportion of these differences can be attributed not only to party differences but also to constitutional structures and veto players. For example, highly centralized unitary states are, in principle, more amenable to partisan influences on public policy than states in which the government is constrained by oversized coalitions or by countermajoritarian powers such as federalism, an influential constitutional court and an autonomous central bank.

Consider two non-majoritarian cases: first, an all-inclusive coalition, such as Switzerland during the Second World War and after 1959, and second, a democracy, in which the major opposition party is co-governing, such as the Federal Republic of Germany in the 1970s and 1990s and also after 2000. Within the context of an all-inclusive coalition, there is not so much leeway for policy-making of the kind suggested by standard partisan theory, i.e. solo runs of the incumbent party A in period one, followed by solo runs of the former opposition party B in the subsequent period. The choice that exists in an all-inclusive coalition for all parties is the freedom to choose between bargaining, exit, and blockade of the decision-making process. When bargaining and compromise-seeking prevail, policy tends to be premised on the lowest common denominator of the coalition partners. This denominator tends to generate policy continuity rather than discontinuity and provides for limited short-term elasticity in policy-making. Because policy results under these circumstances from extended bargaining and compromise-seeking, it is difficult or impossible for the voter to attribute the political output to its origin. However, this means interruption or blockade of the causality that partisan theory predicts for the relationship between voter's preferences, policy choices, policy output and positive feedback from the social constituencies.

A similar logic governs the policy process when state structures allow for co-government of the opposition party. The major example is the 'Grand Coalition State' (Schmidt, 1996b) in the Federal Republic of Germany or in situations of 'divided government' in (semi-)presidential democracies. In both cases the 'incumbent' party (or parties) is dependent on support from the opposition parties.

Co-governing opposition parties pose awkward problems for the parties-do-matter hypothesis, because the latter has centred attention mainly on a clear-cut division of labour between government and opposition. When applied to cases in which the opposition party is de facto co-governing, the methodology of standard partisan theory erroneously attributes policy outputs to the incumbent party, while these outputs, in reality, result from compromises between the incumbent and the opposition party or from anticipation of the constraints the opposition party imposes on the government.[2]

8.5 THE IMPACT OF CONSTITUTIONAL STRUCTURES AND VETO PLAYERS ON PUBLIC POLICY

Democratic states differ not only in the extent to which conservative, liberal, centrist or leftist parties participate in government. It is also the political-institutional design and the relative importance of veto players which vary from country to country. The list of states in Table 8.1 comprises nations with divergent constitutional structures, such as centralized unitary states of the French and the British type, decentralized unitary states, for example the Nordic nations, decentralized federal systems, such as the USA and Switzerland, and the 'unitary federal state' (Hesse, 1962), as typified by the German case (Wachendorfer-Schmidt, 2000).

Moreover, the countries listed in Table 8.1 belong to different types of democracy. Following Lijphart (1999), the United Kingdom in the pre-devolution period and New Zealand before the introduction of proportional representation in 1993 can be regarded as major examples of majoritarian democracy, while Switzerland represents a typical non-majoritarian consensus democracy. Most other countries have more mixed democratic regimes (Lijphart, 1999).

The democratic countries in the OECD-area also differ in the extent to which countermajoritarian institutions narrow the room to manoeuvre available to central government. This dimension is related to, though not identical with, the distinction between majoritarian and consensus democracy. According to indices of countermajoritarian institutions (see Table 8.2), the Federal Republic of Germany, Switzerland and the USA are the major examples of powerful countermajoritarian constraints of central government.

Finally, the role of veto players varies from one advanced industrial democracy to the other (Tsebelis, 1995, 1999). A large number of veto players and, thus, powerful constraints of policy-making and 'significant legislation' (Tsebelis, 1999) have mainly marked Austria, Switzerland, the USA and the Federal Republic of Germany, but also Belgium, France, Italy and The Netherlands. In contrast to this, the total number and the political importance of veto players is much smaller in the Nordic countries and in Westminster-type countries (see Table 8.2).

The indicators in Table 8.2 reveal differences in deep-seated constitutional structures and veto players in OECD-democracies. These indicators suggest that the scope for action available to central government is wide in countries in which the majority in the legislature and the executive is largely unconstrained, or 'sovereign', such as in Britain, and New Zealand, but also in Sweden, Norway, Denmark and in Southern Europe. Very broadly speaking, these countries can be conceived of as 'sovereign democracies' defined in terms of a relatively unconstrained demos or a relatively unconstrained majority in the legislature and the executive (see column 7 in Table 8.3).

In contrast to this, constitutional structures and veto players severely constrain the demos and narrowly circumscribe the government's course of action in a second group of countries. This group includes the federal states in the OECD-area – Australia, Austria, Belgium, Canada, Germany, Switzerland and the USA – as well as Italy. These countries are, broadly speaking, 'semi-sovereign' democracies, defined as a demos or a majority in the legislature and the executive which is tamed by numerous checks and balances as well as other formal and informal constraints.

Table 8.2 *Constitutional structures and veto players in 23 economically advanced democracies in the year 2000*

Country	Type of democracy (majoritarian, consensus or mixed type & federal vs unitary)	Federalism vs unitary state	Counter-majoritarian constraints of central government (Schmidt, 1996)	Veto player-Index (Schmidt, 2000)	Index of constitutional structures (Huber et al., 1993)	Semi-sovereign vs sovereign democracy
Australia	Majoritarian-federal	Decentralised federalism	3	6	4	semisovereign
Austria	Consensus-federal	Centralised federalism	3	9	3	semisovereign
Belgium	Consensus-unitary*	Decentralised federalism	4	7	4	semisovereign
Canada	Majoritarian-federal	Decentralised federalism	3	3	4	semisovereign
Denmark	Consensus-unitary	Decentralised unitary state	3	3	0	sovereign
Finland	Consensus-unitary	Decentralised unitary state	1	4	1	sovereign
France	Majoritarian-unitary	Centralised unitary state	1	7	2	sovereign
Germany	Consensus-federal	Unitarian federalism	5	8	5	semisovereign
Greece	Majoritarian-unitary	Centralised unitary state	1	3	1	sovereign
Iceland	Consensus-unitary	Centralised unitary state	1	1	0	sovereign
Ireland	Consensus-unitary	Centralised unitary state	2	4	0	sovereign
Italy	Consensus-unitary	Centralised unitary state	3	7	1	semisovereign
Japan	Consensus-federal*	Decentralised unitary state	2	5	2	sovereign
Luxembourg	Consensus-unitary	Centralised unitary state	2	6	0	sovereign
Netherlands	Consensus-federal*	Decentralised unitary state	2	7	1	sovereign
New Zealand	Majoritarian-unitary	Centralised unitary state	1	3	1	sovereign
Norway	Consensus-unitary	Decentralised unitary state	1	2	1	sovereign
Portugal	Consensus-unitary	Centralized unitary state	1	2	1	sovereign
Spain	Majoritarian-federal	Decentralised unitary state	2	6	1	sovereign
Sweden	Consensus-unitary	Decentralised unitary state	1	2	0	sovereign

(Continued)

Table 8.2 *Continued*

Country	Type of democracy (majoritarian, consensus or mixed type & federal vs unitary)	Federalism vs unitary state	Counter-majoritarian constraints of central government (Schmidt, 1996)	Veto player-Index (Schmidt, 2000)	Index of constitutional structures (Huber et al., 1993)	Semi-sovereign vs sovereign democracy
Switzerland	Consensus-federal	Decentralised federalism	5	8	6	semisovereign
United Kingdom	Majoritarian-unitary	Centralised unitary state	2	2	3	sovereign
USA	Majoritarian-federal	Decentralised federalism	5	6	7	semisovereign

Note: * = borderline case

Explanation:

Column 1: name of country.

Column 2: based on Lijphart (1999: 189).

Column 3: based on Lijphart (1999: 189) (with revisions), and Wachendorfer-Schmidt (2000), state structure as of 1, January 2000.

Column 4: index of institutional constraints of central state government (Schmidt, 1996: 172) for 1 January, 2000. High values indicate a large number of counter-majoritarian constraints, low values indicate a small number of counter-majoritarian constraints, and thus a larger room to manoeuvre for the central state government. The index is an additive index, composed of six dummy-variables (1 = constraint, 0 = else): 1. constraints due to policy harmonization in the European Union (EU membership = 1, else = 0), 2. degree of centralization of state structures (1 = federalism, 0 = else), 3. difficulty of amending constitutions (1 = very difficult, 0 = else) (major source Lutz, 1994), 4. a strong bicameralism (= 1, else = 0), 5. central bank autonomy (Busch, 1995) (= 1, else = 0), and 6. referendum (1 = frequent, 0 = rare). It is based mainly on Banks et al. (1997), Gallagher et al. (2000), Lijphart (1999).

Column 5: index of veto players for 1 January 2000, based upon Schmidt (2000). The veto player index mirrors the total number of the major veto players. It is based on 10 dummy-variables: 1. consociational democracy, 2. federalism, 3. central bank autonomy, 4. Lijphart index of judicial review (Lijphart, 1999: 314), 5. EU membership, 6. developed protection of minorities, 7. bicameralism, 8. coalition government, 9. self-administration in social policy (social insurance based financing of the social budget according to ILO estimates > 50 %), 10. developed direct democracy.

Column 6: augmented and updated version of Huber, Ragin and Stephens' index of constitutional structures for 1 January 2000 (Huber et al., 1993: 728). The constitutional structure index is an additive index, composed of five indicators: 1. federalism (0 = absence, 1 = weak, 2 = strong), 2. parliamentary government (= 0) versus presidentialism or Swiss type of *Kollegialregierung* (= 1), 3. proportional representation (= 0, modified PR = 1, majoritarian formula and single member district = 2), 4. bicameralism (1 = weak, 2 = strong), 5. referendum (0 = no referendum or rare, 1 = frequent).

Column 7: 'Sovereign' and 'semi-sovereign' democracy are based on columns 2–6 of this table. Semi-sovereignty and sovereignty are defined, following Katzenstein (1987), by the overall extent to which the demos is institutionally constrained. In a 'semi-sovereign democracy', the demos (or the majority in the legislature and the executive) is severely constrained. Within the context of a 'sovereign democracy', however, the demos (or the majority in the legislature and the executive) disposes of a wide room to manoeuvre.

Table 8.3 *Party composition of governments in sovereign and semisovereign democracies 1950–2000*

Dominant party composition of government 1950–2000	Sovereign democracies	Semisovereign democracies
Leftist	Denmark Norway Spain Sweden	Austria
Centre	(Finland) Luxembourg (Netherlands)	Belgium Canada Federal Republic of Germany Italy
Liberal	Iceland Portugal	Switzerland
Conservative	France Greece Ireland Japan New Zealand United Kingdom	Australia USA

Note: Greece, Portugal and Spain: entries for period since democratization in the 1970s. Finland and The Netherlands are borderline cases.

Explanation:

Column 1: Dominant party in government (measured by cabinet seats share between 1950 and 2000).

Column 2: Sovereign democracies: see text.

Column 3: Semi-sovereign democracies: see text.

Is there any systematic relationship between sovereign or semi-sovereign democracies and the long-term partisan composition? For example, does democratic semi-sovereignty covary with a more moderate or centrist partisan complexion of government? This is indeed the case. The partisan composition of government in semi-sovereign democracies is more centrist or liberal than those of sovereign democracies. Moreover, unlike their semi-sovereign counterparts, where coalition government prevails, sovereign democracies tend towards single-party government (above all in the English-speaking family of nations; see: Castles, 1998). Furthermore, the partisan complexion of government in the sovereign democracies is dominated by conservative or leftist tendencies (see Table 8.3).

Institutional characteristics, such as countermajoritarianism and veto players, are potentially important determinants of public policy. Due to a largely unconstrained majority, a significantly larger potential for policy change can be expected in a 'sovereign democracy'. Conversely, a much more limited scope for policy change is likely within a constellation of forces typical of a 'semi-sovereign democracy', such as a federal system, a large number of veto players, and a consensus democracy or a mixed polity, comprising majoritarian and non-majoritarian elements.

Empirical studies support these views. The share of public spending as a percentage of GDP, for example, tends to be significantly smaller in federal states than in non-federal ones (Wachendorfer-Schmidt, 2000). Moreover, the share of GDP allocated to the social budget varies with the index of counter-majoritarian institutions (Schmidt, 1998). This index is also inversely associated with indicators of 'big government', long-term change in the tax burden, labour market policy effort and levels of gender inequality, to mention only a few relationships. Furthermore, the relative size of public employment (as a percentage of total employment) is significantly smaller in countries with a large number of veto-players in contrast to nations in which few veto players are co-governing. Moreover, veto players account for variation in the frequency of labour law legislation. Veto player indices have also contributed to the explanation of tax reforms (Wagschal, 1999) and labour legislation.[3] In contrast to this, significant policy-turnarounds occur when the following criteria are fulfilled: few veto players, small ideological distance between these players, long duration of a government and a large increase in the ideological difference between the current and the previous government, such as a change in power from a leftist to a rightist government (Tsebelis, 1999).

These studies suggest, that the hypothesis of partisan influence on public policy, when applied to a semi-sovereign democracy, must be particularly sensitive to the impact of countervailing powers. Moreover, the total potential for policy change as well as the policy effects from political parties in semi-sovereign democracies are likely to be smaller than those in sovereign democracies. In contrast to this, the parties-do-matter hypothesis is in most policy areas fully applicable to sovereign democracies, such as the majoritarian democracies of Sweden, Britain, New Zealand and Greece. It is not accidental that large partisan effects on public policy were reported from these countries. Examples include the expansion of the welfare state and full employment policy until the late 1980s in Sweden, where a 'Social Democratic Image of Society' (Castles, 1978) has prevailed over a long period (Therborn, 1985; Olsson, 1990). Britain's spectacular policy changes in the period of the Labour governments in 1945–51 and in the era of Thatcherism (Moon, 1993, 1995) also lend support to a strong parties-do-matter hypothesis. A third example is New Zealand in the 1980s, when a Labour government began to introduce radical market-oriented reform (Nagel, 1994; Castles et al., 1996). Greece is the fourth country in which incumbent parties have fully exploited the room to manoeuvre created by majoritarian democracy and hegemonic majority: the PASOK governments of the 1980s used public power for a wide variety of purposes, including the breathtaking expansion of patronage and clientelism in the public sector.

Multivariate explanations of public policy underline the impact of constitutional structures and party composition of government. Take the growth of government in the West from the early 1960s until the late 1990s. In this period, most OECD-nations have experienced a dramatic expansion of public expenditure as a percentage of Gross Domestic Product, and a significant, albeit less steep, increase in government final consumption expenditure. Particularly steep has been the increase in the role of the state above all in the Nordic nations. There, total outlays of government as a percentage of GDP exceeded the 60 per cent mark and in Sweden 70 per cent in 1993, but declined thereafter to a lower level in the second half of the 1990s (OECD, 1999). In another group of nations, the growth of government started from a low level and has remained much more muted, above all in Japan, the United States and Australia.

A substantial proportion of the differences in the growth of government in the West is attributable to economic cycles, rates of unemployment, demographic trends, such as a growing proportion of the population aged 65 and above, and de-inflationary or inflationary trends. But the growth of big government is also caused by political factors, such as inheritance of policy programmes (Rose and Davies, 1984) and the inclination of most politicians not to reject the policy heritage of the past. Among the political factors, incumbent parties and institutional structures also deserve to receive foremost mention.

To illustrate the impact of parties and political institutions, Table 8.4 arrays findings from pooled cross-section-time-series analysis of public spending determinants in democratic OECD-nations from the early 1960s to the late 1990s. To begin with, the growth of government in this period was fuelled by influential policy inheritance factors, such as that mirrored by the strong impact of the lagged dependent variable. Moreover, political-economic factors played a major role. Among these, the 'cost disease' of the public sector – which results from targeting wage bargaining in the (less productive) public sector to wage policy in the (usually more productive) private market sector – deserves to receive first mention. Increasing rates of unemployment also push the share of total outlays of general government. In contrast to this, de-inflation disciplines fiscal policy and tends to lower spending levels.

Public spending determinants include genuinely political factors. Three of them deserve to receive foremost mention. First, leftist parties' participation in government increases public spending. This relationship is particularly pronounced in the Nordic countries and in the Continental European context. In contrast to this, Labour parties in Anglo-American democracies, following 'Third Way' theories or being pushed by neo-liberal policy of their opponents, have adopted a less etatist policy stance since the 1980s. Second, the growth of big government can also be attributed to policy choices of centre or centre-right parties, such parties of Christian democratic persuasion in periods of economic growth. Thus, social democratic and Christian demo-cratic parties have long been major causes of the growth of government in the post-1960 period, largely through the reconstruction and expansion of social policy (van Kersbergen, 1995; Schmidt, 1998: 168, 205–14). In contrast to this, conservative parties, such as Britain's Conservative Party, have been major inhibitors of the role of government in modern democracies.

State structures also make a difference in public spending. For example, countermajoritarian institutions, such as federalism and autonomous central

Table 8.4 *Determinants of public spending as a percentage of gross domestic product in 21 OECD-member states 1960–98*

Determinants	Effect on public spending (% GDP)	Coefficient	Level of significance
• Intercept		1.574	0.000
• Public spending (% GDP) in previous year	expansive	0.950	0.000
• 'Cost disease of the public sector'	expansive	0.052	0.001
• Change in the rate of unemployment against previous year	expansive	0.774	0.000
• Inflation/Deflation	expansive/restrictive	0.080	0.014
Political			
• Countermajoritarian constraints (Schmidt, 1996a)	restrictive	– 0.071	0.036
• Social democratic party in office	expansive	0.004	0.034
• Christian democratic party in office	expansive (until 1982)	0.010	0.001
• Maastricht Treaty effect	restrictive	– 0.725	0.010

The data in Table 8.4 are based on cross-section-cross-time regression of 21 countries and 39 points of observation for each country. Levels of significance were estimated with panel corrected standard errors according to Beck and Katz (1995).

Operational definition of the independent variables:

- Public expenditure in previous year: total outlays of general government as a percentage of GDP in previous year (lag 1). Source: OECD Economic Outlook (various issues).
- 'Cost disease' of the public sector: measured by the total number of public sector employees as a percentage of total labour force. Source: OECD Labour Force Statistics (various issues).
- Change in the rate of unemployment: rate of unemployment minus rate of unemployment in previous year. Source: OECD Labour Force Statistics (various issues).
- Deflation: change of the rate of unemployment against previous year (in percentage point differences); computed from OECD Economic Outlook (various issues).
- Political institutions: countermajoritarian constraints: based on Schmidt (1996a), see Table 8.2; negative sign indicates an inverse relationship: the more powerful the countermajoritarian constraints, the smaller the share of public spending as a percentage of GDP.
- Social democratic party in office: social democratic share of cabinet seats in the period from 1960 to 1998; in order to measure period-effects in the 1980s and 1990s, labour party governments in Anglo-American countries since the early 1980s were coded '0'.
- Christian democratic party in office: Christian democratic share of cabinet seats in the period from 1960 to 1998; in order to account for period-specific effects in the 1980s and 1990s, Christian democratic governments since 1980 were coded '0'.
- Maastricht Treaty effect: period-dummy (from 1993 onwards = 1, else = 0)

Source: Manfred G. Schmidt: File POOLOECD, 1 December 1999 (Centre for Social Policy, Bremen).

banks, have inhibited big government. The exception is Germany's 'unitary federalism' (Hesse, 1962), which tolerated the expansion of a welfare state, largely because the social budget is mainly financed by social insurance contributions rather than taxes and because the pro-welfare statist inclination of the two largest parties in Germany has overridden most of the federal obstacles to big government. The overall relationship, however, is mirrored in the inverse association between public spending and the index of countermajoritarian institutions in Table 8.3.

Last but not least, public spending has also been shaped by international and transnational constellations. The adaptation of fiscal policy to the convergence criteria of the Maastricht Treaty on the European Union, above all a low rate of inflation, a level of public debt not higher than 60 per cent of GDP, and upper limits to budget deficits, has impeded further increases in the share of public spending since 1993 until the end of the period under investigation (see Table 8.4).

8.6 CONCLUSION

Taking the various bits and pieces together, this chapter suggests three conclusions on the explanation of public policy differences in democratic nations. First, the review of the literature fully supports the view that public policy is to a significant extent influenced by policy choices of incumbent parties. This finding lends further support to the parties-do-matter theory. Second, proponents of the parties-do-matter view should take the impact of constitutional structures and veto players into account. A particularly large potential for party-driven policy changes can be expected in sovereign democracies, i.e. majoritarian democracies with few veto players. Much more muted is the potential for policy change (and the extent to which this potential will be exploited) in non-majoritarian democracies, above all where many veto players are de facto co-governing ('semi-sovereign democracies'). Third, the combination of classical parties-do-matter-theory, analysis of constitutional structures and veto player theorem according to Tsebelis (1999) demonstrates that the policy immobility which often results from constitutional constraints of government and powerful veto players, can be overridden by the impact of three variables: first, a Grand Coalition between the major political parties, second, long duration of a government and third, a large increase in the ideological difference between current and previous government, such as a dramatic change in power from a moderate coalition government to a radical single-party government.

NOTES

1 Principal investigators have been – to name just a few: Hibbs (1977, 1987a, 1987b, 1992, 1994); Cameron (1978, 1984); Schmidt (1980, 1982a, 1982b, 1992b, 1996); Tufte (1978); Castles (1982, 1998); Alt (1985); Garrett and Lange (1986); Cusack (1999); Garrett (1998); Budge and Keman (1990) and Keman (1988).

2 The methodology of standard partisan theory, such as Hibbs' contributions, is not well equipped to handle the case of co-governing opposition parties. Co-governance of the opposition party requires more detailed analysis and measurement of constitutional structures and institutional 'veto-points' (Immergut, 1992). But this has been neglected by public choice proponents of the partisan theory of public

policy, such as Hibbs (1987a, 1987b), and power resources theorists, such as David Cameron (1984), and Korpi (1983).

3   As far as significant labour legislation is concerned, the relationship is straight-forward: many veto players, wide ideological distance between them and the government, short duration of a government, and small increase (or no increase at all) in the ideological difference between current and previous government, impede major labour law legislation.

9 COMPARATIVE POLITICS AND THE WELFARE STATE

Kees van Kersbergen and Uwe Becker

9.1 INTRODUCTION

There are many ways to study the welfare state. The economists' major questions obviously deal with the economic conditions and consequences of welfare state interventions in the economy – typically in terms of efficiency, both macro- and micro-economically (see: Barr, 1993). The sociologists' interests concern the social underpinnings of welfare state development and the outcomes of main welfare state policies and programmes – most crucially in terms of equality, labour market behaviour and the life cycle. The host of comparative, empirical studies of the welfare state tend to combine the economic and sociological perspective and can therefore be rightly grouped under the sub-discipline of economic sociology (Esping-Andersen, 1994).

It is conspicuous that, until recently, comparative political science has paid relatively little attention to the welfare state. This is surprising because the welfare state represents one of the major structural (political) changes in post-war democracies. The contrast between the huge body of (economic) sociological literature on the welfare state and the modest contribution of political science is sharp. To the extent that comparative political scientists have investigated welfare state topics in the past, they have predominantly done so in order to test, criticize or denounce the so-called 'politics doesn't matter' cliché (Hofferbert and Cingranelli, 1996). In the 1980s, the 'politics matters' school (Castles, 1982; Chapter 8 in this book) time and again attempted to show that this cliché was indeed more a theoretical and ideological slogan than an empirical reality. In the recent words of the school's then leading spokesman, Francis G. Castles (1998: 27): 'This assertion of the consequentiality of politics was once extremely valuable as an antidote to the prevailing orthodoxy that policy was merely a function of socio-economic forces ...'. Most political science analyses, moreover, have – quite understandably – tended to focus narrowly on the political determinants of welfare state development. Once it was empirically established that politics, particularly the party-political constellation within a nation's overall institutional make-up, did matter, for instance for social spending, political scientists gradually seemed to lose interest.

Essentially and in terms of the logic of research, there have been two main ways to study the welfare state. First, one can look at the welfare state as a dependent variable, that is to say that one is interested in explaining how and why welfare states emerge and in accounting for cross-national variation in welfare state types. Second, the welfare state can be conceptualized as an independent (or intervening) variable. This implies that the main research interest focuses on the extent to which, and the conditions under which, the welfare state explains specific outcomes. These can be social and economic, such as income equality, unemployment, and labour market participation, or political, such as the electoral opportunities of political parties (Schmidt, 1982b; Esping-Andersen, 1985a; Keman, 1988).

It is somewhat of a paradox that precisely at the time that the 'politics matters' protagonists and others (see Castles, 1998; Stephens et al., 1999) conclude increasingly that democratic politics matters less and less for welfare state development and outcomes, welfare state issues have taken a much more prominent place on the research agenda of comparative politics (Pierson, 1998; Levy, 1999).

The first section of this chapter presents an overview of the development of comparative studies of the welfare state. This section deals with theories and approaches that – strictly speaking – do not necessarily belong to the discipline of comparative politics, but do form the core of the body of social scientific knowledge of the welfare state. We think that in order to apprehend fully the current state of affairs, an 'analytic' history of theory-building is necessary. In Section 9.3 we pay attention to the influential theory of welfare state regimes as developed by Esping-Andersen (1990, 1999) and to the institutionalist turn in welfare state research. We examine the so-called resilience thesis that contemporary welfare states are far more resilient and durable than what one would expect, given the enormous challenges to the welfare state (ageing societies, unemployment, globalization, etc.) and given what leading theories of the development of the welfare state seemed to predict. In Section 9.4 we deal in more empirical detail with how nations have coped with the social risks of a market economy and how the regimes have actually adapted. In the concluding Section 9.5 we review the current state of affairs and discuss some main contributions to the debate on democratic welfare state change.

9.2. A HISTORY OF THEORIES[1]

The debate on the origins, growth and nature of the welfare state has been flourishing for more than three decades now. The extensive body of literature finds its justification in the fact that the welfare state is a fundamental structural component of contemporary democracies. The purpose of this section is to introduce theories and empirical studies that attempt to explain the growth of the welfare state and the cross-national variations in the development of social policies in advanced democracies. In other words, the focus is on empirically oriented theories that attempt to identify the causal forces and mechanisms promoting the development of the welfare state and the variation between welfare states.

There have been three main theoretical approaches to the emergence and growth of the welfare state. First, *functionalist* theories have understood the growth of the welfare state in developed nations by and large as the response of the state to the growing needs of its citizens. Second, class mobilization or interest *group theories* have sought the causes for cross-national differences in welfare policies and expenditures among industrial democracies primarily in the varying capacities of collective political actors (labour movements, interest groups, political parties) to articulate, politicize and implement welfare demands. *Institutionalist theories*, finally, have argued that institutions (the rules and regulations of democratic policy-making), operating relatively autonomously from social and political pressures, determined the growth and shape of the welfare state. These contrasting approaches, which will be discussed in some more detail below, did not simply differ in how they construct the causal logic of their argument; above all, they vary with respect to how they have grasped the explanatory problem of welfare state evolution. The principal interest of functional accounts was finding an answer to the question why different nations tended to adopt similar social and economic policies. Their explanatory problem concerned the *convergence* of social policies among nations that had reached an advanced stage of economic development. Political and institutionalist theories, on the other hand, mainly dealt with the question of cross-national variations in social and economic policies among nations that were similar in their economic and social structures. Their explanatory effort focused on the *divergence* of welfare state development in nations that were largely comparable in other respects.

The range of research designs and methods has probably been as wide as the theoretical approaches that can be distinguished. Nevertheless, two distinct and opposite methods figure prominently in the literature. First, the cross-national quantitative research strategy, which is variable-oriented, includes many cases and makes use of statistical techniques to test causal relations between variables. Second, the comparative historical design, which is case-oriented, examines many variables and offers an in-depth study of a single or limited number of cases by looking at complex historical conditions and sequences (Ragin, 1987, 1991; Castles, 1989b; Rueschemeyer et al., 1992; Keman, 1994). As Ragin (1987) has shown, the goals of the two major strategies of comparative social science differ radically. Whereas the comparative historical, case-oriented design acknowledges the complexity of social and historical events and, accordingly, is reluctant to seek general explanations that go beyond the complex and unique conditions of a single case, the cross-national, variable-oriented strategy seeks general explanations precisely by disregarding (or holding constant) many of the distinctive features and historical conditions of single cases. Both methods, moreover, contrast with respect to the role of theory in research: 'the case-oriented approach uses theory to aid historical interpretation and to guide the identification of important causal factors; the variable-oriented strategy, by contrast, usually tests hypotheses derived from theory' (Ragin, 1987: 55).

As a result of the coexistence of these two contrasting methods, the discipline of comparative welfare state research – like other areas of comparative research (e.g. Rueschemeyer et al., 1992: 12–39) – has tended to yield opposite substantial results, particularly when studying the explanatory relevance of political variables. Thus, case-oriented studies typically denied a simple link between social interests and political outputs, whereas several variable-oriented analyses consistently showed the causal association between, for instance, the strength of Leftwing political parties and social spending or other measures of welfare state development. In her institutionalist analysis of health politics in France, Switzerland and Sweden, Immergut (1992: 243) concluded that 'in contrast to approaches that seek the roots of political activity in social forces, the cases discussed here have shown that politics can be independent of social power'. In contrast, in his macro-comparative analysis of 18 welfare states, Esping-Andersen (1990: 1) argued that '... the history of political class coalitions is the most decisive cause of welfare-state variations'.

9.2.1 Functional Accounts

Theories which stress the causal primacy of *industrialization* typically argued that the welfare state was by and large the answer of society to the growing needs of its population. Industrialization created a demand for welfare by destroying the traditional bonds of kinship, family ties, and the guilds, which were the main institutions providing social security. The development of industrial society (and its correlates of economic growth, urbanization, demographic change) at the same time created the possibility of new forms of social security of a more comprehensive character: the welfare state. The prime explanatory problem for these theories concerned the very existence of, rather than the variation among western welfare states (Wilensky and Lebeaux, 1958; Cutright, 1965; Pryor, 1968; Rimlinger, 1971; Kerr et al., 1973; Jackman, 1975; Wilensky, 1975).

For theories that accord causal centrality to *modernization* (economic development, secularization, democratization) comparable considerations hold. The welfare state is seen as an effect of modernization and as one of the mechanisms restoring disrupted societal integration. The explanatory object typically involved the timing rather than the existence of social policy in modern society. The introduction of major social programmes was seen as directly associated with the rhythm and tempo of modernization (Flora and Heidenheimer, 1981; Flora and Alber, 1981; Alber, 1982; Kohl, 1985; Flora, 1983; 1986; Alber, 1989).

Both the argument of the 'logic of industrialism' and the major thesis of the 'logic of modernization' stressed that societal development created the demand for social security that could only be met by means of state inter-vention (Keman, 1998). In other words, the politics of social welfare was a function of the industrialization and modernization of societies. Economic development, industrialization and modernization were preconditions for welfare state development in a dual sense: the welfare state was 'a product of both the new need and the new resources generated by the process of industrialization' (Pierson, 1991: 16). The developmental perspective of the 'logic of industrialism' is most clearly exemplified in the work of Wilensky (1975).

Theories of industrialization and modernization have argued in favour of an objective problem pressure of societal integration. Both industrial and modernization theories are functional accounts, because they assume that societal problem pressures emerge from the wide disruption created by social change and that the welfare state, in turn, was the automatic and functional response to this. A natural consequence of this reasoning was that all nations sharing the experience of modernization and industrialization were assumed to converge in their adoption of social policies. The further nations were on the scale of industrial development, the more they were likely to advance social policies,[2] and the more they tended to look alike. However, it remains obscure how needs and demands can create their own fulfilment. There is little or no account of political intermediation, other than that the growth of the welfare state is 'hastened by the interplay of political elite perceptions, mass pressures, and welfare bureaucracies' (Wilensky, 1975: 47). As theories of the differences between modern welfare states, moreover, these lack the analytical tools because the main variables do not show any variation among the advanced industrial nations. Schmidt (1989b) has argued that an industrialism-thesis does account for differences in social spending between rich and poor nations, but cannot cope with 'exceptions' that either spend too much or too little, given their level of development (see also: Keman, 1998).

9.2.2 Social Democracy as a Model of the Welfare State

The debate on the 'Social Democratization' of capitalism has naturally centred on equality, either in terms of the distributive performance, or in terms of the institutional commitments of welfare states, such as universalism, solidarity, the generosity of social rights, and their capacity to 'de-commodify' workers (Western, 1989; Esping-Andersen, 1990).

The first generation of research was primarily a debate with the 'logic of industrialism' thesis, but increasingly also with the 'median voter' view of democratic politics as represented in particular by Jackman (1975, 1986). Hence, the objective was two-fold: to demonstrate that politics mattered and that the party composition of government and parliament made a decisive difference. Hewitt (1977) was one of the first to examine explicitly the capacity of Social Democratic labour movements to affect redistribution in both these senses. His argument was that the mere presence of democratic structures could not sufficiently explain gains in equality and that Social Democratic rule was a necessary condition of egalitarian outcomes.

The causal effect of Social Democracy on welfare state performance was subsequently corroborated by a large number of studies that employed the variety of research designs identified earlier in this chapter. In the comparative case-approach, some studies emphasized the Scandinavian experience in particular, primarily because of the seemingly close association between Social Democratic dominance and advanced welfare states (Castles, 1978; Korpi, 1978; 1983; Esping-Andersen, 1985a; Esping-Andersen and Korpi, 1986). Others sought to identify the Social Democratic effect via matched comparisons between 'failed' and 'successful' cases, such as Higgins and Apple's (1981) and Pontusson's (1988) British–Swedish contrast, Esping-Andersen and Korpi's (1984) and Scharpf's (1984, 1987) comparison of Austria, Germany and Sweden, and Hage et al.'s (1989) four-nation comparison. By comparing nations in which the welfare state outcomes seemed to diverge despite Social Democratic movements of similar strength, these studies served to identify more concretely the conditions under which Social Democratic movements were capable of introducing change. Three key conclusions emerged from these studies. Castles (1978) has emphasized the weakness of the Right as a basic precondition; Stephens (1979) and Higgins and Apple (1981) have suggested that the political efficacy of Social Democracy was contingent on trade union strength or cohesion; and Castles (1978) as well as Esping-Andersen (1985b) held that the Social Democratic model could only be pursued effectively through the building of political coalitions (especially with the agrarians).

The dominant approach, however, has been the cross-national, quantitative design to test the Social Democratic thesis on the basis of 16 to 20 advanced nations (Hewitt, 1977; Stephens, 1979; Korpi, 1983; Swank and Hicks, 1985; Esping-Andersen, 1985b). Most analyses were cross-sectional, but (pooled-) time series analyses became more common in the late 1980s and early 1990s (Griffin et al., 1989; Korpi, 1989; Alvarez et al., 1996). Using a variety of different measures of both Social Democratic strength, and the policy outcomes (from social spending and redistribution to various institutional characteristics), most of these studies had in common a theory of working class mobilization of political power, i.e. the Social Democratization of capitalism depends on the degree to which the balance of power favoured labour. In most cases, the political parties were identified as the chief causal agents. Swank and Hicks (1985) for instance tested a number of competing explanatory hypotheses on social spending (transfers) and equality, such as level and rate of economic growth, the role of democratic institutions, political power of labour and capital, and increasing needs. They found that the most consistent explanation concerned class-based political actors. The degree of unionization significantly influenced transfer spending as did the presence of large monopoly-sector firms. In addition, the finding was that lower- and working-class protest (demonstrations, strikes) positively affected social spending.

The power resources argument has been most fully developed by Korpi (1983) and the fully developed Social Democratic model can be summarized as follows. The more the mass of the population is organized as wage-earners within the Social Democratic movement, the higher the quality (universalism, solidarity, redistribution) of the welfare arrangements tended to be and, as a result, the higher the extent of equality. A developed welfare state, therefore, was evidence for a decisive shift in the balance of power in favour of the working class and Social Democracy. The distribution of power resources between the main social classes of capitalist society determined political intervention in the economy and the extent of inequality.

This basic power resources model has been subject to several amendments, precipitating the emergence of a second generation of research. Apart from the emphasis on the relative weakness and fragmentation of the Right (Castles, 1978, 1985) and on the distinctiveness of political class alliances (Esping-Andersen, 1985a and b) mentioned above, there arose a consensus in the literature that the political efficacy of Left parties depended on the extent to which they counted on strong trade unionism (Stephens, 1979) and, especially, on a centralized, neocorporatist industrial relations system (Cameron, 1978, 1984; Schmidt, 1983; Scharpf, 1984, 1998; Keman, 1988, 1990; Hicks et al., 1989).

As Shalev (1983) has pointed out, many of these studies assumed the Social Democratic welfare state to be a leap in the direction of socialism or, indeed, an early image of the future 'good society'. At the very least, the Social Democratic welfare state represented an intermediary stage between capitalism and socialism (Stephens, 1979; Stephens and Stephens, 1982; Korpi, 1983). Several authors challenged this kind of embryonic socialism assumption. Tilton's (1990) analysis of Swedish Social Democratic ideology argued that its dominant values had their roots in a radical-liberal commitment to freedom of choice rather than to socialism. Baldwin (1990) rejected the causal link between Social Democracy and solidaristic social policies since, in his analysis, their mainsprings were not necessarily in the working classes. His contribution to the debate was innovative for two reasons. First, he showed that while growing equality may have been a characteristic of modern welfare states, it has not been its goal. The welfare state was more about reapportioning risks than about the redistribution of wealth. Equality referred to risk redistribution. Second, the theory of risk and distribution allowed for a rejection of what Baldwin called the labourist account (i.e. the Social Democratic model with its stress on class power and class coalitions), but at the same time protected the socialist interpretation of the development of the welfare state. The main problem with the labourist approach had been its narrow focus on the working class as the only risk category. The critical insight was that class may, but rarely does, coincide with a risk category. The labourist view mistakenly assumed that welfare policies were explained in terms of a victory of the working class over the bourgeoisie. Certain risks, of course, tended to coincide with class. Occupational injuries and unemployment came with the position of an industrial worker. It was this coincidence that led to the labourist interpretation. More often, however, risk categories cut through the cleavage of class, a fact that established the possibility of varying risk coalitions. The welfare state was a pooling of risk rather than of resources (Baldwin, 1990: 19).

Baldwin's crucial claim was that what historically had determined the solidarity of social policy was not working-class strength, but, on the contrary, the fact that 'otherwise privileged groups discovered that they shared a common interest in reallocating risk with the disadvantaged' (Baldwin, 1990: 292). Similarly, Heclo and Madsen (1986) and Therborn (1989) have argued that the principles of solidarity and equality that characterize Swedish Social Democracy had less to do with socialism than with the Swedish historical tradition. Thus, it may very well have been Swedish history, and not Social Democracy, that constituted the root cause of reform. The implication was that the Swedish model was inapplicable elsewhere (Milner, 1989).

In the debate with the functionalist 'logic of industrialism' and modernization theses (and their Marxist equivalents), the explanatory power of Left parties cum trade union strength seemed to hold up against standard demographic and modernization variables, such as age structure and level of economic development. Yet, the results depended very much on differences in variable measurement and methodological design. Left power explanations tended to vanish when controlling for age structure when the outcome was measured as social expenditure ratios (Pampel and Williamson, 1989; Esping-Andersen, 1990) because such a large share of spending was age-dependent. As Griffin et al. (1989) showed, cross-sectional and time-series models told different stories (see also Keman, 1988; Pampel and Stryker, 1990; Amenta, 1993; Hicks and Misra, 1993).

9.2.3 Challenges to the Social Democratic Thesis

The one-to-one relationship between labour movement power and welfare outcomes was challenged in different ways. In one group one finds those who emphasized the importance of neocorporatist solutions to global economic dependency. Cameron (1978, 1984) suggested that the association between strong Social Democracy and welfare states was linked to a country's position in the international economy. Specifically, he has argued that the vulnerability that small, open economies faced favoured the expansion of the public economy so as to reduce uncertainty via social guarantees, full employment, and more active government management of the economy. As elaborated more fully in the work of Katzenstein (1985), the real causal chain appeared to be that small open nations developed democratic corporatist structures as a way to enhance domestic consensus, facilitate economic adjustments, and maintain international competitiveness. While democratic corporatism was promoted by the presence of strong Social Democratic labour movements, Katzenstein pointed to Switzerland and The Netherlands to suggest that they did not constitute a necessary condition. At this point it became increasingly difficult to separate the neocorporatist argument from the Social Democratic thesis (see also Keman, 1990; Garrett, 1998).

Cameron's argument has often been mistakenly interpreted as an outright rejection of the Social Democratic thesis: the explanatory power attached to 'openness' seemed to suggest that the effect of Social Democracy was spurious. However, the gist of his thesis (see: Cameron, 1984) was more deeply historical, suggesting that the openness of an economy favoured certain structural features in societies which, in turn, enhanced the power of labour. Since small, open economies tended to be industrially concentrated, they also tended to develop strong and unified interest organizations. The capacity to forge broad consensus and to mobilize power was further helped by the homogeneity and concentration of the labour force (Hemerijck, 1993).

The importance of neocorporatist arrangements for Social Democratic success has been stressed in the studies of Schmidt (1983), Keman (1988), and Hicks et al. (1989). They have suggested that Social Democracy was most likely to promote (and defend) welfare statism successfully if its parliamentary power was matched by strong consensus-building mechanisms in both the polity and economy. These studies also suggested that neocorporatist intermediation came to play an especially important role in maintaining welfare policies during economic crises periods: the distributive battles that erupt when growth declines were better managed with 'all-encompassing' interest organizations. Studying income distribution, Hicks and Swank (1984) and Mueller (1989) suggested that the strength of Left parties (and economic openness) influenced income distribution directly, while trade unionization and centralization of wage bargaining had decisive indirect effects by providing the electoral basis for Social Democracy. By the end of the 1980s a consensus had grown that parties or unions alone had little effect and that successful Social Democratization required a configuration of strong Leftwing parties in government supported by an encompassing and centralized trade union movement.

9.3 RETHINKING WELFARE STATE THEORY

In the early 1990s students of 'welfare statism' began rethinking what precisely the theory should explain. The choice of many (especially early) studies to gauge welfare state achievements in terms of social expenditures had been defended on pragmatic grounds (spending data were reliable and easy to collect), and substantially (they should reflect 'effort' or the scope of the social wage). Yet the spending variable was then rightfully criticized for its loose correspondence to the theoretical issues of Social Democratization (Esping-Andersen, 1990). In particular, aggregate spending ratios fail to distinguish the characteristic effects of Social Democracy from those of other political forces. Indeed, politics mattered, but not all politics mattered in the same way.

The choice of a variable that measured income inequality and redistribution appeared to gain face validity to the extent that equality was the traditional socialist goal. Since the early study by Hewitt (1977), there was considerable evidence in favour of a Social Democratic effect on income distribution (Bjorn, 1979; Stephens, 1979; Van Arnhem and Schotsman, 1982; Hicks and Swank, 1984; Swank and Hicks, 1985; Hage et al., 1989; Mueller, 1989). Still, income distribution was for several reasons a problematic variable.

On technical grounds, aggregate data available until the arrival of the Luxembourg Income Study (Mitchell, 1990; Smeeding et al., 1990) were not truly comparable. On theoretical grounds, income distribution was problematic to the extent that the kinds of universalistic and generous welfare programmes associated with successful Social Democratic politics tended to lose their redistributive effect because they increasingly favoured the middle classes (LeGrand, 1982; Goodin and LeGrand, 1987; Esping-Andersen, 1990). Ringen (1987) argued that large welfare states generated greater equality, but this may have been true only of transfers. With the rising importance of collective services, any firm conclusion still must await more research on non-cash income distribution.

There was some evidence to suggest that the Social Democratic effect was more evident when measured against institutional characteristics of welfare states. This is the case in Myles' (1989) study of pension systems, Korpi's (1989) and Kangas' (1991) studies of sickness insurance, Palme's (1990) study of pension rights, and Esping-Andersen's (1990) study of welfare state attributes such as universalism, the public–private mix, the importance of means-tested social benefits, and active labour market policies. Yet as research moved in the direction of studying the institutional properties of welfare states, it also moved away from the kind of linear 'more or less' or 'the bigger, the better' Social Democratization conception that dominated the literature in the 1980s. Thus Kangas' (1991: 52) study of social expenditures and social rights concludes that 'the biggest are not necessarily the best, but the best are rarely the smallest'.

One of the major insights of the debate has been that to equate Social Democracy and the welfare state may have been a mistake. There was considerable variation on both the independent (Social Democracy) and the dependent (the welfare state and equality) variable (Keman, 1990, 1993b). Titmuss (1974) already argued that welfare states differed fundamentally as to their institutionalization of solidarity and equality. Only his 'institutional redistributive' type came anywhere near the Social Democratic ideal. Furniss and Tilton (1977) offered a distinction between the *social security* state and the *social welfare* state, only the latter representing the Social Democratic ideal. Therborn (1986, 1987a) stressed the vital criteria of social policy and a commitment to full employment. Without the commitment to full employment there was no Social Democratic welfare state. He therefore argued in favour of a regeneration of welfare state theory. Hence, this development left behind the Social Democratic bias and this has put once again the political causes of variations in social policies prominently on the research agenda. The reconsideration of the model began with the undeniable fact that early welfare state reforms rarely, if ever, were initiated by Social Democracy, and that several countries (e.g. The Netherlands: Therborn, 1989) pursued equality and welfare statism without the advocacy of a strong Social Democratic labour movement (Castles, 1978, 1985; Stephens, 1979; Wilensky, 1981; Skocpol and Amenta, 1986). This suggested the need to elaborate the political process of welfare state construction. One answer came from those who showed that Christian Democracy (or Catholicism) constituted a functional equivalent or alternative to Social Democracy. This point was raised early on by Stephens (1979: 100), who argued that 'it seemed possible that anti-capitalist aspects of catholic ideology – such as notions of fair wage or prohibitions of usury – as well as the generally positive attitude of the catholic church towards welfare for the poor might encourage government welfare spending'. As a result, one of the basic assumptions of the Social Democratic model, namely that the power of labour equals the power of Social Democracy, had to be relaxed. Stephens has suggested that Christian Democratic parties operating in the centre enjoyed considerable working-class support and were commonly backed by powerful catholic unions (see also: Shalev, 1983) and that this political constellation was highly favourable to welfare state development. Schmidt (1980, 1982a) has asserted that Social Democracy and Christian Democracy could be functionally equivalent, at least during periods of economic prosperity, and Wilensky (1981) has argued that the two movements overlapped considerably in ideological terms, and that catholicism indeed constituted a more important determinant of welfare statism than did Social Democracy.

These attempts to improve upon the Social Democratic model culminated in Esping-Andersen's (1990) thesis that Christian Democracy and Social Democracy result in fundamentally different kinds of welfare states (see also: van Kersbergen, 1995). Most importantly, Christian Democracy is reluc-tant to expand collective social services and does not demonstrate the kind of full employment characteristic of the Social Democratic model. Later research (e.g. Huber et al., 1993; Huber and Stephens, 1993; Castles and Mitchell, 1993) corroborated these findings. These analyses embody real improvements in understanding the political forces that shape welfare state outcomes. However, the farewell to the Social Democratic model was not radical enough to allow of a thorough innovation in the power resources tra-dition that could fully grasp the still problematic association between Christian Democracy and welfare state development. There were two main reasons for this. First, the critique of the assumptions of the Social Demo-cratic model needed to be developed further. Second, the understanding of Christian Democracy was still inadequate and needed to be improved.

The usually unreasoned assumptions of the Social Democratic literature can be summarized as follows: class and class structure are the determinants of political power, and the political power of the working class is founded by the degree of organization of its main political representative, Social Demo-cracy; a developed welfare state is the incarnation of Social Democracy in power; a high level of social spending is a token of a developed welfare state and therefore of a powerful labour movement. The latter two assumptions were major points of reference in Esping-Andersen's (1985b, 1987, 1990) criti-cal contribution to welfare state theory. The first assumption, however, con-tinued to figure in the theory of welfare state regimes. In particular, it was imperative to modify the presupposition of equating labour power and Social Democracy. Like Baldwin (1990), Esping-Andersen made the observation that dominant theories of working-class mobilization fail to explain the origins of social policy, because they were 'essentially premised on the laborist, socialist, or Social Democratic model of collective action, a model that was far from being dominant until well into the twentieth century' (Esping-Andersen, 1990: 109). This suggested that Esping-Andersen was explicitly trying to avoid class reductionism since one 'cannot assume that socialism is the natural basis for wage-earner mobilization' (Esping-Andersen, 1990: 17).

Other parties, for instance, could also take the role of articulating labour demands. This idea points to those countries where Christian Democratic parties have been dominant. Here, such parties had been decisive in the interpretation of labour's social policy needs. In other words, labour had autonomous social policy needs which would normally have led to Social Democratic power mobilization concentrated around the goals of solidarity, equality and universalism, were it not for the fact that such demands were 'filtered' and 're-interpreted' (and implicitly assumed to be 'distorted') by other movements, notably Christian Democracy (see van Kersbergen, 1995, 1999).

9.3.1 The Theory of Welfare State Regimes

Esping-Andersen took seriously the criticism of the Social Democratic model, arguing that there was a striking conceptual indifference in the literature with respect to the object of study itself: the welfare state. Starting from the judgement that 'expenditures are epiphenomenal to the theoretical substance of welfare states' (1990: 19) and the reflection that 'it is difficult to imagine that anyone struggled for spending *per se*' (1990: 21), he has suggested that the study of welfare states has much to gain by looking at the quality of *social rights*, the typical patterns of *stratification*, and the manner in which the *state*, the *market* and the *family* interacted in the production of social welfare. There did not exist any causal linearity between societal power and welfare statism. Welfare states rather cluster along qualitative and political dimensions.

Esping-Andersen distinguishes three types of welfare state regimes: a Social Democratic, a Liberal and a Corporatist or Conservative regime. These regimes differ with respect to the major institutions guaranteeing *social security* (the state, the market or the family); the kind of *stratification* systems upheld by the institutional mix of these institutions (the extent of status and class differentiation, segmentation and inequality typically implied in social security systems); and the degree of *de-commodification*, that is to say 'the degree to which individuals, or families, can uphold a socially acceptable standard of living independently of market participation' (Esping-Andersen, 1990: 37). The Social Democratic regime is characterized by a political commitment to equality; it reduced status and class differentials and modified greatly the market dependence of wage-labour. Particularism and an unwillingness to alter the status and class structure are major features of the conservative regime, which also favours a social policy that

Table 9.1 *Esping-Andersen's regimes and their characteristics*

	Liberal	Social Democratic	Conservative
Role of:			
Family	Marginal	Marginal	Central
Market	Central	Marginal	Marginal
State	Marginal	Central	Subsidiary
Welfare state:			
Dominant mode of solidarity	Individual	Universal	Kinship Corporatism Etatism
Dominant locus of solidarity	Market	State	Family
Degree of decommodification	Minimal	Maximum	High (for bread-winner)
Modal examples	USA	Sweden	Germany Italy

Source: Esping-Andersen (1999: 85).

privileges and preserves the family. In the liberal welfare state regime the market predominated and social rights are generally modest and attached to performance on the labour market. The variations in welfare state regimes are by and large explained by the distinct modes in which classes (particularly the working class) have mobilized politically, the diverging structuration of class alliances and class coalitions, and the different national policy legacies (see Table 9.1).

In the attempts to reconceptualize the welfare state, Esping-Andersen's work stands out as having decisively changed the direction of theoretical and empirical research. In effect, much of the recent literature provides (sometimes overly) critical discussions of the theory of welfare state regimes, but is at the same time greatly indebted to the suggestion that there are various configurations of market, state, and the family, and that variations in welfare state development are 'not linearly distributed, but clustered by regime-types' (Esping-Andersen, 1990: 26).

Studies that appeared since Esping-Andersen's 1990 book increasingly highlighted distinct welfare state types, but also proposed improvements of the classification (see, for example, Lessenich and Ostner, 1998). Many amendments of the basic three-regime typology have been suggested, such as the addition of a type addressing the peculiarities of the Mediterranean world (Lessenich, 1994; Ferrera, 1996a). Others suggest that an Asian type of welfarism should be constructed (Goodman and Peng, 1996). The essence of both amendments is that a fourth element has to be added to the chain Esping-Andersen uses as the criterion for distinguishing welfare states. In the Asian case the chain then would be market–family–state–group/company, because in Japan neighbourhoods and especially companies also perform a crucial role in social security. In the Mediterranean case the fourth element is the patron–client relationship as exemplified with regard to Italy by Ferrera (1996a and b). In Italy, the 'partitocrazia' (i.e. rule by parties) channels large amounts of public resources to party factions and party controlled companies, foundations and institutions functioning as a sort of 'undergovernment' (*sottogoverno*). In exchange for votes and based on specific personal relations between party officials (patrons) and the population (clients) the institutions of the *sottogoverno* distribute welfare benefits, particularly in the field of pensions. Taken together, these two amendments would bring about a typology of five types of welfare systems (Becker, 2000).

Another 'fourth world of welfare capitalism' was put forward by Castles and Mitchell (1993), who attempted to refine the theory of welfare state regimes by referring to peculiarities of the Australian (and New Zealand) system. The means-tested, residual type of welfare state found in Australia had to be considered as the result of a coherent Social Democratic strategy once one took into account labour's success in establishing guaranteed employment and wage growth, accompanied by occupational social rights. Looking at welfare expenditure and benefit equality, taxes and transfers, and redistribution of incomes, Castles and Mitchell demonstrate the relevance of their proposed four-quadrant typology of welfare states. Particularly interesting was their attempt to link these welfare state types to distinct political configurations in democracies, which apparently singled out a Liberal, a Conservative, a 'Radical' and a Social Democratic regime. The existence of a radical regime was explained in terms of a distinct historical, political pattern, 'consisting of a labour movement unable to obtain a degree of partisan control commensurate with its political support base in the community and of a historical legacy of radical egalitarianism' (Castles and Mitchell, 1993: 123). In Australia and New Zealand the market itself produced welfare. And, as Esping-Andersen (1999: 89) recently argued, this implies that 'it may be a fallacy to simply equate markets and Liberalism'.

Esping-Andersen at first agreed with the theoretical relevance of a radical, fourth world, because it showed that the biased focus of much of the literature on the welfare state ran the risk of underrating the possible effects of private or less direct political interventions in the market. However, in his most recent work he seems to have changed his mind:

> It is possible that the Antipodean model provided a package of welfare guarantees that was essentially 'Social Democratic' in the 1960s and 1970s. Like Britain, however, the passage of time is pushing Australia – and certainly New Zealand – toward what appears as prototypical Liberalism: minimal state and maximum market allocation of risks, and the market side of the coin appears increasingly genuinely market. (Esping-Andersen, 1999: 90)

According to Esping-Andersen, then, the regime characteristics summarized in Table 9.1 are still, or even increasingly relevant today. Perhaps he is right. Those, however, who think it is necessary to add a fourth or even fifth type of welfare capitalism, have also good arguments.

Meanwhile, in describing recent welfare state developments, we will largely make use of Esping-Andersen's distinctions. We will, however, shift the attention from abstract relations between the market, the state and the family towards how and why a society approaches material risks. Moreover, we will talk of a paternalist instead of a conservative type. This slight change in terminology reflects the peculiarities of Christian Democracy. Basically, paternalism refers to a 'caring relation' between the 'strong' or the advantaged and the 'weak' or the disadvantaged. In the first case (strong versus weak), paternalism is conservative. In the second case, however, where a balance of advantages and disadvantages without generally classifying groups of people is at stake, this is not necessarily true (Becker, 2000).

9.3.2 The Institutionalist Turn

While the discussion on typologies and suitable standards for comparative analysis went on in the 1990s, the 'new institutionalism', which had become influential a decade earlier, found its way into welfare state research. The social scientific concept of institutions is centred on the notion of 'rules of the game' (Ostrom, 1990: 176; March and Olsen, 1995), and in the social and political field it occupies the whole range of features from rule-based formal structures such as state forms, parliaments and corporatist bodies, to informal rules and norms (North, 1990: 3ff) like those patterning the relationships between parliaments and governments or between welfare agencies and recipients. This is a very broad concept which is often criticized for its vagueness (Guy Peters, 1996), but some institutionalists use it in its narrower meaning of formal structures. In general, institutionalists stress the determining force of institutions in historical processes, a nexus which is called 'path dependence'. In this they are challenged, however, by the criticism that institutional structures are open to historical change too and that, if at all, institutionalism has to be historical institutionalism which takes into account the interplay between structures and action (Steinmo et al., 1992; Czada et al., 1998).

Whatever the theoretical merits of the different institutionalist strands are, in welfare state research this approach concentrates on the explanation of the development of national differences as well as on the success or failure of recent attempts to reform welfare systems and to cut back expenditures. With respect to the first subject the question is whether it really was only historical exigencies, power relations and ideologies which brought about the peculiarities of, for example, the American and Swedish welfare states. What about the importance of these countries' political institutions in this matter? Would it be realistic to expect anything else than a residual welfare system in the context of a weak, fragmented government as in the United States? And is it not just the centralized structure of the Swedish state in combination with a PR election system minimizing the impact of special interests that enabled Swedish politicians to raise the taxes necessary to finance large welfare programmes (Steinmo et al., 1992)? These are good questions, and it seems that the institutional approach scores at least some points. However, in cases of different outcomes in similar institutional settings – Sweden and Italy, for example – the approach gets into trouble. And it cannot explain, particularly in its formal-institutional variety, why just egalitarian conceptions of welfare were so strong in Scandinavia whereas they have been weak most of the time in the Latin countries. And why has political fragmentation not been a strong incentive in US politics to change the entire structure of American democracy instead of enhancing liberal individualism (see also: Weaver and Rockman, 1993; Schmidt, 1996a; Keman, 1997c)?

More attention has gone to institutionalist studies of recent welfare state change than to general examinations, particularly to Paul Pierson's (1994) *Dismantling the Welfare State?* Pierson's main finding is that in spite of mounting pressures from liberal forces in contemporary democracies, symbolized by the names of Reagan and Thatcher, and – in contrast to changes in the arenas of macro-economic policy, industrial relations or regulatory policy – 'the welfare state stands out as an island of relative stability' (1994: 5). In explaining this resistance to change Pierson focuses not only on institutional structures but also on electoral mechanisms. In his view, the former include those networks of welfare bureaucracies and services in the policy areas of social housing, health care, education, public assistance and social security, the very existence of which is bound to the status quo in social policy and which therefore exert powerful pressures against attempts of retrenchment. These professional networks were created by post-war welfare state development of democratic states, and once established they were able to muster substantial veto powers against reform efforts (Pierson, 1996: 147). Because these structures stand for path continuity, a weakening of Social Democratic and Christian Democratic parties and the trade union movement – the main historical supporters of welfare state expansion – need not necessarily translate into commensurate weakening of social policy.

Moreover, Pierson argues, 'frontal assaults on the welfare state carry tremendous electoral risks' (1996: 178). Welfare expansion usually generated a popular politics of credit-claiming for extending social rights and raising benefits to an increasing number of citizens, while austerity policies affront large groups of voters. Since 'welfare state retrenchment generally requires elected officials to pursue unpopular policies' (1996: 143f), these officials are confronted with the problem of 'blame avoidance'. This, however, is particularly difficult to realize in the rather centralized, parliamentary democracies predominant in Europe. Responsibility and accountability are concentrated there (Pierson, 1994: 33). Therefore, even 'retrenchment advocates … confront a clash between their policy preferences and their electoral ambitions' (Pierson, 1996: 146). As a rule, the latter prevail. And in the fragmented USA the institutional logic that prevented the build-up of a generous and comprehensive welfare system also tends to block retrenchment reforms.

Separate welfare programmes have been cut down in a number of countries, Pierson has to admit (1994: 5, 118ff). However, institutional inertia and voter preferences prevent fundamental changes and provide for a considerable degree of path continuity (see also Esping-Andersen, 1996: 24). Esping-Andersen even asserts that although the environment of social policy has changed and welfare states are adapting to new challenges, welfare state regimes by and large persist and react to the challenges and new risks in a manner typical for their institutional path. As he (1999: 165) puts it: 'the inherent logic of our three welfare regimes seems to reproduce itself'. The Social Democratic regime has emphasized the state's role in welfare. Active labour market policies are aimed at maximizing labour market participation, particularly of the young. The conservative welfare regimes have continued to stress passive labour market policies (transfers) and at the same time have transferred the burden of care to the family. The Liberal regimes have increased their traditional reliance on the market (deregulation, privatization, marketization of risks). Below we shall discuss to what extent this diagnosis is correct and what the value is of Pierson's assumption of an electorate overwhelmingly supporting the given welfare state level. After Pierson, however, one can no longer seriously study the struggle about the welfare state without taking institutional structures into consideration.

9.4. RISKS AND SOCIAL SECURITY

9.4.1 Liberalism, Social Democracy, and Paternalism

The existence of a labour market implies the risk of unemployment. In addition, people are sometimes unable to earn a living on the market because of personal circumstances such as illness or disability. An 'atomized' society entails the risk of poverty in old age. Politically, the ideas on how to deal with such risks diverge substantially. *Liberalism* has much confidence in the market. In a free market the risk of unemployment does not exist if labour is cheap enough. If unemployment does occur, the price of labour needs to drop. In an economy that is moving to a new market equilibrium, individual citizens are assumed to insure themselves – individually or collectively (e.g. as unionized workers) – against the risk of unemployment. The same holds for sickness, disability and old age. Social risks are seen as no different from other risks for which one takes out an insurance policy, such as third-party insurance. A minimal system of public social security serves a clientele of people who – for reasons outside their responsibility – are incapable of insuring themselves. Independence and the ability to cope for oneself rather than 'care' occupy centre stage in Liberalism. In the ideal-typical Liberal market economy there is no room for more than minimal solidarity, except in the sense that the right to income is linked with the assumption that one does one's best. The result is what Titmuss (1974: 62) called the 'residual welfare state'.

A profound distrust of the market is characteristic for both the *Social Democratic* and the *paternalistic* attempt to regulate the market economy. Here, the individual citizen is not looked upon as a 'production factor' or solely an individual, but as a social being. Therefore, social security ought to be based on social solidarity, a communitarian idea that is a feature of both currents. The main differences pertain to the Social Democratic assumption of the possibility of universal citizenship and the conviction that political intervention in the form of employment policies is necessary to compensate for market failure. Nobody should suffer from the market. Social Democracy assumes people to live in solidarity rather than as autonomous individuals.

Paternalism in its conservative strand, for instance as a trait of Catholic social doctrine, assumes a natural social cleavage between the 'weak' and the 'strong'. While liberal contract theory emphasizes rights and duties and Social Democracy is rooted in the struggle for the emancipation of the working classes, paternalism one-sidedly stresses the obligations of both the weak and the strong. It is the obligation of the strong to help the weak and the duty of the weak to obey the strong. However, if care and support by the family and by private charities are insufficient, then it is the obligation of the 'caring state' to protect the weak (De Swaan, 1988). Social security is necessary to prevent and combat poverty in order to prevent or combat moral degradation and to restore and maintain the natural, organic harmony of society (Van Kersbergen, 1995).

By contrast, modern paternalism assumes that the democratic ideal of citizenship has not yet been developed. Independence is judged a core value, yet at the same time one has to acknowledge that because of the cumulating of social, cognitive or physical disadvantages not everybody will meet the requirements for citizenship. Paternalism holds that in a rich society that wants to avoid poverty, misery and disintegration the disadvantaged need to be supported by the advantaged.

In spite of the common roots of all contemporary welfare states in industrialization, individualization and democratization, the variation in the emerging social security arrangements has been vast. Although diffusion was a frequent phenomenon, most systems acquired their own logic of development, according to differences in economic structure, level of urbanization, cultural traditions and the structure of the political system. Party-political relations of power largely determined the original choices with respect to the developmental path of social security and made the emerging welfare systems appear as parts of specific democratic regimes.

9.4.2 Systematic Differences

One important distinction between the systems concerns the type of insurance. On the one hand, there are universalist schemes that are tax-financed. On the other hand, one finds social insurances that are by and large contribution-based. Universal schemes pay flat-rate benefits that are unrelated to earned income. Social insurance benefits depend on contributions and are typically earnings-related. A universalist system is sometimes referred to as the *Beveridge-model* (after the Liberal chairman of the British committee that wrote an influential report on a tax-financed flat-rate social system in 1942; Ashford, 1986: 264ff). The social insurance model is referred to as the Bismarck-system or the continental system. Universalist benefits are sometimes means-tested, that is to say a benefit is conditional on what one can contribute oneself, for instance from property from the income of one's spouse. The latter point indicates that even in an individualized society the role of the family in the provision of social security is still important, especially in the southern European countries (Schmidt, 1998; Esping-Andersen, 1999).

A mix of universalist schemes and social insurances is characteristic for all western democracies, but the emphasis on one of the forms determines the type of welfare state system. Universalist arrangements, whether or not means-tested, are typical for child allowances and social assistance in most countries, a (universalist) national health system is to be found in Denmark, Britain and Sweden. In Denmark and Britain the minimum unemployment benefits are tax-financed, while all Scandinavian countries as well as The Netherlands have a universalist basic old age pension system that is not means-tested and supplemented with an earnings-related benefit. Scandinavia leads when it comes to tax-financed social security (a high 81.6 per cent in Denmark in 1992), followed by Britain (42.8 per cent) and the continental welfare states (26 per cent in Germany, 22.6 per cent in The Netherlands and 17.7 per cent in France; Einerhand et al., 1995: 41). Sometimes the difference between tax-financed and contribution-based social security arrangements is purely bureaucratic. The Danish tax-financed unemployment benefit, for instance, is earnings-related. Moreover, many social insurance schemes are subsidized by taxes, while social security contributions are occasionally used for redistributive purposes (also: Schmidt, 1998: 215–28).

According to Esping-Andersen's (1990) original theory, universalism in social security is typical for the Social Democratic welfare state regime, while social insurance is a feature of the Conservative cluster. The idea behind this is that universalist schemes increase equality and appeal to solidarity, while a social insurance system reproduces the income and status differentials that exist in the labour market. However, the contrast between Social Democracy and Conservatism according to the difference between universalist schemes versus earnings-related social insurances does not seem to be entirely logical. Universalism without means-testing and statutory supplements only seems to make sense at a very low level of benefits. But in this form it would be Liberal rather than Social Democratic, because of the minimal redistributive effect. The other possibility is that wages would be universalistically determined, but this is obviously not the case in market economies, and one cannot expect social security (to be distinguished from incomes policies) to correct market inequalities. Moreover, Baldwin (1990: 60ff) has demonstrated that, historically, universalist arrangements originated in those parties and movements that stood up for the interests of the self-employed. Where the advent of industrialization was late, the Social Democratic labour movement accepted universalism (Baldwin, 1990: 114). However, if workers were already embedded in a system of social insurances (as in Germany), Social Democracy tended to resist the universalist arrangements (Baldwin, 1990: 161). In his later work, Esping-Andersen argues that the Social Democratic label should be reserved exclusively for the period since the 1960s. Moreover, the defining characteristics of Social Democracy are 'firstly, the fusion of universalism with generosity and, secondly, its comprehensive socialization of risks' (Esping-Andersen, 1999: 79).

Another important feature of social security concerns the difference between passive and active labour market policies. Benefits are passive measures, while the complex of social policies that are aimed at minimizing labour market risks (such as training, schooling, job subsidies and job creation) are active labour market policies. The latter policies obviously require a critical attitude towards the labour market and are therefore typical for the Social Democratic and not for the Liberal regime. Some types of active policies would also fit where paternalistic and etatist traditions converge. So, it is not a surprise that expenditures for active labour market policy is highest in Scandinavia and lowest in the Anglo-Saxon world, with the continental European countries in between (Empter and Esche, 1997: 182ff).

In addition to active labour market policies such as schooling, training and short-term labour market measures, structural employment can be politically combated by expanding public sector employment or by encouraging labour market participation. The Scandinavian countries – at least since the 1960s – have been public employment leaders: approximately 30 per cent of all jobs are public sector jobs. Public sector employment has been the basis for the high rates of female labour market participation found in Scandinavia. Jobs for women are further promoted by favourable child care facilities and fairly generous arrangements for maternal and paternal leave (for a comparative study of recent developments, see: Bussemaker and van Kersbergen, 1999).

The picture with respect to expenditures for passive labour market policies (including early retirement) is only slightly different. These expenditures are highest in Denmark and the Netherlands and lowest in the USA, where the figure is only one-tenth of the Danish. Especially in Italy, The Netherlands, France and Germany public expenditures for early retirement are substantial. Unemployment benefits (see Becker, 2000: 227f) are highest in Denmark (90 per cent of former earnings) and lowest in Italy and the USA (30 per cent on average). The difference in duration of benefits is similar: a maximum of 5 years in Denmark and 26 weeks in the USA (other countries are located in between these extremes). However, one cannot 'deduce' the type of welfare state regime from the generosity of benefits. Italy, for instance, is hardly a liberal country, but the official unemployment benefits (26 per cent) are lower than in the USA and of shorter duration. The unemployed depend to a large extent on the family and charity, the black market or a disability pension to be acquired in the jungle of the 'sottogoverno' (Ferrera, 1996b: 21–6). Another example is The Netherlands. Here benefits equal the Swedish level, but Social Democratic values were less prevalent until the 1960s. Politics was dominated by Christian Democratic paternalism.

In the context of this chapter it is of course impossible to provide detailed information on all schemes for all welfare states. In Table 9.2 we therefore provide some recent basic indicators of the quality of selected welfare states by looking at the presence or absence of active labour market policies, the presence or absence of basic social security schemes, and the income replacement ratios of benefits.

Table 9.2 *Basic data on western systems of social security, poverty and inequality in the mid-1990s and replacement rates for average production workers*

	AUS	DK	F	G	GB	I	NL	NZ	S	USA
Legal minimum wage	*	N	Y	N	Y	N	Y	Y	N	Y
Level of basic provisions	M	H	M	M	L	L	H	M/L	H	L
Universalist basic pension	N	Y	N	N	N	N	Y	Y	Y	N
General social assistence	N	Y	Y	Y	Y	N	Y	N	N	N
Net repayment rate (%) of an unemployed, SF, 1st month 'NRR', SF, 60th month, incl.	71	83	80	78	77	47	84	70	89	68
Housing assistance	71	83	65	71	77	11	80	70	99	17
Poverty rate (< 50% median income)	9.5	5.0	6.8	9.1	18.9	14.2	6.1		6.7	17.1
Gini-index of net-inequality	0.306	0.217	0.291	0.282	0.337	0.345	0.253		0.234	0.344
Change of Gini mid-1970 to mid-1990s in %	+5.2	−4.9	−1.7	+6.4	+35.9	+12.7	+11.8		+0.9	+34.4

Explanation: H = relatively high, M = medium; L = relatively low; Y = Yes. N = No, ST = standard family with 2 children;

Note: * = Australia has some regulations regarding wage levels.

Sources: OECD (1996–2000); OECD (1997b: 13).

Surprisingly, Denmark and Sweden do not have a legal minimum wage, and it should be added that the replacement rates would be different in non-standard situations. Particularly in the USA, these would be much lower for single people, who only receive 30 per cent for 26 weeks. In Italy the situation is even worse. Here a single person only gets 26 per cent for the same period (juvenile unemployed living at home receive no assistance at all), and in both countries no social assistance exists. To supply-siders, Italy must be a puzzling case. Unit labour costs are low (*The Economist*, 19 December 1998), social security for the working-age population is at the lowest level of the democratic western world, and yet unemployment and non-employment are very high. Is that simply the result of high taxes and tight labour market regulations (which companies often escape by corruption; Regini, 1997: 107)? Or is it the flourishing black economy which in 1994 accounted for 26 per cent of Italy's GDP (estimates for Britain, Denmark and Germany were respectively 12, 13 and 17 per cent; *The Economist*, 3 May 1997). Or is it because the family still plays a key role in providing care for the elderly and the young unemployed (Esping-Andersen, 1999: 63)? It seems that Britain too seems to fare well in welfare terms. In reality, however, many more provisions are subject to means-testing than in European countries with comparable replacement rates. Justifiably or not, means-testing tends to discourage people from taking the full social provisions to which they are entitled (Einerhand et al., 1995). An average replacement rate of about 35 per cent of GDP per capita, as reported by Empter and Esche (1997: 63), seems to be much more realistic than the OECD figure of 77 per cent (related to the Average Production Worker wage, yet still much higher). As a result, the British poverty rate is one of the highest of the countries compared here, and it is the British unemployed who suffer most. The percentage of them living in poverty was 45.5 per cent in 1988, a figure even higher than that of their Italian counterparts (35.2 per cent), whereas in Denmark, the country with the highest benefits (90 per cent of earned wages), only 2.7 per cent of the unemployed are recorded as poor (Eurostat, 1996: 213).

9.4.3 Challenges and Reforms

Contemporary welfare states are confronted with two main problems. First, the social security systems, especially the pension systems and health systems, face great financial problems, as a result of ageing populations. On average about 70 per cent of total social expenditures in the EU member states is going to pensions and health care for the elderly. In Italy it is even more than 80 per cent (Hanisch, 1998: 20). The second major problem concerns mass unemployment which is mainly caused by increasing labour supply resulting from the rising number of women entering the labour market as well as by international competition that has moved a considerable part of production processes relying on unqualified labour to low-wage countries. If one takes into account various kinds of hidden unemployment, the result is a very high level of 'non-employment', especially on the European continent. With officially registered unemployment rates on average below 10 per cent, the OECD provides an estimate of non-employment of about 25 per cent of the labour force. Reinforced by individualization, this implies a rising welfare state clientele. Even in countries where 'registered' unemployment has been decreasing substantially (as in The Netherlands), 'non-employment' and the number of social security beneficiaries have not really declined.

In sum, roughly since the 1980s, the welfare systems of all economically developed democracies have come under pressure because of the rising costs of ageing populations and the sharp increase in non-employment in all its different guises. Most democratic states have reacted with a mix of increasing social security contributions and taxes, introducing incentives to work, cutting back benefits, limiting the duration and indexing of benefits, increasing wage differentiation (particularly by relatively lowering the minimum wage), tightening eligibility criteria, introducing or reinforcing means-tests and sanctions, and abolishing programmes for specific groups (such as young unemployed who live at home; Keman, 1998).

In Britain, the welfare cuts seem to have been very drastic (Bradshow, 1993: 43), while in the USA retrenchment has been concentrated on 'welfare' (as different from the contribution-based 'social security) recipients (Myles, 1996: 128). In Sweden, as in The Netherlands, benefits have been brought down from a comparatively very high level (Palme and Wennemo, 1997; Becker, 2000). France has been the major exception to the extent that major improvements were made in social security (Hantrais, 1996), while in Germany the political stalemate between the upper and the lower house of parliament have made social security reforms very difficult (Hemerijck et al., 2000). In the Italian system, apart from pensions and perhaps health care (see Ferrera, 1996b) there has been little retrenchment, whereas the Danish and Australian systems have kept their level, although there too eligibility rules were tightened.

It is difficult to identify the effects of retrenchment exactly, but a look at poverty rates and the development of employment reveals that countries where, as in Britain and the USA, retrenchment took place on an already low level of welfare benefits, the poverty rate – defined as an income lower than 50 per cent of the median income – has increased to nearly 20 per cent. In the European continental countries approaching the Social Democratic or paternalist types of welfare statism, cuts in the relatively generous benefits or no retrenchment at all have kept poverty rates on a relatively stable low level of about 5 to 9 per cent (OECD, 1997: 54). Unemployment has decreased sharply in a country with a liberal welfare state, the United States, but the same holds for The Netherlands with its cuts in very high levels of benefits as well as for Denmark with very little retrenchment at all. Sweden, by contrast, has experienced a combination of rising unemployment and some drastic cuts in social security. And Italy has not seen any increase in employment or a decrease of unemployment – despite its very low level of social security (OECD, 2000). In other words, the association between the level of benefits and the level of employment seems to be weaker than is often suggested.

Can we conclude, as Pierson does, that by and large the welfare state is an island of relative stability? With the exception of Britain after 1985 (and to some extent Germany) welfare expenditures have increased steadily all over the western world in the 1980s. In the 1990s, this process continued at a lower pace, with The Netherlands, Sweden and Denmark (after 1994) being the exceptions (SCP, 2000: 354). These developments do not provide exact information, however, because the ageing process of western society and the rise of its social costs have accelerated in the past two decades, and because in the 1990s non-employment has risen in most countries. As a result, the total number of people receiving social security benefits has increased and health care expenditures have mounted. In most countries cuts in the smaller part of the social security package – child allowances, social assistance, unemployment insurance – could not compensate this incremental increase. This only happened where basic pensions were also retrenched and where the cuts were either drastic (as in Sweden, though from a high level) or accompanied by high economic growth and stable or declining unemployment (as in Denmark and particularly in The Netherlands).

In our view Pierson's statement appears to be too general, not taking into account the complexity of the processes at stake (moreover, he does not consider the dimension of redistribution by, for instance, taxation). The assumption that there is strong popular support for keeping the existing level of the welfare state seems also untenable. Looking at different parts of social security, it become clear that majorities are against cuts in pensions and health care, but also that these majorities turn into minorities when it comes to unemployment benefits and social assistance, that is to say those fields where risk is unevenly spread. And the differentiation is growing when people are asked for the price they want to pay for a stable or even improved quality of the welfare system (Keman, 1998; Mau, 1998; Goodin et al., 1999).

Finally, Esping-Andersen's idea of an ongoing path dependency in welfare state adjustment at least has to be qualified. His suggestion is largely true if one looks at inequality, which has risen most, for instance by lowering income tax rates, in countries within the liberal type and least or not at all in the Social Democratic Scandinavian cluster. However, the liberal notion of individual responsibility has gained ground everywhere (Cox, 1998), the esteem of the market has grown, and social security cuts have been on average and in relative terms as severe in Social Democratic and paternalist countries as they have been in liberal ones. Cautiously, one could state that in the face of secularization and individualization conservative or traditionally paternalist conceptions of the welfare state are in a process of erosion and that liberal conceptions are prevailing against Social Democratic and modern paternalist ones, at least at the moment. Social Democrats in a number of countries have adopted this idea under the label of the 'third way'. Traditional welfare statism, as described in this chapter, particularly following Esping-Andersen, seems to be in transition.

9.5. POLITICAL ISSUES AND THEORETICAL PERSPECTIVES

9.5.1 Political Issues

Individual responsibility is central to democratic citizenship, so there seems to be no problem with the spread of the liberal conception of welfare. What tends to be overlooked, however, is that risks of unemployment, disability and sickness remain distributed unevenly in society. These risks tend to be concentrated with those who have low labour market qualifications and at the same time poor resources to insure themselves. Hence, more individual responsibility in this sense is bound to bring about either a redistribution of the burden of social security towards those groups already most vulnerable or simply a rise in poverty to the level of countries like the United States. Traditional Social Democrats, still strong in Scandinavia, Portugal and France, as well as paternalistic Christian Democrats are the main political actors still addressing this problem at the moment in a different vein from Liberalism. A crucial question for the future development of the welfare state and the principle of solidarity will be therefore whether a majority of the people will support its basic lay-out, not only with regard to pensions, but particularly also with regard to those areas where risks are distributed unevenly. When public support in these domains declines, Liberalism and the 'third way' are indistinguishable and on the winning road (Giddens, 1998).

A related question concerns the market–state nexus. If the emphasis is put, as currently seems to be the case, on letting market forces be free and flexible, then a conception facilitating increasing inequality is favoured. A free market, it is said, is enhancing employment because it would comprise a flexible labour market and create demand for low-skilled, low-paid labour. This would imply a rising number of working poor as well as increasing income differentiation. Facilitating lower wages, moreover, would require that the level of employment-related social security benefits would have to be brought down too. So, it seems that there is a dilemma of work and welfare. If one wants to keep a generous level of welfare, a certain political protection of labour is necessary and unemployment or – to be more precise – non-employment, can probably no longer be reduced to pre-1980s levels, at least not in all western democracies. Like the case of generous benefits this would also be a question of political support. For large employment programmes require high taxes. To raise these taxes seems to become increasingly difficult in societies where class boundaries and ideologies are losing their relevance in the formation of individual identities as well as in political mobilization.

9.5.2 Theoretical Perspectives

In the introduction two different ways of studying the welfare state were distinguished, depending on whether the welfare state was looked on as a dependent or independent variable. Originally, welfare state researchers were interested in explaining the emergence of welfare states. Then the focus gradually shifted to cross-national variation in the level of development of welfare states as the main explanatory problem. Simultaneously, many studies were undertaken that concentrated on the effects of welfare states.

Precisely at this point, however, there seems to be a major problem in contemporary comparative welfare state studies. There is considerable confusion around the question of what exactly is to be explained. The problem is known as the 'dependent variable problem'. What are compartivists trying to explain? Is it the crisis of the welfare state? Is it cross-national variation in the patterns of retrenchment? Is it the reconstruction of the welfare state? Is it the persistence of welfare states? Is it the convergence of regimes (see: Keman, 1998)?

Pierson observes that there is a lack of consensus on outcomes, particularly with respect to the issue of how much welfare states have actually changed since the Golden Age of economic growth (1960–80). For instance, where Pierson (1996) looks at social spending, particularly transfer payments, and concludes that there has been no radical dismantling of welfare state arrangements, Clayton and Pontusson (1998) criticize this thesis by pointing to the fact that if one looks at the organization of the public sector, particularly regarding the delivery of social services and the development of public employment, one can observe significant levels of retrenchment and market-oriented reforms, even in the Social Democratic welfare state of Sweden. In fact, Clayton and Pontusson go so far as to argue that current reforms (retrenchment) of social services tend to have a bias which is not picked up if one studies transfer payments only. By contrast, Levy (1999) finds that especially welfare state reform in Christian Democratic regimes cannot be described either in terms of pure retrenchments of transfer payments or in terms of a reduction in social services. His argument is that these welfare states 'are not locked into zero-sum trade-offs between the pursuit of efficiency and the pursuit of equity' (Levy, 1999: 265). In fact, successful reform of the welfare state implies turning vice into virtue, that is, 'targeting inequities within the welfare system that are simultaneously a source of inefficiency' (ibidem).

The controversy over the dependent variable is first of all a result of the indistinctness of the concept of the welfare state itself. Too many and quite divergent phenomena are discussed under the same heading. In other words, contemporary welfare state research suffers from a weakness well known in comparative politics: concept stretching. Related to this is the problem of which data to use for the operationalization of the 'welfare state'. Also, most theories so far are still based on the analysis of data of the early 1990s, whereas the most significant changes may well be more recent (van Kersbergen, 2000). Finally, Pierson also notices theoretical weaknesses that concern the implicit assumption in many studies that one can measure welfare state change along a single scale ranging from 'growth' to 'dismantling'. His solution is to define the dependent variable 'welfare state change' in terms of three dimensions: *re-commodification* (strengthening the whip of the labour market), *cost-containment* (the attempt to keep balanced budgets through austerity policies, including deficit reduction and taxation policies) and *recalibration* (the attempt to adjust existing welfare state arrangements to new goals and demands). As Pierson himself points out, this is 'tricky territory analytically', because it may be very hard to 'distinguish the impact of new ideas about how to do things, or efforts to recalibrate errant programs, from simple cutbacks in provision'. The task of comparative political science is:

1. to study, both theoretically and empirically, welfare state reform by carefully elucidating and documenting what kind of changes are taking place;
2. to explain empirically the cross-national variation in change along the various dimensions of welfare state reform as well as trying to uncover the causal forces and mechanisms that drive these processes;
3. to study the effects of these reforms on the political, social and economic performance of advanced democracies.

Evidently, the research agenda of comparative political science is vast, as are the theoretical and methodological problems to be mastered, but it is crucial that political scientists continue to make efforts to contribute to research in an area where economists and sociologists have done already so much work.

This is in particular important since this chapter has demonstrated that at present the political landscape of most contemporary democracies is drastically changing.

BOX 9.1   A NOTE ON METHODOLOGY REGARDING THE COMPARATIVE ANALYSIS OF THE WELFARE STATE

The debate over strategic variables and contradictory or inconsistent empirical findings has had a tendency to slip into a predominantly technical squabble, confusing statistical techniques, methodology and substance. Such controversies were exemplified, for instance, by the critical exchange between O'Connor (1990) and Pampel and Stryker (1990). However, introducing more sophisticated statistical techniques alone could not settle the unresolved issues. The more fundamental methodological issue pertained to the necessity of relating findings of quantitative analyses back to the theoretical assumptions of the various models. Huber et al. (1993) then showed that different conceptualizations and measurements of the welfare state and the factors that encourage its development, may have satisfied diverging theoretical interests, but also caused empirical confusion (see also: Huber and Stephens, 1993). Moreover, although more-sophisticated statistical techniques have certainly helped overcome problems inherent to the linear, cross-sectional (ordinary least squares, OLS) model (such as multicollinearity and the low case-to-variable ratio; Hicks, 1994), multiplying the number of cases by pooling time-series and cross-sectional data does not necessarily solve this confusion.

Hicks and Misra (1993) have identified theoretical fragmentation as the root cause of inconsistent and contradictory findings. Rather than attempting to resolve these discrepancies by technical sophistication, they started looking for a theoretical reconciliation of diverging approaches, because – so to speak – every theory has a point. Their 'political resource' theory was therefore not so much a theory, but a collection of causes of welfare-state development adopted from other theoretical frameworks. The originality of their enterprise lies in underscoring the fact that the causes of welfare-state development are too complex to be comprehended fully by the limited perspectives of mainstream theories.

In his comment on both Hicks and Misra (1993) and Huber et al. (1993), Amenta (1993) made the point that refined quantitative studies have done much to solve unsettled disputes with respect to spending efforts, but have fallen short of providing convincing accounts of social policy phenomena that are not easily operationalized in terms of aggregate expenditures. In fact, he went so far as to suggest that comparative historical analyses of one or a few cases will remain theoretically more fruitful, because this type of research 'can untangle issues of causality for which quantitative indicators are too highly correlated to interpret …' (Amenta, 1993: 760). However, Amenta may have overstated his case to the extent that only in-depth case studies or close comparisons could provide the hypotheses to be tested in macro-comparative analyses (see for this point also: Castles, 1989b). There is no reason to assume that cross-fertilization should be uni-directional. Stressing the absolute friction between macro-comparisons and case studies not only threatens to paralyse the search for generalizations, but also denies the possibility of welcoming rather than explaining away 'outliers', exceptional cases, and 'unexplained variations'. The analysis of residuals in quantitative studies, for instance, constitutes a potentially rich source of new hypotheses that can be tested in closer examinations of crucial cases. Amenta's point on spending, however, was important. The most sensible position is to acknowledge that spending matters, but that focusing on spending data alone is theoretically problematic and is prone to statistical pitfalls.

Fuzzy Set Theory (FST), an important extension of Charles Ragin's Qualitative Comparative Analysis (QCA), is currently being promoted as having the potential of integrating the case oriented and variable oriented approaches (Ragin, 2000). The basic idea is that one needs to view cases as specific *configurations* of variables. In this manner one is able to study a fairly large set of cases without having to sacrifice the historically rich information on the cases or the ability to generalize across a number of cases. The major claim is that FST (like QCA) is able to deal with causality in a more sophisticated fashion than standard regression analysis or pooled-time series analysis is capable of. Whether FST will be adopted in contemporary research, particularly in retrenchment studies, remains to be seen (but see Kvist, 1999).

NOTES

1 This section is partly based on van Kersbergen (1995: Ch. 2).
2 This line of reasoning also implied that there is no conditional relation between welfare state development and democracy or capitalism (Pryor, 1968). Marxist analyses follow by and large the same kind of functional reasoning. See Piven and Cloward (1972), O'Connor (1973), Ginsburg (1979), Gough (1979), Lenhardt and Offe (1984), Mishra (1984).

THE POLITICAL PERFORMANCE OF DEMOCRACIES

The preceding chapters have demonstrated that both parties and governments matter as regards policy-making. Equally obvious is that the institutional design of democracy is important with respect to what parties and government can do. Together they are the ingredients to understand and to explain what, eventually, democratic governance amounts to. In Part Four the focus of attention is on what democracies produce, or – as it is commonly called – the political performance of democratic systems.

In *Chapter 10* the policy performance of post-war representative democracy is assessed. Although Castles supports the argument that 'politics' matters and democracies do function as supposed, he points out that the cross-national variation of policy performance is due to many other factors and circumstances that need to be taken into account as well.

Basically the argument is that democratic policy performance must be understood as the outcome of structural, in particular socio-economic, variables as well as of institutional factors. The added value of political parties need not to be denied but should not be overrated either. Nevertheless, it is obvious that, notwithstanding the complexity of factors that affect policy performances of democracies, they tend to be 'better, kinder and gentler' than other regimes (for example, by having a welfare state).

Exactly this issue is taken up in *Chapter 11* and *Chapter 12*, which complete this volume. Essentially Lane and Ersson examine first the question: whether or not democracies as a regime-type are indeed 'better' than other regimes. Secondly, they analyse to what extent democracies do differ among themselves. Both questions can be answered in the affirmative. This means, among other things, that welfare and well-being do indeed coincide with democracy. Finally, Lane and Ersson draw the conclusion that, although institutional differences between democratic countries explain different performances, this does not lead to a parsimonious model of building a better democratic polity as is put forward by some political scientists. On the contrary, the complexities of national political systems and societal development are often underrated, if not simplified.

In *Chapter 12* the analysis is less focused on the question whether or not democracies are different or better, but more on how well do they perform in terms of public welfare (i.e. Quality of Life) and of the 'level of democraticness' available (i.e. Quality of Democracy). It appears that – controlling for demographic and socio-economic factors – democratic institutions are relevant, if not important, for the Quality of Life in society and such a situation is associated with high(er) levels of democraticness. These results are assessed in view of the institutional differences that exist within 52 democracies and demonstrate that its institutional design is important for achieving and improving *democratic governance* within representative democracy. Yet, the overall conclusion to be drawn from the final part of this book is that indeed institutions matter, but should be studied in a careful way in relation to the specific features of the societal and political actors involved. If this (obvious) point of departure is neglected then the relationship between politics and society will remain abstract and the comparative analysis of democracy will remain the sufficient explanatory power.

10 POLICY PERFORMANCE IN THE DEMOCRATIC STATE: AN EMERGENT FIELD OF STUDY

Francis G. Castles

10.1 INTRODUCTION

Over the past three decades, scholars from across a number of social science disciplines have become more and more interested in the forces shaping the policy outcomes of democratic government. Public policies vary over time and across nations. In the years following the Second World War, governments in Western democratic nations have taken a far more activist stance than in earlier periods. This has been true of public policy across the board: economic policy, labour market policy, policies influencing the lives of families and, above all, the set of policies we describe as the welfare state. The broadest measure of the extent of changing patterns of state intervention is the growth of public expenditure, which, for the average OECD-member state, went from around a quarter of Gross Domestic Product in 1960 to almost a half by the end of the century. Within that total, programmes like Social Security transfers and public spending on Health have increased still more rapidly.

Different nations did not, however, start out with similar public policies or experience the same trajectories of growth. In terms of aggregate public expenditure, the big spenders of the early post-war period were the countries of continental Western Europe followed by a grouping of English-speaking and Scandinavian countries, with the nations of Southern Europe, Japan and Switzerland making up the rear. By the late 1990s, the Scandinavian countries and The Netherlands (Therborn, 1993) were in the vanguard, followed by continental Western Europe and Southern Europe, with some of the English-speaking countries plus, once again, Japan and Switzerland in the rearguard. In terms of economic policy performance, there was no lesser change or cross-national variation. After a generally propitious period in which most nations experienced high levels of economic growth accompanied by low levels of unemployment and inflation, economic performance deteriorated markedly in the early 1970s. However, country profiles varied hugely. Countries like Austria, Japan and Switzerland managed to combine low inflation and unemployment throughout. The Scandinavians managed to achieve lower unemployment, but seemingly at some cost in inflation terms. Countries like Ireland, Italy and the United Kingdom experienced long periods in which both unemployment and inflation were high. Given change and cross-national variation of this magnitude, it was natural that scholars would wish to inquire into the factors determining the extent and trajectory of policy programmes and the factors shaping economic policy outcomes. As research in this area has grown, it has become a specialist field in it own right. That field is, perhaps, most appropriately described as comparative public policy (Heidenheimer et al., 1975 and 1990; Lane, 1985; Castles, 1998).

It is no less natural that, as research in this area has developed, it has tended to become regarded as a sub-discipline of comparative politics. There are, at least, two good reasons why this should have occurred and one further reason, which, as we shall see, is more questionable. The *first* good reason is that studies in comparative public policy concern themselves with an intrinsic aspect of political life; namely, how governments impact on the lives of citizens through the formulation of public policies. The *second* good reason is that the study of comparative public policy shares with comparative politics a methodology, which focuses on patterns of similarity and difference amongst nations. This coincidence is not accidental. The variables, which are the concerns of these fields of research, are system level phenomena, the variation of which can only be demonstrated or explained by contrasting the experience of different nations (see for this: Pennings et al., 1999: Part 1). A *third*, more questionable, reason for regarding the field as a branch of comparative politics is the belief on the part of a substantial group of scholars that the primary sources of variation in public policy outcomes are political in nature (see for this position Chapter 9 in this book).

This is a belief that follows naturally from commonplace political science understandings of the ways in which democratic mechanisms and democratic structures influence the policy-formation processes of the modern state (Castles, 1982; Keman, 1988). It is, however, a belief that has frequently been challenged by evidence demonstrating that social and economic factors are pivotal in determining outcomes and by arguments suggesting that the policy *autonomy* of political actors is much less real than is often assumed by democratic theory.

The main purpose of this chapter is to chronicle the history of the emerging field of comparative public policy and to give some account of these challenges and the controversies they have generated. Early sections focus on the theoretical and empirical debates, which were the crucible of the new sub-discipline. An initial concern was how best to account for policy differences between more and less economically advanced nations, and from this developed a controversy about whether an understanding of the sources of such differences tells us anything meaningful about the factors making for policy variation amongst the more advanced nations. Later sections concentrate on the more recent literature. The focus was now quite explicitly on variation amongst advanced democratic states, with controversy centring on the nature of the causal sequences determining outcomes as well as on the nature of the factors most centrally involved in the policy process.

The earlier literature tended to use comparative public policy as an arena for 'points scoring' between rival theoretical and disciplinary claims. In consequence, it exaggerated differences between rival approaches and often generated as much heat as light. Later studies have also frequently exaggerated the explanatory claims of particular kinds of factors and particular causal sequences. Collectively, however, the more recent literature may be seen as providing the basis for a more genuinely cumulative approach by generating a wider and more detailed inventory of the range of influences shaping public policy in the modern state. Arguably, the most fruitful studies have been those which have been most explicit in embracing a cumulative approach by deliberately combining elements from that inventory to produce genuinely multi-causal accounts of policy development and change.

10.2 WHY THE POST-WAR WORLD WAS DIFFERENT

The initial impetus to the emergence of empirical research in the field of comparative public policy is to be found in a process of intellectual stock-taking undertaken by the social science community in the early post-war decades. Key questions preoccupying scholars of this period were how best to characterize the new society that had risen from the ashes of the Second World War and the nature of the forces most likely to determine the future development of that society. The obvious reference points for debate on these questions were contrasts between inter-war and post-war political and economic realities. Three stood out. First, the inter-war period had seen a dramatic struggle in many Western nations between parties which adhered to the democratic rules of the game and others which sought to supersede them in the name of ideologies of both Right and Left. By the mid-1950s, despite some concerns about the degree of support for communist 'anti-system' parties in a few of the countries of continental Western Europe, the general view was that the Second World War had decisively tipped the scales in favour of democracy. Second, the inter-war period had been characterized by stagnant economic growth and poor economic performance. By the mid-1950s, it was already clear that Western economies had entered a new growth phase, with unemployment levels in most countries quite exceptionally low by inter-war standards. Finally, it was obvious that governments were beginning to take on new responsibilities. Active economic policy management along Keynesian lines was now an orthodoxy and was given much of the credit for lower unemployment, whilst democratic governments everywhere were siphoning at least some of the fruits of burgeoning economic growth into the expansion of the welfare state.

Although such contrasts were part of the intellectual mainstream in the early post-war period, scholars differed as to their implications for reshaping the character of democratic politics and policy formulation. For some, like Seymour Martin Lipset, the victory of democracy had muted rather than replaced the class conflicts intrinsic to capitalist societies. The ideological struggles of the inter-war period had been transformed into a 'democratic class struggle' in which:

> The leftist parties represent themselves as instruments of social change in the direction of equality; the lower-income groups support them in order to become economically better off, while the higher-income groups oppose them in order to maintain their economic advantages. (Lipset, 1959: 229)

In this account, partisan conflict remains important. While the future of democratic institutions is no longer an object of partisan struggle, differences in the class constituencies of political parties translate into different redistributive choices. The clear implication is of real differences in redistributive policy outcomes resulting from diverse patterns of partisan incumbency in Western democratic nations.

Other scholars believed that the victory of democracy had gone further, effectively dissolving all significant differences between the parties. Because the categorical imperative of democratic politics was to obtain an electoral majority, all parties were forced to appeal to a similar constituency of support, leading to policy programmes differing only in terms of their window dressings. A possible logic for such a process was supplied by Anthony Downs' (1957) theory of the 'median voter', which suggests that parties will progressively locate their policy platforms at the centre of the political spectrum. Symptoms of such an ideological convergence were not difficult to observe. The Swedish political scientist, Herbert Tingsten (1955: 145) noted that '(t)he actual words "socialism" or "liberalism" are tending to become mere honorifics, useful in connection with elections and political festivities'. The French sociologist, Raymond Aron (1955) pointed to an increasing awareness that 'the political categories of the last century – Left and Right, liberal and socialist, traditional and revolutionary – have lost their relevance'. Otto Kirchheimer (1964, 1966b), a German political scientist, saw the class parties of an earlier era being replaced by cross-class, 'catch-all' parties, and saw the inevitable consequence as a 'waning of opposition' in Western democratic systems. In a book entitled *The End of Ideology* (1960: 402–3), the American sociologist, Daniel Bell identified a 'consensus among intellectuals on political issues: the acceptance of a Welfare State; the desirability of decentralized power; a system of mixed economy and political pluralism'. With substantial consensus on acceptable policy goals as well as on the democratic rules of the game, politics was unlikely to be a source of substantial cross-national differences in policy outcomes.

Most of the writers mentioned here saw an intimate connection between economic progress, democracy and the emergence of political consensus, with greater affluence serving as the solvent for the extreme political divisions of an earlier era. Others, however, viewed the linkage between policy outcomes and the economic progress as more direct, with industrial modernization creating the need for progressively greater intervention by the state. This was by no means a novel position. As long ago as 1877, Alfred Wagner, a German public finance theorist, had advanced a 'law of increasing state activity'. It postulated that the very process of industrialization through which societies became more affluent produced problems which forced them to devote ever greater proportions of national income to the provision of collective goods (see Larkey et al., 1981). This hypothesis of a link between economic modernization and the growth of the state was now restated as part of a wider thesis of the 'logic of industrialism' through which the imperatives of modern technology strip away all significant sources of national difference (Kerr, 1960). In the process, modern societies experience a process of convergence of both economic (Galbraith, 1967) and social (Wilensky and Lebeaux, 1958) policy. The state becomes more active and it becomes bigger, but, paradoxically, politics in the traditional sense become less and less significant, since they no longer have a claim to being a formative influence on policy choice.

10.3 THE 'POLITICS-DOES-MATTER' DEBATE

Early empirical studies of variation in policy outcomes were designed to provide evidence relevant to the claims made by the 'end of ideology' and industrial modernization schools. Governmental outputs, and most conspicuously, measures of the extent of government spending, were a natural focus for such research for two reasons. One was data availability. Governments routinely produce data – national accounts statistics – that provide information on their spending. This makes cross-national comparison of expenditure totals easier than almost any other kind of policy outcomes research. The other reason was theoretical relevance. The view that politics in advanced Western societies can be likened to a 'democratic class struggle' rests on the notion that where parties supported by the lower classes in society control the reins of government, public spending on welfare and on measures furthering egalitarian goals will be higher. Evidence that partisan control of government in such societies was not associated with spending on welfare and on policies designed to achieve wider egalitarian goals would imply that this view was incorrect. On the other hand, evidence that, in such societies, spending for such purposes was associated with factors such as affluence, urbanization, occupational or demographic structure would suggest that what mattered most was not politics, but economic modernization.

The earliest research was based on comparisons of the American states. It came down heavily in favour of the view that apparent links between state expenditure and party competition disappear once we take account of various aspects of economic development, including per capita income, occupational structure, urbanization and education level (see Dawson and Robinson, 1963; Dye, 1966, but cf. Sharkansky and Hofferbert, 1969). Studies comparing communist and capitalist nations arrived at rather similar conclusions (Pryor, 1968; Rimlinger, 1971). What mattered most were not ostensible differences in political ideology, but differences in the degree of industrialization manifested by such nations, and hence differences in the nature of the problems they confronted and in their organizational capacity to cope with them. Finally, there were a number of sociological studies that sought to account for variation in welfare state development amongst nations at widely divergent economic levels. These studies concluded that the main determinants of early programme adoption (Cutright, 1965) and of aggregate spending levels (Wilensky, 1975) were primarily socio-economic in character.

Harold Wilensky's *The Welfare State and Equality* (1975) is generally regarded as the classic study in what, by the mid-1970s, had become the sociological orthodoxy. On the basis of an analysis of social security spending in 1966, he concludes that:

> For this sixty-country sample, the primacy of economic level and its demographic and bureaucratic correlates is support for a convergence hypothesis; economic growth makes countries with contrasting cultural and political traditions more alike in their strategy for constructing the floor beneath which no one sinks. (Wilensky, 1975, 27)

For Wilensky, the crucial aspect of socio-economic development is population ageing, with an increasing proportion of older people exerting irresistible pressure for welfare programmes catering to the needs of the old. In a sense that pressure is political, since it is manifested in demands for greater state activity, but the demands are no more prevalent in democratic than in communist systems and are directed at parties and governments, irrespective of their ideological preferences. Wilensky's findings, like those of the majority of the studies cited here, derive from *cross-sectional* research using multivariate techniques of a relatively sophisticated kind. They seem to offer strong evidence in support of the industrial modernization thesis and to be broadly compatible with the implications which follow from the 'end of ideology' hypothesis. They appear to leave little scope for the possibility that public policy in the modern state is decisively shaped by the outcomes of the 'democratic class struggle'.

By the mid-1970s, the sociological orthodoxy was at its zenith. A decade later, it had become a minority view. Focusing their attention on policy differences exhibited by advanced democratic nations, empirical researchers of the period re-examined the 'end of ideology' hypothesis and the industrialization thesis and found them wanting. This rediscovery of politics did not have a single voice. Many studies pointed to Leftwing partisan control of government as the key variable determining a nation's expenditure on welfare objectives (Hewitt, 1977; Cameron, 1978; Stephens, 1979) and the character of its economic policy choices (Hibbs, 1977; Tufte, 1978). Countries in which parties of the Left were strong had bigger welfare states, lower unemployment and utilized Keynesian demand management techniques more actively than countries in which the Left was less strong. Others argued that national differences in welfare spending and economic inequality could be better accounted for by the negative impact of parties of the

Right in government (Castles, 1978; Castles and McKinlay, 1979; van Arnhem and Schotsman, 1982). Still others saw class rather than party as the critical variable. To Korpi (1978, 1983), public policies favouring working-class interests emerged where a solidaristic labour movement worked together with a Social Democratic government. Gough (1979), developing earlier insights of Piven and Cloward (1972), noted the correspondence between working class militancy and government initiatives in the area of social amelioration. Finally, the emergent literature on corporatist modes of interest intermediation (Lehmbruch, 1977; Schmitter and Lehmbruch, 1979) linked economic policy performance to differences in the capacities of political systems to compromise class interests (Schmidt, 1982b; see also Chapter 8 in this book). These nuances apart, this was a literature with, at least, two common themes. The first was that the linkages between socio-economic modernization and policy outcomes stressed by the sociological orthodoxy were either absent or much exaggerated. The second was that observed differences in the balance of political forces in Western nations corresponded closely to differences in the degree to which the state took an activist stance in the areas of economic and social policy (Keman, 1993b).

What is both fascinating and more than a little paradoxical is, of course, the fact that conclusions as widely variant as those of the sociological orthodoxy and the 'politics matters' literature could be drawn from what was ostensibly the same body of evidence concerning the socio-economic and political correlates of public policy development in the modern state. The key to understanding this discrepancy in findings lies in the diverse strategies of comparison employed by the two approaches. Studies in the 'end of ideology' -cum- industrialization mode adopted the strategy of focusing on contrasts between the extent of ideological polarization in the inter-war and post-war eras or between policy outcomes in countries at widely divergent levels of economic development (see Dryzek, 1978; Castles and McKinlay, 1979). This strategy is sometimes described as the 'most different' approach to comparative analysis (Przeworski and Teune, 1970: 31–9). The conclusions that ideological difference has declined and that less industrialized nations tend to be characterized by a lesser degree of state activism are undoubtedly true, but have few, if any, implications for our understanding of differences in public policy outcomes amongst more developed nations. It is on these latter nations that studies in the 'politics matters' mode have concentrated their attention, adopting the alternative ('most similar') strategy of comparing nations which are relatively alike in terms of economic development and democratic participation (Pennings et al., 1999: Part III). What these studies claim to have demonstrated is that, within the far smaller ambit of policy diversity that distinguishes such nations, differences in class mobilization and in partisan incumbency are amongst the factors influencing the diversity that does exist (Keman, 1988).

The obvious implication, therefore, is that the findings of both kinds of studies could be simultaneously true, with the sociological orthodoxy describing differences over time and between countries at diverse economic levels and the 'politics matters' hypothesis capturing at least part of the dynamic of policy divergence in advanced nations. However, that was not, for the most part, how the protagonists of the two schools saw the issue. Because they saw themselves as addressing the same set of issues, the factors associated with the rise of the modern state, their divergent findings were widely interpreted as disagreements about facts, with studies in the socio-logical tradition explicitly rejecting the relevance of political factors and studies in the 'politics matters' mode largely dismissing the importance of socio-economic explanations. Moreover, the fact that the views of the two schools found their natural homes in different social science disciplines transformed ostensible differences about the factors associated with the rise of the modern state into polemical arguments concerning the explanatory primacy of sociology and political science. Although, in retrospect, this con-flict of theoretical perspectives and empirical findings was the crucible from which the sub-discipline of comparative public policy emerged, it was, for many years, an arena in which one-sided disciplinary 'points scoring' was often no less prominent than the search for greater scientific understanding.

10.4 PATHWAYS TO POLICY

Since the early 1980s, work in the field of comparative public policy has largely focused on accounting for policy differences amongst advanced democratic states. A problem with such an approach is that it tends to divert attention from the key socio-economic and political parameters that distin-guish patterns of policy development in rich and poor nations and in demo-cratic and undemocratic ones (see: Schmidt, 1989b; Lane and Ersson, 1997). It has also meant that a number of nations which are now moderately affluent and democratic, but which were poor and undemocratic in earlier decades, have been much under-represented in the comparative literature. Greece, Portugal and Spain are the obvious instances. Only now are scholars turning to the question of whether public policy development in these nations has mirrored that of other Western nations or whether it has reflected the special circumstances of Southern European social, economic and cultural develop-ment (see: Leibfried, 1993; Castles, 1995; Ferrera, 1996a; MIRE, 1997).

The big advantage of a more concentrated focus on advanced democratic states is that it has facilitated the elaboration of a wider range of hypotheses. In part, that is because the subtleties of public policy variation in this rela-tively homogeneous grouping of nations are not obscured by massive diver-gences in economic level and forms of government as they were in comparisons involving less developed countries. In part, it is because the far greater data availability for the advanced countries allowed scholars to explore and test a wider variety of hypotheses than previously and to do so across a wider range of policy issues. The elaboration of an ever increasing body of hypotheses and findings across an ever wider span of policy areas has been the basis for transforming an intellectual debate on the antecedents

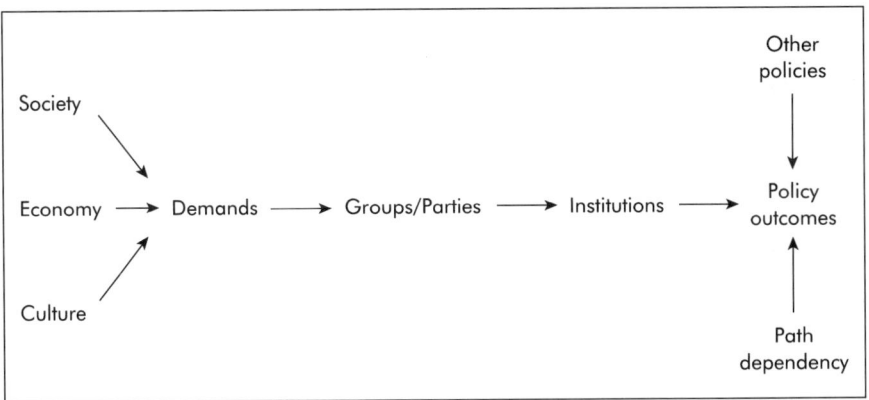

Figure 10.1 *Paths to public policy formation*

of post-war policy development into an area of specialized study in its own right. It has also held out the promise of a more cumulative and scientific approach to research in this field.

The model shown in Figure 10.1 provides a schematic rendering of the kinds of factors and the varieties of causal sequences featuring in the recent literature. The model identifies the generic components of a set of potential sequences through which demands emerging from a particular social, economic and cultural matrix are transformed into policy outcomes. This process of transformation takes place in a political system in which interest groups and political parties are the main political actors, but in which institutional arrangements condition their scope for independent activity. Theories in the field are distinguished both by the components on which they focus and by the causal sequences linking those components to final outcomes. In other words, different theories identify different pathways to policy.

What distinguishes policy-making under *democratic* conditions is that groups and parties are free to express and organize interests and that electoral and legislative arrangements provide institutionalized devices by which ordinary citizens can influence policy. Ostensibly this seems to guarantee that politics will be of great significance in the policy process of the democratic state. There are, however, influential accounts which argue that is not the case. Their common theme is that undoubted differences in interest group politics, partisan complexion of government and institutional arrangements in different countries do not translate into different policy outcomes, because, even under democratic conditions, political actors enjoy only limited autonomy.

10.5 CONSTRAINED AUTONOMY AND POLICY CONVERGENCE

At least four arguments of this kind have featured in the literature in recent decades. One, which is frequently encountered in discussions of social policy development, relates to changing patterns of population need. The argument is that democratic politicians, irrespective of ideological persuasion, find it extremely difficult to resist demands from large sections of the population adversely affected by social change. Moreover, because, in the course of the past century, responses to need have been institutionalized into a huge panoply of welfare entitlements, the expenditure impact of changing patterns of need is frequently automatic. According to Wilensky (1975), population ageing has been much the most significant source of emergent population need and, hence, has been the major factor shaping the rise of the modern welfare state. A belief that similar mechanisms will prevail in future underpins prophecies of expenditure crisis arising from the further 'greying' of the population over coming decades (World Bank, 1994; OECD, 1996). There is also beginning to be some major concern about the likely policy consequences of declining fertility trends in many Western nations (Castles, 1998; Esping-Andersen, 1999). Whenever social policy analysts predict the shape of future policy developments on the basis of changing patterns of need, they are implicitly arguing that the hands of democratic politicians are to a greater or lesser degree tied by the exigencies of large-scale economic and social change (compare this with the arguments of policy targeting in Chapter 4 in this book).

Another argument premised on the limited autonomy of political actors in a democratic environment was widely used to account for the crisis that marked the end of the Golden Age of welfare state expansion (OECD, 1981). The main theme of the debate was the view that the growth of public spending had now outstripped the willingness of a democratic electorate to finance that spending through taxes. In essence, the argument was the needs thesis writ large. Democratic governments were caught between a rock and hard place. On the one hand, they could not resist the demands of any reasonably large body within the electorate, because to do so gave a competitive edge to opposition parties ready to make irresponsible promises in order to gain office. On the other, giving in to such demands inevitably meant spiralling deficits and increased levels of public debt. Such accounts came from both Left and Right. On the Left, the dilemma was viewed as one of the latest manifestations of the inherent contradictions of capitalism, with popular demands being ultimately frustrated by the need to maintain a regime favourable to the interests of private capital accumulation (Offe, 1972; O'Connor, 1973). On the Right, it was seen as a crisis marking the outer limits of the post-war, interventionist-state, with governments progressively immobilized by demands way beyond their capacity to respond (King, 1975; Brittan, 1977).

Both of the above arguments suggest that there are major limitations on the capacity of democratic governments to resist calls for greater public spending. The most recent variant of the limited autonomy argument suggests that changing economic realities leave political actors with little option but to reduce the size of the state (Scharpf, 1997; Jessop, 1996; Rhodes, 1997). The substance of that change is the shift to a more globalized world economy.

Under circumstances where international trade dominates domestic markets and where there are few impediments to capital movements across national boundaries, domestic policy autonomy is severely constrained by the freedom of investors to seek better returns in other markets (see: Ohmae, 1991; Cerny, 1994; Pauly, 1995; cf. Hirst and Thompson, 1996). The logic of globalization confronts the logic of escalating demands head-on. Because footloose capital will tend to gravitate to environments in which taxation is lower, Keynesian fiscal strategies premised on adjustments to domestic tax-rates are no longer viable. Because states must compete to attract new sources of capital and to prevent existing capital moving elsewhere, there will inevitably be a 'run to the bottom' across most categories of social and public spending. Although it is politicians who make the decisions that usher in the leaner, meaner state, the imagery of the globalization rhetoric is of an absence of any genuine political choice, of policies dictated by the sheer brute force of economic realities. The claim of globalization theory is the claim so often made by Margaret Thatcher (Britain's Prime Minister: 1979–91): that there is *no alternative* to the policies currently on offer!

Whatever their disagreements on the likely trajectory of state intervention, all of these arguments see the ultimate determinants of public policy outcomes as interests emanating from the economic and social environment. However, a final class of argument suggests that the factor, which most restricts freedom of policy manoeuvre, is the constraining impact of *prior policy choices*. Such arguments have a variety of forms. In some cases, outcomes are self-perpetuating, as in economists' accounts of the adverse effects of what they call 'hysteresis', where the declining job readiness of the unemployed makes it increasingly less likely that they will find employment in the future (see: Layard et al., 1991). In other words, high unemployment causes higher unemployment. In others cases, prior policy choices – either in the area in question or in related areas – modify popular preferences and/or repertoires of probable institutional responses so that the policies of yesteryear persist as the template of policies in the here and now. As Myles and Quadagno (1997) show, pension reformers in welfare states designed on Bismarckian, contributory, principles are confronted with quite different options from reformers operating in the context of flat-rate, exchequer-funded, Beveridge systems (cf. Overbye, 1994). What is common to all forms of such arguments is the notion that public policy is substantially path dependent; that it is highly resistant to change once its initial parameters are firmly established (Keman, 1993b; Hicks et al., 1995).

Although not logically required by arguments from constrained autonomy, most of these accounts have also been associated with claims concerning the *policy convergence* of modern states. Population ageing ultimately means that all advanced nations will have large welfare states. The inherent tendency of democratic demands to outstrip the democratic willingness to pay taxes produces universal welfare state crisis. Competing in a globalized economy means that nations have no alternative but to reverse the tide of post-war interventionism and downsize the state. Research in the comparative tradition properly treats such assertions of emergent similarity with an inherent scepticism, since they contradict the essential premise of the comparative approach, that differences amongst nations are of sufficient magnitude to be worthy of study. Indeed, the fact of continuing cross-national diversity provides a method and a spur to researchers who seek to challenge the deterministic implications of such arguments. The evidence of three or more decades of work in the field of comparative public policy is that supposedly universal trends are frequently of limited duration and never sufficient to cancel out significant variation from other sources (Castles, 1998: 312–36).

10.6 THE IMPACT OF INTERESTS

For pathways to policy to allow of politics influencing policy variation amongst nations, it is necessary that national differences in the character of interest groups, political parties and institutional arrangements have independent effects on policy outcomes. Studies identifying such effects have employed two basic approaches. The simplest has been to seek to demonstrate patterns of co-variation between political and outcome variables, showing, for example, that, where a certain type of party has been strong, there has been a strong tendency to adopt policies of a particular type. A more complex approach has been to move beyond the identification of policy-relevant political actors to locate the circumstances under which such actors become strong in the first place. That this latter approach makes the forces shaping the main actors in the democratic struggle central to the task of understanding policy variation in the democratic state is a further reason why research in comparative public policy has found a natural home within the comparative politics sub-discipline.

Studies identifying interest groups as the key actors shaping policy outcomes have had a highly circumscribed focus. That is because interest group systems are, in most respects, country-specific, rendering virtually impossible the kind of common categorization which is the essential precursor to comparative analysis. The only obvious exception is the inherent duality of the opposed interests of labour and capital as represented by trade unions and business associations, which occurs in some form in all advanced democratic societies (Streeck and Schmitter, 1995). Early neo-Marxist contributions to the literature tended to view such organizations as class actors pressing for the collective economic interests of their members (Gough, 1979). The main focus of theorizing in this area has, however, been on the potential of corporatist institutional arrangements to produce superior economic outcomes by reducing levels of overt conflict between labour and capital (see Chapter 7 in this book).

There have been many variants on this theme, not all of them particularly consistent (see: Therborn, 1987b; Braun, 1989; Woldendorp, 1995; Siaroff, 1999), but the core idea was that appropriate institutional arrangements could promote increased awareness of the long-term advantages of collaboration between economic interests and of the destructive potential of short-term, sectional conflict. The implication was that countries like Austria, The Netherlands, Norway, Germany and Sweden, which all commentators agreed possessed the required kind of 'encompassing' labour market institutions, would have better economic outcomes than countries like Britain, France, Italy and the USA, which were widely seen as lacking them. Optimism about the economic benefits of corporatism was at its height in the late 1970s and early 1980s (see: Goldthorpe, 1984). However, weaker economic performance in a number of corporatist countries in the 1990s disappointed earlier expectations (Kitschelt et al., 1999). As a result, research on the policy implications of diverse modes of managing conflict between interests in the labour market is now taking new forms, with contrasts between corporatist and non-corporatist systems giving way to more nuanced comparisons of the policy profiles associated with diverse 'production regimes' or 'varieties of capitalism' (Hollingsworth et al., 1994; Soskice, 1999).

The view that comparative research on the link between interest group activity and policy outcomes is necessarily restricted to conflicts between labour and capital is seemingly contradicted by recent work by Paul Pierson (1996, 2001) on what he calls 'the new politics of the welfare state'. Pierson argues that one of the things which distinguishes the contemporary politics of retrenchment from the earlier stage of building the welfare state is a shift from the primacy of parties to the primacy of interests. The very success of the welfare state project in earlier post-war decades has altered the dynamics of policy-making.

With these massive programmes have come dense networks of interest groups and strong popular attachments to particular policies, which present a considerable obstacle to reform (Pierson, 1996: 146).

According to Pierson, the 'old politics of the welfare state' largely concerned the role of parties of the Left in building the welfare edifice. In contrast, the 'new politics' of the contemporary era are about the way in which interests mobilize to frustrate those seeking to dismantle that edifice (see Chapter 9 in this book).

The conclusions of Pierson's 1996 article on this theme are ostensibly based on observations of retrenchment politics in four countries – Britain, Germany, Sweden and the USA – and, therefore, seemingly transcend the specificity of national interest group systems. In fact, the only country for which he provides firm evidence of group mobilization to protect welfare programmes is the USA. However, there is nothing new about interest groups playing a major role in welfare politics in that country. Indeed, the original Social Security Act of 1935 was partly a response to an organized movement of elderly Americans (the Townsend Movement) pressing for the introduction of age pensions (Orloff, 1988: 68–9). What distinguished the USA from other Western countries in the welfare state building stage is what distinguishes the USA now: that, in the absence of ideologically based parties, interest group politics are much more vital in the USA than elsewhere. In reality, then, the 'new politics of the welfare state' are nothing new in the

USA and, outside of the USA, interest group politics remain subordinate to party. Pierson may well be justified in arguing that inter-party differences on welfare issues are no longer as salient as they once were (see Stephens et al., 1999; Castles, 2000). However, on the basis of the evidence he provides, he is clearly not justified in arguing that interest groups have become the dominant political actors in the policy processes of modern democracies.

10.7 THE COMPLEXITIES OF PARTISANSHIP

Although, as previously noted, the rediscovery of politics of the late 1970s had many voices, the theme that was strongest, and which has remained strongest, was the impact of party in shaping public policy performance and, in particular, outcomes relating to the welfare state. This should occasion little surprise. By the second half of the twentieth century, party politics had clearly superseded legislative politics as the major force determining the complexion of government in the parliamentary democracies of Western Europe and the Anglo-Saxon world. Given that government, in turn, initiates and administers policy, it is natural to assume a flow-on from the input to the output side of politics. Indeed, it is the presumption of such a flow-on that is generally seen as giving party government its legitimacy as a democratic form of governance. Party rule is compatible with rule by the people because the mandate to govern results from a popular choice amongst rival policy platforms (Klingeman et al., 1994). That, in turn, is what makes the claim that parties influence policy formation so important. Demonstrating the truth of this claim is not just a matter of showing the relevance of politics; it is also a matter of showing that the democratic form of government functions as it is supposed to function (see Chapter 4 in this book).

There are a variety of empirical strategies by which one might go about seeking to establish a link between the partisan complexion of government and policy outcomes. Arguably, the most direct is to assess the extent to which electoral promises are carried out when parties win office. This has been the strategy adopted by recent comparative research on party manifestos, with findings which reveal just the kind of correspondence between party programmes and policy outcomes assumed by the theory of party government. Generally, however, research in the comparative public policy tradition has taken a somewhat different tack. This has involved the generation of hypotheses concerning the probable policy consequences of rule by parties of a given type and the use of cross-national data to test such hypotheses. It is this approach which has led to a focus on the role of parties of the Left. The historic agenda of such parties has been to use state intervention to promote greater economic and social equality, suggesting the obvious hypotheses that, where they have been dominant, the state will be bigger and equality will be greater. Early work supporting such conclusions has already been cited. Later studies using more sophisticated statistical techniques, a variety of specifications of Left strength and a range of control variables, have replicated their findings for various time-points and periods in the post-war era (Hicks and Swank, 1984; Korpi, 1989; Esping-Andersen, 1990; Huber et al., 1993; Keman, 1988, 1993a; Schmidt, 1996a).

Although parties of the Left have been the predominant focus of research, there has also been work on other types of party. Early findings by Castles (1982) that Right incumbency has been associated with a less interventionist public policy stance have been extended in a variety of contexts including issues of sexual equality (Norris, 1987), foreign development aid (Imbeau, 1988) and educational spending (Castles, 1989a, 1998). There has also been considerable interest in the impact of Christian Democratic parties. Research has now demonstrated that countries in which such parties have been a dominant influence in the post-war era spend as much for social purposes as countries in which the Left has been strong (Wilensky, 1981; Huber et al., 1993; Castles, 1998). However, the content of social policy is very different. In Christian Democratic, continental, Western Europe, Catholic social policy doctrines in particular have favoured status preservation and income maintenance through contribution-based income transfer systems; in Leftist Scandinavia, Social Democratic ideas have favoured economic equality and direct provision by the state (see: Esping-Andersen, 1990; van Kersbergen, 1995). Finally, comparative historians have added a note of caution to more sweeping generalizations about the policy consequences of Left hegemony. Even where the ultimate impact of such parties has been plain to see, as in Social Democratic, Scandinavia, it has been shown that middle-class parties have sometimes played a crucial part in initiating welfare programmes and in shaping the trajectory of subsequent social policy development (Baldwin, 1990; Swenson, 1991).

The claim that the old (partisan) politics of the welfare state has been superseded by a 'new politics of the welfare state' based on interest group politics has already been noted. The comparable claim in the economic policy literature has been that the kind of differences that once distinguished economies presided over by Leftist and corporatist regimes have diminished or disappeared in the face of common global economic imperatives. However, research findings are now emerging, which show that currently fashionable arguments about the policy implications of globalization are either incorrect or very much exaggerated (see: Garrett, 1998; Swank, 2001). More interesting still is recent work suggesting that any weakening of partisan impact on the demand-side of the economy has been more than compensated for by emergent supply-side differences. In path-breaking research, Boix (1998) has noted that what distinguishes parties of the Left is no longer their emphasis on tax and spend policies, but rather their use of interventionist strategies, including active labour market policies and infrastructure investment, to raise the productivity of labour and capital. In contrast, the distinguishing characteristic of the conservative side of politics is no longer an emphasis on small government as such, but rather on the potential of strategies such as privatization and reduced marginal tax rates to encourage private provision of physical and human capital. Findings such as these once again confirm the key role of parties in shaping a wide variety of public policy outcomes, whilst also demonstrating that the nature of that role is often far more complex than initially supposed.

10.8 THE INSTITUTIONS OF GOVERNMENT

Accounts of policy determination emphasizing the role of interest groups and parties highlight the influence of the major input mechanisms of democratic politics. In contrast, institutional accounts, which have been a major growth area in comparative public policy research over the past decade, concentrate on the ways in which the output structures of government shape the character of policy outcomes. The core premise of such accounts is that different kinds of structures process policy demands in different ways. This may be a matter of capacity. Some kinds of governmental structures are more efficient and effective in accomplishing particular tasks than are others. More usually, it is a matter of more or less explicit institutional design (Scharpf, 1991; Colomer, 1996; Shepsle, 1997). The authors of the American constitution designed their governmental institutions around the idea of checks and balances precisely because they wished to put obstacles in the way of ill-considered and precipitate change. However, the fact that governmental structures are often fashioned with broader or more narrowly defined objectives in mind does not mean that their policy consequences are necessarily ones that would be welcomed by a democratic majority. The whole point of constitutional documents, and what gives them their powerful policy impact, is that they constrain subsequent generations to behave in particular ways whether they wish to or not.

Within the institutions literature, there are two rival accounts of the way in which governmental structures impinge on the growth of the state. One rests on the mechanics of the policy process, identifying veto points in the structure of decision-making, and arguing that the more players it takes to change the status quo, the less will be the likelihood of radical change (Immergut, 1992; Huber et al., 1993; Tsebilis, 1995; see also Chapter 8 of this book). Each veto point multiplies opportunities to mount campaigns against proposals, which impose costs on those who benefit from existing policies. Hence, institutional arrangements like strong bicameralism and federalism, which proliferate the number of relevant veto points, are likely to be conducive to a weaker development of the state than arrangements such as unicameralism and unitary government, which concentrate the locus of political power. In line with this reasoning, there is strong agreement in the literature that federal states exhibit weaker social expenditure development than unitary ones (see: Wilensky, 1975; Cameron, 1978; Castles and McKinlay, 1979; Gordon, 1988; Lane and Ersson, 1997).

An alternative account of the impact of governmental structures focuses on the ways in which institutional arrangements foster conflict or consensus amongst decision-makers, leading to more or less competitive or consensual policy styles (Guy Peters et al., 1977; Keman, 1996, 1999; Birchfield and Crepaz, 1998). In the latest working of this theme, Arend Lijphart (1999) suggests that there is evidence that a consensual style of politics is conducive to more successful macro-economic management. More directly relevant to issues concerning the size of the state, he provides evidence that consensus politics produces a 'kinder, gentler' democracy characterized by higher social expenditure, lesser economic inequality, a less punitive criminal justice system and more generous foreign aid (see also Chapter 7 of this book).

Discussion of the impact of governmental structures on policy outcomes is not restricted to the size of the state. There has also been a strong interest in the ways in which economic policy outcomes are shaped by institutional arrangements, with public choice theory providing much of the intellectual impetus for analysis and research. Theoretical work on the link between fiscal policy arrangements and economic performance is illustrative. Within the public choice tradition, institutions are seen as sets of rules, determining optimum strategies for self-interested players. From this perspective, it can be argued that the 'dispersal of fiscal authority among different levels of government' optimizes the probability of constraining 'Leviathan's overall fiscal appetites' (Brennan and Buchanan, 1980: 181). Given an assumption that high tax levels are inimical to economic efficiency, this implies that economic policy outcomes in federal states are likely to be better – all other things being equal – than those in unitary states. While empirical tests have failed to confirm such a relationship, they have shown that less formalized indicators of the extent of tax decentralization are associated with higher levels of economic growth and greater price stability (Castles, 1999).

The ways in which institutional arrangements contribute to or restrain inflation have been a major theme of the literature over several decades. This concern does not come out of public choice theory alone. As previously noted, earlier debates on the potential of corporatist labour market institutions to contain distributional conflict in the wages policy arena originated from class-based analysis. The public choice school's more recent contribution to the literature has concentrated attention on the role of independent central banks in promoting price stability. Essentially, the argument is that labour market actors will be more conscious of the inflationary consequences of their actions, where they have strong expectations that the authorities will maintain tight monetary policies, and that this is more likely to occur where central banks are free of governmental interference. Despite serious conceptual difficulties in classifying degrees of central bank independence in different nations, the broad consensus of findings supports such a conclusion (Alesina, 1989; Grilli et al., 1991; Busch, 1993).

We conclude this section by noting a significant contrast between accounts of policy variation resting on differences in institutional arrangements and accounts resting on differences in demands, interests and parties. Whereas differences of the latter type are not readily susceptible to manipulation or social engineering, institutional arrangements can, in principle, at least, be reshaped and redesigned through the conscious decision of political actors.

Because this is so, institutional accounts assert that politics matter in a sense above and beyond that implied by the mere demonstration that differences in the input mechanisms of democratic politics contribute to differences in policy outcomes. If there is evidence that corporatist institutions favour diminished labour market conflict, governments may deliberately choose – as, in many countries, they did in the late 1970s and early 1980s – to foster the development of tripartite links between labour, business and government. If there is evidence that fiscal decentralization promotes economic efficiency or that central bank independence is conducive to price stability, then it makes sense to think of modifying policy arrangements to achieve such outcomes. Thus, when we argue that institutions matter, we are doing something more than simply offering a scientific account of the forces driving the policy process. We are also making the very significant point that the shape of public policy is, at least in part, a function of our organization of democratic choices.

10.9 CONCLUSIONS

The latter sections of this chapter have attempted to summarize recent work in comparative public policy by discussing the wide variety of pathways to policy identified in the literature. There has, however, been some degree of artificiality in the presentation. Because our main purpose has been to identify differences amongst the types of explanatory account featuring in the literature, we have paid little explicit attention to efforts by a variety of scholars to integrate and build bridges between such accounts. Work of this nature can be found in a variety of methodological traditions: the historical sociology of Peter Flora and his colleagues, the 'power resources' approach of the Stockholm Institute of Social Research, and the hugely complex pooled time-series designs employed in contemporary quantitative research (see: Janoski and Hicks, 1994). Once we reject the over-determinism of the early sociological orthodoxy and of later assertions of circumscribed policy autonomy, complexity becomes the natural object of study. Pathways to policy are many, they differ from policy area to policy area and they change over time. The mark of the increasing maturity of comparative public policy as a field of study within political science is that it less frequently addresses such undifferentiated questions as whether politics matters, and instead asks how, when and to what extent particular aspects of democratic politics influence particular policy outcomes.

11   DEMOCRATIC PERFORMANCE: ARE THERE INSTITUTIONAL EFFECTS?

Jan-Erik Lane and Svante Ersson

11.1 INTRODUCTION

As the universe of democratic regimes has expanded considerably since 1989 we face greater institutional variation in the constitutional organization of democracies. The political institutions vary not only in terms of Montesquieu's *trias politica*, but also in terms of other institutional arrangements such as electoral systems (and related formulae), the state format, the nature of the constitution (codified or not) as well as the position of independent public bodies. The new institutional approach tends to describe merely all the similarities and differences between democratic institutions, but theorizing this cross-national variety in the 'new' Europe is an even greater challenge.

If the old institutionalism was chiefly descriptive, parochial and legalistic, then the new institutionalism should do better. Just as the new institutionalist scholar may arm himself/herself with a plethora of approaches and models from different schools, so he/she may pay as much attention to the small European democracies as to the large nations, e.g. Germany, France and the UK. Neo-institutionalist research would not stop where the written constitution ends but would examine what Max Weber called the 'real' constitution, or the rules that are actually operated in a political system, codified or not (Czada et al., 1998).

Distinctive of the new institutionalism is the idea that: *Institutions Matter*. Outcomes are not to be analysed merely by means of preferences or culture, but it is believed that institutions play a role in determining political performance. This is basically a causal notion, meaning that we must be able to observe some form of constant conjunction between an institution and its effect(s). One may distinguish between a micro and a macro-version of institutions in relation to institutional effects. On the one hand, there is the micro-perspective dealing with one institution at a time, focusing upon its minute effects. On the other hand, there is the macro-perspective dealing with a pattern of institutions at the societal level. The purpose of this chapter is to examine democratic institutional performance at the *macro*-level, and especially search for the occurrence of institutional effects among policy outputs and outcomes (see also: Weaver and Rockman, 1993; Colomer, 1996; Keman, 1997c).

11.2 INSTITUTIONAL EFFECTS

Institutional or neo-institutional analysis would take a huge step forward towards a set of testable models if it could show that institutions matter for outcomes. In this chapter we will attempt to advance neo-institutionalism by showing how *democratic* institutions are important for policy outputs as well as for political, social and economic outcomes. We will use a Humean methodology, correlating an institutional variation with a variation in outputs and outcomes. The relationships between institutional items and policy outputs and outcomes to be examined below will be derived from democratic theory. However, whether or not alternative hypotheses about the impact of institutions are true can only be decided on the basis of empirical tests.

Two questions would be central in a so-called Humean approach to institutional importance: (1) What is the *average* institutional performance? (2) Does institutional performance involve institutional *causality*? We approach these two problems in a macro analysis, meaning that we examine data about whole societies and their macro-political institutions. Democratic theory is sufficiently contested and contestable to allow for a number of alternative models about institutional performance which can be tested. Alternative hypotheses about the effects of different democratic institutions, competing for allegiance, are also considered.

Such a macro-analysis is based upon two requirements. First, institutions can be clearly identified at the macro-level as well as separated from other types of entities in the social reality, such as social and economic conditions or the interests of actors, and culture. Second, there is a set of policy outputs and outcomes which do vary and warrant a search for institutional effects. In the institutionalist literature the set of outputs and outcomes includes public policies such as welfare state expenditures or public sector efforts, and socio-economic outcomes such as the level of human development, social and gender equality, as well as political outcomes such as political or constitutional stability. It is the case that all these outputs and outcomes show ample cross-national variation across the set of democratic countries to warrant such an investigation. At present, the universe of countries adhering to a democratic regime today is almost one third of the some 190 states of the world (Derbyshire and Derbyshire, 1996).

As we will look at the impact of democratic institutions, we wish to distinguish between the difference that democracy and non-democracy makes for outcomes (*genus proximum*), on the one hand, and the effects of a variety of democratic institutions, on the other hand (*differentia specifica*). Thus, we first ask what difference does it make for policy outputs or outcomes whether a country is democratic. Second, we inquire into whether alternative sets of democratic institutions indeed implicate a difference for policy outputs and outcomes at the macro-level.

11.3 DEMOCRATIC INSTITUTIONS: INTRINSIC OR EXTRINSIC IMPORTANCE?

Institutions are important, we are being told by all the versions of neo-institutionalism (Williamson, 1985; March and Olsen, 1989; North, 1990; Keman, 1997c). We ask: *for what*? The search for institutional effects would, if successful, strengthen neo-institutionalism or the new institutionalism. The mere claim about institutional importance would be replaced by a set of theoretically derived models that have been tested in empirical research with confirmation. Proclaiming 'institutional importance' is, however, ambiguous, as long as the following two critical distinctions are not made.

11.3.1 Institutional Importance: Intrinsic or Extrinsic

Institutions are the rules or norms which are upheld by means of sanctions. Thus, behaviour is oriented in terms of rules where failure to comply with the rules results in sanctions. The institutionalization of norms is the entire process through which norms are brought to apply in societies. Institutions are intrinsically important when their norms are being complied with. Thus, institutions may be considered absolutely vital to any society because much behaviour in all societies tends to comply with norms. Institutions, however, are failing if societal behaviour does not comply with its norms. In all societies there always occurs behaviour which is deviant in relation to its norms. When deviance is prevelant, then the existence of the institution is in jeopardy.

Institutions that are upheld often receive moral support, i.e. they come to be recognized as legitimate. Much of political life in a democracy is institutionalized. For instance, the behaviour in legislatures tends to follow explicit or implicit norms, resulting in standard procedures for voting and for work in committees. One can state that such institutions are important, meaning that they structure behaviour and receive support in terms of widespread legitimacy (Tsebelis, 1990). Although parliaments operate different institutions, one may claim that they all are important in this intrinsic sense of 'importance', meaning only that norms are complied with. And, to take another example, it is an important question where an economy successfully institutionalizes much economic interaction and induces market behaviour with low transaction costs (North, 1990).

Extrinsic importance is something completely different, as it refers to the consequences of the operation of institutions. Institutions, when strongly in place, can bring about outcomes in the causal sense. Thus, norms when firmly institutionalized may be conducive to political, social or economic results. This is not a question of whether the norms are complied with or not, but whether the operation of the institutions brings about outcomes that go beyond the mere institutionalization of the norms.

For instance, a parliament recruited by means of majoritarian election techniques may display a different performance profile from a parliament recruited by means of a Proportional Representation system, or result in different policy outputs and outcomes. Similarly, an economy which institutionalizes a high degree of economic freedom may achieve a higher rate of economic growth than an economy with institutions that allow for less economic freedom. 'Being important' here stands for the consequences of the institution beyond mere compliance.

11.3.2 Institutions: Rules or Actors

Discussing 'institutional importance' or the concept of institutional effects implies that one conceives of institutions as rules that constrain or empower individual or collective actors. In this chapter we will pursue institutionalism in its rational-choice version, because it is the type of institutionalism that offers a distinct conceptualization of institutions, separating institutions from other entities in social life. Sociological institutionalism, identifying institutions with not only norms but also culture as well as organizations, may cast its nets too widely, meaning that 'institution' stands for everything and thus nothing (see, for example: Powell and Di Maggio, 1991; Streeck, 1992; March and Olsen, 1995).

In order to derive testable models about institutions, it is necessary to distinguish them from actors, preferences or culture. 'Institutions' stand for the norms that society complies with. And the key question is whether or not institutional variation does produce a difference in outputs and outcomes. We know that outputs and outcomes vary strongly among the countries of the world. Thus, socio-economic outcomes are very different measured in terms of affluence, economic growth, human development and equality. The same is true of political outputs and outcomes such as the size of the public sector, the respect for human rights and political stability. Do institutions play a role in explaining this variation in outputs and outcomes? More specifically, we ask: Do democratic institutions make a difference?

A theory on the impact of democratic institutions may be developed in two ways: focusing on the *genus proximum* of democracy or on those institutions that are characteristic for *any democratic regime*. We will use Tocqueville's model about the general consequences of a democratic society, with regard to indicating the *genus proximum*. Presently the most discussed model about democratic effects is probably the Lijphart theory about the differential consequences of the operation of Westminster democracy and Consensus democracy (Lijphart, 1984, 1999). Before we evaluate this *differentia specifica* model, we will discuss the *genus proximum* model: institutional effects that deals with the distinction between democracy and non-democracy.

11.4 IMPACT OF DEMOCRACY: DE TOCQUEVILLE'S MODEL

What is democracy? Which regimes enter the set of non-democracies? These questions about the definition of democratic institutions can be answered in various ways (see: Woldendorp et al., 2000; Chapter 3 of this book). One may focus upon institutions that secure government of the people or by the people. Here, the *genus proximum* of democracy is group decision-making where votes are allocated to choose participants and the group decision is the aggregation of the preferences of the participants. Hence, what democracy in its minimum sense excludes is the imposition of the will of an external person or the declaration of the preference of one participant as the group choice against all the preferences of the other participants. Democratic decisions are non-dictatorial from within the group nor imposed from outside of the group.

In political democracy, there is an institution that safeguards equality, as implied by the one-man, one-vote rule. All citizens – men and women – are equal and count for the same. In addition there is the idea of making decisions by one group decision-making rule, meaning simple majority voting. Although political democracy may employ qualified majority decision-making, real life democratic countries tend to use simple majority in most of their institutions. Thus, we shall use a minimalist definition of the *genus proximum* of democracy: equal citizen voting rights and simple majority decision-making is prevalent.

Equal voting rights and simple majority is, of course, a very thin definition of democratic institutions, which is sometimes called 'populist democracy' or Rousseaun democracy. One may arrive at thick definitions of democracy by increasing the number and types of citizen rights, including negative or positive freedoms, group rights and immunities: for instance, property rights (see for this: Held, 1987). Another method for arriving at a thick definition of democracy is to make the group decision-making rules more complex, including a variety of qualified decision-making or the allocation of veto possibilities to various players. Precisely *differentia specifica* definitions of democracy follow from various thick definitions of the concept (Saward, 1994; Beetham, 1994).

Focusing upon the separation between democracies and non-democracies in the countries of the world today, we employ a *human rights index*. The set of non-democracies includes a variety of different regimes: personal dictatorships, one party regimes, military juntas and traditional regimes. The non-democratic regimes, of whatever kind they may be, do not satisfy the minimalist criteria on democracy: equal citizen voting rights and the prohibition against dictators from inside or outside the choice group. There are a variety of indices measuring the institutionalization of political and civil rights, ranking countries from 0 to 10 in terms of the extent of their democraticness (see also Chapter 3 in this book).

In contrast to these regimes the argument is that democracies would enhance outputs such as the welfare state or socio-economic performance, because democratic institutions promote the interests of most of its citizens. This is the classical position in Tocqueville's predictions about the future of democracy, stated in his second volume of *Democracy in America* published in 1840.

Tocqueville distinguished between the aristocratic and the democratic society. The future of mankind is linked to with the latter type of society, argued Tocqueville. A democratic society would promote the level of human

Table 11.1 *Democratic performance: correlation analysis*

	RGDP/ca	HDI	SOC	CGR	GINI	FEM REP
Democracy 1970s	r = 0.74	0.81	0.58	0.36	−0.17	−0.19
	(0.000)	(0.000)	(0.000)	(0.000)	(0.097)	(0.025)
Democracy 1980s	r = 0.53	0.80	0.64	0.34	−0.09	−0.04
	(0.000)	(0.000)	(0.000)	(0.000)	(0.239)	(0.330)
Democracy 1990s	r = 0.70	0.70	0.73	0.51	−0.23	0.37
	(0.000)	(0.000)	(0.000)	(0.000)	(0.037)	(0.000)

RGDP = Real GDP per capita in US$; HDI = human development index; SOC = social security payments as a % of GDP; CGR = central government revenue as a % of GDP; GINI = Gini indices measuring inequality in income distribution; FEM REP = female parliamentary representation in %; Pearson product moment correlations are used; numbers in parentheses denote the level of significance; p-value close to or < 0.050 indicates that the correlation in question is significant.

Source: See Appendix 1 to this chapter.

development, as it emphasizes individualism and the pursuit of personal happiness. Since it favours equality before freedom, a democratic society favours public sector expansion, which will provide government with the resources it needs to equalize conditions between classes or income strata as well as between men and women (Tocqueville, 1990, Volume II: 168–214).

Is it true that democracies perform differently in the Tocqueville sense from non-democracies if data about the realities of the word today are examined? Table 11.1 suggests an answer using cross-sectional information from the 1970s, 1980s and 1990s, where the occurrence of democracy is measured by means of indices tapping the institutionalization of civil and political rights.

It is not an exaggeration to state that all of the Tocqueville ideas are confirmed in the data about policy outputs and socio-economic outcomes among democratic and non-democratic countries around the world. The significant results in Table 11.1 validate Tocqueville's image of democracy as being associated with high economic outputs and a high level of human development (HDI). Democracy also gives a major role to the state in the form of the provision of welfare by means of large social expenditures oriented towards income maintenance (transfer payments). At the same time democracies appear to promote equality by reducing income differences and recognizing the status of women. What Tocqueville warned against was government centralization, which prediction is also corroborated in the data about the size of Central Government Revenues (CGR).

In sum: the features of Tocqueville's type of *genus proximum* democracy is positively related to societal performance. How about causality? Are the democratic institutions indeed contributing to the outputs and outcomes listed in Table 11.1? It could well be that there is some underlying factor which accounts for both the occurrence of democracy and the performance config-uration. Conversely, one could argue that democracy is the *effect* and the per-formance the *cause*. We need to establish therefore the institutional effects of democracy. In Table 11.2 we report the regression analyses concerning the level of human development, the size of welfare state policies and equality.

Table 11.2 *Regression analysis: level of human development, welfare state policies and equality*

Independent variables		HDI 1980	HDI90	SOCB85	SOCB93	GINI 80	GINI 90	FEM 80	FEM90
				Dependent variables					
Democracy	Coeff	0.060	0.048	0.517	0.479	0.700	0.469	−0.601	0.029
		(11.24)	(7.00)	(0.91)	(1.00)	(1.31)	(0.74)	(−2.06)	(0.09)
Econ Freedom	Coeff	0.026	0.045	–	–	–	–	–	–
		(2.20)	(3.91)						
Trade Union	Coeff	–	–	0.109	0.322	–	–	–	–
				(2.21)	(6.23)				
LN RGDPCH	Coeff	–	–	5.932	3.842	−0.026	−4.251	0.246	0.413
				(3.25)	(2.84)	(−0.01)	(−1.92)	(0.25)	(0.39)
Protestants	Coeff	0.000	−0.000	–	–	−0.034	0.009	0.150	0.197
		(1.29)	(−0.14)	(0.19)		(−0.72)	(0.19)	(5.14)	(7.12)
Family systems	Coeff	–	–	–	–	1.939	0.541	−1.196	−0.799
						(2.64)	(0.59)	(−2.82)	(−1.81)
Constant	Coeff	0.099	0.136	46.505	−33.756	25.840	68.898	13.846	7.960
		(2.07)	(2.63)	(−3.94)	(−3.60)	(1.44)	(3.45)	(1.60)	(0.84)
Adj. R^2		0.70	0.58	0.57	0.79	0.11	0.20	0.28	0.46
N		92	93	51	36	71	55	105	100

LN RGDPCH; LN stands for natural logarithm; RGDPCH refers to Real GDP/capita in Appendix 1 for the 1970s, 1980s and the 1990s; Spearman's rho is the coefficient in this table; for the classification of democratic regimes, see Appendix 2; *t*-values are in parentheses; when *t* has an absolute value of close to or > 2 it indicates that the regression coefficient in question is 'significant'.

Source: See Appendix 1 to this chapter.

The findings in Table 11.2 about institutional effects of democracy on performance indicate that, apart from institutions, other factors must be taken into account. Obviously the coefficients reported are not only varied, but also insignificant in many cases. Human development is hardly causally related to 'democracy' and 'economic freedom', whereas indicators of the welfare state appear to be. Let us therefore discuss in more detail the Tocquevillean dimensions of democracy in relation to societal performance.

11.4.1 Level of Human Development

The Human Development Index (HDI) allows us to rank most of the countries of the world. It is basically a composite index taking into account first and foremost total economic output or the GDP but it adds measures of other dimensions of affluence such as literacy, life expectancy and educational enrolment. In the 1990s the variation in the HDI is substantial: ranging from 200 for the poorest countries to close to 1000 for the more affluent countries. Is democracy an explanatory factor for the variation in the 1990s in the HDI?

Since the HDI includes the GDP, we would expect to find among its determinants, factors that promote affluence, for instance economic institutions that allow for economic freedom. Since the HDI includes, in addition to the GDP, such matters as the quality of life, we expect socio-cultural factors also to play a role, for instance a religion that underlines well-being and individualism such as Protestantism. Table 11.2 reports a regression model for the HDI comprising besides democratic institutions also economic institutions and religion. From the results it appears that the level of human development remains strongly linked with the institutionalization of civil and political rights, even when other factors have been taken into account.

Can we conclude that Tocqueville was right about democracy resulting in affluence and a decent standard of living? Perhaps this institutional effect could manifest itself in the long run. In the short run, however, such an impact is not very likely, as rights cannot produce economic outputs. Yet, a high level of human development may well stimulate demands for the introduction of democracy, as occurred in South East Asia during the 1990s.

11.4.2 Welfare State Policies

There is a huge literature discussing the determinants of welfare state effort (see for an overview Castles, 1998 and Chapter 9 in this book), which varies considerably today among the countries of the world. Some countries are fully developed welfare states with high levels of social expenditures, both with an allocative and redistributive nature, whereas other democracies provide for little of state guaranteed welfare and are rather trusting of the market mechanism or are simply refraining from doing much in the social sphere. Why this variation in terms of welfare effort, measured by means of public expenditures as a percentage of GDP?

Theory claims that there are two main determinants – economic resources and societal preferences – for instance in the form of the strength of the Left in politics and society (see Chapters 8 and 9 in this book). An affluent society would make a welfare state possible but the strength of the Left in government induces the welfare state. One must not only have enough economic resources to develop a tax state, but one must also have the ambition to do so, because the political majority prefers a welfare state to a welfare or market society (Esping-Anderson, 1990; Keman, 1993b; Pierson, 1996).

To test this hypothesis, one could analyse the cross-national variation in welfare state expenditures: Transfer Payments. *Transfer Payments* cover all forms of income maintenance programmes, which tend to vary considerably not only between states in general, but also within the set of democratic countries. Why? An answer is suggested in the models in Table 11.2, where level of Transfer Payments as a percentage of GDP is regressed with the growth of the GDP (i.e. Wagner's Law), with the duration of the Left in government, for which we here use trade union strength as a proxy, and finally with democracy, or the institutionalization of civil and political rights.

The findings in Table 11.2 suggest that resources and preferences are more important when explaining the variation in one key policy output, i.e. Transfer Payments, than democracy itself. High levels of Transfer Payments tend to emerge when there is a culture or average profile of preferences favouring egalitarianism, according to Wildavsky (Wildavsky, 1986). Tocqueville predicted that democracy in itself would generate such an egalitarian society, calling for public sector expansion. However, this is not necessarily the case, as democracies with an individualistic culture would favour the welfare society model (Thompson et al., 1990).

11.4.3 Equality

Democracy opens up the possibility for the government to correct the inequalities in society. To Tocqueville, the search for real equality would be the most dominant tendency in the democratic era. We approach equality from two angles: income equality and gender equality. Both dimensions of equality vary considerably among countries. However, they are not the same phenomenon. Does democracy reduce both kinds of inequalities? If so, then this would also be the case if one adds other factors, for instance economic ones like affluence, or cultural ones like a Protestant religion, or the structure of the family system?

Table 11.2 estimates a model predicting two outcomes: income inequalities in the form of GINI-scores and gender equality as measured by female representation in Parliament as a result of GDP, democracy, Protestantism and the family system. It is argued by economists that there exists a Kuznets' curve meaning that income inequalities even out as countries grow richer. In addition, there is sociological theory which links in-egalitarian outcomes with a collectivist culture or family system (Todd, 1983, 1984) and egalitarian outcomes with a religion that emphasizes individualism (e.g. Protestantism).

The regression analyses in Table 11.2 concerning these two aspects of equality, income equality and gender equality, hardly supports the claim by Tocqueville that democracy in itself matters. Instead, both the economic hypothesis and the sociological hypotheses receive some empirical support.

11.4.4 Summing Up

We have found that democratic institutions tend to be strongly associated with major differences in policy outputs and social and economic outcomes. However, this is all institutional performance. When searching for institutional effects of democracy, following Tocqueville's predictions about the general impact of democracy, then things are not quite so transparent. Other factors must be taken into account than simply the institutionalization of civil and political rights *per se* (see also Chapter 12 in this book).

In the literature on empirical democratic theory one encounters an even stronger claim, namely that different kinds of democratic regimes have different performance profiles in terms of outputs and outcomes. Beyond that, it is stated that specific democratic institutions bring about certain outcomes. We will examine these claims below in relation to a variety of particular democratic institutions.

11.5 DEMOCRACY: THE *DIFFERENTIA SPECIFICA*

By extending the set of democratic institutions in the working concept of democracy, one moves away from the minimalist criteria of equal citizen voting rights and the use of simple majority rule discussed so far. There are a variety of extended definitions of democracy, focusing upon how alternative institutions are combined into complex mechanisms. Let us use the already classical statement of Arend Lijphart of the *differentia specifica* models of democracy.

In *Democracies* (1984) and *Patterns of Democracy* (1999) Lijphart outlined two ideal-types of democracy by – in a Weberian fashion – exaggerating and combining certain features into two polar types of democracy that have no counterparts in real life political systems. Yet, his own empirical work demonstrated already that there is still much institutional variation to allow for only two ideal-types (Lijphart et al., 1988; see for this also Chapter 8 in this book).

The Lijphart typology raises a number of interesting questions for research about democratic institutions, their performance and impact. One may add other *differentia specifica*, e.g. Lijphart himself later talks about corporatism and democracy (Keman and Pennings, 1995). According to Lijphart himself *Consensus Democracy* outperforms *Westminster Democracy* on several evaluation criteria and performs always at least equally well as Westminster Democracy. Below, the logic of the Lijphart model is elaborated. Thereafter we shall test various hypotheses about institutional effects on the structuration of democratic institutions.

11.5.1 Two Ideal-types of Democracy?

Basically, Westminster Democracy is the logic of executive government, emanating from the sovereignty of parliament. What institutions are involved in this kind of power fusion or executive dominance? If the logic of Westminster Democracy is power fusion, then we must ask: Do all the institutional items in this ideal-type entail executive dominance and do they form a coherent pattern to that effect?

More specifically, Westminster Democracy harbours the following institutions: (a) minimum winning and minimum sized coalitions; (b) unicameral or asymmetrical bicameral parliaments; (c) plurality or majoritarian election formulas; (d) no legal review; (e) unitary state; and (f) flexible constitution. What we wish to pin down is the mechanisms behind Westminster Democracy, i.e. how it comes about that these six Westminster Democracies institutions are conducive to power fusion. Two interpretations are feasible:

1. When there is executive dominance, then we find $a + b + c + d + e + f$.
2. When there is a or b or c or d or e or f, what degree of power fusion is apparent?

The first version states a mechanism about one complex necessary condition, whereas the second version states a mechanism involving many sufficient conditions for power fusion. Below, each of the institutions mentioned will be discussed separately in terms of its necessity and sufficiency.

An uncodified or highly flexible constitution is hardly necessary for power fusion. It is true that in British parliamentarism, the government is the first executive of parliament and all public powers emanate from the legislative supremacy of parliament. Yet, codified constitutions may enshrine the very same institutions that constitute conventions in British constitutional practice – see for instance the Nordic democracies. French presidentialism would adhere to the same logic of power fusion, i.e. executive dominance, especially if one bypasses *Cohabitation*,[1] but it is certainly bolstered by the 1959 constitution. Hence, power fusion does not need by definition on unwritten condition. However, one may argue that a 'rigid' constitution impairs power fusion.

Actually, one major disadvantage in the Lijphart model is that *presidentialism*, which is a most important executive institution both in terms of power and in terms of frequency of occurrence, does not really fit. For what is the logic of presidentialism: power fusion or power sharing? It appears that the relevance of presidentialism in Europe after 1989 – strong head of state and strong prime minister – just increases, as more and more countries move towards this non-American model. Presidentialism or semi-presidentialism in Western and Central Europe – could be considered as typical for executive dominance as well (see for this also: Duverger, 1980; Elgie, 1998; Keman, 2000b).

A unitary state does not imply power fusion, as lower levels of government may well exercise considerable financial autonomy and may be responsible for a large number of state competencies at their own discretion. A unitary state may allow its local governments complete financial autonomy as in Denmark and Sweden, or by means of devolution delegate powers to large areas, like Scotland and Wales in the United Kingdom. In short, unitary states may be centralized as in The Netherlands, France, Greece and Portugal or decentralized as in Northern Europe and in Spain and Italy.

The occurrence of legal review, or the power of judges or a constitutional court, to test statute laws for their constitutionality, implies clearly a major restriction on executive dominance. However, the conclusion that the lack of legal review implies executive dominance is a conjecture. In any democracy that adheres to the Rule of Law there will be judicial institutions that limit the power of the executive branch of government. Thus, almost all countries in Europe with no legal review have various judicial or quasi-judicial institutions where citizens may seek redress against public administration. Parliaments in Scandinavia have their own Ombudsman for examining the executive branch of government. The French Conseil Constitutionel limits executive dominance more than it enhances it. Finally all Central European democracies recognize legal review by means of a constitutional court, although they can be characterized as centralized government (Keman, 2000a).

It is also true that one kind of election system reinforces power fusion, according to the Duverger principle that the plurality method or majoritarian formula brings about 'manufactured majorities', upon which simple majority governments may be formed.[2] However, the opposite conclusion does not hold, namely that PR electoral systems entail lack of executive dominance. Long periods of executive dominance such as the Christian Democratic rule in Italy, the Social Democratic governments in Scandinavia, and the Gonzales government in Spain stemmed from PR election systems. A most spectacular change of the election system took place in Italy in 1994, but this movement in favour of Westminster Democracy did not change much in terms of executive dominance.

A unicameral parliament or an asymmetric bicameral parliament where the lower house prevails over the upper house does not imply executive dominance by definition. This depends on the constellation of forces in each particular parliament and their specific rights. However, a *symmetrical* two-chamber parliament could limit executive dominance, if the two chambers have a different composition of political forces. The capacity of a one-chamber parliament or asymmetrical bicameralism to bolster power fusion is thus entirely dependent upon the specific institutions by which it is empowered (Tsebelis and Money, 1997). Hence, we argue that unicameralism is *neutral* in relation to executive dominance, although executive dominance is more likely in unicameralism.

The distinction between one-chamber and two-chamber parliaments seems of very limited relevance in Western and Central Europe, especially if one inserts the symmetrical/asymmetrical restriction. Almost all European democracies would end up in the asymmetrical one-chamber category, as if they were all Westminster Democracies. Only the federal countries are different. Yet, the degree of executive dominance is quite variable in Germany, Austria and Switzerland, taking into account that only the Helvetian Republic can be considered as a dual federal system (Schmidt, 2000; Wachendorfer-Schmidt, 2000).

Finally, executive dominance appears to foster minimum winning-sized coalitions. But is it also true that executive dominance could not occur under another type of government, for instance a minority government or an over-sized government?[3] The obvious candidate for executive dominance would be a grand coalition of the Austrian type, where the two large parties have managed to monopolize political power for decades (until, 2000), ruling Austria from Vienna. Minority coalitions on the other hand would have to be based upon compromising in parliamentary committees (Strøm, 1990).

The argument about the Westminster Democracy logic is basically a theory about which institutions are necessary for having executive dominance: the conditions a + b + c + d + e + f must have been met. This statement is, however, not correct since executive government can occur under a different set of combinations of conditions, for instance, where there is a 'pivot' party like the DC (in Italy), the CDU (in Germany), the SAP (in Sweden) and DNA (in Norway), or the CDA in The Netherlands (Keman, 1994). The fact that each of the Westminster institutions appears neither sufficient nor necessary for executive dominance implies the possibility that each condition as such may well occur without leading to executive dominance.

Conversely, Consensus Democracy is constructed by proceeding in the same manner as with the Westminster Democracy, but, of course, stating the opposites to the institutional items listed in (a) to (f). The institutions of Consensus Democracy are supposed to be conducive to *power sharing*, which, again, raises the question about necessary or sufficient conditions to be met.

Governments under Consensus Democracy would have to be coalitions between two or more parties, as one-party government with a simple majority is typical for Westminster Democracy. But what type of coalition is typical of Consensus Democracy? It is difficult to tell which in Consensus Democracy is the polar type to the Westminster Democracy cabinet: grand coalitions as in consociational theory, or any kind of coalition government that is not minimum winning and minimum sized. Power sharing, however, may also occur in the form of a single-party minority government that negotiates temporary coalitions in parliament. In fact, since the 1990s the 'oversized' type as well as 'minority' governments do not occur that often anymore. And, where they occur, they appear to become less frequent (like in the Benelux countries and Austria). The major exceptions are: Denmark, Norway and Switzerland. In the new democracies – in Central Europe – the major type of government is either 'one party' or 'minimal winning' (see: Woldendorp et al., 2000: Chapter 2).

The idea that power sharing is basically a consequence of symmetrical bicameralism, is definitely in agreement with the predictions from game theory (Tsebelis and Money, 1997). But the caveat is that this only applies if the two chambers are politically different. If a majority is in command of both houses, then perhaps power sharing must rely on other institutions. Until 1994 Italian bicameralism, which leaned towards symmetry, has not been conducive to power sharing. Another example is the German 'semi-sovereign state' (Schmidt, 1995).

A PR electoral system would clearly be a candidate for a necessary condition for power sharing, yet it is not a sufficient condition. If there is power sharing, then there is PR, but the reverse is not true. One can imagine a single party receiving a majority of the votes under a PR electoral system (if it is not highly proportional in its outcomes). This would then mean that the majority party could rule in the form of executive dominance. Take the cases of Spain and Portugal in the 1980s and 1990s as empirical examples. Hence, an additional condition of power sharing would be the extent to which a party system is fragmented or not (see: Pennings and Lane, 1998).

Does power sharing really entail legal review, or the capacity of judges to squash legislation by testing laws against criteria of constitutionality? Switzerland is considered as a typical Consensus Democracy, but Switzerland neither accepts nor endorses legal review. And rightly so: How could judges squash what the people wish in a referendum democracy? The same observation holds for The Netherlands and Sweden: there is only a 'technical' legal review and the ultimate powers are with parliament.

One could have such power of the judicial branch of government in a country, ruled by a one-chamber parliament, as is actually the case in most of Central Europe. There can be legal review in a country with one dominant party – e.g. in Japan under the Liberal Party rule. All of the Central European countries recognize legal review, but power sharing does not occur frequently in these new democracies.

Concerning the federal state format, one may ask whether it is a necessary or sufficient condition for power sharing. Austrian federalism is not considered to be conducive to a power-sharing mechanism. And for Belgian federalism it is too early to say. On the other hand, power sharing between the centre and the regions seem to take place to some extent in some unitary states, such as Spain, Italy and France. Yet, Germany and also Switzerland are considered as power-sharing political systems (see: Linder, 1994; Schmidt, 2000; Braun, 2000).

Power sharing would necessitate a written constitution in Consensus Democracy. The distinction between a written and an unwritten constitution is not clear-cut. All constitutions that have been codified at one stage need to develop conventions in order to operate. Power sharing in Switzerland is based upon the 'Magic Formula' from 1959, but it is not codified. The German 1949 Basic Law says little about interlocking federalism and the resulting grid-lock. If there is a codified constitution such as in Sweden from 1809 to 1974 and another one from 1975 onwards, is there ipso facto power sharing? All constitutions are a mixture of codified law and conventions or case law. All countries have constitutional documents of one kind or another, supplemented by legal interpretation and conventions.

One must arrive at the conclusion that the Consensus Model is less coherent than the Westminster Model. It is probably not correct to argue that power sharing exists, only if conditions a + b + c + d + e + f apply altogether. It is also not correct to argue that if a or b or c or d or e or f is available, then power sharing is by definition present. In other words: other factors than *formal* institutionalization are relevant for explaining the occurence of Consensus Democracy.

11.5.2 How much Institutional Convergence?

The institutionalist par excellence of the founders of the modern theory on constitutional government, Montesquieu, argued that each country has its own spirit of laws and norms. The institutions of a country have emerged from an institutional evolution over the centuries, institutional legacies reflecting the past history of the country. This tends toward a holistic position, claiming that each institution makes sense when it is understood as a single piece of a larger puzzle and as a result of a country's historical development (Putnam, 1993; Lehmbruch, 1996).

Conversely Max Weber does not claim institutional coherence or convergence to exist. On the contrary, he considered institutions as (single) norms that carry sanctions against non-compliance. In Weber's view institutionalization is connected with the universal drive towards rationality, and his legal-rational type of authority comprises the concept of an institution as a key element, making this kind of domination different from patrimonial, feudal and charismatic authority (Keman, 1997c).

Following Weber we take up the atomistic position, treating each political institution as a separate entity. The electoral system is one such institution with a few basic alternatives that appear to be capable of occurring together with a large variety of other political institutions. PR electoral systems occur in unitary as well as federal states, in countries with or without legal review, where government can be of any type of coalition, and together with uni- or bicameralism. Hence, a multitude of combinations of institutions do exist and each configuration is more or less different. Therefore, we contend, institutional convergence is a myth.

Thus, the argument that there are two ideal-types of democracy, one adhering to the spirit of power fusion and the other converging upon the opposite spirit of power sharing, if scrutinized carefully, falls victim to its emphasis on similarity of institutions. Democratic political institutions vary along a number of dimensions, and this high degree of cross-national variation of different mechanisms for democratic government implies that there are more than only two logics of institutional coherence.

One must therefore be careful about assuming institutional coherence in the real world. When one brings together institutions into a model of democracy, then it is always a question of probabilities whether or not two or more institutions do go together in the real world. This can be illustrated by means of 'presidentialism' in relation to Westminster Democracy and Consensus Democracy. On the one hand, presidentialism implies in our view power sharing between the executive and the legislature. Thus, presidentialism, if it works according to the Montesquieu model or as in the American constitution, should be placed with Consensus Democracy. This is in agreement with the analysis of Westminster Democracy as executive dominance over the legislature, where the power of prime minister is fused with the power of the majority group in parliament. This can be observed in British parliamentarism, where the cabinet is simply the most powerful committee of parliament. However, in all analyses of regime transitions Lijphart (1992) advocates parliamentarism ahead of presidentialism, warning for the dangers of 'presidentialism' as a system of power concentration by the head of state (Linz, 1990, 1994).

Yet, following the logic of a strong preference for Consensus Democracy, institutional coherence would imply that one should accept also that presidentialism, at least in the American version with its counter-weighting powers called 'Madison democracy', is different from it. However, according to Lijphart (1999) parliamentarism displays better outcomes than presidentialism. This contradiction can only be resolved by the making of a distinction between two types of parliamentarism: Westminster Democracy and Consensus Democracy. Consensus Democracy would not lead to power sharing, but rather to power diffusion by its employment of the grand coalition as the form of cabinet, avoiding adversarial democracy which is characterized by its concentration of power with a simple majority. From this perspective,

Table 11.3 *Institutional foci in democracies*

1.	Electoral system:	majoritarian versus proportional
2.	State format:	unitary–federal
3.	Executive:	parliamentary–presidential
4.	Judiciary:	legal review
5.	Legislature:	unicameral–bicameral
6.	State-society:	degree of corporatism
7.	Elite co-operation:	degree of consociationalism
8.	Autonomy:	independence of central banks

it appears that 'presidentialism' often is closer to Consensus Democracy than to Westminster Democracy. Actually, the logic of institutional coherence is that institutional convergence will probably occur in reality.

One perspective upon institutional coherence and eventual convergence is to look at institutional performance. Is it the case that different types and combinations of democratic institutions result in different kinds of policies and outcomes? In order to examine this question one should proceed along the atomistic route, taking one institution at a time, and not combine them into ideal-types in order to explain the related performance.

11.6 INSTITUTIONAL PERFORMANCE IN DEMOCRACIES

In Table 11.3 eight macro institutional foci of democracies have been distinguished which may result in alternative outcomes. These institutional possibilities include a set of alternative macro-institutions which may also be looked upon as competing institutional mechanisms.

This classification – derived from Lijphart (1999) – is outcome based, meaning that these institutions figure prominently in the institutionalist literature as explanations of policy outputs and performance. Actually, there is no limit to the number of institutional items that one may wish to include. Often legislative institutions are very important for the explanation of micro-outcomes, such as when the use of a rule like the referendum or the standard alternative aggregation rules in parliamentary voting means a difference for one special decision. Thus, one could cover also the institutional variation in legislative rules. And what would be for instance the macro-outcomes from the use of one or another method of voting, that is, the electoral system?

As most of these institutional items change very slowly, it is possible to probe institutional effects by examining data about policy outputs and outcomes in the 1980s and 1990s, using the institutional classification of democratic institutions listed in Table 11.3. Below we shall scrutinize the performance profile of the different institutions of democracy, focusing upon the same policy outputs and outcomes discussed above in connection with the general effects of democracy (see Table 11.3).

Welfare state expenditures can be interpreted as a measure of welfare state effort. This is a policy output variable. The level of human development, on

Table 11.4 *Performance profiles: correlation analysis for democratic regimes*

		Human Development index		Female parliament representation		Gini index		Social security index	
		1980	1990	1980	1990	1980	1990	1980	1990
Election	r =	−0.08	−0.04	0.26	0.32	−0.22	−0.24	0.23	0.42
system		(0.325)	(0.402)	(0.060)	(0.029)	(0.109)	(0.145)	(0.092)	(0.008)
Federalism	r =	0.15	0.14	−0.14	−0.11	0.21	0.03	−0.16	−0.09
		(0.191)	(0.200)	(0.205)	(0.256)	(0.128)	(0.455)	(0.174)	(0.320)
Presidentialism	r =	−0.42	−0.44	−0.33	−0.27	0.72	0.72	−0.59	−0.41
		(0.005)	(0.003)	(0.023)	(0.050)	(0.000)	(0.000)	(0.000)	(0.010)
Legal review	r =	−0.08	−0.09	−0.48	−0.42	0.18	0.30	−0.15	−0.22
		(0.321)	(0.305)	(0.001)	(0.005)	(0.166)	(0.088)	(0.195)	(0.115)
Legislature	r =	0.14	0.16	−0.29	−0.15	0.05	−0.08	−0.11	−0.07
bicameral		(0.206)	(0.180)	(0.039)	(0.184)	(0.401)	(0.361)	(0.257)	(0.347)
Corporatism	r =	0.36	0.34	0.56	0.60	−0.48	−0.47	0.53	0.54
		(0.015)	(0.018)	(0.000)	(0.000)	(0.003)	(0.014)	(0.000)	(0.001)
Consocia-	r =	0.26	0.34	0.31	0.26	−0.42	−0.61	0.51	0.51
tionalism		(0.059)	(0.018)	(0.029)	(0.057)	(0.008)	(0.001)	(0.001)	(0.001)
Central bank	r =	0.27	0.28	0.20	0.29	−0.27	−0.39	0.28	0.16
independence		(0.052)	(0.049)	(0.120)	(0.042)	(0.064)	(0.039)	(0.049)	(0.185)

Note: Spearman's rho is the coeficient used for this table; when the *p* value is close to or < 0.050 it indicates that the correlation in question is significant; for the classification of democratic regimes, see Appendix 2.

Source: See Appendix 1 to this chapter.

the other hand, is an outcome variable (i.e. performance) which taps the level of socio-economic development in a country. The Gini index of income inequalities is also a performance measure, whereas the variable measuring the extent of gender equality, i.e. women's representation in political life, may be seen as partly an outcome and partly a policy output.

Policy outputs and outcomes vary depending upon different factors, of course. We focus upon the contribution of alternative democratic institutions as an aid to understanding cross-national variation. Since institutions are only one kind of factor that explains outputs and outcomes in addition to, for instance, social structure and culture, one cannot expect to find very strong correlations between institutions, on the one hand, and outputs and outcomes, on the other hand. Nevertheless the analysis of simple correlations can be employed to draw up a picture of institutional performance. Here we treat the various democratic regimes as dichotomies; see Appendix 2 for the classification of the various democratic regimes.

The correlations in Table 11.4 indicate bivariate relations, which need to be researched in a more profound manner by means of regression analysis. Table 11.4 has a few strong relationships between various democratic institutions and policy outputs as well as socio-economic outcomes. Yet, the distinction between majoritarian and proportional election systems, on the one hand, and corporatism as well as consociationalism, provides for the transparent contrasts in performance profile of institutions.

Thus, there seems to be a clear institutional impact from presidentialism upon all the outputs and outcomes included. Presidentialism tends to perform in a distinct manner, involving low public expenditures, high-income inequalities as well as a poor socio-economic performance. Corporatist institutions tend to display the very opposite performance profile, which is also true of consociational institutions with the important exception of much less gender equality in the latter than in the former (Birchfield and Crépaz, 1998).

In relation to the other institutions, the general result is that one needs to specify the presumed institutional effect in a more precise manner, as the correlations tend to be rather weak and thus lack theoretical import. One may note that PR electoral systems tend to favour gender equality and high levels or transfer payments as well as appearing to reduce income inequalities. The bicameral institution is weakly related to gender equality in the form of female representation in the parliament, but bicameralism seems to reduce the amount of income redistribution. Although there seems to be a certain pattern of institutional arrangements, it is too early to claim intrinsic coherence and consistency with policy outputs and performance.

11.7 ARE THERE DEMOCRATIC INSTITUTIONAL EFFECTS?

The neo-institutionalist claim that institutions indeed matter can empirically be confirmed if one demonstrates that an institutional factor has a clear *partial* impact upon outcomes when the contribution of other factors has been taken into account. This procedure will help to address the difficult problem of causal induction with respect to the actual impact of institutions.

Below we employ regression analysis in order to substantiate the claim that various types of democratic institutions contribute to certain policy outputs and outcomes. We will analyse a specific set of institutional effects that concern important aspects of the democratic state:

- democratic stability
- centralization of the state
- size of the public sector.

Democratic stability concerns how a country scores on the human rights scale from one decade to another. Political institutions may be crucial for stabilizing a democracy, especially if the surrounding social, economic and cultural conditions have a negative impact upon democratic endurance. If federalism makes a difference, then – we argue – it must concern the fiscal centralization or decentralization of the state. Finally, although we consider Wagner's Law (see also Chapter 8 in this book) as being an important explanation of big(ger) government, it could well be the case that the substantial variation in the size of the public sector among rich countries is also related to the occurrence of an institutions factor like corporatism. It would mean that – in addition to parliament – societal interests are strongly influenced by

Table 11.5 *Regression analyses: democracy and centralization*

Independent variables		DEMO	DEMO	DEMO	CENTRAL	CENTRAL
				Dependent variables		
Legal review	coeff	-0.53 (-2.00)	-	-0.61 (-2.92)	-	-
federalism	coeff	-	-	-	-11.18 (-3.10)	-11.16 (-3.13)
Presidential	coeff	-0.69 (-2.18)	-0.76 (-2.36)	-	-	-
Sclerosis	coeff	-	-	-	0.02 (50)	-
Lnrgdp70	coeff	1.15 (5.96)	1.15 (5.72)	1.33 (7.23)	4.35 (1.43)	5.41 (2.54)
Constant	coeff	-0.56 (-0.33)	-0.77 (-0.44)	-2.26 (-1.43)	-6.61 (-0.30)	-12.85 (-0.71)
Rsq adj		0.65	0.62	0.61	0.25	0.27
N		37	37	37	35	35

Note: T-statistic in parentheses; lnrgdp70: ln stands for natural logarithm; rgdp70 refers to Real GDP/capita in Appendix 1 for the 1970s.

Source: See Appendix 1 to this chapter.

institutionalized interest intermediation. Table 11.5 tests these models about the occurrence of institutional effects.

Democratic stability, Table 11.5 informs us, involves a clear institutional effect. The adherence to presidential institutions does not increase the probability of democratic stability. On the contrary, presidentialism reduces the probability of sustainable democracy as compared with its institutional competitor: parliamentarism. This observation opens up the debate on the pros and cons of *semi*-presidentialism as a viable alternative (Keman, 2000b; see also Chapter 3 in this book).

Interestingly, we cannot detect a positive institutional effect from the main judicial institution which has received much attention in constitutional debates, namely legal review. One must remind oneself of the distinction between institutions on paper and institutional realities, as several countries which provide for legal review in their constitutions have as a matter of fact failed to implement such provisions. On the contrary, we have a corroboration of the institutional hypothesis that federalism means a lower level of fiscal decentralization than unitarism (Braun, 2000). Similarly, in Table 11.6 when looking at the OECD set of nations we have corroboration of another much discussed institutional effect (Keman and Pennings, 1995). Corporatist institutions among the rich democratic countries of the world drive up public expenditures, indicating that at high levels of affluence the Wagner effect is cancelled out by preferences or by organized interest intermediation (Olson, 1982). When rich countries face the choice between state or market, they tend to choose not primarily on the basis of the resources available. Rather, so it appears, their preference for the welfare state or the welfare

Table 11.6 *Regression: total public sector output*

Independent variables		Dependent variables	
		Total 95	Total 95
Corp-1	coeff	5.06	–
		(2.99)	
Corp-2	coeff	–	0.88
			(2.52)
Lnppp95	coeff	−25.40	−20.29
		(−1.80)	(−1.32)
Constant	coeff	300.20	242.28
		(2.15)	(1.58)
Rsq adj		0.35	0.37
N		18	17

Note: Lnppp95: ln stands for natural logarithm; ppp95 refers to ppp in Appendix 1 for 1995; *t*-statistics in parentheses.

Source: See Appendix 1 to this chapter.

society depends on party programmes, as a strong electoral position for the Left often implies a preference for the welfare state.

11.8 WHICH TYPE OF DEMOCRACY IS BEST?

Democracy is considered at the end of the twentieth century to be the system of political institutions that basically triumphed over alternative systems: communism and fascism. To some, this is the end of a long process of institutional choice (Fukuyama, 1992), but to others it is the beginning of a new period of institutional deliberations. The relevant question now is whether one type of democracy performs better than another type, or in our approach to the problem: does one democratic institution result in different outcomes than another?

Institutional superiority or institutional improvement may be based upon political, social or economic outcomes. In the theory about two types of democracy – Westminster Democracy and Consensus Democracy – all three types of evaluation criteria play a role. Lijphart claims that institutions representing Consensus Democracy tend to outperform Westminster Democracy on all three evaluation criteria. At least Consensus Democracy institutions never do worse than Westminster Democracy institutions (Lijphart, 1999). We wish to argue that it is much more a question about a *trade-off* than a positive 'win-set' altogether.

Examining data about policy outputs and outcomes in the 1990s, there are a few interesting differences between countries that score low and countries that score high on power sharing, which point to the existence of a major institutional trade-off in the set of stable democracies, i.e. those belonging to the so-called OECD-world.

The countries that score low on power sharing are the countries with strong institutionalization of majoritarian institutions in the form of the

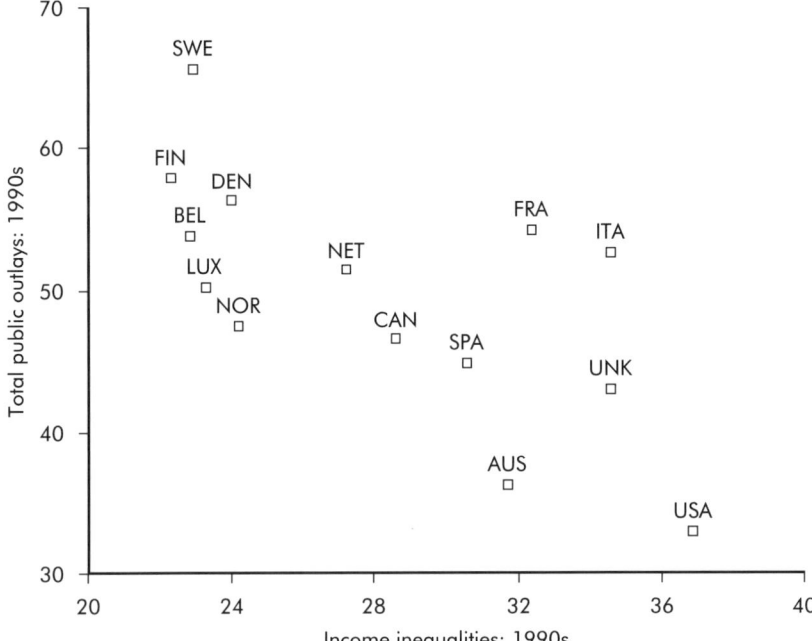

Figure 11.1 *Total public outlays and income inequalities in the 1990s.*
Key: AUS = Australia; BEL = Belgium; CAN = Canada; DEN = Denmark;
FIN = Finland; FRA = France; ITA = Italy; Lux = Luxembourg;
NET = Netherlands; NOR = Norway; SWE = Sweden; SPA = Spain;
UK = United Kingdom; US = United States of America. Source: See Appendix 1

electoral system or the executive. These countries include the Anglo-Saxon world: the UK, the USA, Canada, Australia and New Zealand. On the other hand, there are countries which perform high on power sharing, for instance the small European democracies and the Scandinavian countries, which countries favour PR election systems and consociational or corporatist institutions (Colomer, 1996; Keman, 1997c).

The most obvious difference in performance connected with the Anglo-Saxon democracies and with the continental European democracies concerns in particular:

- public sector size
- income inequality.

The Anglo-Saxon democracies tend to have low public expenditures whereas the continental European democracies are characterized by a large public sector. And the former countries are also characterized by considerable income inequalities, whereas the latter countries show a more even distribution of income, especially in the Nordic countries. We portray this trade-off between small public sector and large income inequalities in Figure 11.1.

The connection between total public sector size and income inequality is persistently and significantly negative whatever measure we use.[4] Perhaps this institutional trade-off can be related to the Tocqueville model and its basic confrontation between two values in a democratic regime, namely freedom from government and equality for all? In other words: equal citizen rights do not imply socio-economic equality. The type of democratic institutions in place appears to direct this very relationship *within* democracies.

11.9 CONCLUSIONS

Democratic regimes can be structured in alternative ways. A number of institutions may be employed to aggregate the preferences of citizens into a government decision. We have looked at eight institutional foci comprising institutional alternatives in a dichotomous manner, including the Montesquieu institutions (division of powers), the electoral system (mode of representation) and the organization of the state. Analysing how these institutions relate to each other and how they perform in terms of outputs and outcomes, we arrive at two conclusions, as follows.

1. The amount of institutional variation in the set of democratic states is greater than is often thought. Polities may combine institutions in a number of different ways with few restrictions deriving from any norm about coherence or institutional convergence. In the future, we may thus see new mixtures of the eight institutional foci that have been analysed. The degrees of freedom in institutional reform are apparently quite large. A reduction to two ideal-types of democracy is therefore producing a dichotomy that is insufficient to study contemporary developments, for instance in Central European countries.
2. The performance record of various institutions demonstrate striking differences. One majoritarian institution, presidentialism, displays a performance record that is distinct from the other majoritarian institution, the electoral system. Whereas 'presidentialism' is associated with a lower performance record, this is not necessarily the case with a plurality electoral system. Corporatism performs in the opposite fashion to presidentialism. The performance profile of consociationalism is close to that of corporatism with the exception of gender equality, but both corporatism and consociationalism have much more distinctive performance profiles within politics with a PR electoral system. Federalism matters particularly for fiscal decentralization.

All in all, one may well conclude that our analysis shows that mixtures of institutions matter more than certain *models* of democracy with a prescribed set of institutions.

NOTES

1 Cohabitation is the situation where government is composed of a different party (or: parties) than the president's party.
2 Manufactured majority is the result of the fact that a 'first past the post' electoral system is not based on Proportional Representation. See for this Bogdanor and Butler (1983).
3 Oversized governments are those where there are more parties participating than is necessary to have a majority in parliament. See: Woldendorp et al. (2000).
4 The correlations between total public sector size in 1995 and various income inequality measures for the 1990s are: −0.69 (lis), −0.68 (lis90), −0.47 (gini) and −0.58 (gini90).

APPENDIX 1 TO CHAPTER 11: VARIABLES AND SOURCES

Variables	Sources
Central Bank independence	Cukierman (1992)
Central government revenue	World Bank (1997, 1992)
Consociationalism	our own classification
Corporatism	classification based upon ILO (1997)
Corporatism	index: 1 Lijphart, A. and Crépaz, M. (1991)
Corporatism	index: 2 Calmfors, L. and Drifill, J. (1988)
Democracy scores	Freedom House (ed.) (annuals)
Economic freedom	Gwartney et al. (1996)
Electoral system	IPU (1995)
Family system	Todd (1983)
Federalism	Encyclopedia Britannica (1996); Europa Yearbook (1985); Banks (1978); Blondel (1969)
Female parliamentary representation	IPU (1995)
Gini-index	Deiniger, K. and Squire, L. (1997); Tabatabai, H. (1996)
Human development index	UNDP (1994)
Legal review	Maddex (1996); Blondel (1973, 1969)
Legislature	Encyclopedia Britannica (1996, 1985); Tsebelis and Money (1997); Banks (1978);
LIS: gini-index	LIS (1998)
PPP: purchasing power parties	OECD (1998)
Presidentialism	Encyclopedia Britannica (1996, 1985); Alvarez et al. (1996); Banks (1978); Blondel (1969)
Protestantism	Encyclopedia Britannica (1996); Barrett (1982)
Real GDP/capita	Summers and Heston (1994)
Social security benefits payment	UNDP (1997); ILO (1992)
Sclerosis	Black (1966) and our own data
Total95: total public outlays	OECD (1998)
Trade union strength	ILO (1997)

APPENDIX 2 TO CHAPTER 11: CLASSIFICATION OF DEMOCRATIC REGIMES

Country	Electoral System	Federalism	President- ialism	Legal review	Legis- lature	Corpor- atism	Consoci- ationalism	Central Bank
AUSL	0	1	0	1	1	0	0	0
AUT	1	1	0	1	1	1	1	1
BEL	1	0	0	0	1	1	1	0
BOT	0	0	1	0	0	0	0	0
BRA	1	1	1	1	1	0	0	0
CAN	0	1	0	0	1	0	0	1
COL	1	0	1	1	1	0	0	0
COSRI	1	0	1	0	0	0	0	1
DEN	1	0	0	0	0	1	0	1
DOM	1	0	1	0	1	0	0	0
ECU	1	0	1	1	0	0	0	0
ELSA	1	0	1	0	0	0	0	0
FIN	1	0	0	0	0	1	1	0
FRA	0	0	0	1	1	0	1	0
GER	1	1	0	1	1	0	0	1
GRE	1	0	0	0	0	0	0	1
ICE	1	0	0	0	0	1	0	1
INDIA	0	1	0	1	1	0	0	1
IRE	1	0	0	1	1	0	0	1
ISR	1	0	0	0	0	0	0	1
ITA	1	0	0	1	1	0	1	0
JAM	0	0	0	0	1	0	0	0
JAP	0	0	0	1	1	0	0	0
LUX	1	0	0	0	0	1	1	1
MAUU S	0	0	0	0	0	0	0	0
MEX	0	1	1	1	1	0	0	0
NET	1	0	0	0	1	0	1	1
NEWZ	0	0	0	0	0	0	0	0
NOR	1	0	0	0	0	1	0	0
POR	1	0	0	1	0	0	0	0
SPA	1	0	0	1	1	0	0	0
SWE	1	0	0	0	0	1	0	0
SWI	1	1	1	0	1	0	1	1
TRI	0	0	0	0	1	0	0	0
UNIK	0	0	0	0	1	0	0	0
USA	0	1	1	1	1	0	0	1
VEN	1	1	1	1	1	0	0	0

Notes: electoral system: proportional = 1; plurality/majoritarian = 0; federalism: federal = 1; non-federal = 0; presidentialism: presidential = 1; non-presidential = 0; legal review: more legal review = 1; less legal review = 0; legislature: bicameralism = 1; unicameralism = 0; corporatism: corporatist (i.e. strong trade unionism) = 1; non-corporatism = 0; consociationalism: consociational (i.e. frequently grand coalition) = 1; non-consociationalism = 0; central bank independence: more autonomy = 1; less autonomy = 0.

12 DEMOCRATIC INSTITUTIONS, GOVERNANCE AND POLITICAL PERFORMANCE

Hans Keman with the collaboration of Malika Aït Mallouk

12.1 THE MEANING OF THE CONCEPT OF DEMOCRATIC GOVERNANCE

If one were to ask what governance is and means in relation to government, then most people would be puzzled. Puzzled because 'government' is a self-evident concept and as such it appears to be a 'natural' phenomenon of contemporary society. Yet, it is not that easy to define what governance is and what it entails. Samuel Finer (1970), for instance, attributes at least four different meanings to the term 'government' in relation to society. First of all government denotes exercising a measure of control over others. Secondly, government is a condition of ordered rule. Thirdly, it refers to a body of people charged with the duty of governing. Fourthly, according to Finer, government is the method of ruling a particular society. In short, government in relation to governance can be seen as an *epi*-phenomenon which is obvious and obscure at the same time.

In this chapter we set out to analyse the *relationship* between the structure of democratic government and its societal performance. Central in the analysis is the cross-national variation of governance due to the organization of the state and the type of government by means of policy outputs and outcomes. Together this shapes the extant modi of democratic governance. This will lead us to the question of what governments do and what this means for society in terms of democratic and material performances (Keman, 1997a; Castles, 1998; Lane and Ersson, 2000).

In the next section we shall first develop some kind of definition of government which is not *per se* encompassing, but is universally (more or less) recognizable and empirically applicable. In addition we shall endeavour to conceptualize what democratic governance entails in relation to the polity in which it is positioned.

12.1.1 Government and Governance: Multifarious Concepts

In addition to a descriptive definition of what the structure of government entails, an *analytical* approach will be elaborated for *empirical* use. First of all, government is not the same as politics. This is a contested notion: many political scientists (and others too) see politics basically as an activity that amounts to what concerns the state. Taken in this sense political science is the study of government, if not the analysis of the public exercise of authority within a society. This is a rather limited view of what politics is, and it is restricted to what is often called the *polity*: the existence and operation of government on the basis of a constitution (or 'basic laws') according to the Rule-of-Law. Hence, equating 'politics' with 'government' is not only a too simple and a limited view, it also would lead to circular reasoning as regards what governments do and why they are (supposedly) doing it. In this chapter therefore the meaning of government is considered to be different from 'politics' – which is a public activity among people – with the purpose to organize the public domain (Putnam, 1993; Heywood, 1997). Governance is then the term we shall use to denote the relationship between the public at large (as, for instance, represented by the electorate) and policy-making actvities of representative government. Yet, the term also implies that governmental power is shared with other agents and is increasingly influenced by institutional structures in which national (or central) government is embedded. These developments have not only altered the functioning of government as an actor, but also are considered to be a part of multi-level and multi-actor governance. In sum: in this chapter the term governance is used with respect not only to its *systemic* relationship (with, for instance, parliament and parties), but also its *embeddedness* in institutional structures and societal actors (see: Colomer (ed.), 1996).

Governance is thus not identical to the 'polity' (i.e. the rules of the political game). Yet, the idea of the 'polity' has an implication for the meaning of governance which cannot and should not be discarded: it defines by and large what is considered to be part of the 'public domain' within a society. As early as Aristotle the distinction is regularly made between *public and private*, on the one hand, and between *authority and autonomy*, on the other. Of course, these distinctions are related to the meaning of constitutional government and also to good and effective governance.

From this point of view the meaning of government can be seen as 'governance', which is both a normative and material concept. In the words of Finer (1970: 6):

> ... in a given society not all political activity is governmental; some may be societal. And ... not all governmental activity is political: some may be routine administration. Government and politics come into contact at the point where the course of action has to be selected for the whole of society – under certain conditions.

The *normative* impact of democratic governance is then, in addition to the debate about the distinction between public and private, to what extent and under which conditions government is, and can be held, *responsible* for the enhancement of public welfare and thus the 'common good', i.e. the quality of life within a society. The *material* side of governance refers more to its type, scope of action and how this affects the social and economic life of the citizens. In modern times the normative and material significance of government surfaces, for example, by means of the 'welfare state' (Titmuss, 1974; Esping-Andersen, 1990). Yet, whatever idea is dominant about the role of government, and however obscure its meaning may be in relation to 'good and effective governance', the concept must be defined before its structure and actual role in and for a society can be assessed and understood.

12.1.2 Towards a Definition of Government

Although most authors do not converge on the meaning of what government is (or is supposed to be), they do agree on the fact that the executive is the irreducible core of government. Its history is the development of political authority; from ancient times to absolute monarchs, government was an almost universal phenomenon. The political executive predates constitutional and democratic government and the concomitant emergence of separate legislatures, bureaucracies, judiciaries and other branches of the (semi-) public services. Every country has an executive body called government which is thus considered as responsible for running the public affairs within and for a society. Taken in this sense it is *the* key point of political life (Tilly, 1975).

This remains true – so argues Blondel (1990) – even if one tends to doubt whether or not government and its executive organization is able to direct effectively the course of events (nationally and internationally), let alone to influence the social and economic structure of their country. Yet, on the other hand, government is the sole organization with authority, more than any other body, with an opportunity to shape society: either by public action or by doing nothing (Dye, 1966; Klingemann et al., 1994).

The crucial point made is that it might appear easier to understand 'government' by referring to the formal and institutional *processes* which operate at the *national* level to maintain *public order* and to enhance *collective action*. Taken in this sense the related actions and performances of government can then be considered as 'governance'.

In summary: government should be considered as a (more or less) institutionalized process that defines its 'room to manoeuvre' to govern. In general this means that the structure of government is basically characterized by mechanisms through which 'ordered rule' is maintained: *governments are the machinery for making and enforcing collective decisions by means of public action for a society*. This definition implies a number of distinct but interdependent functional roles: managing the apparatus of government; regulating public affairs; making decisions and directing society; implementation and co-ordination of policy formation, exerting leadership (Finer, 1970; Blondel, 1982; Page and Wright, 1999).

These elements will be elaborated and discussed in the remainder of this chapter, attempting to show how governments are institutionally structured and thus how they affect society by means of their policy performances.

12.2 GOVERNMENT AND THE POLITICAL SYSTEM: GOVERNANCE

In the preceding section it was emphasized that the 'body government' is a distinctive phenomenon, yet at the same time the core actor within any political system. In addition government was defined in terms of its functional characteristics. In other words, it can be seen as the 'power room' of societal development, albeit that it cannot function on its own: it is part of society and embedded in the existing political system. In this section the structural relationship between government and society will be elaborated. In addition the position and role of *governance* – the process of making collective decisions for a society in a more or less binding way – shall be highlighted. In the second part of this section we will dwell upon the characteristics of government in relation to the existing political regime (as the formation of a political system as a whole) and its implications for democratic governance in particular.

12.2.1 Government as a Structural Element of Society

A widespread approach in political science is systems theory, originally developed by David Easton (see also Chapter 4 in this book). Although it is a contested approach, it nevertheless forms a good point of departure for studying and understanding the 'structure of government'. In this view government is considered as machinery engaged in various activities, which we discussed in Section 12.1.2. Central in the activities of government is that it is concerned with the determination and implementation of *public* policies, both material (the distribution and redistribution of goods and services, such as education, defence, infrastructure, welfare provisions, etc.) and immaterial or 'moral' values (deciding and, often, prescribing for the population what is allowed or not). An important assumption is then that the government speaks and decides for society as a whole. Hence, action by government is seen as *binding* for the whole nation and as *directing* the systems by means of 'the authoritative allocation of material and immaterial values' to cite David Easton (1981).

The general framework of reference regarding government as a part of the political system is depicted in Figure 1.1 (see Chapter 1 of this book). The general idea behind this systems approach is that external pressure – or the 'context' – generates action by politics and government, resulting in political decision-making or 'choices' and concomitant policy-formation. The extent to which the policy-making process eventually addresses the societal pressures, i.e. *demands*, will influence the extent of *support* for government (and the political system at large). In other words, both the stability of society and the 'proper' functioning of the political system is indicated by the way government is capable of producing an 'authoritative allocation of values' that appears to be required. However abstract this may seem to the reader, it is a useful tool for describing the role and position of government in reality in relation to governance and political performance (see also: Lane and Ersson, 1994: 17; Keman, 1997a: 15; Pennings et al., 1999: Part III).

The main point to make here is that the relationship between government and politics, on the one hand, and the political system and society, on the other, is that the *structure* of government indicates how and to what extent it is capable of 'ordered ruling' of society and thus sharing the degree of governance. Conversely, the way the political system is organized and works indicates the *constraints* of public governance in particular in an *indirect* democracy. This brings us to the role of *institutions* and *political actors* that characterize the political system and determine their working in empirical-analytical terms (Shepsle and Bonchek, 1998; Czada et al., 1998; Lane and Ersson, 2000).

12.2.2 Political Institutions and the Structure of Government

Institutions, or the formal and informal rules of the political system, have always shaped the role of politics in society and thus the position and activities of government. In the first place there is *constitutional government*, which can be seen as a set of basic rules that direct the opportunities for and limits of governmental action *vis-à-vis* society or the 'context' (see: Heywood, 1997; Lijphart, 1999; Keman, 2000b).

Firstly the existing 'Rule of Law' prescribes the scope of action available for government as well as the control of these actions by others than the members of government and its apparatus (civil service and the military). *Secondly*, the basic rules also define how government is organized and, hence, how the conversion of demands into policy-making is supposed to take place. It makes a difference, for example, whether the state is a federation or a unitary system. Or, whether government is centralized or not, democratically organized or not, and so on. *Thirdly*, these rules also define by and large which actors are part of the political system and government, and how they interact. For instance, almost always the relationship between the Head of State and the Head of Government and their respective relations to representative bodies is defined by informal and formal rules. This, of course, also applies to the rules concerning the electoral system and who is eligible for office and, hence, whether or not parties (can) exist or how many are allowed and what rights these actors have for *co*-governing and for conducting effective forms of *opposition* as is, for instance, elaborated in the concept of 'polyarchy' (see Chapter 3 in this book).

In summary: the constitution and related basic laws are the rules that institutionalize the structure of government and shape the actual working of the political system in terms of governance. These rules also define which actors are involved and what their role and position are in relation to government.

So, these rules define the relations between the executive and legislative, on the one hand, and the impact of parties and interest groups on decision-making, on the other. In addition, *informal* rules – the development of conventions, routines and accepted patterns of behaviour – do exist everywhere. They are more often than not the result of practices grown over time that facilitate the day-to-day working of formal rules, or have been accepted by all actors involved because they seem to enhance the stability of the political system regardless of its formal organization (Olsen, 1998; Lehmbruch, 1998).

Knowledge of these informal rules is vital, since they enable the student of government to understand why and how in seemingly similar political systems the position and role of governments can be so different. In most books on 'Comparative Government' one can find a bewildering cross-national variation of the institutions of government and their impact on the working of government. Only a few authors have been capable to produce a more systematic treatise on the structure of government. Jean Blondel (1990) is one of these, and another seminal author on this subject is Arend Lijphart (1999). Whereas Blondel focuses on the functional activities of government given the institutional structure, Lijphart is more concerned with the actual patterns of interaction between the political actors – inter alia government – given the existing rules of the political game. Both authors emphasize the idea that the structure of government must be understood in terms of the political systems of which it is the core. Both Lijphart and Blondel also stress the importance of institutions, actors and performance for the study of government to explain *democratic* governance. These ideas can be seen as the 'background' of much of what follows.

12.3 POLITICAL REGIMES AND THE SHAPING OF GOVERNMENT

There have been and always will be classifications of political regimes. The term 'regime' means: system of ruling society. Numerous indicators have been used but here we shall concentrate on the *constitutional system*, i.e. the formal and informal *institutionalization* of government.

Under the influence of the so-called 'new' institutionalism more attention is presently paid to the fact that, in addition to the formal rules (i.e. constitutional ones and basic laws), there exist informal rules that exist either to make the formal rules work (in practice), or imply a practice that brings about the intended result (Weaver and Rockman, 1993; Schmidt, 1996a; Keman, 1998; Lane and Ersson, 2000). In addition the focus on government has changed towards the 'style' of governance and thus to the relations between other political actors that either co-decide or ultimately (can) control government (Colomer, 1996; Lijphart, 1999; Keman, 1999).

The institutional approach enables the student of government to define more precisely the particular (and sometimes peculiar!) *complexion* of government. This is quite important since it enables us to define the relationship between the structure of democratic government itself and the eventual performance in terms of public governance.

Table 12.1   *Types of constitutional government*

Type	N	% of total (N = 197)
Parliamentary	55	27.9
Presidential	77	39.1
Dual executive	12	6.1
Other	53	23.9

Source: Derbyshire and Derbyshire (1996: 40).

12.3.1 Representative Government

Central to representative democracy is that the *executive* is elected indirectly by the population, assuming that the population (or more precisely: the electorate) through its representation in the assembly directs and controls government. Hence, the way the relationship between executive and legislative is institutionalized, shapes the role and position of democratic government. This relationship is almost everywhere *constitutionally* driven, or laid down in a basic law. In addition to the type of representation and the formal relationship between the executive and legislative, the informal rules do affect and thereby shape the working of government. These are the 'conventions' that shape in addition the structure of representative government. Both the formal and informal rules determine the 'room for manoeuvre' for government and more often than not, will be conducive to its 'leadership'. In the literature this feature of government is often denoted as 'Styles of Leadership' (see: Lijphart, 1977; Blondel, 1990; Heywood, 1997). For instance, differences in the formal relationship between the executive and legislative, on the one hand, and the type of electoral system, on the other, influence the modes of behaviour and composition of government. In turn, this particular mode of behaviour results in a *pattern* of behaviour, which becomes common over time (Thelen and Steinmo, 1992).

Three types of representative government can be distinguished:

* presidential government;
* parliamentary government;
* dual power government.

According to Derbyshire and Derbyshire, (1996) the cross-national distribution of these types is as shown in Table 12.1.

First of all, it should be noticed that the division of Derbyshire and Derbyshire is rather lenient with regard to the achieved level of democraticness. If we compare this distribution with that of Alvarez (1996) then the percentage of *representative* government is around 50 per cent (of 157 countries). Secondly, we can observe from Table 12.1 that presidentialism is the most prevalent system across the world. However, one should also notice that this is not true for the European continent (70 per cent is parliamentary or dual executive government). Finally, most noteworthy is the fact that after the late 1980s the number of dual power governments has doubled. Below we shall focus on the three types of representative government that are characteristic for democratic governance.

12.3.2 Presidential Government

For each type the role and position of the *Head of State* is crucial. Although most states have a president as Head of State, in many cases the presidency is merely symbolic and its main function is to represent the sovereignty of the nation and government. In this sense presidents are comparable to most constitutional monarchs. However, in other systems – e.g. the USA – the president has been assigned the role of executive and the related power is *separated* from the legislative powers of the (elected) assembly. In most cases the executive Head of State cannot be removed by the legislative, he or she appoints the other members of government, and derives legitimacy from his/her popular election to office (i.e. elected leadership).

This formal separation of powers clearly affects the conventions as regards the relationship between assembly and the presidency. First of all, the president can direct policy, but not law-making. This results in the convention that the president must seek loyal members in the assembly to propose bills. Hence, although the president is not by definition dependent on a stable majority, he or she must find majorities which can be different from policy issue to policy issue at the political agenda. The implication is that presidential governments may tend to volatile policy-making and are often characterized by fragmented policy concertation, i.e. the internal co-ordination of the over-all policy of government is weak (see: Guy Peters et al., 2000). On the other hand, presidential government is considered to be beneficial if and when a crisis occurs, depending, of course, on the available 'style of leadership'. Governmental action can be redirected in the course needed on a short notice by the *one-person* executive. However, this potential advantage can and is often counteracted by the occurrence of 'divided governments'. This is the situation where the majority of the assembly is not supporting the president (or his party). Finally, both the formal and informal rules do affect the style of leadership. Obviously, the foremost feature is that of a one-person executive who dominates the politics of government. He or she can call upon the public, by whom he or she is elected, and represents national government at home and abroad. This feature of a one-person executive also reinforces the type of governance that prevails: it varies from a more inter-active style of leadership (such as, for instance, Roosevelt during the Second World War) to a more plebiscitary mode of governance (such as the style of Charles de Gaulle in France).

12.3.3 Parliamentary Government

Parliamentary government is organically linked to the legislative, or *parliament*. The government emerges from the assembly and can be dismissed by a vote of no-confidence (and often also needs a vote of investiture by the same parliament). At the same time government can – often after consultation with the Head of State – dissolve parliament and call for a new election. Whereas presidential government appears as strong and relatively independent, parliamentary government is often considered to be weak because of the mutual dependence between the executive and legislature. In other words a typical consequence of parliamentary government is that both powers are *fused*.

A *second* feature is that government consists of ministers who are basically appointed by parliament (though often formally by the symbolic Head of State, i.e. a president or monarch). This implies that each member of government is directly responsible to parliament. Parliamentary government can be characterized as a collegial body with traditionally a Prime Minister who is seen as first among equals (i.e. 'Primus-inter-Pares'). Constitutionally the main differences between presidentialism and parliamentarism is vested in the relationship between the executive and the legislative. Parliament is essentially the supreme power – the symbol of governance, but at the same time it is clear that this supremacy is conventionally tilted towards government. For, contrary to presidential government, parliamentary government can propose bills; often every minister has the right to do so.

Thirdly, parliamentary government is characterized by its organization as a *cabinet*, a collegial body with a relative collective responsibility. This feature is determined by its informal relationship with parties in parliament. For this reason parliamentary government is more often than not depicted as 'party-government' in which the office of Head of Government is separated strictly from the office of Head of State (Woldendorp et al., 2000).

Given these differences with presidentialism, it is usual to differentiate parliamentary government by means of its conventional shape and working. On the one hand, there is the 'one-party government' which is defined by the fact that the majority party in parliament forms government. On the other, there is 'coalition government' where a combination of parties forms a government, which is supported by a majority in parliament. A third sub-type is, of course, the minority government (one-party or coalition government). In short, in parliamentary types of government the political representation is always mediated by means of parties. This feature also implies that the conventions as regard their role and position is more or less directed by the relative strength of parties in parliament, and the way these interact on the basis of their party programmes (Klingemann et al., 1994).

Budge and Keman (1990) have studied in great detail this relationship between parties and coalition government and concluded that much depends on the interaction of parties, i.e. the 'party system', and the way parties are represented in government. In essence, the formal requirements to govern are (much) less important than the way *inter-party relations* are shaped in relation to finding and establishing a consensus. This particular feature, which is a necessary condition for the stability of parliamentary government, spills over in the variable 'style of leadership' (see: Lijphart, 1984, 1999; Blondel, 1982).

In some parliamentary democracies, the formal power of the Prime Minister is enhanced. For instance, in Germany and Spain, and also in the

United Kingdom, the Prime Minister can dismiss and appoint ministers at her/his own discretion. This enhanced power of the Prime Minister is said to be a more general situation, be it formally enshrined or not in many European democracies (Blondel and Müller-Rommel, 1993).

All in all: Parliamentary government is structured differently from presidential government. The formal powers of the executive and legislative are largely fused, consensus formation between parties in government and in parliament is a conventional prerequisite to make policies, and therefore negotiations take place in both government and parliament where, in the final instance, parties do really matter. Hence, as is often put forward, parliamentary systems of governance are indeed an *indirect* form of democracy. Whereas in presidential systems the Head of Government is primarily *directly* elected, this is not the case in parliamentary systems (with a few exceptions, like Israel where the Prime Minister is directly elected). To push this argument further: in parliamentary democracies *parties* are the key factor linking the electorate to parliamentary government. However, the representative character of parliamentary governments is often doubted because of their lack of accountability and responsiveness and therefore impaired democratic governance (Keman, 1997b).

12.3.4 Dual Power Government

This type of government has often been considered as an anomaly or as a residual category. But, as a consequence of the criticisms raised with regard to both presidential and parliamentary government, dual power government is taken much more seriously nowadays (Duverger, 1980). Another development that has brought about more attention to this type of government – more often than not labelled as 'semi-presidentialism' – is the fact that during the so-called 'Fourth Wave of Democratization' (see: Chapter 3 in this book) in many of the emergent democracies the new or renewed constitutions were developed in such a way that the disadvantages of both presidentialism and parliamentarism were to be avoided (Lijphart, 1992; Linz, 1994; Hague et al., 1998).

In contrast to presidential and parliamentary government the executive and legislative powers are neither fused nor distributed across both institutions, but rather *co-exist*. For example a dual power system would avoid the potential (and occurring) deadlocks between the executive and legislature, i.e. between the president and parliament. By sharing the powers to some extent and having separated elections for parliament and president the advocates of semi-presidentialism argue that the advantages of a directly *elected* Head of State in combination with the flexibility of a parliamentary cabinet with a *selected* Head of Government are combined. This would avoid the rigidity of the presidential executive (to some extent) as well as dominating the executive and legislative powers.

In other words: the supposed stability of a president is juxtaposed with the representation of a parliamentary majority. Hence the central characteristic of dual power government is the constitutional co-existence of executive and legislative in government. This implies that conventions must develop that are based on 'power-sharing' between the president, the cabinet-government and parliament. However, this can also and easily lead to forms of divided government due to bicameralism (as also happens in federal states and in presidential systems), on the one hand, or due to 'cohabitation' where the president's party has no majority in the assembly (France is the most notorious example), on the other. These situations of difficult and delicate power sharing appear however not to jeopardize regime stability nor the expedition of governmental business (Weaver and Rockman, 1993).

Notwithstanding the advantages of the dual system of executive and legislative leadership there are relatively few constitutions that allow for this type of government. The majority of the cases can be found in Europe: France, Portugal, Finland, the Czech Republic, Estonia, Lithuania, Slovenia and Poland. It should be noted that most of these states have developed this dual system only recently (with the exception of Finland and France). This may well be an expression of a growing dissatisfaction with the apparent disadvantages of both the straightforward presidential and parliamentary systems of democratic government and their affects on society. Another sign of this growing dissatisfaction is constitutional debates on this subject, which are predominantly held in South America (e.g. in Argentina, Brazil and Colombia: Lijphart, 1992; Linz, 1994; Keman, 2000b).

The working of dual power government is heavily influenced by constitutional rules and the multiple relations that exist between the executive and legislative. Hence, the main disadvantage is the delicate interrelations between *all* powers. This may well imply that imbalances and disruption lead to stalemates and gridlocks. Nevertheless, the fact that the electorate has a more direct influence on *both* the executive and legislative than in the other types of representative government can be seen as an advantage in terms of achieving democratic governance.

In conclusion: three types of representative government have been discussed by means of their formal rules, conventions and style of leadership. It appears that these three types – presidential, parliamentary and dual power government – are indeed different from each other. It has also become clear that all types can be adjudicated in terms of advantages and disadvantages with respect to democratic governance. The question that remains to be answered is, however, how well they are in fact and reality capable of producing materially and democratically adequate performances. This question will be dealt with in Section 12.5.

12.4 THE FORM OF GOVERNMENT: FORMAT AND ORGANIZATION

As was outlined in Section 12.1.1, two of the main functions of any government are policy-making and policy-implementation. Obviously the way governments are organized is of importance here. In addition, and this was

Table 12.2 *State format and organization in liberal democracies (N = 52)*

	Number	Percentage
Format		
Unitary state	33	63.5
Semi-federal	6	11.5
Federal	13	25.0
Organization		
Centralized	18	34.6
Devolution	19	36.5
Decentralized	15	28.8

Source: Woldendorp et al. (2000: 34–5) and own computations.

also emphasized earlier, leadership comes prominently into play here. By the *organization* of government is meant the rules that determine the decision-making process within and between members of government and parliament. At the same time the policy-making capacity of government is influenced by the degree of *vertical and horizontal* organization of the polity. This will be discussed below by discussing the comparative features of the state *format* in relation to the shaping of governmental powers.

12.4.1 State Format and the Shaping of Government

The powers of government are strongly related to the responsibility for the whole of a state's territory and those units of government concerned with only a part of it. In other words: the degree of *institutional autonomy* of government as the executive branch in terms of functional capacities, on the one hand, and in terms of geographic jurisdiction, on the other, is a vital part of the analysis of governments in terms of competencies. Hence, the state format has certain implications for the overall degree of democratic governance.

The *state format* refers then to distinctions like federal and unitary, centralized and decentralized, and also the degree of power-sharing among the political units (such as provinces and communities) that make up the complexion of national government.

It is immediately clear from Table 12.2 that 36.5 per cent of all nations under review have a federal or a semi-federal state format. Secondly, it should be observed that many of these countries are characterized by a large territory (e.g. Australia, Brazil, Canada, India, Russia and the USA), or by a history of ethno-religious or linguistic divisions (e.g. Belgium, Canada and Switzerland). However, this is not by definition the sole reason for establishing a federal government (Schultze, 1992; Elazar, 1995; Hague et al., 1998).

As has been put forward in the 'Federalist Papers' – a political debate in the USA preceding the formulation of its constitution – another important argument has been the principle of local sovereignty and self-government (as in Switzerland). It is important therefore to distinguish between the need for effective government given 'tyranny of distance' and the wish of self-regulation or local autonomy. The latter principle is often laid down in the constitution in a detailed fashion, whereas the former justification is hardly ever mentioned. More often than not, as for instance in Australia and India, the executive powers of the federal government tend to become stronger over time. The crosscutting dimension of federalism is therefore in many cases the development towards centralization of executive powers by means of derived law-making and by the increased 'power of the purse' of the *national* government of the federation (Castles, 2000).

The stricter and more elaborated, however, the federal constitution is, the stronger the institutional *autonomy* of the constituting parts will be. In a truly federal system, the changing of the distribution of executive and legislative powers cannot be undertaken arbitrarily by the national government but must involve the non-central units, either by overcoming their 'blocking powers' or by finding consent through political compromise (Lijphart, 1999; Wachendorfer-Schmidt, 2000). Hence, a federal state is mostly characterized by an elaborate constitution or set of 'basic laws' which are difficult to alter and are quite specific concerning the balance of power between the centre and the constituting geographic parts of the realm. Some authors have therefore called the central government within a federal polity the 'semi-sovereign state' (Schmidt, 1996b). Of course this has implications for the room for action of national government. Parallel to the national government the non-central layers of government have considerable powers of decision-making and policy-implementation (and often of taxation). As with dual executive government it is a system of *co-existent* governance. In most federal polities this situation can easily lead to gridlocks, in particular if certain policy competencies are overlapping or, conversely, are completely separated. It is therefore a matter of dispute whether or not the policy performance of federalism equals that of a unitary state (Elazar, 1995; Lane and Ersson, 1997; Keman, 2000a).

Federalism is often, and quite logically, characterized by a decentralized state organization. Yet, it should be noticed that in many unitary nation-states similar provisions are made and often over time developed. And, indeed, one can surmise a number of institutional arrangements that allow for institutional autonomy of specific minorities or regions within the unitary state. This again influences the structure of government. On the one hand, this is brought about by means of geographic decentralization, on the other, through so-called *functional* decentralization, i.e. leaving certain policies to semi-governmental or even semi-public bodies; an example is The Netherlands (Lane and Ersson, 1998). A good example of functional *and* geographic decentralization is Scandinavia: in the Scandinavian countries the local communities have extensive powers of regulation and taxation. This type of state format is often considered as 'decentralized' and concerns 28.8 per cent of the states under review (see Table 12.2). In the United Kingdom the government has recently given some form of 'home rule' to the Welsh and Scottish regions. In South Africa the constitution has been amended to give greater autonomy to the Provinces, whereas regionaliza-tion has been extended and institutionalized in Spain (to a large extent) and

Italy. Hence, in addition to the formal but rigid division between Federal and Unitary States, one should take into account the possibilities of executive and legislative devolution of powers. This may well imply that the institutional format and organization of the state can be expected to have a variable impact on the political performance of representative government.

In conclusion: the powers of government can in part be derived by the institutional arrangement in terms of its state format and organization. The *distribution* of power in unitary states can also be divided geographically and organized functionally in terms of institutional *autonomy*. It depends therefore in an equal measure, on how the constitution provides for the separation of powers, on the one hand, and on how and to what extent the government is constrained in its exercise, regardless of whether it concerns a federal or unitary system. This kind of formal arrangement of power division influences, of course, the working of representative government and its policy performance. Below we shall discuss the decision-making powers of representative government *per se*.

12.4.2 The Organization of Representative Government

Contrary to presidential systems government in a parliamentary system depends very much on the balance between cabinet, Prime Minister and ministers. The executive involves a particular tension between collegiality and hierarchy between a pre-eminent chief minister and a ministerial college of *political equals*. In most presidential systems ministers are merely dependent on the leadership of the Head of State, if not in fact subservient.

The principle of 'collegiality' involves not only equality in rank-and-file within government, but also the idea that all decisions are made *collectively*. That is to say: an individual minister must abide to the collective responsibility and share this with the whole cabinet, also *vis-à-vis* parliament. If not, than the minister is expected to resign. This convention is becoming, however, rare since in most of these systems it means nowadays, more often than not, that the whole cabinet-government resigns. If it concerns a *coalition*-government – and in practice this is often the case – this is almost a fixed but informal rule. The reason is that the parties in government do not allow for upsetting of the delicate inter-party balance established.

This type of organization of government is almost exclusively West European and affects democratic governance. There are two other types of cabinet-government: Prime Ministerial cabinets, on the one hand, and Ministerial governance, on the other.

Prime Ministerial cabinets have either developed as a practice, which is a consequence of the division of the party system, or has been the results of the institutional design of the polity. In most Anglo-Saxon countries, because of the 'first-past-the-post' electoral system, there is (almost) always a majority party in parliament. Hence, this party is government and the party leader forms his or her government and is in a position to dismiss and to appoint ministers. Yet, *Prime Ministerial government* also exists in parliamentary systems where a coalition is necessary to govern. Here the Prime Minister derives his or her dominant position from the *formal* relations between the executive and legislative: the Prime Minister is often less vulnerable because of the 'constructive vote of no confidence'.[1] In this type of cabinet government it is the 'Chancellor' who deals with parliament primarily and controls the individual ministers. In a sense, the chancellor is the 'conductor' and supervisor with respect to policy co-ordination (Blondel, 1990; Gallagher et al., 2000).

Finally, there is the *ministerial cabinet-government*. Here, the ministers have no collegial obligations, nor is the Prime Minister a supremo. Each and every minister is responsible for his or her policy area and, consequently, there is little policy co-ordination. In fact, the Prime Minister is basically a power broker who is involved in two arenas: *within* government and *vis-à-vis* parliament. It will not come as a big surprise that ministerial cabinet-governments are seen as less efficient in decision-making compared with other types of representative government. It is obvious that ministerial cabinet-government is the least hierarchical of the three parliamentary forms of government. It is also clear that its organization is strongly influenced by the constitutional rules and related conventions and is strongly influenced by existing party system (Budge and Keman, 1990; Laver and Shepsle, 1996).

12.5 POLITICAL PERFORMANCE AND DEMOCRATIC GOVERNANCE

Recall that in *Section 12.1.2* government was defined as those 'mechanisms' through which ordered rule is maintained, on the one hand, and as 'the machinery for making and enforcing collective decisions by means of public action for a society', on the other. In other words: the structure of government is considered as a *means to an end*. This relationship between means and ends has been described with the help of a structural-functional approach and is called the *systemic* analysis of political life. The central idea is that government is the *core* of the political system and that it (re)acts in order to promote the systems maintenance. The extent to which government is indeed functionally capable of doing this, is what is often called a 'structured induced equilibrium' (Colomer, 1996; Shepsle, 1997; Keman, 1999). The fact that the political system endures (or not) is then the first sign of *political performance*. Yet, system stability is not enough to assess the political performance in relation to the various features of government enhancing democratic governance.

For empirical-analytical purposes a useful distinction is made by Lane and Ersson (2000): between *policy* performance, on the one hand, and *democratic* performance, on the other, to operationalize political performance. Policy performance refers to the extent to which government is indeed capable of producing fiscal means and regulative measures to enhance public welfare for its citizens. Democratic performance refers to the extent to which government, according to the existing institutions is responsible to society as well as accountable for its publicly enforced actions. Both concepts can be considered as indicators of system performance, in terms of democratic governance. Below the relationship between the features of representative government and the types of political performance that are distinguished are examined. The guiding question being, of course, whether or not there is a relation between types of government and features of democratic governance.

12.5.1 The Policy Performance within Democracies

The core business of government is to rule to ensure stability through the exercise of authority. This, in turn, requires that the structure and activities government is fit to perpetuate its own existence and ensure the survival of the political system as a whole. Hence, the longevity and endurance of a regime and the related shape of governance indicates the ability of a system to contain or reconcile societal conflicts. According to Heywood (1997) stable government is based upon consensus and consent. This would mean that a political system, and its government in particular, must be responsive to popular demands and pressures. Conversely, if this were not the case then it can be expected that the support for government is inadequate for its survival. This systems perspective (Easton, 1981) is often put forward to point to the strength of democratic government. For, the longevity and endurance of democratic systems is not only high but such systems are also characterized by the absence of intra-system conflict by means of violence. Hence, it is expected that representative democratic government is more capable of coping with conflict and turmoil than most other (non-democratic) governmental structures. However, the caveat regarding democracy and stability is that it is founded upon a delicate balance between responsive policy-making and the need for efficient and effective policy implementation. This is the art of steering the ship of state through problematic social and economic 'problems', and thereby enhancing public welfare and with it policy and democratic performance (Keman, 1997b; Castles, 1998).

Among others, Bingham Powell (1982) and Lane and Ersson (2000) have attempted to measure the performance of political systems across the world by means of comparative data on the level of democracy, the number of years of the present constitution and of univeral suffrage, on the one hand, and rates of protest and violence over the last 30 years, on the other hand. We replicate this descriptive analysis by inspecting 52 democratic systems under review here in order to assess how variable representative govern-ments have established 'peaceful' relations with society and *vice versa*.

From Table 12.3 it is obvious that high levels of democraticness are associ-ated with the period for which a country has had a constitution and experi-enced a democratic polity. Conversely, this is expressed in the absence of high levels of protest and violence. In short, the more enduring a democracy is, the more 'ordered' society appears to be. However, one may wonder whether this also the case if, for instance, the socio-economic situation is less prosperous and – for instance – the levels of unemployment are high(er).

Table 12.3 *Correlation table*

	Democraticness	Pluralism	Polyarchy
Constitutional years	0.50	0.52	0.33*
Duration undisturbed	0.74	0.71	0.48
Duration disturbed	0.72	0.66	0.47
Protest	−0.41	−0.50	−0.25
Strikes	0.21*	0.11*	0.23*
Violence	−0.72	−0.81	−0.49

Note: All correlations are Pearson product moment coefficients and all results are significant at 0.01 level (one-tailed) unless they are flagged (*).

From regression-analysis these circumstances appear only to be relevant in terms of the effect produced by low(er) levels of economic wealth, which is associated with higher levels of protest and having together a negative bearing on the level of democraticness. Hence, it transpires that *cyclical* effects of economic misery (like inflation and unemployment) are not directly affecting the democratic governance. It appears to be rather a matter of a *structural* deficiency, i.e. a poor nation is not only associated with less democraticness, but also (apparently) has less 'room for manoeuvre' to remedy such a situation and thereby develop democratic governance.

This conclusion is in accordance with a large part of the literature that focuses on the determinant of democratization and democratic development (see: Landman, 2000): economic developments are important *conditions* for democratic governance. Yet, as Manfred Schmidt (1989b, 2000) has demonstrated, there is more to it. Although 'economics' matters, it does not and cannot explain satisfactorily the cross-national variation in the political performance of nations across the world. This can easily be demonstrated by replicating the so-called 'Zöllner Model' to our universe of discourse (N = 52; see the Appendix to this chapter for the list of countries included).

The 'Zöllner Model' assumes that both demographic factors (such as the level of the dependent population) and economic affluence (e.g. the level of GNPpC) determine the provision of public welfare by governments. In other words: governments, democratic and non-democratic alike, will produce social policies depending on 'objective' developments of the society they rule. Yet, so it is argued, this may be true to a certain extent, but it does not fully account for the cross-national variation in social policy provision, nor – and that is our main point – for what other factors are relevant as well and to what degree (see: Keman, 1997a; Schmidt, 2000).

In Table 12.4, we examine to what extent the 'Zöllner Model' indeed explains the policy outputs of democratic government. The results demonstrate that indeed the demographic situation and economic circumstances are *relevant* for understanding the cross-national variations of policy outputs. At the same time it is also obvious that there is ample room for further explanation, as the explained variance (Adjusted R^2) is at the most not higher than 66.1 per cent (re. Social Policy Expenditures).

Table 12.4 *Application of the Zöllner Model (N = 52)*

Dependent variables	Independent variables			Explained variance
	Population	Level of affluence	Original level	
Central government expenditures	−0.07	0.04	0.46*	18.0%
Social policy	0.10	0.40*	0.57*	66.1%
Health care	−0.04	0.57*	0.052*	51.5%
Education	0.21	0.24	0.43*	25.1%
Defence	−0.06	−0.17	0.87*	65.0%

Note: All models are OLS-regressions; the significant results are flagged (*); the coefficients are expressed as standardized values; see the Appendix for further information.

Second, it should be noted that the *size* of the public economy is hardly the result of the central variables of the Zöllner Model. Conversely, we observe that the *policy choices* made show a certain degree of priority: social welfare and health care are predominant, whereas this is less the case with education. Hence, there are other factors at work that direct the size and functional allocations of the public economy.

Thirdly, the parameter which is significant in all equations in Table 12.4 is the *previous level* of expenditures (in the 1970s), and this accounts for most of the explained variance. This does not support the Zöllner Model, but rather demonstrates that the *original choices* made also determine the present levels of policy output by governments. This implies two additional explanations: one, that political decisions made and put into effect have a strong tendency to be 'path dependent' (Thelen and Steinmo, 1992; Putnam, 1993) or that policy-making tends to be influenced by incrementalism (Tarschys, 1985; Keman, 1993b). Whatever way one looks upon this, it is apparent other factors than 'objective' developments alone do account for policy making in democratic systems. For it is an accepted point of view in the literature on 'new' institutionalism and public policy analysis that the institutional design of political systems by and large produces effects such as incrementalism, inertia and path dependency, which in turn affect the policy outcomes, that is: political performance (see, for example, Guy Peters, 1996; Keman, 1997c; Castles, 1998; Pennings et al., 1999). It appears valid therefore to pursue the examination of the central hypothesis of this chapter: how and to what extent do *institutional* factors account for the political performance of representative government, on the one hand, and how does the cross-national variation in policy and democratic performance affect the degree of democratic governance of a society?

12.5.2 Types of Democratic Government and Policy Performance

In the previous section we found that 'time' has an effect on *policy* performance (by means of path dependency and incremental developments). As the

Table 12.5 *Duration and constitutional type of democracy and policy performance*

	Social policy	Education	Health care
Intercept	−1.97	2.42	2.08
Duration of democracy	0.42	0.31	0.22
	(3.17)	(1.99)	(1.46)
Universal suffrage	0.24	0.24	0.25
	(1.73)	(1.66)	(1.60)
Parliamentary executive	0.51	0.21	0.19
	(2.30)	(1.38)	(1.34)
Presidential executive	−0.39	−0.15	−0.22
	(−3.19)	(−1.04)	(−1.59)
Dual power government	0.42	0.22	0.17
	(3.10)	(1.54)	(1.20)
Adj. R^2	39.3%	11.3%	12.3%

Note: Based on OLS-regression technique; T-values in parentheses; the coefficients are standardized values; see the Appendix for the operationalization of the variables.

size of the public economy (total expenditures by government) is irrelevant within our universe of discourse (see Table 12.4) and as regards the analysis of policy choices, we shall focus on those policy areas that represent the development of *public welfare*: Social policy, Education and Health Care. These areas represent the core of the 'welfare state' (see also: Flora and Heidenheimer, 1981; Esping-Andersen, 1990; Castles, 1998). The research question we need to answer is then: to what extent do 'age' and 'type of government' influence the policy choices made, as reflected in the allocated levels of expenditure. In other words: does it make a difference whether a democratic regime exists longer or not, and, whether it is a presidential, parliamentary or a dual power system?

The results of this exercise (Table 12.5) show that the duration of democracy has an impact on the levels of expenditure for all policy areas and in particular on social policy. This reinforces the conclusions drawn from Table 12.4: the longer a political system has been in operation the more 'welfare statism' has been developed. The impact of universal suffrage can also be noticed, but to a lesser extent than is often thought. For instance, Lipset (1959) and Wilensky (1975) argued that the introduction of universal suffrage would not increase the political influence of the working class, but also would strongly enhance the urge for 'welfare statist' policy-making. Yet, as Castles has shown in Chapter 10 in this book (see also: Castles, 1998: 180–94) there is not a direct link between the institutional design of the political system and the *level* of expenditure. However, at the same time it appears relevant whether constitutional government is presidential or not. Presidentialism is obviously not promoting the extension of a welfare state related policy performance, if and when compared with parliamentarism and dual power governance.[2] Hence, the policy performance of *power sharing* governments is (positively) different from systems that are characterized by a *separation* of powers and *one-actor* executive.

12.5.3 The Impact of State Format and Organization of Government on Policy Performance

Earlier in this chapter we have proposed that the state format, on the one hand, and the organization of government, on the other, could well influence the policy performance. The *state format*, i.e. whether a political system is unitary or not and centralized or not, so it was argued, would make a difference as to the levels of expenditure as well as to the effect in terms of societal performance. In addition, it has been argued that the way *government* is organized – more or less hierarchically, on the one hand, and more or less directly related to parliament – would affect policy performance. In Table 12.6 we present the results of our investigation by means of regression analysis. First, we examine the state format, and secondly, the organization of governments across 52 countries.

It is immediately clear from Table 12.6 that the format of the state is of minor influence on the actual policy-performance of government. However, a closer inspection of the results also shows a paradox that is often disregarded: a unitary structure does not necessarily preclude identical mechanisms to those considered 'natural' for federalism (see: Lane and Ersson, 1997; Wachendorfer-Schmidt, 2000; Keman, 2000a). Many unitary states have institutional equivalents which produce similar effects on the policy performance, and this produces the apparent paradox. Although federal states have lower levels of public expenditures, which seems to be reinforced if and when there is symmetrical bicameralism (Tsebelis and Money, 1997; Lijphart, 1999), this appears to be counteracted by a decentralized organization of the state. And, so we argue, one should take into account the extent to which the state format is federal or not *and* genuinely decentralized or not (as is indicated by institutional autonomy; see: Colomer, 1996; Lane and Ersson, 1998). Hence, the conclusion must be that although the state format *per se* is only indirectly relevant for the policy performance.

The same line of argument can be applied to the organization of *national* (or: central) government. As we have observed, there is a difference between presidentialism and the other types of democratic governance. We can, however, refine this statement by inspecting how the 'body' government is organized in terms of hierarchical features, on the one hand, and its relationship with the assembly or parliament, on the other hand. Two hypotheses can be formulated:

- The more hierarchically government is organized, the more presidential is its style of leadership and related performance.
- The stronger the dominance of government, in particular the Head of State and Head of Government, over parliament, the more presidential is the style of leadership and related performance.

In other words: we expect that the hierarchical features of government have a bearing on the degree of power sharing and on political consensus and

Table 12.6 *Unitary-centralized versus federal-decentralized states and policy performance (1990)*

Independent variables	Policy performance			
	General government		Social policy	
Intercept	13.33		22.91	
Federalism	−0.45	(−2.48)	−0.71	(−2.52)
Decentralization	0.49	(3.46)	0.75	(2.70)
Bicameralism	−0.35	(−2.27)	0.02	(0.13)
Adj. R^2	13.7%		15.4%	

Note: See Table 12.5 for explanations.

Table 12.7 *The effects of hierarchically organized government and dominating executives on policy performance*

Independent variables	Policy performance	
	General government	Social policy
1. Intercept	39.03	28.19
PM dominant	−0.02 (−0.14)	−0.14 (−1.14)
HOS dominant	−0.39 (−2.59)	−0.65 (−5.28)
Adj. R^2	15.3 %	38.9%
2. Intercept	28.0	19.0
Government dominant	0.35 (2.40)	0.56 (4.40)
Parliament dominant	0.08 (0.40)	−0.35 (−1.82)
Balanced relationship	0.32 (1.61)	0.74 (3.97)
Adj. R^2	30.2%	43.6%

Note: See Tables 12.5 For explanation.

co-operation and thus on democratic governance (see: Lijphart, 1999: Chs 15 and 16).

Judging the results in Table 12.7 it appears that the first hypothesis is tenable. At the same time it is also obvious that a dominant position of the Prime Minister and a 'strong' parliament is not translated into the associated policy performance. It is therefore interesting to note that, regardless of whether a political system is presidential or not, the position of the Head of State seems to be more influential than is often thought. If the prerogatives of the Head of State allow for (active) intervention the evidence points to the fact that it impedes higher levels of spending, if not to a veto position. Yet, in democracies where government is dominant over parliament or where the relations between the executive and legislative is balanced, it appears to promote (active) policy-making. Hence, the second hypothesis is not supported by our analysis.

We conclude from this that the role of government is more central to policy performance than parliament is. If the Head of State, whether or not in a so-called presidential system, is institutionally strong, this affects policy-making. If government is dominant, regardless of whether or not its 'primus-inter-pares' has special powers, this also influences the policy-making capacity of government. The same inference can be made for democratic systems where the executive–legislative relations are balanced. Hence, there is not only a difference between parliamentarism and presidentialism *per se* (Linz, 1994), but also between democracies where the Head of State, on the one hand, and parliament, on the other, prevail in terms of prerogatives. This observation leads us to conclude that the way the constitutional powers are distributed is more important than the way they are separated or shared. In other words: not the constitutional powers as such, but the related exercise on the basis of derived prerogatives is what counts for the consequential policy performance (see also: Weaver and Rockman, 1993; Shepsle, 1997; Woldendorp et al., 2000). Such a conclusion would point to the importance of the role of political actors (parties and organized interests) with regard to the process of policy-making and related performance. This has been extensively analysed in Parts Two and Three of this book, demonstrating *inter alia* how crucial parties are in translating popular demands into public policies as well as showing that the political complexion of government is essential in order to overcome institutional veto-points within the state format.

The overall conclusion of this section is therefore that in democracies the institutional design of the state matters in conjunction with the constitutional organization of government. These features do indeed shape policy performance. Hence, the institutional fabric of democracy is conducive to democratic governance in terms of its policy performance.

12.6 DEMOCRATIC GOVERNMENT AND DEMOCRATIC GOVERNANCE

The question that is still begging for an answer is: to what extent is democratic government conducive to the *democratic* performance of its society? Or to put it differently: are democratic institutions and policy-making significantly related to the features that represent democratic qualities in terms of a *shared* governance.

In Chapters 2, 3, 8 and 11, aspects of this question – central to the comparative analysis of democratic politics – have been dealt with. On the one hand Daalder and Lane and Ersson have argued that institutional devices as such may be important but do not unequivocally produce 'good governance' or a 'good society'. On the other hand, Keman and Schmidt have shown that particular institutional features produce better performances than others (see also: Bingham Powell, 1982; March and Olsen, 1995; Lijphart, 1999; Dahl, 1998).

In this section we shall attempt to inspect whether or not the various types of democracy are indeed conducive to democratic governance. Democratic governance is defined here as the level of democraticness achieved within a nation. The level of democraticness is a measure of the extent to which the institutional design of a democratic polity actual promotes societal pluralism, on the one hand, and safeguards the civil and political rights of (groups of) individuals, on the other hand (see Chapter 3 in this book). Hence, the level of democraticness indicates the extent of the liberty and of the influence of the population at large. In other words: it shows to what extent the citizen is *free to* participate and act in the democratic system in which he or she lives. Conversely, the quality of democracy indicates to what extent the citizen and the population at large is indeed *free from* social and economic hazards as produced by the fabric of society (see: Marshall, 1950; Lipset, 1959; Titmuss, 1974; Bingham Powell, 1982; Held, 1987; Castles, 1998; see also Chapters 9 and 10 in this book).

In the remainder of this section we shall review both indicators of democratic performance cross-nationally. In addition, we shall inspect to what extent a relative underperformance results in societal protest or political defection by citizens.

Such a cross-national analysis will allow us to draw conclusions of the effects of democracy as an institutional system on both aspects of *democratic governance*: democraticness and the related quality of life.

12.6.1 State Format, Type of Government and Level of Democraticness

There are two normative lines of reasoning which argue that differences of state format and government type have an impact on the level of democraticness.

First, many 'federalists' argue that federal arrangements tend to be more democratic than unitary states (see, for example: Ducacheck, 1970; Riker, 1975; Elazar, 1997; Lane and Ersson, 1997). The main advantage of federalism is considered to be that it is based on *parallel* power sharing and enhances political control and allocative justice and thus produces (more) democratic governance.

The *second* line of thought concerns the debate on the deficiencies of presidentialism *vis-à-vis* parliamentary systems (Lijphart, 1992; Linz, 1994; Stepan and Skach, 1994; Keman, 2000b). Although presidential systems are recognized for their separation of powers, they are also characterized by their relative *political instability*. On the one hand, this is due to the separation of powers, which can easily lead to *gridlocks* in decision-making. On the other hand, a feature of presidential government is that it is dependent on one person, who often feels legitimized (due to his or her direct election) to deviate from standing procedures, or even to resort to *unconstitutional* practices.

In summary: it is argued that both federalism and presidentialism have specific effects on the level of democraticness: the former a positive, and the latter a negative effect.

The correlations reported in Table 12.8 appear to be quite conclusive: Presidential systems are strongly and significantly related to lower levels of democraticness, pluralism and polyarchy. The claim that federalist institutions of democracy are superior cannot be sustained, nor does the opposite conclusion appear valid. Yet, these results are to a certain extent misleading. If we control the bivariate results for the levels of affluence of a country and the constitutional age of the polity, it appears that presidentialism can indeed be conducive to certain abuse and thus affect the level of democraticness. However, if and when socio-economic conditions are (becoming)

Table 12.8 *Bivariate relations between indicators of democraticness and features of the state format*

	Democraticness	Polyarchy	Pluralism
Indicators of federalism and presidentialism			
Presidentialism (Derbyshire, 1996)	−0.62*	−0.63*	−0.46*
Federalism (Woldendorp et al., 2000)	−0.7	0.02	0.01
Unitary/federal (Woldendorp et al., 2000)	0.21	0.07	0.29
Presidential power (in this chapter)	−0.44	−0.50*	−0.53
Decentralization (Woldendorp et al., 2000)	0.30	0.14	0.42*

Note: All Pearson product moment correlation; significant results (p ≤ 0.01) are flagged (*); N = 46; see Appendix to Chapter 3 for the operationalization of democraticness.

favourable and democratic institutions prevail over time, the negative relationship between democratic performance and presidentialism is less significant.

12.6.2 Policy Performance, Democratic Performance and the Quality of Life

In much political science and economic literature the relationship between (liberal) democracy and the quality of social and individual life is emphasized (Castles et al., 1987; Potter et al., 1997). Some even suggest that after the fourth wave of democratization (with the ending of the Cold War), that democracy was not only the sole option for organizing the polity and government, but also the natural course to enhancing public welfare and (thus) the quality of life (see e.g. Fukuyama, 1992; Huntington, 1991).

This argument is in part derived from the idea that a democratically organized society will not only lead to a better *policy* performance, but will also be conducive to more-stable patterns of *democratic* governance. Along this road of democratic consolidation it is expected that this development is expressed in an encompassing situation of 'democraticness'. At the same time the expectation is that such a development towards democratic governance is associated with improving material conditions for a society as a whole in terms of the 'quality of life'.[3]

Democratic and material performance are thus seen as *outcomes* of democratic polities and public policy performance. It follows then that a positive relationship is reflected in an ordered and legitimized rule by government. Conversely, if the performances are absent or below par, this may well lead to protest, turmoil and defection. Such a situation could be characterized as leading to a diminished democratic governance.

We have seen in Section 12.5 the relationship between the democratic organization of society and policy performance. Inter alia it depends on how state and government are organized as well as to what extent the relations between the executive and legislature are shaped. With this caveat in mind we present in Table 12.9 evidence regarding the relationship between policy performance and democratic and material performance. For obvious reasons

Table 12.9 *Democratic performance and quality of life in relation to policy performance*

Policy performance	Democratic and material performance					
	HDI	Misery	Gini	Dem	Plural	Poly
HDI	1.0	−0.28*	−0.48*	0.57*	0.50*	0.51*
Misery	−0.28	1.0	0.15	−0.35*	−0.46*	−0.21
Gini	−0.48*	0.15	1.0	−0.71*	−0.53*	−0.70*
Change GDP	0.57*	0.44*	−0.73*	0.66*	0.54*	0.60*
Change dependent population	−0.27*	0.04	0.50*	−0.56*	−0.33*	−0.57*
Central government expenditures	0.35*	−0.14	−0.52*	0.56*	0.41*	0.55*
Social policy	0.63*	−0.26*	−0.65*	0.71*	0.53*	0.69*
Welfare services	0.35*	−0.30*	−0.35*	0.48*	0.47*	0.34*

Note: All Pearson product moment correlation; significant results (p ≤ 0.01) are flagged(*); see Appendix for elaboration of variables.

we control this relationship by the parameters of the Zöllner model (see Table 12.4). It is immediately clear that policy performance of democratic government is highly associated with all indicators of democratic and material performance. To some extent 'Misery' is less consistently related to the different policy types. In addition it should be noted that both the 'objective' factors (belonging to the Zöllner model) and the interrelations between democratic and material performance are, again, quite high.

We can safely say therefore that democraticness and quality of life in society do go together with both favourable 'objective' conditions and public policy outputs across the 52 democracies under review. In our view this allows for the conclusion that if and when the material performance within a society is favourable, in part due to democratic policy-making and related performance, then it is associated with a higher level of democraticness. In turn, this attained level reflects a situation of democratic governance of both government and the population at large.

12.6.3 Dissatisfaction, Underperformance and Democraticness

Obviously, favourable conditions and performances are in reality mirrored by reversed situations, where socio-economic factors and public policy efforts do not enhance public welfare nor the quality of life. The consequence of a deteriorating social and economic situation can develop in two directions: *one*, it prevents a democratic system from achieving a higher level of democraticness; and *two*, it may develop into lower levels of democraticness (Hibbs, 1973).

Cross-national studies of democratization have paid much attention to the explanation of the occurrence of protest and violence. On the one hand, the literature focuses on the causes and consequences of protest and violence with respect to societal instability and revolutionary developments (Gurr, 1970;

Table 12.10 *Democratic performance and levels of societal protest*

	Democraticness	Pluralism	Polyarchy
Intercept	0.78	0.07	−0.18
Protest	−0.35 (−2.78)	−0.27 (1.81)*	−0.35 (−2.36)
Violence	−0.38 (−3.16)	−0.43 (−3.07)	−0.29 (−1.95)
Strikes	0.28 (2.43)	0.33 (2.38)	0.49 (2.83)
Misery	−0.32 (−3.18)	−0.32 (−2.67)	−0.37 (−2.26)
HDI	0.25 (1.88)	0.14 (0.91)*	0.28 (1.80)
Adj. R^2	60.0%	56.7%	51.2%

N = 34.

Muller and Seligson, 1987; Landman, 2000). On the other hand, attention has been paid to the occurrence of dissatisfaction, popular dissent and protest through social movements with regard to political stability and democratic behaviour (Bingham Powell, 1982; Kriesi et al., 1995; Inglehart, 1997; Foweraker and Landman, 1997). Yet, although a lot of research has been done into this subject, there is little unanimity as regards its effects on democraticness. How does political dissent affect the attained level of surveillance of political and civil rights, and does societal dissatisfaction affect the existing polyarchic conditions of democracy in a country where protest, violence and, for instance, strikes do occur regularly? In other words: is democratic governance a genuine asset of the political systems under review here?

The answer to this question is presented in Table 12.10, where the impact of violence, protest and strikes have been modelled together with the extant degree of misery, on the one hand, and the index of human development, on the other hand.[3] We think that these factors together can be expected to influence the available levels of democraticness. For if the quality of life is low and the level of misery is high then one may expect that manifestations of societal dissatisfaction and political dissent will rise. In turn this will, so we expect, have a negative impact on the level of democraticness (i.e. democratic performance) and hence affect the extent of democratic governance of politics and society.

The results of the regression analysis clearly shows that high(er) levels of violence and protest negatively affect the levels of democraticness of a political system as well as the associated indicators. Whereas high(er) levels of protest have effects for political competition and the rule-of-law, more violent manifestations of protest have a strong(er) impact on the maintenance and surveillance of civil and political rights in a country. This is not the case with strike activity. Apparently this is a widely accepted and recognized mode of protest across the countries under review in this chapter. Both the levels of human development and of misery are conditional factors influencing the achieved level of democratic governance.

Hence, our analysis demonstrates that low levels of public welfare, as exemplified in the Misery Index and the Human Development Index appear to go together with higher levels of societal dissatisfaction and political dissent. Hence, such circumstances, wherever they occur, are relevant for the development and maintenance of democratic governance.

12.7 CONCLUSIONS

The central argument of this chapter has been that the institutional design of democracy structures the role and position of government and its 'room for manoeuvre'. This idea has been elaborated theoretically and empirically in order to analyse and interpret the nexus between democratic governance and its related performance. It could be shown that various indices of demo-cratic government produce different types of governance. The main distinc-tions used and elaborated are the existing format of the state, the type of government in terms of executive–legislative relations, and the organiza-tional features of the 'body' government. The question begging for an answer has been whether or not the cross-national variation in the institu-tional design of governance in democracies would lead to certain distinctive patterns of policy performance (policy output) and subsequently to variable patterns of democratic performance (material and procedural outcomes). The overall expectation throughout this chapter was not only that 'institutions matter' but also would imply a differentiation in terms of more or less demo-cratic governance of the political systems under review. This has been, of course, the main thrust of this book as a whole: bringing together existing theories of democracy and confronting these with empirical evidence by means of comparative methods of political analysis (Keman, 1993a; Lane and Ersson, 1994; Mair, 1996; Pennings et al., 1999; Landman, 2000; Schmidt, 2000).

The cross-national empirical analysis presented in this chapter has demon-strated not only that there is ample variation across the 52 democracies under review, but also that these differences in the structure of the state and the organization of government produce different policy outcomes and related performances. By and large this result reinforces the arguments put forward in this book, in particular in Parts Three and Four, focusing on the role of democratic government and its policy-making efforts. Hence, 'government matters', and this is for a large part due to its institutional position and concomitant organization. It appears, for instance, that the distinction between federal and unitary states is *not* a crucial one but that the decen-tralized organization of the state is. In addition, so it has been observed, there is a difference between presidentialism and other types of government in terms of policy performance and political stability. Such conclusions are not only supportive of this type of macroscopic comparative analysis, but also demonstrate the importance of linking theory with evidence. It allows us to dispel myths and controversies about democratic governance and the performance of such systems.

Another central concern throughout this book has been the development of empirically based 'middle range' theories on democratic politics and governance. In much literature, however, this is underrated (of course, there are also examples that are not tarred with this brush!). In particular, the logical step to link the fabric of democracy in all its variations with the actual performance is still underdeveloped. Too much political science research does not examine the actual output and outcomes of the systems under review. Again, throughout this book this has been, implicitly and explicitly, one of our ambitions: to study the *performances* of democratic systems. In this chapter this ambition has been highlighted by means of inspecting cross-nationally the performance of democracies by looking into the achieved 'quality of life' in a society and the attainment of a desired level of 'democraticness'. The analysis reveals that there is a relationship between public policies produced and democratic performance. Of course, non-political factors remain relevant as well (as has been illustrated by means of the Zöllner model), but it appears equally clear that democratic politics matters with regard to their policy production and societal performance. This seems good news, or at least hopeful news. Yet, at the same time one can observe that the consolidation and extension of democraticness around the globe is a complex process that is, more often than not, characterized by volatile patterns. Hence, conditional factors such as demographic change and economic development are important – not only as conditions for (further) democratization, but also as priorities for governments with respect to developing public welfare and enhancing the quality of life in the societies for which they are and must be held responsible. If not, and this is not only a consequence for 'late comers' or less wealthy nations, democratic performance is easily jeopardized and will impair a further development to genuine democratic government and concomitant democratic governance.

NOTES

1 Such a motion is only allowed if and when there is an alternative Prime Minister *with* a parliamentary majority.
2 This conclusion is reinforced by means of residual analysis: on the one hand, it appears that it can be upheld if controlled for affluence (change in GNPpC), and on the other hand, if controlled for old versus new democracies, or 'first waves' against the others.
3 This concept is operationalized by means of the following indicators:

   • *Human Development Index*: which reflects the availability of a wide range of services and opportunities that are associated with 'welfare'.
   • *Gini Index*: a commonly used measure for assessing income inequality across the population.
   • *Misery Index*: this measure indicates the extent to which the purchasing power and employment of the population is improving or not.

   These indexes have been discussed already in the previous chapter of this book (by Lane and Ersson), except for the 'misery index' (but see for this: Keman, 1984; Castles et al., 1987; Janoski and Hicks, 1994).

APPENDIX TO CHAPTER 12: VARIABLES AND SOURCES

Variables	*Sources/computations*
Bicameralism	Based on Woldendorp et al., (2000, Table 2.1); Maddex (1996) and Banks et al. (1997)
Balanced relationship	Woldendorp et al. (2000: Table 2.5) and own computations
Central government expenditures	World development indicators at www.worldbank.org/data/
Constitutional years	Maddex (1996) and Banks et al. (1997)
Decentralization	Woldendorp et al. (2000) and own computations
Defence	World development indicators at www.worldbank.org/data/
Democraticness	Computed as the standardized sum of polyarchy and pluralism
Dual executive	Derbyshire and Derbyshire (1996)
Duration of democracy	1 = new democracy established after 1988 2 = recent democracy, established after 1946 3 = old democracy, established before 1945 When disturbed the score is lessened by 0.5.
Duration of democracy undisturbed	Adapted from Derbyshire and Derbyshire (1996) and Banks et al. (1997) 1 = new democracy established after 1988 2 = recent democracy, established after 1946 3 = old democracy, established before 1945 When disturbed the case loses the whole score.
Education	UNDP Human Development Report, 1998
Gini	World development indicators at www.worldbank.org/data/
Health care	UNDP Human Development Report, 1998
Hos dominant	Woldendorp et al. (2000: Table 2.5) and own computations
Misery	Computed as: [rates of unemployment + inflation]/2 Based on data from World development indicators at www.worldbank.org/data/
Parliament dominant	Woldendorp et al. (2000: Table 2.5) and own computations
Parliamentary system	Derbyshire and Derbyshire (1996)
PM dominant	Woldendorp et al. (2000: Table 2.7) and own computations
Pluralism	Factor score of the indexes of political rights, civil rights and Coppedge and Reinicke
Polyarchy	Factor score of the indexes of Jaggers and Gurr (1995) and Vanhanen (1997)
Population	ILO: World Labour Report (2000)

Presidential system	Derbyshire and Derbyshire (1996)
Protest	Banks (1996)
Social policy	ILO: World Labour Report (2000)
State format	Woldendorp et al. (2000: Table 2.2) and own computations
State organization	Woldendorp et al. (2000: Table 2.2) and own computations
Strikes	Banks et al. (1997)
Universal suffrage	Based on Woldendorp et al. (2000: Table 2.4) and Banks et al. (1997)
Violence	Banks (1996)
Welfare services	Sum of social policy, health care and education

BIBLIOGRAPHY

Alber, J. (1982) *Vom Armenhaus zum Wohlfahrtsstaat. Analysen zur Entwicklung der Sozialversicherung in Westeuropa.* Frankfurt and New York: Campus Verlag.

Alber, J. (1989) *Der Sozialstaat in der Bundesrepublik, 1950–1983.* Frankfurt and New York: Campus Verlag.

Alber, J. (1986) 'Germany', in P. Flora (ed.), *Growth to Limits. The Western European Welfare States since World War II.* Vols 1, 2, 4. Berlin: Walter de Gruyter.

Alesina, A. (1989) 'Politics and business cycles in industrial democracies', *Economic Policy,* 8: 55–98.

Alesina, A. and Rosenthal, H. (1995) *Partisan Politics, Divided Government, and the Economy.* Cambridge, Mass.: Cambridge University Press.

Almond, G.A. (1956) 'Comparative political systems', *Journal of Politics,* 18: 391–409.

Almond, G.A. and Coleman, J.S. (eds) (1960) *The Politics of the Developing Areas.* Princeton, N.J.: Princeton University Press.

Almond, G.A. and Powell, G.B. (1966) *Comparative Politics: A Developmental Approach.* Boston: Little Brown.

Almond, G.A. and Powell, G.B. (1978) *Comparative Politics* (2nd edn). Boston: Little Brown.

Almond, G.A. and Powell, G.B., Jr. (1996) *Comparative Politics Today.* Glenview, Ill: Scot, Foresman and Company.

Almond, G.A. and Verba, S. (1963) *The Civic Culture: Political Attitudes and Democracy in Five Nations.* Princeton, N.J.: Princeton University Press.

Alt, J. (1985) 'Political parties, world demand and unemployment: domestic and international sources of economic activity', *American Political Science Review,* 79: 1016–40.

Alvarez, R.M., Garrett, G. and Lange, P. (1991) 'Government partisanship, labor organization, and macroeconomic performance', *American Political Science Review,* 85: 539–56.

Alvarez, R.M. et al. (1996) 'Classifying political regimes', *Studies in Comparative International Development,* 31 (2): 3–36.

Amenta, E. (1993) 'The state of the art in welfare state research on social spending efforts in Capitalist democracies since 1960', *American Journal of Sociology,* 99 (3): 750–63.

Anderson, C.J. and Guillory, C.A. (1997) 'Political institutions and satisfaction with democracy: a cross-national analysis of consensus and majoritarian systems', *American Political Science Review,* 91 (1): 66–81.

Andeweg, R.B. (1996) 'Élite-Mass linkages in Europe: Legitimacy crisis or party crisis', in J. Hayward (ed.), *Élitism, Populism, and European Politics.* Oxford: Clarendon Press.

Andrain, C.F. (1980) *Politics and Economic Policy in Western Democracies.* N. Scituate, Mass.: Duxbury Press.

Apter, D.E. (1965) *The Politics of Modernization.* Chicago: Chicago University Press.

Armingeon, K. (1983) *Neo-korporatistische Einkommenspolitik. Eine vergleichende Untersuchung von Einkommenspolitiken in westeuropäischen Ländern.* Frankfurt am Main: Haag & Herchen.

Armingeon, K. (1994) *Staat und Arbeitsbeziehungen. Ein internationaler Vergleich.* Opladen: Westdeutscher Verlag.

Armingeon, K. (1996) 'Konkordanzzwänge und Nebenregierungen als Handlungshindernisse?', in K. Armingeon and P. Sciarini (eds), *Deutschland, Österreich und die Schweiz im Vergleich. Sonderheft der Revue Suisse de Science Politique,* 2 (4): 277–303.

Armingeon, K. (1997) 'Swiss corporatism in comparative perspective', *West European Politics,* 20 (4): 164–79.

Armingeon, K. (1999a) 'Consociationalism and economic performance in Switzerland 1968–1998', in T. Ertman (ed.), *The Fate of Consociationalism.* London: Oxford University Press.

Armingeon, K. (1999b) 'Politische Reaktionen auf steigende Arbeitslosigkeit', in A. Busch and T. Plümper (eds), *Nationaler Staat und Internationale Wirtschaft. Anmerkungen zum Thema Globalisierung.* Baden-Baden: Nomos.

Armingeon, K. and Sciarini, P. (eds) (1996) 'Die politischen systeme Deutschlands, Österreichs und der Schweiz', *Sonderheft der Revue Suisse de Science Politique,* 2 (3).

Arnhem, J.C. and Schotsman, J.G. van (1982) 'Do parties affect the distribution of incomes? The case of advanced capitalist democracies', in Castles, F.G. (ed.), *The Impact of Parties, Politics and Polities in Democratic Capitalist States.* London: Sage.

Aron, R. (1955) 'Fin de l'age idéologique', in T.W. Adorno and W. Dirks (eds), *Sociologica.* Frankfurt: Europaische Verlagsanstalt.

Ashford, D.E. (1986) *The Emergence of the Welfare States.* Oxford: Basil Blackwell.

Axelrod, R. (1984) *The Evolution of Cooperation.* London: Penguin.

Baldwin, P. (1990) *The Politics of Social Solidarity. Class Bases of the European Welfare State 1875–1975.* Cambridge: Cambridge University Press.

Banks, A. (1996) 'Cross-national time series data archive', Binghampton, N.Y.: CSA.

Banks, A. (ed.) (1978) *Political Handbook of the World 1978.* New York: McGraw-Hill.

Banks, A.S., Day, A.J. and Muller, T.C. (eds) (1997) *Political Handbook of the World: 1997.* Binghampton, N.Y.: CSA.

Barnes, S.H. and Kaase, M. (eds) (1979) *Political Action: Mass Participation in Five Western Democracies.* London: Sage.

Barr, N. (1993) *The Economics of the Welfare State.* Oxford: Oxford University Press.

Barrett, D.B. (ed.) (1982) *World Christian Encyclopaedia: A Comparative Study of Churches and Religions in the Modern World, AD 1900–2000.* Nairobi: Oxford University Press.

Barry, B (1978) *Sociologists, Economists and Democracy.* Chicago: University of Chicago Press.

Bartolini, S. and Mair, P. (1990) *Identity, Competition and Electoral Availability: The Stabilisation of European Electorates 1885–1985.* Cambridge: Cambridge University Press.

Beck, N. and Katz, J.N. (1995) 'What to do (and not to do) with time-series-cross-section data in comparative politics', *American Political Science Review,* 89: 634–47.

Becker, U. (2000) 'Welfare state development and employment in the Netherlands in comparative perspective', *Journal of European Social Policy,* 10 (3): 219–39.

Becker, U. (2001) 'A Dutch model? Employment growth by corporatist consensus and wage restraint: A critical account of an idyllic view', *New Political Economy,* 6 (1).

Beer, S. and Ulam, U. (eds) (1958) *Patterns of Government: The Major Political Systems of Europe.* New York: Random House.

Beetham, D. (ed.) (1994) *Defining and Measuring Democracy.* London: Sage.

Bell, D. (1960) *The End of Ideology.* Glencoe, Ill. Free Press.

Berger, S. (ed.) (1981) *Organizing Interests in Western Europe: Pluralism, Corporatism and the Transformation of Politics.* Cambridge: Cambridge University Press.

Berg-Schlosser, D. and Meur, G. de (1996) 'Conditions of authoritarianism, fascism, and democracy in interwar Europe: systematic matching and contrasting of cases for "small N" analysis', *Comparative Political Studies,* 29 (4): 423–68.

Berg-Schlosser, D. and Müller-Rommel, F. (1987) *Vergleichende Politikwissenschaft: ein einführendes Handbuch.* Opladen: Leske & Budrich.

Betz, H.-G. (1994) *Radical Rightwing Populism in Western Europe.* Basingstoke: Macmillan.

Beyme, K. von (1970) *Die Parlamentarischen Regierungssysteme in Europa.* München: Piper Verlag.

Beyme, K. von (1985) *Political Parties in Western Democracies.* Aldershot: Gower.

Beyme, K. von (1994) *Systemwechsel in Osteuropa.* Frankfurt am Main: Campus.

Binder, L. et al. (1971) *Crises and Sequences in Political Development.* Princeton: Princeton University Press.

Bingham Powell, G. (1982*) Contemporary Democracies: Participation, Stability and Violence.* Cambridge, Mass.: Harvard University Press.

Bingham Powell, G. (2000) *Elections as Instruments of Democracy: Majoritarian and Proportional Visions.* New Haven and London: Yale University Press.

Birchfeld, V. and Crépaz, M.M.L. (1998) 'The impact of constitutional structures and collective and competitive veto points on income inequality in industrialized democracies', *European Journal of Political Research,* 34 (2): 175–200.

Bjorn, L. (1979) 'Labor parties, economic growth, and redistribution in five capitalist countries', *Comparative Social Research,* 2: 93–128.

Black, C.E. (1966) *The Dynamics of Modernization: A Study in Comparative History.* New York: Harper & Row.

Blais, A., Blake, D. and Dion, S. (1993) 'Do parties make a difference? Parties and the size of government in liberal democracies', *American Journal of Political Science,* 37: 40–62.

Blais, A. and Dobrzynska, A. (1998) 'Turnout in electoral democracies', *European Journal of Political Research,* 33 (2): 239–61.

Blais, A. and Massicotte, L. (1996) 'Electoral systems', in L. LeDuc, R.G. Niemi and P. Norris (eds), *Comparing Democracies: Elections and Voting in Global Perspective.* Thousand Oaks, Calif.: Sage.

Blondel, J. (1969) *Introduction to Comparative Government.* London: Weidenfeld and Nicholson.

Blondel, J. (1973) *Comparative Legislatures.* Englewood Cliffs, N.J.: Prentice-Hall.

Blondel, J. (1982) *The Organization of Governments: A Comparative Analysis of Governmental Structures.* London: Sage.

Blondel, J. (1990) *Comparative Government: An Introduction.* Hertfordshire: Philip Allan.

Blondel, J. and Müller-Rommel (eds) (1993) *Governing Together: the Extent and Limits of Joint Decision-Making in Western European Cabinets.* Basingstoke: Macmillan.

Blondel, J. and Thiebault, J.-L. (eds) (1991) *The Profession of Government Minister in Western Europe.* Houndsmill: Macmillan.

Bogaards, M. (1998) 'The favourable factors for consociational democracy: A review, *European Journal of Political Research*, 33 (1): 475–96.

Bogdanor, V. and Butler, D. (eds) (1983) *Coalition Government in Western Europe.* London: Heinemann.

Boix, C. (1998) *Political Parties, Growth and Equality.* Cambridge: Cambridge University Press.

Bollen, K.A. (1979) 'Political democracy and the timing of development', *American Political Science Review*, 44: 572–87.

Bollen, K.A. (1993) 'Liberal democracy: validity and method factors in cross-national measures', *American Journal of Political Science*, 37 (4): 1207–30.

Bollen, K.A. and Paxton, P. (2000) 'Subjective measures of liberal democracy', *Comparative Political Studies*, 33 (1): 58–86.

Borchert, J. (1995) *Die konservative Transformation des Wohlfahrtsstaates.* Frankfurt a.M.: Campus.

Bradshow, J. (1993) 'Developments in social security policy', in C. Jones (ed.), *New Perspectives on the Welfare State in Europe.* Part II: 'Issues from Britain'. London: Routledge.

Braun, D. (1989) *Grenzen Polotischer Regulierung Der Weg in die Massenarbeitslosigkeit am Beispiel der Niederlande.* Wiesbaden: Deutscher Universitätsverlag.

Braun, D. (ed.) (2000) *Public Policy and Federalism.* Aldershot: Ashgate.

Brennan, G. and Buchanan, J.M. (1980) *The Power to Tax: Analytical Foundations of a Fiscal Constitution.* Cambridge: Cambridge University Press.

Brittan, S. (1977) *The Economic Consequences of Democracy.* London: Temple Smith.

Browne, E.C. and Dreijmanis, J. (eds) (1982) *Government Coalitions in Western Democracies.* New York: Longman.

Bryce, J. (1929) *Modern Democracies.* 2 vols. London: Macmillan.

Budge, I. (1993) 'Rational choice as comparative theory: beyond economic self interest', in H. Keman (ed.), *Comparative Politics.* Amsterdam: VU University Press.

Budge, I. (1994) 'A new spatial theory of party competition: uncertainty, ideology and policy equilibria viewed comparatively and temporally', *British Journal of Political Science*, 24: 443–67.

Budge, I. (1996a) *The New Challenge of Direct Democracy.* Cambridge: Polity Press.

Budge, I. (1996b) 'Great Britain and Ireland: Variations on dominant party government', in J.M. Colomer (ed.), *Political Institutions in Europe.* London: Routledge.

Budge, I. (2000) 'Expert judgements of party policy positions: uses and limitations in political research', *European Journal of Political Research*, 37 (1): 103–13.

Budge, I., Crewe, I. and Farlie, D. (eds) (1976) *Party Identification and Beyond. Representations of Voting and Party Competition.* London: John Wiley.

Budge, I. and Farlie, D. (1976) 'A comparative analysis of factors related with turnout and voting choice', in I. Budge, I. Crewe and D. Farlie (eds) (1976) *Party Identification and Beyond. Representations of Voting and Party Competition.* London: John Wiley.

Budge, I. and Farlie, D. (1983) *Explaining and Predicting Elections: Issue Effects and Party Strategies in Twenty-Three Democracies.* Winchester: Allen and Unwin.

Budge, I. and Keman, H. (1990) *Parties and Democracies. Coalition Formation and Government Functioning in 20 States.* Oxford: Oxford University Press.

Budge, I., Klingemann, H.-D., Volkens, A., Bara, J. et al. (2001) *Mapping Policy Preferences: Parties, Governments, Electors 1945–1998.* Oxford: Oxford University Press.

Budge, I., Newton, K. et al. (1997) *The Politics of the New Europe. Atlantic to Urals.* London: Longman.

Budge, I., Robertson, D. and Hearl, D.J. (eds) (1987) *Ideology, Strategy and Party Change.* Cambridge: Cambridge University Press.

Burin, F.S. and Shell, K.L. (eds) (1969) *Politics, Law and Social Change: Selected Essays of Otto Kirchheimer*. New York: Columbia University Press.

Burkhart, R.E. and Lewis-Beck, M.S. (1994) 'Comparative democracy: the economic development thesis', *American Political Science Review*, 88: 903–10.

Busch, A. (1993) 'The politics of price stability: why the German-speaking nations are different', in F.G. Castles (ed.), *Families of Nations. Patterns of Public Policy in Western Democracies*. Aldershot: Dartmouth.

Busch, A. (1995) *Preisstabilitätspolitik*. Opladen: Leske & Budrich.

Bussemaker, J. and Kersbergen, K. van (1999) 'Contemporary social-capitalist welfare states and gender inequality', in D. Sainsbury (ed.), *Gender and Welfare State Regimes*. Oxford: Oxford University Press.

Calmfors, L. and Drifill, J. (1988) 'Centralisation of wage bargaining', *Economic Policy*, 6: 13–61.

Cameron, D.R. (1978) 'The expansion of the public economy,' *American Political Science Review*, 72: 1243–61.

Cameron, D.R. (1984) 'Social democracy, corporatism, labour quiescence, and the representation of economic interest in advanced capitalist society', in J.H. Goldthorpe (ed.), *Order and Conflict in Contemporary Capitalism*. Oxford: Oxford University Press.

Cameron, D.R. (1985) 'Does government cause inflation? Taxes, spending, and deficits', in L.N. Lindberg and C.S. Maier (eds), *The Politics of Inflation and Economic Stagnation. Theoretical Approaches and International Case Studies*. Washington, D.C.: Brookings.

Campbell, A., Converse, P.E., Miller, W.E. and Stokes, D.E. (1960) *The American Voter*. New York and London: Wiley.

Casper, G. (1995) *Fragile Democracies*. Pittsburgh: University of Pittsburgh Press.

Castles, F.G. (1978) *The Social Democratic Image of Society. A Study of the Achievements and Origins of Scandinavian Social Democracy in Comparative Perspective*. London: Routledge and Kegan Paul.

Castles, F.G. (ed.) (1982a) *The Impact of Parties. Politics and Policies in Democratic Capitalist States*. London: Sage.

Castles, F.G. (1982b) 'The impact of parties on public expenditure', in F.G. Castles (ed.) (1982a) *The Impact of Parties. Politics and Policies in Democratic Capitalist States*. London: Sage.

Castles, F.G. (1985) *The Working Class and Welfare: Reflections on the Political Development of the Welfare State in Australia and New Zealand, 1890–1980*. London: Allen and Unwin.

Castles, F.G. (1986a) 'Social expenditure and the political Right: a methodological note', *European Journal of Political Research*, 14: 669–76.

Castles, F.G. (1986b) 'Under what circumstances does change really matter?', *European Journal of Political Research*, 14: 681–3.

Castles, F.G. (1989a) 'Explaining public education expenditures in OECD nations', *European Journal of Political Research*, 17: 431–49.

Castles, F.G. (ed.) (1989b) *The Comparative History of Public Policy*. Cambridge: Polity Press.

Castles, F.G. (ed.) (1993) *Families of Nations. Patterns of Public Policy in Western Democracies*. Aldershot: Dartmouth.

Castles, F.G. (1995) 'Welfare state development in Southern Europe', *West European Politics*, 18 (2): 291–313.

Castles, F.G. (1998) *Comparative Public Policy. Patterns of Post-war Transformation*. Cheltenham: Edgar Elgar.

Castles, F.G. (1999) 'Decentralization and the post-war political economy', *European Journal of Political Research*, 36: 27–53.

Castles, F.G. (2000a) 'The dog that didn't bark: economic development and the post-war welfare state', *European Review*, 8 (3): 313–32

Castles, F.G. (2000b) 'Federalism, fiscal decentralization and economic performance', in U. Wachendorfer-Schmidt (ed.), *Federalism and Political Performance*. London: Routledge.

Castles, F.G., Gerritsen, R. and Vowles, J. (eds) (1996) *The Great Experiment: Labour Parties and Public Policy Transformation in Australia and New Zealand*. Sydney: Routledge.

Castles, F.G., Lehner, F. and Schmidt, M.G. (eds) (1987) *Managing Mixed Economies*. Berlin and New York: Walter de Gruyter.

Castles, F.G. and Mair, P. (1984) 'Left-Right political scales: some expert judgements', *European Journal of Political Research*, 12: 73–88.

Castles, F.G. and Marceau, J. (1989) 'The transformation of gender inequality in tertiary education', *Journal of Public Policy*, 9: 493–508.

Castles, F.G. and McKinlay, R. (1979) 'Does politics matter? An analysis of the public welfare commitment in advanced democratic states', *European Journal of Political Research*, 7: 169–86.

Castles, F.G. and Mitchell, D. (1993) 'Worlds of welfare and families of nations', in F.G. Castles (ed.) (1993) *Families of Nations. Patterns of Public Policy in Western Democracies*. Aldershot: Dartmouth.

Cerny, P. (1994) 'The dynamics of financial globalization: technology, market structure and policy response', *Policy Sciences*, 27: 319–42.

Cerny, P.G. (1999) 'Globalization and the erosion of democracy', *European Journal of Political Research*, 36 (1): 1–26.

Clayton, R. and J. Pontusson (1998) 'Welfare-state retrenchment revisited: entitlement cuts, public sector restructuring, and inegalitarian trends in advanced capitalist societies', *World Politics*, 51: 67–98.

Coleman, J.S. (ed.) (1965) *Education and Political Development*. Princeton, N.J.: Princeton University Press.

Collier, D. and Mahon, J. (1993) 'Conceptual stretching revisited: adapting categories in comparative analysis', *American Political Science Review*, 87(4): 845–55.

Colomer, J.M. (ed.) (1996a) *Political Institutions in Europe*. London: Routledge.

Colomer, J.M. (1996b) 'Introduction', in J.M. Colomer (ed.) *Political Institutions in Europe*. London: Routledge.

Compston, H. (1994) 'Union participation in economic policy-making in Austria, Switzerland, The Netherlands, Belgium and Ireland, 1970–1992', *West European Politics*, 17 (1): 123–45.

Compston, H. (1995a) 'Union participation in economic policy making in Scandinavia, 1970–1993', *West European Politics*, 18 (1): 98–115.

Compston, H. (1995b) 'Union participation in economic policy making in France, Italy, Germany and Britain, 1970–1993', *West European Politics*, 18 (2): 314–39.

Compston, H. (1997) 'Union power, policy making and unemployment in western Europe, 1972–1993', *Comparative Political Studies*, 30 (6): 732–51.

Conover, P.J. and Searing, D.D. (1994) 'Democracy, citizenship and the study of political socialisation', in Ian Budge and David McKay (eds), *Developing Democracy*. London: Sage.

Coppedge, M. and Reinicke, W.H. (1990) 'Measuring polyarchy,' *Studies in Comparative International Development*, 25 (1): 51–72.

Cox, R.H. (1998) 'The consequences of welfare reform: how conceptions of social rights are changing', *Journal of Social Policy*, 27 (1): 1–16.

Crépaz, M.M.L. (1996a) 'Consensus versus majoritarian democracy. Political institutions and their impact on macroeconomic performance and industrial disputes in 18 industrialized democracies', *Comparative Political Studies*, 29 (1): 4–26.

Crépaz, M.M.L. (1996b) 'Constitutional structure and regime performance in 18 industrialized democracies: a test of Olson's hypothesis', *European Journal of Political Research*, 29 (1): 87–104.

Crewe, I. and Denver, D.T. (eds) (1985) *Electoral Change in Western Democracies*. New York: St Martin's.

Crouch, C. (1993) *Industrial Relations and European State Traditions*. Oxford: Clarendon Press.

Cukierman, A. (1992) *Central Bank Strategy, Credibility, and Independence. Theory and Evidence*. Cambridge, Mass.: Cambridge University Press.

Cusack, T. (1995) *Politics and Macroeconomic Performance in the OECD Countries during the period 1950 through 1990*. Berlin: Wissenschaftszentrum Berlin für Sozialforschung.

Cusack, T. (1997) 'Partisan politics and public finance: changes in public spending in the industrialized democracies, 1955–1989', *Public Choice*, 9 (3): 375–95.

Cusack, T. (1999) 'Partisan politics and fiscal policy', *Comparative Politics*, 32: 464–84.

Cutright, P. (1965) 'Political structures, economic development and national security programs', *American Journal of Sociology*, 70: 537–50.

Czada, R. (1995) 'Der Kampf um die Finanzierung der deutschen Einheit', in G. Lehmbruch (ed.), *Einigung und Zerfall. Deutschland und Europa nach dem Ende des Ost-West-Konflikts*. Opladen: Leske & Budrich.

Czada, R.M., Heritier, A. and Keman, H. (eds) (1998) *Institutions and Political Choice: on the Limits of Rationality*. Amsterdam: VU-University Press.

Daalder, H. (1966) 'The Netherlands: opposition in a segmented society', in R.A. Dahl (ed.) (1966) *Political Oppositions in Western Democracies*. New Haven, Conn.: Yale University Press.

Daalder, H. (1974) 'The consociational democracy theme', *World Politics*, 26: 604–21.

Daalder, H. (1979) 'Stein Rokkan 1921–1979: a memoir', *European Journal of Political Research*, 7: 337–55.

Daalder, H. (1987) 'Countries in comparative European politics', *European Journal of Political Research*, 15: 3–21.

Daalder, H. (1995) *Van Oude en Nieuwe Regenten. Politiek in Nederland*. Amsterdam: Bert Bakker.

Daalder, H. (ed.) (1997) *Comparative European Politics: the Story of a Profession*. London: Pinter.

Daalder, H. and Mair, P. (eds) (1983) *Western European Party Systems: Continuity and Change*. London: Sage.

Dahl, R.A. (ed.) (1966) *Political Oppositions in Western Democracies*. New Haven, Conn.: Yale University Press.

Dahl, R.A. (1970) *Modern Political Analysis*. Englewood Cliffs, N.J.: Prentice-Hall.

Dahl, R.A. (1971) *Polyarchy. Participation and Opposition*. New Haven and London: Yale University Press.

Dahl, R.A. (1984) 'Polyarchy, pluralism, and scale', *Scandinavian Political Studies*, 7 (4): 225–40.

Dahl, R.A. (1989) *Democracy and its Critics*. New Haven and London: Yale University Press.

Dahl, R.A. (1998) *On Democracy*. New Haven and London: Yale University Press.

Dalton, R.J. (1984) 'Cognitive mobilization and partisan dealignment in advanced industrial democracies', *Journal of Politics*, 42 (2): 264–84.

Dalton, R.J., Flanagan, S.C. and Beck, P.A. (eds) (1984) *Electoral Change in Advanced Industrial Democracies: Realignment or Dealignment?* Princeton, N.J.: Princeton University Press.

Dalton, R.J. and Wattenberg, M.P. (1993) 'The not so simple act of voting', in A.W. Finifter (ed.), *Political Science: The State of the Discipline II*. Washington, D.C.: The American Political Science Association.

Davis, O.A., Dempster, A.H. and Wildavsky, A. (1966) 'A theory of the budgetary process', *American Political Science Review*, 60: 529–47.

Dawson, R.E. and Robinson, J.A. (1963) 'Inter-party competition, economic variables and welfare politics in the American states', *Journal of Politics*, 25: 265–89.

Deininger, K. and Squire, L. (1997) *The Deininger-Squire data set*; available at: <http://www.worldbank.org/html/prdmg/grthweb/dddeisqu.htm>.

Derbyshire, J.D. and Derbyshire, I. (1996) *Political Systems of the World*. New York: St Martin's Press.

De Swaan, A. (1988) *In Care of the State. Health Care, Education and Welfare in Europe and the USA in the Modern Era*. Cambridge: Polity Press.

Deth, J. van and Scarbrough, E. (eds) (1995) *The Impact of Values*. Oxford: Oxford University Press.

Diamond, L., Linz, J.J. and Lipset, S.M. (eds) (1988) *Democracy in Developing Countries*. 4 vols. Boulder: Westview Press.

Diamond, L. and Marks, G. (1992) *Reexamining Democracy: Essays in Honor of Seymour Martin Lipset*. Newbury Park, Calif.: Sage.

Diamond, L. and Plattner, M.F. (eds) (1993) *The Global Resurgence of Democracy*. Baltimore: Johns Hopkins University Press.

Diamond, L. and Plattner, M.F. (eds) (1994) *Nationalism, Ethnic Conflict, and Democracy*. Baltimore: Johns Hopkins University Press.

Dogan, M. and Pelassy, D. (1990) *How to Compare Nations: Strategies in Comparative Politics*. Chatham: Chatham House.

Domke, W.C., Eichenberg, R.C. and Keleker, C.M. (1983) 'The illusion of choice: defense and welfare in advanced industrial democracies', *American Political Science Review*, 77 (1): 19–35.

Downs, A. (1957) *An Economic Theory of Democracy*. New York: Harper & Row.

Dryzek, J. (1978) 'Politics, economics and inequality: a cross-national analysis', *European Journal of Political Research*, 6: 399–410.

Ducachek, I.D. (1970) *Comparative Federalism: the Territorial Dimension of Politics*. New York: Holt, Rinehart and Winston.

Dunleavy, P. and Margetts, H. (1994) 'The experiental approach to auditing democracy', in D. Beetham (ed.), *Defining and Measuring Democracy*. London: Sage.

Duverger, M. (1954) *Political Parties: Their Organization and Activity in the Modern State*. London: Methuen.

Duverger, M. (1980) 'A new political system model: semi-presidential government', *European Journal of Political Research*, 8: 165–87.

Dye, T.R. (1966) *Politics, Economics, and the Public*. Chicago: Rand McNally.

Easton, D. (1953) *The Political System*. New York: Knopf.

Easton, D. (1965) *A Systems Analysis of Political Life*. New York: Wiley.

Easton, D. (1981) 'The political system besieged by the state', *Political Theory*, 9 (3): 303–25.

Easton, D. and Dennis, J. (1969) *Children in the Political System: Origins of Political Legitimacy*. New York: McGraw-Hill.

Eckstein, H. (1966) *Division and Cohesion in Democracy: A Study of Norway*. Princeton, N.J.: Princeton University Press.

Eckstein, H., and Apter, D.E. (eds) (1963) *Comparative Politics: A Reader*. Glencoe, Ill.: Free Press.

Eijk, C. van der and Franklin, M.N. (eds) (1996) *Choosing Europe? The European Electorate and National Politics in the Face of Union*. Ann Arbor: University of Michigan Press.

Eijk, C. van der, Franklin, M.N. and Oppenhuis, E. (1996) 'The strategic context: party choice, ', in C. van der Eijk and M.N. Franklin (eds) (1996) *Choosing Europe? The European Electorate and National Politics in the Face of Union*. Ann Arbor: University of Michigan Press.

Einerhand, M., Kerklaan, M., Metz, H., Siegelaer, E. and Vliegenhart, M. (1995) *Sociale Zekerheid: Stelsels en Regelingen in Enkele Europese Landen*. Den Haag: Vuga/ Ministerie van Sociale Zaken en Werkgelegenheid.

Eisenstadt, S.N. (ed.) (1971) *Political Sociology: A Reader*. New York: Basic Books.

Eisenstadt, S.N. (1973) *Tradition, Change and Modernity*. New York: Wiley.

Elazar, D.J. (1995) 'Federalism', in S.M. Lipset (ed.), *The Encyclopedia of Democracy*. London: Routledge.

Elazar, D.J. (1997) 'Contrasting unitary and federal systems', *International Political Science Review*, 18 (3): 237–51.

Elgie, R. (1998) 'The classification of democratic regime types: conceptual ambiguity and contestable assumptions', *European Journal of Political Research*, 33 (2): 219–38.

Empter, S. and Esche, A. (eds) (1997) *Eigenverantwortung und Solidarität. Neue Wege in der Sozial- und Tarifpolitik*. Gütersloh: Bertelsmann.

Encyclopaedia Britannica (annually) *Britannica World Data*. Chicago: Encyclopaedia Britannica.

Esping-Andersen, G. (1985a) *Politics Against Markets. The Social Democratic Road to Power*. Princeton, N.J.: Princeton University Press.

Esping-Andersen, G. (1985b) 'Power and distributional regimes', *Politics and Society*, 14: 223–56.

Esping-Andersen, G. (1986) 'From poor relief to institutional welfare states: the development of Scandinavian social policy', in R. Erikson et al. (eds), *The Scandinavian Model: Welfare States and Welfare Research*. Armonk: Sharpe.

Esping-Andersen, G. (1987) 'The comparison of policy regimes: an introduction', in M. Rein, G. Esping-Andersen and L. Rainwater (eds), *Stagnation and Renewal. The Rise and Fall of Policy Regimes*. Armonk and New York: Sharpe.

Esping-Andersen, G. (1990) *The Three Worlds of Welfare Capitalism*. Cambridge: Cambridge University Press.

Esping-Andersen, G. (1994) 'Welfare and the economy', in N. Smelser and R. Swedberg, *Handbook of Economic Sociology*. Princeton, N.J.: Princeton University Press.

Esping-Andersen, G. (ed.) (1996) *Welfare States in Transition: National Adaptations in Global Economies*. London: Sage.

Esping-Andersen, G. (1999) *Social Foundations of Post-Industrial Economies*. Oxford: Oxford University Press.

Esping-Andersen, G. and Korpi, W. (1984) 'Social policy as class politics in post-war capitalism: Scandinavia, Austria and Germany', in J.H. Goldthorpe (ed.), *Order and Conflict in Contemporary Capitalism*. Oxford: Clarendon Press.

Esping-Andersen, G. and Korpi, W. (1986) 'From poor relief to institutional welfare states', in R. Erikson, E.J. Hansen, S. Ringen and H. Uusitalo (eds), *The Scandinavian Model: Welfare States and Welfare Research*. New York: M.E. Sharpe.

Europa Yearbook (1985) London: Europa Publications.

Eurostat (1996) *Social Portrait of Europe*. Luxembourg: Office for Official Publications of the European Communities.

Evans, P.B., Rueschemeyer, D. and Skocpol, Th. (eds) (1985) *Bringing the State Back In*. Cambridge, Mass.: Harvard University Press.

Farr, J., Dryzek, J.S. and Leonard, S.T. (eds) (1997) *Political Science in History. Research Programs and Political Traditions*. Cambridge: Cambridge University Press.

Farrell, D.M. (1997) *Comparing Electoral Systems*. London: Prentice Hall Harvester Wheatsheaf.

Faure, A.M. (1994) 'Some methodological problems in comparative politics', *Journal of Theoretical Politics*, 6 (3): 307–22.

Ferejohn, J. (1997) 'The development of the spatial theory of elections', in J. Farr, J.S. Dryzek and S.T. Leonard (eds) (1997) *Political Science in History. Research Programs and Political Traditions*. Cambridge: Cambridge University Press.

Ferrera, M. (1986) 'Italy', in P. Flora (ed.) (1986) *Growth to Limits. The Western European Welfare States since World War II. Vols 1, 2, 4*. Berlin: Walter de Gruyter.

Ferrera, M. (1996a) 'The southern model of welfare in social Europe', *Journal of European Social Policy*, 6 (1): 17–37.

Ferrera, M. (1996b) 'The partitocracy of health. Towards a new welfare politics in Italy', *Res Publica*, 38 (2): 447–59.

Finer, H. (1949) *Theory and Practice of Modern Government* (revised edition). New York: Holt.

Finer, S.E. (1970) *Comparative Government*. Harmondsworth: Penguin.

Finkle, J.L. and Gable, R.W. (eds) (1966) *Political Development and Social Change*. New York: Wiley.

Flora, P. (1974) *Modernisierungsforschung: Zur Empirischen Analyse der Gesellschaftlichen Entwicklung*. Opladen: Westdeutscher Verlag.

Flora, P. (1975) *Indikatoren der Modernisierung: Ein Historisches Datenhandbuch*. Opladen: Westdeutscher Verlag.

Flora, P. (1983) *State, Economy and Society in Western Europe, 1815–1975*. 2 vols. Chicago: St James.

Flora, P. (ed.) (1986) *Growth to Limits. The Western European Welfare States since World War II. Vols 1, 2, 4*. Berlin: Walter de Gruyter.

Flora, P. and Alber, J. (1981) 'Modernization, democratization, and the development of the welfare states in western Europe', in P. Flora and A.J. Heidenheimer (eds) (1981) *The Development of Welfare States in Europe and America*. New Brunswick and London: Transaction Books.

Flora, P. and Heidenheimer, A.J. (eds) (1981) *The Development of Welfare States in Europe and America*. New Brunswick and London: Transaction Books.

Flora, P., Kuhnle, S. and Urwin, D. (eds) (1999) *State Formation, Nation-Building and Mass Politics in Europe: the Theory of Stein Rokkan*. Oxford: Oxford University Press.

Foweraker, J. and Landman, T. (1997) *Citizenship Rights and Social Movements: A Comparative and Statistical Analysis*. Oxford: Oxford University Press.

Franklin, M.N. (1996) 'Electoral participation', in L. LeDuc, R.G. Niemi and P. Norris (eds) (1996) *Comparing Democracies: Elections and Voting in Global Perspective*. Thousand Oaks, Calif.: Sage.

Franklin, M.N., Mackie, T.T. and Valen, H. (1992) *Electoral Change: Responses to Social and Attitudinal Structures in Western Countries*. Cambridge: Cambridge University Press.

Freedom House (1999) *Freedom in the World. The Annual Survey of Political Rights &*
Civil Liberties 1998–1999.

Friedrich, C.J. (1941) *Constitutional Government and Democracy: Theory and Practice of*
Modern Government. Boston: Little Brown.

Friedrich, C.J. (ed.) (1954) *Totalitarianism.* Cambridge, Mass.: Harvard University Press.

Friedrich, C.J. and Brzezinski, Z.R. (1956) *Totalitarian Dictatorship and Autocracy.*
Cambridge, Mass: Harvard University Press.

Fuchs, D. and H.-D. Klingemann (1995) 'Citizens and the state: a changing relationship?', in H.-D. Klingemann and D. Fuchs (eds), *Citizens and the State.* Oxford:
Oxford University Press.

Fukuyama, F. (1992) *The End of History and the Last Man.* New York: Free Press.

Furniss, N. and Tilton, T. (1977) *The Case for the Welfare State. From Social Security to*
Social Equality. Bloomington: Indiana University Press.

Fusilier, R. (1960) *Les Monarchies Parlementaires: étude sur les Systèmes de Gouvernement:*
Suède, Norvège, Danemark, Belgique, Pays-Bas, Luxembourg. Paris: Editions Ouvrières.

Galbraith, J.K. (1967) *The New Industrial State.* Boston: Houghton Mifflin.

Gallagher, M. (1997) 'Electoral systems and voting behaviour', in M. Rhodes,
P. Heywood and V. Wright, *Developments in West European Politics.* Basingstoke:
Macmillan.

Gallagher, M, Laver, M. and Mair, P. (2000) *Representative Government in Modern*
Europe (3rd edn). New York: McGraw-Hill.

Garrett, G. (1993) 'The politics of structural change. Swedish social democracy and
Thatcherism in comparative perspective', *Comparative Political Studies,* 25: 521–47.

Garrett, G. (1998) *Partisan Politics in the Global Economy.* Cambridge: Cambridge
University Press.

Garrett, G. and Lange, P. (1986) 'Performance in a hostile world: economic growth in
capitalist democracies, 1974–1980', *World Politics,* 38: 517–45.

Garrett, G. and Lange, P. (1991) 'Political responses to economic decline: What's "left"
for the left?', *International Organization,* 45: 539–64.

Gastil, R.D. (1990) 'The comparative survey of freedom: experiences and sugges-
tions', *Studies in Comparative International Development,* 25: 25–50.

Geertz, C. (1983) *Dichte Beschreibung.* Frankfurt a.M.: Suhrkamp.

Giddens, A. (1998) *The Third Way. The Renewal of Social Democracy,* Cambridge: Polity
Press.

Ginsburg, N. (1979) *Class, Capital and Social Policy.* London and Basingstoke: Macmillan.

Goldthorpe, J.H. (ed.) (1984) *Order and Conflict in Contemporary Capitalism.* Oxford:
Oxford University Press.

Goodin, R.E., Headey, B., Muffels, R. and Dirven, H.-J. (1999) *The Real Worlds of*
Welfare Capitalism. Cambridge: Cambridge University Press.

Goodin, R.E. and H.-D. Klingemann (eds) (1996) *A New Handbook of Political Science.*
Oxford: Oxford University Press.

Goodin, R.E. and LeGrand, J. (1987) *Not Only the Poor: The Middle Classes and the*
Welfare State. London: Allen and Unwin.

Goodman, R. and Peng, I. (1996) 'The East Asian welfare states: peripatetic learning,
adaptive strategy, and nation-building', in G. Esping-Andersen (ed.), *Welfare States*
in Transition: National Adaptations in Global Economies. London: Sage.

Gordon, M.S. (1988) *Social Security Policies in Industrial Countries.* Cambridge:
Cambridge University Press.

Gough, I. (1979) *The Political Economy of the Welfare State.* London: Macmillan.

Gould, C.C. (1993) *Rethinking Democracy: Freedom and Social Cooperation in Politics,*
Economy, and Society. Cambridge: Cambridge University Press.

Greene, W.H. (1999) *Econometric Methods*. Englewood Cliffs, N.J.: Prentice Hall.

Grew, R. (ed.) (1978) *Crises and Political Development in Europe and the United States*. Princeton, N.J.: Princeton University Press.

Griffin, L.J., O'Connell, P.J. and McCammon, H.J. (1989) 'National variation in the context of struggle: postwar class conflict and market distribution in the capitalist democracies', *Canadian Review of Sociology and Anthropology*, 26 (1): 1–37.

Griffin, L.J., Walters, P.B., O'Connell, P.J. and Moor, E. (1986) 'Methodological innovations in the analysis of welfare-state development: pooling cross sections and time series', in N. Furniss (ed.), *Futures for the Welfare State*. Bloomington: Indiana University Press.

Grilli, V., Masciandaro, D. and Tabellini, G. (1991) 'Political and monetary institutions and public financial policies in the industrial countries', *Economic Policy*, 13: 341–92.

Gunnell, J.G. (1997) 'The declination of the "state" and the origins of American pluralism', in J. Farr, J.S. Dryzek and S.T. Leonard (eds) (1997) *Political Science in History. Research Programs and Political Traditions*. Cambridge: Cambridge University Press.

Gurr, T.R. (1970) *Why Men Rebel*. Princeton, N.J.: Princeton University Press.

Gwartney, J. et al. (1996) *Economic Freedom of the World 1975–1995*. Vancouver: Fraser Institute.

Hadenius, A. (1992) *Democracy and Development*. Cambridge: Cambridge University Press.

Hage, J., Hanneman, R. and Gargan, E.T. (1989) *State Responsiveness and State Activism. An Examination of the Social Forces and State Strategies that Explain the Rise in Social Expenditure in Britain, France, Germany and Italy 1870–1968*. London: Unwin Hyman.

Hague, R., Harrop, M. and Breslin, S. (1998) *Comparative Government and Politics. An Introduction*. Basingstoke: Macmillan.

Hall, P. (1986) *Governing the Economy*. Oxford: Polity Press.

Hanisch, W. (1998) 'Soziale Sicherung im Europäischen Vergleich', *Aus Politik und Zeitgeschichte*, B: 34–35.

Hanley, D. (ed.) (1994) *Christian Democracy in Europe*. London and New York: Pinter.

Hantrais, L. (1996) 'France: squaring the welfare triangle', in V. George and P. Taylor-Gooby (eds), *European Welfare Policy. Squaring the Circle*, London: Longman.

Hardin, R. (1982) *Collective Action*. Baltimore and London: Johns Hopkins University Press.

Hayward, J. (ed.) (1996) *Elitism, Populism, and European Politics*. Oxford: Clarendon Press.

Heckscher, G. (1957) *The Study of Comparative Government and Politics*. London: Allen & Unwin.

Heclo, H. (1974) *Modern Social Policies in Britain and Sweden*. New Haven, Conn.: Yale University Press.

Heclo, H. and Madsen, H.J. (1986) *Policy and Politics in Sweden*. Philadelphia: Temple University Press.

Heidenheimer, A.J., Heclo, H. and Adams, C.T. (1975) *Comparative Public Policy* (1st edn). New York: St Martin's Press.

Heidenheimer, A.J., Heclo, H. and Adams, C.T. (1990) *Comparative Public Policy* (3rd edn). New York: St Martin's Press.

Held, D. (1987) *Models of Democracy*. Cambridge: Polity Press.

Hemerijck, A. (1993) 'The historical contingencies of Dutch corporatism', unpublished Ph.D. thesis, University of Oxford.

Hemerijck, A., Manow, P. and Kersbergen, K. van (2000) 'Welfare without work? Divergent experiences of reform in Germany and the Netherlands', in S. Kuhnle (ed.), *The Survival of the European Welfare State*. London and New York: Routledge.

Hériteir, A. (1998) 'Institutions, interests and political choice', in R.M. Czada, A. Héritier and H. Keman, *Institutions and Political Choice: on the Limits of Rationality*. Amsterdam: VU-University Press.

Héritier, A. et al. (1994) *Die Veränderung der Staatlichkeit in Europa*. Opladen: Leske & Budrich.

Hermens, F.A. (1941) *Democracy or Anarchy? A Study of Proportional Representation*. South Bend, Ill.: University of Notre Dame Press.

Hesse, K. (1962) *Der unitarische Bundesstaat*. Karlsruhe: Müller.

Hewitt, C. (1977) 'The effect of political democracy and social democracy on equality in industrial societies: a cross-national comparison', *American Sociological Review*, 3: 508–22.

Heywood, A. (1997) *Politics*. Basingstoke: Macmillan.

Hibbs, D.A., Jr. (1973) *Mass Political Violence: A Cross-National Causal Analysis*. New York: Wiley.

Hibbs, D.A., Jr. (1977) 'Political Parties and Macroeconomic Policy', *American Political Science Review*, 71: 1467–87.

Hibbs, D.A., Jr. (1987a) *The Political Economy of Industrial Democracies*. Cambridge, Mass.: Harvard University Press.

Hibbs, D.A., Jr. (1987b) *The American Political Economy*. Cambridge, Mass.: Harvard University Press.

Hibbs, D.A., Jr. (1992) 'Partisan theory after fifteen years', *European Journal of Political Economy*, 8: 361–73.

Hibbs, D.A., Jr. (1994) 'The partisan model of macroeconomic cycles: more theory and evidence for the United States', *Economic and Politics*, 6 (1): 1–23.

Hicks, A.M. (1994) 'The social democratic corporatist model of economic performance in the short- and medium-run perspective', in T. Janoski and A.M. Hicks (eds), *The Comparative Political Economy of the Welfare State*. Cambridge: Cambridge University Press.

Hicks, A. and Misra, J. (1993) 'Political resources and the growth of welfare in affluent capitalist democracies, 1960–1982', *American Journal of Sociology*, 99: 668–710.

Hicks, A., Misra, J. and Ng, T.N. (1995) 'The programmatic emergence of the social security state', *American Sociological Review*, 60 (3): 329–49.

Hicks, A. and Swank, D.H. (1984) 'On the political economy of welfare expansion: a comparative analysis of 18 advanced capitalist democracies, 1960–1971', *Comparative Political Studies*, 17: 81–119.

Hicks, A., Swank, D.H. and Ambuhl, M. (1989) 'Welfare expansion revisited: policy routines and their mediation by party, class and crisis, 1957–1982', *European Journal of Political Research*, 17: 401–30.

Hicks, A.M. and Swank, D.H. (1992) 'Politics, institutions, and welfare spending in industrialized democracies, 1960–82', *American Political Science Review*, 86: 658–74.

Higgins, W. and Apple, N. (1981) *Class Mobilization and Economic Policy: Struggles over Full Employment in Britain and Sweden*. Stockholm: Arbetslivcentrum.

Hirst, P. and Thompson, G. (1996) *Globalization in Question*. Cambridge: Polity.

Hirter, H. (1988) 'Koordinierte Verkehrspolitik. Die Entstehung und Verwirklichung einer Gesamtkonzeption', in P. Hablützel, H. Hirter and B. Junker (eds), *Schweizerische Politik in Wissenschaft und Praxis. Festschrift für Prof. Dr. Peter Gilg*. Bern: Forschungszentrum für schweizerische Politik.

Hix, S. (1999) *The Political System of the European Union*. Basingstoke: Macmillan/ New York: St Martin's Press.

Hockerts, H.G. (1980) *Sozialpolitische Entscheidungen im Nachkriegsdeutschland. Alliierte und deutsche Sozialversicherungspolitik 1945 bis 1957*. Stuttgart: Klett-Cotta.

Hofferbert, R.I. (1966) 'The relation between public policy and some structural and environmental variables in the American states', *American Political Science Review*, 60 (1): 73–82

Hofferbert, R.I and Cingranelli, D.L. (1996) 'Public policy and administration: comparative policy analysis', in R.E. Goodin and H.-D. Klingemann (eds), *A New Handbook of Political Science*. Oxford: Oxford University Press.

Hollingsworth, J.R., Schmitter, P. and Streeck, W. (eds) (1994) *Governing Capitalist Economies*. New York: Oxford University Press.

Höpner, M. (1997) *Politisch koordinierte Oekonomien 1973–1996*. Düsseldorf: Wirtschafts- und Sozialwissenschaftliche Institut (WSI-Diskussionspapier Nr. 42).

Huber, E., Ragin, C. and Stephens, J.D. (1993) 'Social democracy, Christian democracy, constitutional structure, and the welfare state', *American Journal of Sociology*, 99: 711–49.

Huber, E. and Stephens, J.D. (1993) 'Political parties and public pensions. A quantitative analysis', *Acta Sociologica*, 36: 309–25.

Huntington, S.P. (1968) *Political Order in Changing Societies*. New Haven, Conn.: Yale University Press.

Huntington, S.P. (1984) 'Will more countries become democratic?', *Political Science Quarterly*, 99 (2): 193–218.

Huntington, S.P. (1991) *The Third Wave: Democratization in the Late Twentieth Century*. Norman: University of Oklahoma Press.

Huyse, L. (1970) *Passiviteit, Pacificatie en Verzuiling in de Belgische Politiek: Een Sociologische Studie*. Antwerpen: Standaard Wetenschappelyke Uitgeverly.

Ignazi, Piero (1992) 'The silent counter-revolution: hypotheses on the emergence of extreme rightwing parties in Europe', *European Journal of Political Research*, 22 (1): 3–34.

ILO (1992) *The Cost of Social Security: Thirteenth International Inquiry, 1984–1986*. Geneva: ILO.

ILO (1997) *World Labour Report 1997–98: Industrial Relations, Democracy and Social Stability*. Geneva: ILO.

ILO (2000) *World Labour Report 2000: Income Security and Social Protection in a Changing World*. Geneva: ILO.

Imbeau, L. (1988) 'Aid and ideology', *European Journal of Political Research*, 16 (1): 3–28.

Immergut, E.M. (1992) *Health Politics. Interests and Institutions in Western Europe*. Cambridge: Cambridge University Press.

Inglehart, R. (1977) *The Silent Revolution: Changing Values and Political Styles among Western Publics*. Princeton, N.J.: Princeton University Press.

Inglehart, R. (1990) *Culture Shift in Advanced Industrial Society*. Princeton, N.J.: Princeton University Press.

Inglehart, R. (1997) *Modernization and Postmodernization. Cultural, Economic and Political Change in 43 Societies*. Princeton, N.J.: Princeton University Press.

Inglehart, R. and Klingemann, H.D. (1976) 'Party identification, ideological preference and the left-right dimension among Western mass publics', in I. Budge, I. Crewe and D. Farlie (eds) (1976) *Party Identification and Beyond. Representation of Voting and Party Competition*. London: John Wiley.

Inter-Parliamentary Union (IPU) (1995) *Women in Parliaments 1945–1995: A World Statistical Survey*. Geneva: IPU.

Inter-Parliamentary Union (IPU) (annually) *Chronicle of Parliamentary Elections and Developments*. Geneva: IPU; also available at: http:://ipu.org/english/parlweb.htm

Jackman, R.W. (1975) *Politics and Social Equality: A Comparative Analysis*. New York: Wiley.

Jackman, R.W. (1986) 'Elections and the democratic class struggle', *World Politics*, 39: 123–46.

Jackman, R. (1987) 'Political institutions and voter turnout in the industrial democracies', *American Political Science Review*, 81 (2): 405–23.

Jackman, R. and Miller, R. (1995) 'Voter turnout in the industrial democracies during the 1980s', *Comparative Political Studies*, 27 (4): 467–92.

Jaggers, K. and Gurr, T.R. (1995) 'Tracking democracy's Third Wave with the Polity III data,' *Journal of Peace Research*, 32 (4): 469–82.

Janoski, T. and Hicks, A.M. (eds) (1994) *The Comparative Political Economy of the Welfare State*. Cambridge: Cambridge University Press.

Jesse, E. (1994) 'Wahlsysteme und Wahlrecht', in O. Gabriel and F. Brettschneider (eds), *Die EU-Staaten im Vergleich. Strukturen, Prozesse, Politikinhalte*. Opladen: Westdeutscher Verlag.

Jessop, B. (1996) 'Post-Fordism and the state', in B. Greve (ed.), *Comparative Welfare Systems: The Scandinavian Model in a Period of Change*. New York: St Martin's Press.

Jones, M.P. (1995) *Electoral Laws and the Survival of Presidential Democracies*. South Bend, Ill: University of Notre Dame Press.

Kaase, M. and Newton, K. (eds) (1995) *Beliefs in Government*. Oxford: Oxford University Press.

Kalleberg, L. (1966) 'The logic of comparison: a methodological note on the comparative study of political systems', *World Politics*, 12 (1): 69–82.

Kaltefleiter, W. (1970) *Die Funktionen des Staatsoberhauptes in der Parlamentarischen Demokratie*. Köln: Westdeutscher Verlag.

Kangas, O. (1991) *The Politics of Social Rights. Studies on the Dimensions of Sickness Insurance in OECD Countries*. Stockholm: Swedish Institute for Social Research.

Katz, R.S. and Mair, P. (eds) (1992) *Party Organizations. A Data Handbook on Party Organizations in Western Democracies, 1960–90*. London: Sage.

Katzenstein, P.J. (1985) *Small States in World Markets: Industrial Policy in Europe*. Ithaca, N.Y.: Cornell University Press.

Katzenstein, P.J. (1987) *Policy and Politics in West Germany. The Growth of a Semisovereign State*. Philadelphia: Temple University Press.

Keeler, J.T. (1993) 'Opening the windows for reform', *Comparative Political Studies*, 25: 433–86.

Keman, H. (1984) 'Politics, policies and consequences: a cross national analysis of public policy formation (1967–1981)', *European Journal of Political Research*, 12 (2): 147–70.

Keman, H. (1987) 'Welfare and warfare. Critical options and conscious choice in public policy', in F.G. Castles, F. Lehner, M.G. Schmidt (eds), *Managing Mixed Economies*. Berlin and New York: De Gruyter.

Keman, H. (1988) *The Development Toward Surplus Welfare: Social Democratic Politics and Policies in Advanced Capitalist Democracies (1965–1984)*. Amsterdam: CT Press.

Keman, H. (1990) 'Social democracy and the politics of welfare statism', *West European Politics*, 17 (4): 17–34.

Keman, H. (ed.) (1993a) *Comparative Politics.* Amsterdam: VU University Press.

Keman, H. (1993b) 'The politics of managing the mixed economy', in H. Keman (ed.) (1993a) *Comparative Politics.* Amsterdam: VU University Press.

Keman, H. (1994) 'The search for the centre: pivot parties in West European party systems', *West European Politics,* 17 (4): 124–48.

Keman, H. (1996) 'The low countries. Confrontation and coalition in segmented societies', in J. Colomer (ed.) (1996a) *Political Institutions in Europe.* London: Routledge.

Keman, H. (ed.) (1997a) *The Politics of Problem-Solving in Postwar Democracies.* Basingstoke: Macmillan.

Keman, H. (1997b) 'The politics of problem-solving in postwar democracies: institutionalising conflict and consensus in western Europe', in H. Keman (ed.) (1997a) *The Politics of Problem-Solving in Postwar Democracies.* Basingstoke: Macmillan.

Keman, H. (1997c) 'Approaches to the analysis of institutions', in B. Steunenberg and F. van Vught (eds), *Political Institutions and Public Policy.* Dordrecht: Kluwer.

Keman, H. (1998) 'The waning of solidarity? Securing work and income and welfare statism at present', in H. Cavanna (ed.), *Challenges to the Welfare State: Internal and External Dynamics for Change.* Cheltenham and Northampton, Mass.: Edward Elgar.

Keman, H. (1999) 'Political stability in divided societies: a rational-institutional explanation', *Australian Journal of Political Science,* 34 (2): 249–68.

Keman, H. (2000a) 'Federalism and policy performance. A conceptual and empirical inquiry', in U. Wachendorfer-Schmidt (ed.), *Federalism and Political Performance.* London: Routledge.

Keman, H. (2000b) 'The structure of government', in M. Sekuchi (ed.), *Encyclopedia of Life Support Systems.* Oxford: Oxford University Press.

Keman, H. and Pennings, P. (1995) 'Managing political and societal conflict in democracies: Do consensus and corporatism matter?' *British Journal of Political Science,* 25 (2): 271–81.

Keman, H. and van Dijk, T. (1987) 'Policy formation as a strategy to overcome the economic crisis', in H. Keman, H. Paloheimo and P.F. Whiteley (eds), *Coping With the Economic Crisis.* London: Sage.

Keman, H., Paloheimo, H. and Whitely, P.F. (eds) (1987) *Coping With the Economic Crisis.* London: Sage.

Keman, H., Woldendorp, J. and Braun, D. (eds) (1985) *Het Neo-Korporatisme als Nieuwe Politieke Strategie.* Amsterdam: CT-Press.

Kennedy, P. (1987) *The Rise and Fall of Great Powers.* New York: Vintage Books.

Kenworthy, L. (2000) *Qualitative Indicators of Corporatism: A Survey and Assessment* (discussion paper 00/4). Cologne: Max-Planck Institut für Gesellschaftsforschung.

Kerr, C. (1960) *Industrialism and Industrial Man.* Cambridge, Mass.: Harvard University Press.

Kerr, C., Dunlop, F., Harbison, H. and Myers, C.A. (1973) *Industrialism and Industrial Man.* London: Penguin.

Kersbergen, K. van (1995) *Social Capitalism. A Study of Christian Democracy and the Welfare State.* London: Routledge.

Kersbergen, K. van (1997) 'Between collectivism and individualism: the politics of the centre', in H. Keman (ed) (1997a) *The Politics of Problem-Solving in Postwar Democracies.* Basingstoke: Macmillan.

Kersbergen, K. van (1999) 'Contemporary Christian Democracy and the demise of the politics of mediation', in H. Kitschelt, G. Marks, P. Lange and J.D. Stephens (eds), (1999) *Continuity and Change in Contemporary Capitalism.* Cambridge: Cambridge University Press.

Kersbergen, K. van (2000) 'The declining resistance of national welfare states to change?', in S. Kuhnle (ed.), *The Survival of the European Welfare State*. London and New York: Routledge.

Kim, H. and Fording, R.C. (1998) 'Voter ideology in Western democracies, 1946–1989', *European Journal of Political Research*, 33 (1): 73–97.

King, A. (1975) 'Overload: problems of governing in the 1970s', *Political Studies*, 23 (2–3): 283–96.

Kirchheimer, O. (1964) 'The waning of opposition', in R. Macridis and B.E. Brown (eds), *Comparative Politics*. Homewood, Ill.: Dorsey Press.

Kirchheimer, O. (1966a) 'The transformation of Western European party systems', in J. LaPalombara and M. Weiner (eds) (1966) *Political Parties and Political Development*. Princeton, N.J.: Princeton University Press.

Kirchheimer, O. (1966b) 'Germany: the vanishing opposition', in R.A. Dahl (ed.) (1966) *Political Oppositions in Western Democracies*. New Haven, Conn.: Yale University Press.

Kirchner, E.J. (ed.) (1988) *Liberal Parties in Western Europe*. Cambridge: Cambridge University Press.

Kitschelt, H. (1997) 'European party systems: continuity and change', in M. Rhodes, P. Heywood and V. Wright (eds), *Developments in West European Politics*. Basingstoke: Macmillan.

Kitschelt, H., Lange, P., Marks, G. and Stephens, J.D. (eds) (1999) *Continuity and Change in Contemporary Capitalism*. Cambridge: Cambridge University Press.

Klingemann, H.-D. (1987) 'Election programmes in West Germany: 1949–1980, explorations in the nature of political controversy', in I. Budge, D. Robertson and D. Hearl (eds) (1987) *Ideology, Strategy and Party Change*. Cambridge: Cambridge University Press.

Klingemann, H.-D., Hofferbert, R.I. and Budge, I. and others (1994) *Parties, Policies and Democracy*. Boulder, Colo.: Westview Press.

Knutsen, O. (1995a) 'The impact of old politics and new politics values orientations on party choice – a comparative study', *Journal of Public Policy*, 15: 1–64.

Knutsen, O. (1995b) 'Party choice', in J.W. van Deth and E. Scarbrough (eds), *The Impact of Values*. Oxford: Oxford University Press.

Kohl, J. (1985) *Staatsausgaben in Westeuropa*. Frankfurt a.M.: Campus.

Korpi, W. (1978) *The Working Class in Welfare Capitalism*. London: Routledge and Kegan Paul.

Korpi, W. (1983) *The Democratic Class Struggle*. London: Routledge and Kegan Paul.

Korpi, W. (1989) 'Power, politics, and state autonomy in the development of social citizenship: social rights during sickness in eighteen OECD countries since 1930', *American Sociological Review*, 54: 309–28.

Krämer, J. and Rattinger, H. (1997) 'The proximity and the directional theories of issue voting: comparative results for the USA and Germany', *European Journal of Political Research*, 33 (1): 1–29.

Kriesi, H. (1995) *Le Système Politique Suisse*. Paris: Economica.

Kriesi, H. et al. (ed.) (1995) *New Social Movements in Western Europe: A Comparative Analysis*. London: UCL Press.

Kriesi, H. (1997) 'The transformation of cleavage politics', *European Journal of Political Research*, 33 (2): 165–85.

Krouwel, A. (1999) *The catch-all party in Western Europe 1945–1990: a study in arrested development*. PhD dissertation, Vrije Universiteit Amsterdam.

Kunz, Volker (1999) *Parteien und kommunale Haushalte im Städtevergleich*. Opladen: Leske & Budrich.

Kurzer, P. (1993) *Business and Banking. Political Change and Economic Integration in Western Europe.* Ithaca and London: Cornell University Press.

Kvist, J. (1999) 'Welfare reform in the nordic countries in the 1990s: using fuzzy-set theory to assess conformity to ideal types', *Journal of European Social Policy,* 9 (3): 231–25.

Landman, T. (2000) *Issues and Methods in Comparative Politics: An Introduction.* London: Routledge.

Lane (1996) *The Public Sector: Concepts, Models and Approaches.* London: Sage.

Lane, J.-E. (1996) '"Losing touch" in a democracy: demands versus needs', in J. Hayward (ed.), *Élitism, Populism, and European Politics.* Oxford: Clarendon Press.

Lane, J.-E. and Ersson, S.O. (1994) *Comparative Politics: An Introduction and New Approach.* Oxford: Polity Press.

Lane, J.-E. and Ersson, S.O. (1997) 'The institutions of Konkordanz and Corporatism: how closely are they connected?', *Revue Suisse de Science Politique,* 3 (1): 5–29.

Lane, J.-E. and Ersson, S.O. (1998) *Politics and Society in Western Europe.* London: Sage.

Lane, J.-E. and Ersson, S.O. (2000) *The New Institutional Politics: Performance and Outcomes.* London: Routledge.

Lane, J.-E., Mackay, D.H. and Newton, K. (1995) *Political Data Handbook of OECD Countries.* Oxford: Oxford University Press.

LaPalombara, J. (ed.) (1963) *Bureaucracies and Political Development.* Princeton, N.J.: Princeton University Press.

LaPalombara, J. and Weiner, M. (eds) (1966) *Political Parties and Political Development.* Princeton, N.J.: Princeton University Press.

Larkey, P.D., Stolp, C. and Winer, M. (1981) 'Theorizing about the growth of government: a research assessment', *Journal of Public Policy,* 1 (2): 157–220.

Laver, M. (1981) *The Politics of Private Desires.* Harmondsworth: Penguin.

Laver, M. (ed.) (2001) *Estimating the Policy Position of Political Actors.* London and New York: Routledge.

Laver, M. and Budge, I. (1992) *Party Policy and Government Coalition.* Basingstoke: Macmillan.

Laver, M. and Hunt, B. (1992) *Policy and Party Competition.* New York and London: Routledge.

Laver, M. and Schofield, N. (1990) *Multiparty Government: The Politics of Coalition in Europe.* Oxford: Oxford University Press.

Laver, M. and Shepsle, K.E. (eds) (1994) *Cabinet Ministers and Parliamentary Government.* Cambridge: Cambridge University Press.

Laver, M. and Shepsle, K.E. (1996) *Making and Breaking Governments.* Cambridge: Cambridge University Press.

Lawson, K. and Merkl, P.H. (eds) (1988) *When Parties Fail: Emerging Alternative Organizations.* Princeton, N.J.: Princeton University Press.

Layard, R., Nickell, S. and Jackman, R. (1991) *Unemployment: Macroeconomic Performance and the Labour Market.* Oxford: Oxford University Press.

LeDuc, L., Niemi, R.G. and Norris, P. (eds) (1996) *Comparing Democracies: Elections and Voting in Global Perspective.* Thousand Oaks, Calif.: Sage.

LeGrand, J. (1982) *The Strategy of Equality.* London: Allen and Unwin.

Lehmbruch, G. (1967) *Proporzdemokratie. Politisches System und politische Kultur in der Schweiz und Österreich.* Tübingen: Mohr (Siebeck).

Lehmbruch, G. (1974) 'A non-competitive pattern of conflict management in liberal democracies: the case of Switzerland, Austria and Lebanon', in K.D. McRae (ed.) (1974) *Consociational Democracy: Political Accommodation in Segmented Societies*. Toronto: McClelland and Steward.

Lehmbruch, G. (1977) 'Liberal corporatism and party government', *Comparative Political Studies*, 10 (1): 91–126.

Lehmbruch, G. (1979) 'Liberal corporatism and party government', in P.C. Schmitter and G. Lehmbruch (eds) (1979) *Trends Towards Corporatist Intermediation*. London: Sage.

Lehmbruch, G. (1984) 'Concertation and the structure of corporatist networks', in J.H. Goldthorpe (ed.) (1984) *Order and Conflict in Contemporary Capitalism*. Oxford: Oxford University Press.

Lehmbruch, G. (1989) 'Marktreformstrategien bei alternierender Parteiregierung: Eine vergleichende institutionelle Analyse', in T. Ellwein et al. (eds), *Jahrbuch zur Staats- und Verwaltungswissenschaft*, vol. 3. Baden-Baden: Nomos.

Lehmbruch, G. (1993) 'Consociational democracy and corporatism in Switzerland', *Publius: The Journal of Federalism*, 23 (2): 43–60.

Lehmbruch, G. (1996) 'Die korporative Verhandlungsdemokratie in Westmitteleuropa', in K. Armingeon and P. Sciarini (eds), *Deutschland, Österreich und die Schweiz im Vergleich. Sonderheft der Revue Suisse de Science Politique*, 2 (4): 277–303.

Lehmbruch, G. (1998) 'The organization of society: administration strategies and policy networks', in R.M. Czada, A. Heritier and H. Keman (eds), *Institutions and Political Choice: on the Limits of Rationality*. Amsterdam: VU-University Press.

Lehmbruch, G. (1999) 'Negotiated democracy, consociationalism and corporatism in German politics: The legacy of the Westphalian Peace', in T. Ertman (ed.), *The Fate of Consociationalism*. Cambridge: Cambridge University Press.

Lehmbruch, G. (2000) 'Segmented corporatism, the party system, and welfare retrenchment in Germany', in G. Lehmbruch and F. van Waarden (eds), *Renegotiating the Welfare State*. London: Routledge and Kegan Paul.

Lehmbruch, G. and Schmitter, P.C. (eds) (1982) *Patterns of Corporatist Policy Making*. London and Beverly Hills: Sage.

Leibfried, S. (1993) "Sozialstaat" oder "Wohlfahrtsgesellschaft"? Thesen zu einem japanisch-deutschen Sozialpolitikvergleich', *Soziale Welt*, 45: 389–410.

Lenhardt, G. and Offe, C. (1984) 'Social policy and the theory of the state', in C. Offe *Contradictions of the Welfare State*. London: Hutchinson.

Lepsius, M.R. (1978) 'From fragmented party democracy to government by emergency decree and National Socialist takeover: Germany,' in J. Linz and A. Stepan (eds) (1978) *The Breakdown of Democratic Regimes*. 4 vols. Baltimore: Johns Hopkins University Press.

Lerner, D. (1958) *The Passing of Traditional Society: Modernizing the Middle East*. Glencoe, Ill.: Free Press.

Lessenich, S. (1994) 'Three Worlds of the Welfare Capitalism – oder vier? Strukturwandel arbeits- und sozialpolitischer Regulierungsmuster in Spanien', *Politische Vierteljahresschrift Zeitschrift*, 35 (2): 224–44.

Lessenich, S. and Ostner, L. (eds) (1998) *Welten des Wohlfahrtskapitalismus*. Frankfurt am Main: Campus Verlag.

Lessmann, S. (1987) *Budgetary Politics and Elections*. Berlin and New York: Walter de Gruyter.

Levy, J.D. (1999) 'Vice into virtue? Progressive politics and welfare reform in continental Europe', *Politics and Society*, 27 (2): 239–74.

Lewis, P.G., Potter, D.C. and Castles, F.G. (eds) (1978) *The Practice of Comparative Politics*. London: Longman.

Lijphart, A. (1968) 'Typologies of democratic systems', *Comparative Political Studies*, 1: 3–44.

Lijphart, A. (1975) *Politics of Accommodation: Pluralism and Democracy in the Netherlands* (2nd edn). Berkeley: University of California Press.

Lijphart, A. (1977) *Democracy in Plural Societies: A Comparative Exploration*. New Haven, Conn.: Yale University Press.

Lijphart, A. (1984) *Democracies: Patterns of Majoritarian and Consensus Government in Twenty-One Countries*. New Haven and London: Yale University Press.

Lijphart, A. (1989) 'From the politics of accommodation to adversarial politics in the Netherlands: a reassessment', *West European Politics*, 12 (1): 139–53.

Lijphart, A. (1992) *Parliamentary versus Presidential Government*. Oxford: Oxford University Press.

Lijphart, A. (1993) *Electoral Systems and Party Systems in 26 Democracies*. Oxford: Oxford University Press.

Lijphart, A. (1994) 'Democracies: forms, performance, and constitutional engineering', *European Journal of Political Research*, 25: 1–17.

Lijphart, A. (1996) 'The Puzzle of Indian Democracy: A Consociational Interpretation', *American Political Science Review*, 90 (2): 258–68.

Lijphart, A. (1997) 'Changement et Continuité dans la Théorie Consociative', *Revue Internationale de Politique Comparée*, 4 (3): 679–97.

Lijphart, A. (1999) *Patterns of Democracy: Government Form and Performance in Thirty-Six Countries*. New Haven: Yale University Press.

Lijphart, A, Bruneau T.C., Diamondoros, P.N. and Gunther, R. (1988) 'A Mediterranean model of democracy? The Southern European democracies in comparative perspective', *West European Politics*, 11 (1): 7–25.

Lijphart, A. and Crépaz, M.M.L. (1991) 'Corporatism and consensus democracy in eighteen countries: conceptual and empirical linkages', *British Journal of Political Science*, 21: 235–46.

Linder, W. (1994) *Swiss Democracy. Possible Solutions to Conflict in Multicultural Societies*. Basingstoke: Macmillan.

Linz, J.J. (1990) 'The perils of presidentialism', *Journal of Democracy*, 1: 51–69.

Linz, J.J. (1994) 'Presidential or parliamentary democracy: does it make a difference?', in J.J. Linz and A.A. Valenzuela (eds) (1994) *The Failure of Presidential Democracy*. Baltimore: Johns Hopkins University Press.

Linz, J.J. and Stepan, A. (eds) (1978) *The Breakdown of Democratic Regimes*. 4 vols. Baltimore: Johns Hopkins University Press.

Linz, J.J. and Valenzuala, A.A. (eds) (1994) *The Failure of Presidential Democracy*. Baltimore: Johns Hopkins University Press.

Lipset, S.M. (1959) *Political Man*. Garden City, N.Y.: Doubleday.

Lipset, S.M. and Rokkan, S. (1967a) 'Cleavage structures, party systems and voter alignments: an introduction', in S.M. Lipset and S. Rokkan (eds) (1967b) *Party Systems and Voter Alignments: Crossnational Perspectives*. New York: Free Press.

Lipset, S.M. and Rokkan, S. (eds) (1967b) *Party Systems and Voter Alignments: Crossnational Perspectives*. New York: Free Press.

LIS (Luxembourg Income Study) (1998) LIS inequality indices; available at: http://lisweb.ceps.lu/keyfigures.htm.

Lively, J. (1978) *Democracy, Consensus and Social Contract*. London: Sage.

Lowell, A.L. (1896) *Government and Parties in Continental Europe*. London: Longman.

Luhmann, N. (1988) *Die Wirtschaft der Gesellschaft*. Frankfurt a.M.: Suhrkamp.

Lupia, A. and McCubbins, M.D. (1998) *The Democratic Dilemma: Can Citizens Learn What They Need to Know?* New York: Cambridge University Press.

Lutz, D.S. (1994) 'Toward a theory of constitutional amendment', *American Political Science Review*, 88: 355–70.

Mabbett, D. (1995) *Trade, Employment and Welfare. A Comparative Study of Trade and Labour Market Policies in Sweden and New Zealand, 1880–1980*. Oxford: Clarendon Press.

Mackie, T. and Rose, R. (1991) *The International Almanac of Electoral History* (2nd edn). London: Macmillan.

Macridis, R.C. (1955) *The Study of Comparative Government*. New York: Random House.

Macridis, R.C. (1986) *Modern Political Regimes*. Boston: Little Brown.

Macridis, R.C. and Brown, B.E. (1961) *Comparative Politics: Notes and Readings*. Homewood, Ill.: Dorsey Press.

Macridis, R.C. and Cox, R. (1953) 'Research in comparative politics'. (Report of the SSRC Inter-university Research Seminar on Comparative Politics, Evanston, 1952), *American Political Science Review*, 47: 641–75.

Macridis, R.C. and Ward, R.C. (eds) (1963) *Modern Political Systems*. 2 vols. Englewood Cliffs, N.J.: Prentice Hall.

Maddex, R.L. (1996) *Constitutions of the World*. London: Routledge.

Mair, P. (ed.) (1990) *The West European Party System*. Oxford: Oxford University Press.

Mair, P. (1995) 'Political parties, popular legitimacy and public privilege', *West European Politics*, 18 (3): 40–57.

Mair, P. (1996) 'Party systems and structures of competition', in L. LeDuc, R.G. Niemi and P. Norris (eds) (1996) *Comparing Democracies: Elections and Voting in Global Perspective*. Thousand Oaks, Calif.: Sage.

Mair, P. (1997) *Party System Change: Approaches and Interpretations*. Oxford: Clarendon Press.

Mair, P. (1999) 'New political parties in long-established party systems: How successful are they?', in E. Beukel, K.K. Klausen and P.E. Mouritzen (eds), *Elites, Parties and Democracy: Festschrift for Mogens N. Pedersen*. Odense: Odense University Press.

Mair, P. (2001) 'The freezing hypothesis: an evaluation', in L. Karvonen and S. Kuhnle (eds), *Party Systems and Voter Alignments: Looking Back, Looking Forward*. London: Routledge.

Mair, P., Müller, W.C. and Plasser, F. (eds) (1999) *Parteien auf komplexen Wählermärkten: Reaktionsstrategien politischer Parteien in Westeuropa*. Wien: Signum Verlag.

March, J.G. and Olsen, J.P. (1989) *Rediscovering Institutions: The Organizational Basis of Politics*. New York: Free Press.

March, J.G. and Olsen, J.P. (1995) *Democratic Governance*, New York: Free Press.

Marsh, M. and Franklin, M. (1996) 'The foundations: unanswered questions from the study of European elections, 1979–1994', in C. van der Eijk and M.N. Franklin (eds) (1996) *Choosing Europe? The European Electorate and National Politics in the Face of Union*. Ann Arbor: University of Michigan Press.

Marsh, M. and Norris, P. (eds) (1997) 'Political representation in the European parliament', Special issue of the *European Journal of Political Research*, 32 (2).

Marshall, T.N. (1950) *Citizenship and Social Class and Other Essays*. Cambridge: Cambridge University Press.

Mau, S. (1998) 'Zwischen Moralitaet und Eigeninteresse', *Politik und Zeitgeschichte*, B 34–35.

Mayntz, R. and Scharpf, F.W. (eds) (1995) *Gesellschaftliche Selbstregelung und politische Steuerung*. Frankfurt a.M.: Campus.

McDonald, M.D., Budge, I. and Hofferbert, R.I. (1999) 'Party mandate theory and time series analysis', *Electoral Studies*, 18: 587–96.

McLean, I. (1987) *Public Choice*. Oxford: Oxford University Press.

McRae, K.D. (ed.) (1974) *Consociational Democracy: Political Accommodation in Segmented Societies*. Toronto: McClelland and Steward.

Merkel, W. (1993) *Ende der Sozialdemokratie?* Frankfurt a.M.: Campus.

Merkel, W. (1999) *Systemtransformation. Eine Einführung in Theorie und Empirie der Transformationsforschung*. Opladen: Leske & Budrich.

Miller, W. and Stokes, D. (1963) 'Constituency influence in Congress', *American Political Science Review*, 57 (1): 5–23.

Milner, H. (1989) *Sweden: Social Democracy in Practice*. Oxford: Oxford University Press.

MIRE (1997) *Comparing Social Welfare Systems in Southern Europe*. Paris: Mission Recherche, Ministère de l'Emploi et de la Solidarité.

Mishra, R. (1984) *The Welfare State in Crisis. Social Thought and Social Change*. Brighton: Wheatsheaf.

Mitchell, D. (1990) *Income transfer systems: a comparative study using microdata*, unpublished PhD dissertation, Australian National University.

Moon, J. (1993) *Innovative Leadership in Democracy. Policy Change Under Thatcher*. Aldershot: Dartmouth.

Moon, J. (1995) 'Innovative leadership and policy change: lessons from Thatcher', *Governance*, 8: 1–25.

Moore, B. (1966) *Social Origins of Dictatorship and Democracy: Lord and Peasant in the Making of the Modern World*. Boston: Beacon Press.

Morlino, L. (1998) *Democracy Between Consolidation and Crisis: Parties, Groups, and Citizens in Southern Europe*. Oxford: Oxford University Press.

Moses, J.W. (1994) 'Abdication from national policy autonomy. What's left to leave?', *Politics & Society*, 22 (2): 125–48.

Mudde, Cas (2000) *The Ideology of the Extreme Right*. Manchester: Manchester University Press.

Mueller, D.C. (1989) *Public Choice II*: a revised edition, Cambridge: Cambridge University Press.

Muller, E.N. and Seligson, M.A. (1987) 'Inequality and insurgency', *American Political Science Review*, 61: 425–51.

Müller-Rommel, F. (1998) 'The new challengers: Greens and Rightwing populist parties in Western Europe', *European Review*, 6 (2): 191–202.

Myles, J. (1989) *Old Age in the Welfare State: The Political Economy of Public Pensions* (revised edn). Lawrence: University Press of Kansas.

Myles, J. (1996) 'When markets fail: social welfare in Canada and the United States', in G. Esping-Andersen (ed.), *Welfare States in Transition: National Adaptations in Global Economies*. London: Sage.

Myles, J. and Quadagno, J. (1997) 'Recent trends in public pension reform: a comparative view', in K.G. Banting and R. Boardway (eds), *Reform of Retirement Income Policy: International and Canadian Perspectives*. Kingston: School of Policy Studies, Queen's University.

Nagel, J.H. (1994) 'What political scientists can learn from the 1993 electoral reform in New Zealand', *Political Science & Politics*, 27: 525–29.

Naschold, F. and Vroom, B. de (eds) (1994) *Regulating Employment and Welfare. Company and National Policies of Labour Force Participation at the End of Worklife in Industrial Countries*. Berlin: Walter de Gruyter.

Neidhart, L. (1970) *Plebiszit und pluralitäre Demokratie. Eine Analyse der Funktionen des schweizerischen Gesetzesreferendums.* Bern: Francke.

Neubauer, D.E. (1967) 'Some conditions of democracy', *American Political Science Review,* 61 (4): 1002–9.

Neumann, S. (ed.) (1956) *Modern Political Parties: Approaches to the Study of Comparative Politics.* Chicago: University of Chicago Press.

Niedermayer, O. and Schmitt, H. (eds) (1994) *Wahlen und Europaische Einigung.* Opladen: Westdeutscher Verlag.

Niedermayer, O. and Sinnott, R. (1995) *Public Opinion and Internationalized Governance.* Oxford: Oxford University Press.

Norris, P. (1987) *Politics and Sexual Equality. The Comparative Position of Women in Western Democracies.* Boulder, Colo.: Rienner.

Norris, P. (ed.) (1999) *Critical Citizens: Global Support for Democratic Governance.* New York: Oxford University Press.

North, D. (1990) *Institutions, Institutional Change and Economic Performance.* Cambridge: Cambridge University Press.

Notermans, T. (1993) 'The abdication from national policy autonomy: Why the macroeconomic policy regime has become so unfavorable to labor', *Politics & Society,* 21 (2): 133–67.

Nozick, R. (1974) *Anarchy, State, and Utopia.* Oxford: Blackwell.

Nullmeier, F. and Rüb, F.W. (1993) *Die Transformation der Sozialpolitik.* Frankfurt a.M.: Campus.

Oatley, T. (1999) 'How constraining is capital mobility? The partisan hypothesis in an open economy', *American Journal of Political Science,* 43 (4): 1003–27.

O'Donnell, G., Schmitter, Ph.C. and Whitehead, L. (eds) (1986) *Transitions from Authoritarian Rule.* 4 vols. Baltimore: Johns Hopkins.

O'Connor, J. (1973) *The Fiscal Crisis of the State.* New York: St Martin's Press.

O'Connor, J. (1988) 'Convergence or divergence? Change in welfare effort in OECD countries, 1960–1980', *European Journal of Political Research,* 16: 277–99.

O'Connor, J.S. (1990) 'Definition and measurement of welfare effort and its correlates in cross-national analysis. A reply to Pampel and Stryker', *British Journal of Sociology,* 41: 25–8.

OECD (1981) *The Welfare State in Crisis.* Paris: OECD.

OECD (1982–93) *Economic Surveys: Greece.* Paris: OECD.

OECD (1996) 'Ageing in OECD countries: a critical policy challenge', *Social Policy Studies,* No. 20, Paris.

OECD (1996–2000) *Employment Outlook.* (various issues). Paris: OECD.

OECD (1997a) *Historical Statistics 1960–1995.* Paris: OECD.

OECD (1997b) *Economic Outlook 62.* Paris: OECD.

OECD (1998) *OECD in Figures: Statistics on the Member Countries.* Paris: OECD.

OECD (1999) *OECD Historical Statistics 1960–1997.* Paris: OECD.

Offe, C. (1972) 'Advanced capitalism and the welfare state', *Politics and Society,* 4: 479–88.

Ohmae, K. (1991) *The Borderless World: Power and Strategy in the Interlinked Economy.* New York: HarperCollins.

Olsen, J. (1998) 'Political science and organization theory: parallel agendas but mutual disregard', in Czada et al. (eds), *Institutions and Political Choice: On the Limits of Rationality.* Amsterdam: VU-University Press.

Olson, M. (1965) *The Logic of Collective Action: Public Goods and the Theory of Groups.* Cambridge, Mass: Harvard University Press.

Olson, M. (1982) *The Rise and Decline of Nations: Economic Growth, Stagflation, and Social Rigidities.* New Haven and London: Yale University Press.

Olson, M. (1986) 'An appreciation of the tests and criticisms', *Scandinavian Political Studies*, 91 (1): 65–80.

Olsson, S.E. (1990) *Social Policy and Welfare State in Sweden.* Lund: Arkiv.

Oppenhuis, E. (1995) *Voting Behavior in Europe.* Amsterdam: Het Spinhuis.

Oppenhuis, E., Eijk, C. van der and Franklin, M.N. (1996) 'The party context: outcomes', in C. van der Eijk and M.N. Franklin (eds) (1996) *Choosing Europe? The European Electorate and National Politics in the Face of Union.* Ann Arbor: University of Michigan Press.

Organski, K. (1965) *The Stages of Political Development.* New York: Knopf.

Orloff, A.S. (1988) 'The political origins of America's belated welfare state', in M. Weir, A.S. Orloff and T. Skocpol (eds), *The Politics of Social Policy in the United States.* Princeton, N.J.: Princeton University Press.

Ostrom, E. (1990) *Governing the Commons: The Evolution of Institutions for Collective Action.* New York: Cambridge University Press.

Overbye, E. (1994) 'Convergence in policy outcomes: social security systems in perspective', *Journal of Public Policy*, 14: 147–74.

Page, E.C. and Wright, V. (eds) (1999) *Bureaucratic Elites in Western European States.* Oxford: Oxford University Press.

Palme, J. (1990) *Pension Rights in Welfare Capitalism. The Development of Old-Age Pensions in 18 OECD Countries, 1930 to 1985.* Stockholm: Swedish Institute for Social Research.

Palme, J. and Wennemo, I. (1997) 'Swedish social security in the 1990s: Reform and Retrenchment', IPSA: 17th World Congress.

Pampel, F.C. and Stryker, R. (1990) 'Age structure, the state, and social welfare spending: a reanalysis', *British Journal of Sociology*, 41: 16–24.

Pampel, F.C. and Williamson, J.B. (1989) *Age, Class, Politics, and the Welfare State.* Cambridge: Cambridge University Press.

Panebianco, A. (1988) *Political Parties: Organization and Power.* Cambridge: Cambridge University Press.

PáŠálasy, D. (1992) *Qui gouverne en Europe?* Paris: Fayard.

Pauly, L.W. (1995) 'Capital mobility, state autonomy and political legitimacy', *Journal of International Affairs*, 48: 369–88.

Pedersen, M.N. (1979) 'The dynamics of European party systems: changing patterns of electoral volatility', *European Journal of Political Research*, 7 (1): 1–26.

Pekkarinen, J. and Pohjola, M. (eds) (1992) *Social Corporatism: A Superior Economic System?* Oxford: Clarendon Press.

Pelassy, D. (1992) *Qui Gouverne en Europe?* Parise: Fayard.

Pempel, T.J. (1982) *Creative Conservatism. Policy and Politics in Japan.* Philadelphia: Temple University Press.

Pennings, P. (1997a) 'Consensus democracy and institutional change', in H. Keman (ed.), *The Politics of Problem-Solving in Postwar Democracies.* Basingstoke: Macmillan.

Pennings, P. (1997b) 'Socioeconomic problem-solving between conflict and consensus', in H. Keman (ed.) *The Politics of Problem-Solving in Postwar Democracy.* Basingstoke: Macmillan.

Pennings, P. (1998) 'The triad of party system change: votes, office and policy', in P. Pennings and J.-E. Lane (eds) (1998) *Comparing Party System Change.* London: Routledge.

Pennings, P. and Hazan, R.Y. (eds) (2001) 'Special issue: democratizing candidate selection: causes and consequences', *Party Politics*, 7 (3): 267–380.

Pennings, P., Keman, H. and Kleinnijenhuis, J. (1999) *Doing Research in Political Science. An Introduction to Comparative Methods and Statistics.* London: Sage.

Pennings, P. and Lane, J.-E. (eds) (1998) *Comparing Party System Change.* London: Routledge.

Peters, B. Guy, Doughtie, J.C. and McCulloch, M.K. (1977) 'Types of democratic systems and types of public policy', *Comparative Politics*, 10 (2): 237–55.

Peters, B. Guy (1996) 'Political institutions: old and new,' in R.E. Goodin and H.-D. Klingemann (eds) (1996) *A New Handbook of Political Science.* Oxford: Oxford University Press.

Peters, B. Guy (1998) *Comparative Politics. Theory and Methods.* Basingstoke: Macmillan.

Peters, B. Guy, Rhodes, R.A.W. and Wright, V. (eds) (2000) *Administering the Summit. Administration of the Core Executive in Developed Countries.* Basingstoke: Macmillan.

Pierson, C. (1991) *Beyond the Welfare State? The New Political Economy of Welfare.* Cambridge: Cambridge University Press.

Pierson, C. (1998) 'Contemporary challenges to welfare state development', *Political Studies*, 46 (4): 777–94.

Pierson, P. (1994) *Dismantling the Welfare State? Reagan, Thatcher, and the Politics of Retrenchment.* Cambridge: Cambridge University Press.

Pierson, P. (1996) 'The new politics of the welfare state', *World Politics*, 48: 143–79.

Pierson, P. (ed.) (2001) *The New Politics of the Welfare State.* Oxford: Oxford University Press.

Pinkey, R. (1993) *Democracy in the Third World.* Buckingham: Open University Press.

Piven, F.F. and Cloward, R.A. (1972) *Regulating the Poor: The Functions of Public Welfare.* London: Tavistock.

Plamenatz, J. (1973) *Democracy and Illusion.* London: Longman.

Pontusson, J. (1988) *Swedish Social Democracy and British Labour: Essays on the Nature and Conditions of Social Democratic Hegemony.* Ithaca, N.Y.: Cornell University Press.

Potter, D.C., Goldblatt, D., Kiloh M. and Lewis P. (eds) (1997) *Democratization.* Cambridge: Polity Press.

Powell, W.W. and DiMaggio, P.J. (1991) *The New Institutionalism in Organizational Research.* Chicago, Ill.: University of Chicago Press.

Pridham, G. (ed.) (1986) *Coalitional Behaviour in Theory and Practice: An Inductive Model for Western Europe.* Cambridge: Cambridge University Press.

Pryor, F.L. (1968) *Public Expenditure in Communist and Capitalist Countries.* London: Allen and Unwin.

Przeworski, A. (1985) *Capitalism and Social Democracy.* Paris: Cambridge University Press.

Przeworski, A. (1987) 'Methods of cross-national research, 1970–1983', in M. Dierkes, H. Weiler and A.B. Antal (eds), *Comparative Policy Research. Learning from Experience.* Aldershot: Gower.

Przeworski, A. (1991) *Democracy and the Market: Political and Economic Reforms in Eastern Europe and Latin America.* Cambridge: Cambridge University Press.

Przeworski, A. and Sprague, J. (1986) *Paper Stones: A History of Electoral Socialism.* Chicago: University of Chicago Press.

Przeworski, A. and Teune, H. (1970) *The Logic of Comparative Social Enquiry.* New York: Wiley.

Putnam, R.D. (1993) *Making Democracy Work. Civic Traditions in Modern Italy.* New York: Princeton University Press.

Putnam, R.D. (1995) 'Bowling alone: America's declining social capital', *Journal of Democracy*, 6 (1): 65–78.

Pye, L.W. (ed.) (1963) *Communications and Political Development*. Princeton, N.J.: Princeton University Press.

Pye, L.W. (1966) *Aspects of Political Development*. Boston: Little Brown.

Pye, L.W. and Verba, S. (eds) (1965) *Political Culture and Political Development*. Princeton, N.J.: Princeton University Press.

Rabinowitz, G. and Macdonald, S.E. (1989) 'A directional theory of issue voting', *American Political Science Review*, 83: 93–121.

Ragin, C.C. (1987) *The Comparative Method: Moving Beyond Qualitative and Quantitative Strategies*. Berkeley: University of California Press.

Ragin, C.C. (ed.) (1991) *Issues and Alternatives in Comparative Social Research*. Leiden: Brill.

Ragin, C.C. (2000) *Fuzzy-Set Social Science*. Chicago and London: University of Chicago Press.

Rawls, J. (1972) *A Theory of Justice*. Oxford: Clarendon Press.

Regini, M. (1997) 'Social institutions and production structure: the italian variety of capitalism in the 1980s', in C. Crouch and W. Streeck (eds), *Political Economy of Modern Capitalism. Mapping Convergence and Diversity*. London: Sage.

Rhodes, M. (1997) 'The welfare state: internal challenges, external constraints', in M. Rhodes, P. Heywood and V. Wright (eds) (1997a) *Developments in West European Politics*. Basingstoke: Macmillan.

Rhodes, M., Heywood, P. and Wright, V. (eds) (1997) *Developments in West European Politics*. Basingstoke: Macmillan.

Rhodes, M., Heywood, P. and Wright, V. (1997b) 'Towards a new Europe?' in M. Rhodes, P. Heywood and V. Wright (eds) (1997a) *Developments in West European Politics*. Basingstoke: Macmillan.

Riker, W.H. (1975) 'Federalism', in F.I. Greenstein and N.W. Polsby (eds), *Governmental Institutions and Processes*. Reading, Mass.: Addison-Wesley.

Rimlinger, G.V. (1971) *Welfare Policy and Industrialization in Europe, America and Russia*. New York: Wiley.

Ringen, S. (1987) *The Possibility of Politics. A Study in the Political Economy of the Welfare State*. Oxford: Clarendon Press.

Roberts (1978) 'The explanation of politics: comparison, strategy and theory', in P.G. Lewis, D.C. Potter and F.G. Castles (eds), *The Practice of Comparative Politics*. London: Longman.

Rokkan, S. (1970) *Citizens, Elections, Parties: Approaches to the Comparative Study of the Processes of Development*. Oslo: Universitetsforlaget.

Rokkan, S. (1975) 'Dimensions of state-formation and nation-building', in Ch. Tilly (ed.) (1975) *The Formation of National States in Western Europe*. Princeton, N.J.: Princeton University Press.

Rokkan, S. and Urwin, D. (1983) *Economy, Territory, Identity: Politics of West European Peripheries*. London: Sage.

Rokkan, S. and Urwin, D. (eds) (1982) *The Politics of Territorial Identity: Studies in European Regionalism*. London: Sage.

Roozendaal, P. van (1992) 'The effect of dominant and central parties on cabinet composition and durability', in *Legislative Studies Quarterly*, 17: 5–36.

Rose, R. (ed.) (1974) *Electoral Behavior: A Comparative Handbook*. New York: Free Press.

Rose, R. (1984) *Do Parties Make a Difference?* London: Macmillan.

Rose, R. and Davies, P.L. (1984) *Inheritance in Public Policy: Change Without Choice in Britain*. New Haven and London: Yale University Press.

Rose, R. and Urwin, D.W. (1970) 'Persistence and change in western party systems since 1945', *Political Studies*, 18 (3): 287–319.

Rosenow, B. von and Naschold, F. (1994) *Die Regulierung von Altersgrenzen*. Berlin: Sigma.

Rueschemeyer, D., Huber, E., Stephens, E. and Stephens, J.D. (1992) *Capitalist Development and Democracy*. Oxford: Polity Press.

Rustow, D.A. (1967) *A World of Nations: Problems of Political Modernization*. Washington: Brookings.

Sainsbury, D. (ed.) (1994) *Gendering Welfare States*. London: Sage.

Sartori, G. (1970) 'Concept misformation in comparative politics', *American Political Science Review*, 64: 1033–53.

Sartori, G. (1976) *Parties and Party Systems: A Framework for Analysis*. New York: Cambridge University Press.

Sartori, G. (ed.) (1984) *Social Science Concepts: A Systematic Analysis*. Beverly Hills: Sage.

Saward, M. (1994) 'Democratic theory and indices of democratization', in D. Beetham (ed.) (1994) *Defining and Measuring Democracy*. London: Sage.

Scharpf, F.W. (1984) 'Economic and institutional constraints of full employment strategies: Sweden, Austria and Germany, 1973–1982', in J.H. Goldthorpe (ed.) (1984) *Order and Conflict in Contemporary Capitalism*. Oxford: Oxford University Press.

Scharpf, F.W. (1987) 'A game-theoretical interpretation of inflation and unemployment in Western Europe', *Journal of Public Policy*, 7: 227–57 [Special Issue edited by H. Keman].

Scharpf, F.W. (1991) *Crisis and Choice in European Social Democracy*. Ithaca, N.Y.: Cornell University Press.

Scharpf, F.W. (1997) *Games Real Actors Play*. Boulder, Colo.: Westview Press.

Scharpf, F.W. (1998) 'Political institutions, decision styles and policy choices', in Czada et al. (eds) *Institutions and Political Choice*. Amsterdam: VU-University Press.

Scharpf, F.W. (1999) *Governing in Europe. Effective and Democratic?* Oxford: Oxford University Press.

Schmid, J. (1995) *Wohlfahrtsverbände in modernen Wohlfahrtsstaaten: Entwicklung und Vergleich nationaler Konfigurationen in Deutschland, den Niederlanden, Großbritannien und in Schweden*. Opladen: Leske & Budrich.

Schmidt, M.G. (1978) 'The politics of domestic reform in the Federal Republic of Germany', *Politics & Society*, 8 (2): 165–200.

Schmidt, M.G. (1980) *CDU und SPD an der Regierung. Ein Vergleich ihrer Politik in den Ländern*. Frankfurt a.M.: Campus.

Schmidt, M.G. (1982a) *Wohlfahrtsstaatliche Politik unter bürgerlichen und sozialdemokratischen Regierungen. Ein internationaler Vergleich*. Frankfurt a.M.: Campus.

Schmidt, M.G. (1982b) 'The role of the parties in shaping macroeconomic policy', in F.G. Castles (ed.) (1982a) *The Impact of Parties. Politics and Policies in Democratic Capitalist States*. London: Sage.

Schmidt, M.G. (1983) 'The welfare state and the economy in periods of economic crisis: a comparative study in twenty-three OECD nations', *European Journal of Political Research*, 11: 1–26.

Schmidt, M.G. (1985) 'Allerweltsparteien in Westeuropa? Ein Beitrag zu Kirchheimers These vom Wandel des westeuropäischen Parteiensystems', *Leviathan*, 13: 376–97.

Schmidt, M.G. (1986) 'Comment on "Social Expenditure and the Political Right" (by F.G. Castles)', *European Journal of Political Research*, 14: 677–80.

Schmidt, M.G. (1987) 'The politics of labour market policy', in F.G. Castles, F. Lehner and M.G. Schmidt (eds), *Managing Mixed Economies*. Berlin: Walter de Gruyter.

Schmidt, M.G. (1989a) 'Learning from Catastrophes. West Germany's public policy', in F.G. Castles (ed.) (1989b) *The Comparative History of Public Policy*. Cambridge: Polity Press.

Schmidt, M.G. (1989b) 'Social policy in rich and poor countries: socio-economic trend and political-institutional determinants', *European Journal of Political Research*, 17: 641–59.

Schmidt, M.G. (1992a) 'Regierungen – parteipolitische Zusammensetzung', in M.G. Schmidt (ed.), *Die westlichen Länder*. Münich: C.H. Beck.

Schmidt, M.G. (1992b) *Regieren in der Bundesrepublik Deutschland*. Opladen: Leske & Budrich.

Schmidt, M.G. (1993a) 'Theorien der international vergleichenden Staatstätig-keitsforschung', in A. Héritier (ed.), *Policy-Analyse* (Politische Vierteljahresschrift Sonderheft 24). Opladen: Westdeutscher Verlag.

Schmidt, M.G. (1993b) 'Gendered labour force participation', in F.G. Castles (ed.) (1993) *Families of Nations. Patterns of Public Policy in Western Democracies*. Aldershot: Dartmouth.

Schmidt, M.G. (1996a) 'When parties matter: A review of the possibilities and limits of partisan influence on public policy', *European Journal of Political Research*, 30: 155–83.

Schmidt, M.G. (1996b) 'The grand coalition state', in J.M. Colomer (ed.) (1996a) *Political Institutions in Europe*. London: Routledge.

Schmidt, M.G. (1997) *Demokratietheorien* (2nd edn). Opladen: Leske & Budrich.

Schmidt, M.G. (1998) *Sozialpolitik in Deutschland. Historische Entwicklung und interna-tionaler Vergleich* (3rd edn). Opladen: Leske & Budrich.

Schmidt, M.G. (1999) 'On the political productivity of democracies', Mauno Koivisto Lecture, *Scandinavian Political Studies*, 22 (4): 281–94.

Schmidt, M.G. (2000) *Demokratietheorien* (3rd edn) Opladen: Leske & Budrich.

Schmitt, H. and Thomassen, J. (eds) (1999) *Political Representation and Legitimacy in the European Union*. Oxford: Oxford University Press.

Schmitter, P.C. (1979) 'Still the century of corporatism'?, in P.C. Schmitter and G. Lehmbruch (eds) (1979) *Trends Towards Corporatist Intermediation* London: Sage.

Schmitter, P.C. (1981) 'Interest intermediation and regime governability in contem-porary Western Europe and North America', in S. Berger (ed.), *Organizing Interests in Western Europe*. Cambridge. Cambridge University Press.

Schmitter, P.C. (1997) 'Autobiographical reflections: or how to live with a conceptual albatross around one's neck', in H. Daalder (ed.), *Comparative European Politics. The Story of a Profession*. London and Washington: Pinter.

Schmitter, P.C. and Grote, J.R. (1997) 'Der korporatistische Sisyphus: Vergangenheit, Gegenwart und Zukunft', *Politische Vierteljahresschrift*, 38 (3): 530–54.

Schmitter, P.C. and Lehmbruch, G. (eds) (1979) *Trends Towards Corporatist Intermediation*. London: Sage.

Schneider, F. and Frey, B.S. (1988) 'Politico-economic models of macroeconomic policy: a review of the empirical evidence', in Thomas D. Willett (ed.), *Political Business Cycles. The Political Economy of Money, Inflation, and Unemployment*. Durham, N.C.: Duke University Press.

Schultze, R. (1992) 'Föderalismus', in D. Nohlen *Lexikon der Politik. Band 3. Die westlichen Länder* (Hrsg: M.G. Schmidt). München: Verlag C.H. Beck.

Schumpeter, J.A. (1942) *Capitalism, Socialism and Democracy*. New York: Harper & Row.

SCP (2000) *Trends, Dilemmas en Beleid*. Den Haag: SDU.

Shalev, M. (1983) 'The social democratic model and beyond: two generations of comparative research on the welfare state', *Comparative Social Research*, 6: 315–51.

Sharkansky, I. and Hofferbert, R. (1969) 'Dimensions of state politics, economics and public policy', *American Political Science Review*, 63: 867–79.

Sharpe, L.J. and Newton, K. (1984) *Does Politics Matter? The Determinants of Public Policy.* Oxford: Clarendon Press.

Shepsle, K.A. (1997) 'Studying institutions: some lessons from the rational choice approach', in J. Farr, J.S. Dryzek and S.J. Leonard (eds) (1997) *Political Science in History. Research Programs and Political Traditions.* Cambridge: Cambridge University Press.

Shepsle, K.E. and Bonchek, M.S. (1998) *Analyzing Politics. Rationality, Behavior and Institutions.* New York and London: Norton.

Shonfield, A. (1965) *Modern Capitalism. The Changing Balance of Public and Private Power.* London: Oxford University Press.

Siaroff, A. (1999) 'Corporatism in 24 industrial democracies: meaning and measurement', *European Journal of Political Research*, 36 (2): 175–205.

Skocpol, T. (1985) 'Bringing the state back in', in P.B. Evans, D. Rueschmeyer and T. Skocpol (eds) (1985) *Bringing the State Back In.* Cambridge, Mass.: Harvard University Press.

Skocpol, T. and Amenta, E. (1986) 'States and social policies', *Annual Review of Sociology*, 12: 131–57.

Smeeding, T.M., O'Higgins, M. and Rainwater, L. (1990) *Poverty, Inequality and Income Distribution in Comparative Perspective. The Luxembourg Income Study (LIS).* New York: Harvester Wheatsheaf.

Smith, G. (1972) *Politics in Western Europe: A Comparative Analysis.* London: Heinemann.

Soskice, D. (1999) 'Divergent production regimes: coordinated and uncoordinated market economies in the 1980s and 1990s', in H. Kitschelt, P. Lange, G. Marks and J.D. Stephens (eds) (1999) *Continuity and Change in Contemporary Capitalism.* Cambridge: Cambridge University Press.

Steiner, J.A. (1974) *Amicable Agreement versus Majority Rule: Conflict Resolution in Switzerland.* Chapel Hill: University of North Carolina Press.

Steiner, J.A. (1986) *European Democracies.* New York: Longman.

Steiner, J.A. (1999) 'The consociational theory and Switzerland – revisited thirty years later', in T. Ertman (ed.), *The Fate of Consociationalism.* Cambridge: Cambridge University Press.

Steinmo, S. et al. (1992) *Structuring Politics: Historical Institutionalism in Comparative Perspective.* Cambridge: Cambridge University Press.

Stepan, A. and Skach, C. (1993) 'Constitutional frameworks and democratic consolidation: presidentialism versus parliamentarism', *World Politics*, 46: 1–22.

Stepan, A. and Skach, C. (1994) 'Presidentialism and parliamentarism in comparative perspective,' in J.J. Linz and A. Valenzuela (eds) (1994) *The Failure of Presidential Democracy.* Baltimore: Johns Hopkins University Press.

Stephens, J.D. (1979) *The Transition from Capitalism to Socialism.* London and Basingstoke: Macmillan.

Stephens, E., Huber, E. and Stephens, J.D. (1982) 'The labor movement, political power and workers participation in western Europe', *Political Power and Social Theory*, 3: 215–50.

Stephens, J.D., Huber, E. and Ray, L. (1999) 'The welfare state in hard times', in H. Kitschelt, P. Lange, G. Marks and J.D. Stephens (eds) (1999) *Continuity and Change in Contemporary Capitalism.* Cambridge: Cambridge University Press.

Stimson, J., MacKuen, M.B. and Erikson, R. (1995) 'Dynamic representation', *American Political Science Review*, 89: 543–65.

Streeck, W. (1984) 'Neo-corporatist industrial relations and the economic crisis in West Germany', in J. Goldthorpe (ed.) (1984) *Order and Conflict in Contemporary Capitalism*. Oxford: Oxford University Press.

Streeck, W. (1992) *Social Institutions and Economic Performance*. London: Sage.

Streeck, W. and Schmitter, P.C. (1995) *Private Interest Government: Beyond Market and State*. London: Sage.

Strøm, K. (1990a) 'A behavioral theory of competitive political parties', *American Journal of Political Science*, 34 (2): 565–98.

Strøm, K. (1990b) *Minority Government and Majority Rule*. Cambridge: Cambridge University Press.

Summers, R. and Heston, A. (1994) *Penn world tables*, mark 5.6; available at: <http://www.nber.org/pwt56.html>.

Swank, D. (2001) 'Political institutions and welfare state restructuring', in P. Pierson (ed.), *The New Politics of the Welfare State*. Oxford and New York: Oxford University Press.

Swank, D.H. and Hicks, A. (1985) 'The determinants and redistributive impacts of state welfare spending in the advanced capitalist democracies, 1960–1980', in N.J. Vig and S.E. Schier (eds), *Political Economy in Western Democracies*. New York: Holmes and Meier.

Swenson, P. (1991) 'Bring capital back in, or social democracy reconsidered', *World Politics*, 43 (4): 513–44.

Tabatabai, H. (1996) *Statistics on Poverty and Income Distribution: An ILO Compendium of Data*. Geneva: ILO.

Talos, E. (1981) *Staatliche Sozialpolitik in Österreich*. Vienna: Verlag für Gesellschaftskritik.

Tarschys, D. (1985) 'The Scissors Crisis in public finance', *Policy Sciences*, 15 (3): 205–24.

Taylor, C.T. and Jodice, K. (1983) *World Handbook of Political and Social Indicators*. New Haven and London: Yale University Press.

Thelen, K. and Steinmo, S. (1992) 'Historical institutionalism in comparative politics', in S. Steinmo, K. Thelen and F. Longstreth (eds), *Structuring Politics*. Cambridge: Cambridge University Press.

Therborn, T. (1977) 'Capital and suffrage', *New Left Review*, 103: 3-42.

Therborn, G. (1985) *Arbeitslosigkeit. Strategien und Politikansätze in den OECD-Ländern*. Hamburg: VSA.

Therborn, G. (1986) *Why Some Peoples Are More Unemployed than Others. The Strange Paradox of Growth and Unemployment*. London: Verso.

Therborn, G. (1987a) 'Welfare states and capitalist markets', *Acta Sociologica*, 30: 237–54.

Therborn, G. (1987b) 'Does corporatism really matter? The economic crisis and issues of political theory', *Journal of Public Policy*, 7 (3): 259–84.

Therborn, G. (1989) 'Pillarization and popular movements. Two variants of welfare state capitalism: the Netherlands and Sweden', in F.G. Castles (ed.), *The Comparative History of Public Policy*. Cambridge: Polity Press.

Therborn, G. (1992) 'Lessons from "Corporatist" theorizations', in J. Pekkarinen, M. Pohjola and B. Rowthorn (eds), *Social Corporatism: A Superior Economic System?* Oxford: Clarendon Press.

Therborn, G. (1993) 'The politics of childhood: the rights of children in modern times', pp. 241–92 in F.G. Castles (ed.) *Families of Nations. Patterns of Public Policy in Western Democracies*. Aldershot: Dartmouth.

Therborn, G. (1995) *European Modernity and Beyond. The Trajectory of European Societies 1945–2000*. London: Sage.

Thomas, J.C. (1980) 'Policy convergence among political parties and societies in developed nations', *Western Political Quarterly*, 23: 233–46.

Thomassen, J. and Schmitt, H. (1997) 'Policy representation', in M. Marsh and P. Norris (eds) (1997) 'Political representations in the European parliament', Special issue of the *European Journal of Political Research*, 32 (2).

Thompson, M., Ellis, R. and Wildavsky, A. (1990) *Cultural Theory*. Boulder, Colo.: Westview Press.

Tilly, Ch. (ed.) (1975) *The Formation of National States in Western Europe*. Princeton, N.J.: Princeton University Press.

Tilly, Ch. (1990) *Coercion, Capital and European States AD 990–1990*. Cambridge, Mass.: Harvard University Press.

Tilton, T. (1990) *The Political Theory of Swedish Social Democracy. Through the Welfare State to Socialism*. Oxford: Clarendon Press.

Tingsten, H. (1955) 'Stability and vitality in Swedish social democracy', *The Political Quarterly*.

Titmuss, R.D. (1974) *Social Policy. An Introduction*. London: Allen and Unwin.

Tocqueville, A. de (1990 [1840]) *Democracy in America: I–II*. New York: Vintage Books.

Todd, E. (1983) *La troisiéme planète: Structures familiales et sytemes idéologiques*. Paris: Seuil.

Todd, E. (1984) *L'enfance du monde: Structures familiales et développement*. Paris: Seuil.

Traxler, F. (1992) 'Austria: still the country of corporatism', in A. Ferner and R. Hyman (eds), *Industrial Relations in the New Europe*. Oxford and Cambridge: Blackwell.

Traxler, F. (1995) 'From demand-side to supply-side corporatism? Austria's labour relations and public policy', in C. Crouch and F. Traxler (eds), *Organized Industrial Relations in Europe: What Future?* Aldershot: Avebury.

Traxler, F. (1998) 'Der Staat in den Arbeitsbeziehungen. Entwicklungstendenzen und ökonomische Effekte im internationalen Vergleich', *Politische Vierteljahresschrift*, 39 (2): 235–60.

Traxler, F. (1999) 'The state in industrial relations: a cross-national analysis of developments and socioeconomic effects', *European Journal for Political Research*, 36 (1): 55–85.

Traxler, F., Blaschke, S. and Kittle, B. (2001) *National Labour Relations in Internationalized Markets*. Oxford: Oxford University Press.

Truman, D.B. (1962) *The Governmental Process. Political Interests and Public Opinion*. New York: Alfred A. Knopf.

Tsebelis, G. (1990) *Nested Games: Rational Choice in Comparative Politics*. Berkeley, Calif.: California University Press.

Tsebelis, G. (1995) 'Decision making in political systems: veto players in presidentialism, parliamentarianism, multicameralism and multipartism', *British Journal of Political Science*, 25: 289–325.

Tsebelis, G. (1999) 'Veto players and law production in parliamentary democracies: an empirical analysis', *American Political Science Review*, 93: 591–608.

Tsebelis, G. and Money, J. (1997) *Bicameralism*. Cambridge: Cambridge University Press.

Tufte, E.R. (1978) *Political Control of the Economy*. Princeton, N.J.: Princeton University Press. United Nations Development Programme (UNDP) (annual from 1990) *Human Development Report*. New York: Oxford University Press.

Vanhanen, T. (1989) 'The level of democratization related to socioeconomic variables in 147 states in 1980–85', *Scandinavian Political Studies*, 12 (2): 95–127.

Vanhanen, T. (1990) *The Process of Democratization: A Comparative Study of 147 States, 1980–88*. New York: Crane Russak.

Vanhanen, T. (1997) *Prospects of Democracy: A Study of 172 Countries*. London: Routledge.

Veen, H.-J. (ed.) (1983–94) *Christlich-demokratische und konservative Parteien in Westeuropa*. 4 vols. Paderborn: Schöningh.

Verba, S. (1986) 'Comparative politics: where have we been, where are we going?', in H.J. Wiarda (ed.) *New Directions in Comparative Politics*. Boulder, Colo.: Westview Press.

Verba, S., Nie, N.H. and Kim, J. (1978) *Participation and Political Equality: A Seven-Nation Comparison*. New York: Cambridge University Press.

Visser, J. (1990) 'In search of inclusive unionism', *Bulletin of Comparative Labour Relations, 18*. Deventer: Kluwer Law and Taxation Publishers.

Visser, J. and Hemerijck, A. (1997) *A Dutch Miracle. Job Growth, Welfare Reform, and Corporatism in the Netherlands*. Amsterdam: Amsterdam University Press.

Wachendorfer-Schmidt, U. (ed.) (2000) *Federalism and Political Performance*. London: Routledge.

Wagner, A. (1893) *Grundlegung der Politischen Ökonomie, Teil I: Grundlagen der Volkswirtschaft* (3rd edn). Leipzig: C.F. Winter'sche Verlagshandlung.

Wagner, A. (1911) 'Staat (in nationalökonomischer Hinsicht)', in *Handwörterbuch der Staatswissenschaften*, 7: 727–39.

Wagschal, U. (1996) *Bestimmungsfaktoren der Staatsverschuldung in westlichen Industrieländern*. Opladen: Leske & Budrich.

Wagschal, U. (1999) 'Blockieren Vetospieler Steuerreformen?', *Politische Vierteljahresschrift*, 40: 628–40.

Wallerstein, I. (1974–1989) *The Modern World System*. 3 vols. New York: Academic Press.

Ward, R.E. and Rustow, D.A. (ed.) (1964) *Political Modernization in Japan and Turkey*. Princeton, N.J.: Princeton University Press.

Ware, A. (1996) *Political Parties and Party Systems*. Oxford: Oxford University Press.

Weaver, R.K. and Rockman, B.A. (eds) (1993) *Do Institutions Matter? Government Capabilities in the United States and Abroad*. Washington, D.C.: The Brookings Institution.

Webber, D. (1992) 'Kohl's Wendepolitik after a decade', *German Politics*, 1 (2): 149–80.

Weir, M., Orloff, A.S. and Skocpol, T. (1988) *The Politics of Social Policy in the United States*. Princeton, N.J.: Princeton University Press.

Western, B. (1989) 'Decommodification and the transformation of capitalism: welfare state development in seventeen OECD countries', *Australian and New Zealand Journal of Sociology*, 25: 200–21.

Wheare, K.C. (1963) *Legislatures*. Oxford: Oxford University Press.

Whiteley, P. (ed.) (1980) *Models of Political Economy*. London: Sage.

Whiteley, P. (1986) *Political Control of the Macro-Economy*. London: Sage.

Wiarda, H.J. (1986) *New Directions in Comparative Politics*. Boulder, Colo.: Westview Press.

Wildavsky, A. (1980) *How to Limit Government Spending or, How a Constitutional Amendment Tying Public Spending to Economic Growth will Decrease Taxes and Lessen Inflation*. Berkeley, Calif.: University of California Press.

Wildavsky, A. (1986) *Budgeting*. New Brunswick, N.J.: Transaction.

Wilensky, H.L. (1975) *The Welfare State and Equality*. Berkeley: University of California Press.

Wilensky, H.L. (1981) 'Leftism, Catholicism, and democratic corporatism: the role of political parties in recent welfare state', in P. Flora and A.J. Heidenheimer (eds)

(1981) *The Development of Welfare States in Europe and America*. New Burnswick and London: Transaction Books.

Wilensky, H.L. and Lebeaux, C.N. (1958) *Industrial Society and Social Welfare. The Impact of Industrialization on the Supply and Organization of Social Welfare Services in the United States*. New York and London: Free Press and Macmillan.

Williamson, O.E. (1985) *The Economic Institutions of Capitalism*. New York: Free Press.

Williamson, Peter J. (1989) *Corporatism in Perspective: An Introductory Guide to Corporatist Theory*. London: Sage.

Wittfogel, K. (1957) *Oriental Despotism: A Comparative Study of Total Power*. New Haven, Conn.: Yale University Press.

Woldendorp, J. (1995) 'Neo-corporatism as a strategy for conflict regulation in the Netherlands (1970–1990)', *Acta Politica*, 30 (2): 121–50.

Woldendorp, J. (1997) 'Corporatism and socioeconomic conflict-regulation', in H. Keman, (ed.) (1997a) *The Politics of Problem-Solving in Postwar Democracies*. Basingstoke: Macmillan.

Woldendorp, J., Keman, H. and Budge, I. (1993) 'Political data 1945–1990. Party government in 20 democracies', *European Journal of Political Research*, 24 (1): 1–120.

Woldendorp, J., Keman, H. and Budge, I. (2000) *Party Government in 48 Democracies (1945–1998). Composition – Duration-Personnel*. Dordrecht: Kluwer Academic Publishers.

World Bank (1992) *World Development Report 1992*. New York: Oxford University Press.

World Bank (1994) *Averting the Old Age Crisis*. New York: Oxford University Press.

World Bank (1997) *World Development Indicators 1997*. Washington, D.C.: The World Bank.

Wright Mills, C. (1956) *The Power Elite*. Oxford: Oxford University Press.

Zolberg, A.R. (1966) *Creating Political Order: The Party States of West Africa*. Chicago: Rand McNally.

INDEX